Maureen Junker-Kenny
"The Bold Arcs of Salvation History"

Maureen Junker-Kenny

"The Bold Arcs of Salvation History"

Faith and Reason in Jürgen Habermas's Reconstruction of the Roots of European Thinking

DE GRUYTER

ISBN 978-3-11-135850-5
e-ISBN (PDF) 978-3-11-074667-9
e-ISBN (EPUB) 978-3-11-074673-0

Library of Congress Control Number: 2021941797

Bibliographic information published by the Deutsche Nationalbibliothek
The Deutsche Nationalbibliothek lists this publication in the Deutsche Nationalbibliografie;
Detailed bibliographic data are available in the Internet at http://dnb.dnb.de.

© 2023 Walter de Gruyter GmbH, Berlin/Boston
This volume is text- and page-identical with the hardback published in 2022.
Cover illustration: Sta Maria di Pomposa; Photo: Corinne Poleij / iStock / Getty Images Plus
Printing and binding: CPI books GmbH, Leck

www.degruyter.com

To Helmut and Ursula Peukert
In gratitude for their friendship
and for forty years of conversation on pursuits of agency

and in memory of Seán Freyne (1935–2013)
Historical Jesus Scholar
and Professor of Theology at Trinity College Dublin 1980–2002
for opening up the Scriptures to students and colleagues.

Contents

Preface —— XV

Abbreviations —— XVII

Introduction —— 1

1 Recent Philosophical Debates on the Hermeneutics of Past Events and Their Relevance for Biblical Research —— 5
1.1 Debates on the "objectivity" achievable in research —— 5
1.2 Key terms in the study of history —— 9
1.2.1 "Memory" – individual, communicative, collective, cultural? —— 9
1.2.2 "Interpretation" through forging a "plot" out of critically ascertained sources —— 12
1.2.3 "History of effects" as the awareness of the incompleteness of the past —— 14
1.3 Memory, plot, and history of effects in biblical interpretation and the premise of God as acting in history —— 15
1.3.1 Attempting to constitute facts from memory, testimony, and eyewitness accounts —— 16
1.3.2 A "plot" that does justice to the context of the past —— 18
1.3.3 A case study of "plots": Jesus as a Cynic wisdom teacher? —— 19
1.3.4 A framework of the possible, resurrection included? —— 22
1.4 Questions to pursue in Chapters Two, Three and Four —— 24

2 Reconstructing the Position of Paul in Early Christianity —— 27
2.1 Enquiring into Christian origins: Contested issues —— 27
2.1.1 The exegetical task of assessing the sources —— 28
2.1.2 An overview of early Christian self-understandings: Four groupings —— 30
2.1.3 Uncovering the religious symbolism of Jesus' actions, travels and preaching —— 35
2.1.3.1 The symbolism of the Twelve —— 35
2.1.3.2 The Kingdom of God as a counter-vision to existing oppressive powers —— 36
2.1.3.3 Temple critique as a religious and political challenge —— 37
2.1.3.4 A unique combination of apocalyptic thinking and wisdom —— 39

2.2	Paul's theological approach —— 42
2.2.1	A soteriology of atonement —— 43
2.2.2	An ethics structured by the distinction of gospel and grace from law —— 46
2.2.3	The role of Abraham as the model of faith for Jews and Gentiles —— 48
2.2.3.1	From Galatians to Romans —— 49
2.3.3.2	Shared by Jesus and Paul: An Abrahamic view —— 51

3	**Tracing the Origins of the Doctrine of Christ —— 54**
3.1	Christolatry as the origin of Christology? —— 54
3.1.1	Cultic worship of Christ based on a revelatory experience: Larry Hurtado's thesis —— 54
3.1.1.1	"Without analogy": Six factors in the worship of Jesus Christ —— 55
3.1.1.2	Jesus as God's "principal agent" —— 57
3.1.1.3	A ministry with polarising effect —— 58
3.1.1.4	Religious experience as the cause of a "binitarian mutation" of Jewish monotheism —— 59
3.1.2	Prayer *to* God *through* Christ: James Dunn's analysis —— 62
3.1.2.1	The sacredness of places, times, meals, and people in Judaism and early Christianity —— 62
3.1.2.2	Jesus' death as sacrifice – an inevitable interpretation? —— 65
3.2	The role of the Psalms in enabling a transition to Christology and the question of the "*Kyrios*" —— 67
3.2.1	The Psalms as a locus of Christological reinterpretation: Margaret Daly-Denton's analysis —— 68
3.2.1.1	A transfer at the level of images —— 68
3.2.1.2	The model of "intertextuality" —— 70
3.2.2	Philippians 2 as a case study of addressing Christ as *Kyrios* —— 72
3.2.2.1	Which background for *Kyrios*? —— 72
3.2.2.2	"Self-emptying" as implying pre-existence? —— 73

4	**Assessing the Pauline Strand: Exegetical, Methodological and Theological Disputes and Conclusions —— 77**
4.1	Paul, the oral tradition, and the Gospels —— 77
4.1.1	An enquiry into the references in Paul's Letters to the tradition about Jesus: Christine Jacobi's reconstruction —— 78
4.1.1.1	No direct links, just "analogies" —— 78

4.1.1.2	Making decisions in conflicts: How does Paul justify them? —— 79	
4.1.1.3	"In Christ": Paul's "quasi-mystical" appropriation —— 81	
4.1.2	Before and beyond Paul: Understandings of Jesus' life and of discipleship —— 82	
4.2	A dispute on methods —— 84	
4.3	The principle of analogy in history and the claim of Jesus' resurrection —— 89	
4.3.1	Jesus' death and resurrection in terms of sacrifice, or of vindication? —— 89	
4.3.2	A horizon of the "possible", not the "plausible": Elisabeth Schüssler Fiorenza's call for a shift in criteria —— 91	
4.3.3	Resurrection as a practical claim of meaning —— 93	
4.4	Conclusions on the three premises of Habermas's New Testament interpretation —— 94	
4.4.1	Post-Easter Christianity – a formation of spirit inherently marked by Hellenism? —— 95	
4.4.2	Christology from post-Easter conclusions with no basis in Jesus' self-understanding? —— 96	
4.4.3	The interpretation of Jesus' death as atonement – as significant in the history of reception as his proclamation and ethics? —— 97	
5	**The Patristic Era as Setting the Course for Relating Religion to Reason —— 100**	
5.1	Correspondences and points of conflict between the Christian message of salvation and philosophy —— 101	
5.2	The "inner person" in her freedom —— 103	
5.3	Developing soteriology into a conceptual Christology —— 106	
5.3.1	Substance ontology as a "trap" —— 107	
5.3.2	Countering Arius's Neoplatonic interpretation of "Logos" as the instrument of creation —— 109	
5.3.3	The premise of Habermas's critique: the "incarnation of God in the crucified Jesus" —— 111	
5.4	The human freedom of naming in Gregory of Nyssa's reading of Genesis —— 113	
5.5	Creation ending in damnation? The ambiguous theological heritage left by Augustine —— 115	
5.5.1	An era-transcending legacy: Augustine's analysis of interiority —— 116	
5.5.2	Inherited "original sin": A doctrinal innovation based on a misreading of Paul —— 118	

5.5.3	The outcome of the history of a humanity created by God —— 120
6	**The Origins of Modernity in the Late Middle Ages —— 124**
6.1	Taking substance ontology to its limits: Maximus Confessor on the will as capacity and as concrete decision —— 125
6.2	Anselm of Canterbury's philosophical argument for God's incarnation —— 128
6.3	Thomas Aquinas: Refining the role of reason in theology and ethics —— 132
6.3.1	Safeguarding accessibility while respecting dissimilarity: "Analogical" talk about God —— 133
6.3.2	Thomas's soteriology —— 135
6.3.3	Under dispute: The role of human reason regarding the Natural Law —— 137
6.4	John Duns Scotus as the turning point to Modernity —— 140
6.4.1	The univocity of "being" (*ens*) as a category valid for God and for humans —— 140
6.4.2	A supralapsarian Christology —— 142
6.4.3	The human will as a primordial faculty of self-determination —— 145
6.4.4	An open-ended future of creation: God's history with humans and the question of God's "acceptation" —— 147
6.5	William of Ockham's step to Nominalism and its legacy —— 148
6.5.1	Voluntarism developed in a Nominalist direction —— 149
6.5.2	Distinctions between Scotus and Ockham on the relationship between philosophy and theology —— 151
6.6	Two late medieval points of departure for modern thinking —— 153
7	**"Faith" and "Knowledge" after the Copernican Turn in Kant's Critiques of Reason —— 157**
7.1	Modernity as grounded in, or as a revolt against, the late Middle Ages? Hans Blumenberg's critique —— 157
7.1.1	Epochs distinguished by "reoccupations" —— 159
7.1.2	Modernity as a counterproposal to late medieval theocentrism —— 160
7.1.3	The problems of evil and of theodicy as the main thread of reconstruction —— 162

7.1.4	Incarnation as the guideline: Wolfhart Pannenberg's theological response —— 164	
7.1.5	Ongoing theological questions and answers relevant for Modernity —— 167	
7.2	The anthropological turn achieved through Kant's transcendental method —— 169	
7.2.1	Breaking with substance ontology: Theological factors, and a new method —— 170	
7.2.2	Reconceiving theoretical reason based on philosophical or theological distinctions? —— 173	
7.3	Practical reason and the question of meaning —— 177	
7.3.1	Finding parallels between the Augustinian heritage and Kant —— 178	
7.3.2	The "world concept" of philosophy and the public sphere —— 180	
7.3.3	Overtaxed by too great a scope for morality? The antinomy of practical reason and the postulate of God —— 182	
7.3.4	The "ethical commonwealth": Borrowing from Augustine, or supporting the will's capability for self-legislation? —— 185	
8	**Post-Kantian Theories of Language – Pacemakers for the Paradigm Change from Subject Philosophy to Linguistic Interaction —— 190**	
8.1	Discovering language as the medium of reason: Herder, Schleiermacher and Humboldt —— 190	
8.1.1	"Situating reason" in language – an overdue revision of foundations, or a question of levels? —— 191	
8.1.2	Individuality as a result of intersubjectivity? —— 195	
8.1.3	Models of relating speech acts and the language system —— 198	
8.2	Schleiermacher as language theorist —— 202	
8.2.1	Radicalising the starting point of hermeneutics: Non-understanding —— 203	
8.2.2	Interpretation as a dual task, grammatical and technical/psychological —— 205	
8.2.3	The irreplaceable position of individuality —— 209	
8.3	Schleiermacher as a post-Kantian theologian —— 212	
8.3.1	Three misinterpretations —— 213	

8.3.2	"Feeling or immediate self-consciousness" as the object of a transcendental enquiry —— 216	
8.3.2.1	Determining piety in a general theory of self-consciousness, or as a chosen "performance" and "conduct" of religious persons? —— 217	
8.3.2.2	The method used in arguing for "absolute dependence" —— 219	
8.3.3	Two directions of interpreting the "immediate" or "pre-reflective" consciousness – egological or monist? —— 220	
8.4	Consequences of the framework for analysing Schleiermacher and its effect on relating "faith" and "knowledge" —— 225	
8.4.1	Continuities in postmetaphysical thinking on religion —— 226	
8.4.2	Problems of fitting Schleiermacher into a postmetaphysical approach —— 228	
9	**Reappraising the Counterparts: Secular Reason as the Default Position, Religion as "Other"? —— 232**	
9.1	A summary of the course of enquiry —— 232	
9.1.1	Its guiding thesis and steps —— 232	
9.1.2	Assessments of the course of European thought depending on their starting points —— 234	
9.1.2.1	The origins of Christianity in the context of Hellenisation, as assumed in Paul's theology and the Gospels —— 235	
9.1.2.2	Turning points in the history of reception of the New Testament —— 238	
9.2	Rituals as anchor points of religion, or as sites of discursive contestation? —— 242	
9.2.1	The promise of forgiveness: Contesting the Temple's rituals of sacrifice —— 244	
9.2.2	Confirming a new doctrine: The shift to infant baptism —— 245	
9.2.3	Interpreting the Eucharist —— 247	
9.2.4	Ritual as on a par with non-linguistic art, or as part of a discursively accessible practice? —— 250	
9.3	"Faith" and "knowledge" as alternatives, or as distinct pursuits of reason? —— 253	
9.3.1	Which categories after substance metaphysics? —— 254	
9.3.2	Principled autonomy and its price: Not a case of justification, but of meaning —— 255	
9.3.3	Finding the "otherness" of religion in history as the location of God's agency —— 259	

Bibliography —— 263
    Works by Jürgen Habermas —— 263
    Other works —— 264

Person Index —— 278

Subject Index —— 282

Preface

The monumental two-volume work on religion completed by Jürgen Habermas in 2019 which is the subject of this study has allowed me to bring two formative fields of discovery together: the Continental theology, philosophy and ethics I encountered in Tübingen and Münster, and the new perspectives in Biblical Studies I got to know in Trinity College Dublin. As for many students of theology, it was Helmut Peukert who opened up for me the path to the work of Jürgen Habermas and the Critical Theory of the Frankfurt School. For comprehensive, challenging and motivating perspectives on theories of agency and creativity from early childhood to the depths of history, sincere thanks to both Ursula and Helmut Peukert. Sharing in the dedication of the book is Seán Freyne, Founding Professor, Head of Department and Historical Jesus scholar, for his friendship and for insights into the traditions of the Hebrew Bible and Christian origins that move theology in new directions. For continuing the instructive conversations that began with him and Andrew D. H. Mayes and public lecture series with eminent scholars, I thank my colleagues Dr Margaret Daly-Denton and Professor Daniele Pevarello for insightful exchanges. I am grateful to Dr Albrecht Döhnert and Katharina Zühlke and the staff at De Gruyter for their effective and cheerful help also when working under lockdown conditions. My family, Dr Peter Kenny, Fiona Kenny and Kilian Kenny, are to be thanked for enriching a year's confinement to the home office with resourceful and imaginative ideas, and for their in-house tech support. Once again, I owe a debt of gratitude to Fiona Kenny for her precision and good spirits in the intricate task of copy-editing.

Dublin, April 25, 2021, Feast Day of St Mark, Author of the first Gospel

Abbreviations

Jürgen Habermas

Auch eine Geschichte der Philosophie, 2 Vols. (Berlin: Suhrkamp, 2019)
Vol. I Die okzidentale Konstellation von Glauben und Wissen
Vol. II Vernünftige Freiheit. Spuren des Diskurses über Glauben und Wissen

Biblical:

Cor	Corinthians, 1 and 2
Deut	Deuteronomy
Did	Didache
Ezek	Ezekiel
Gen	Genesis
Heb	Hebrews
Isa	Isaiah
Jer	Jeremiah
Lev	Leviticus
Mk	Mark
Mt	Matthew
Lk	Luke
Jn	John
Prov	Proverbs
Rev	Revelation
Rom	Romans
Thess	Thessalonians

Bible translations into English:

CSB	Christian Standard Bible
ESV	English Standard Version
NAB	New American Bible
NEB	The New English Bible
NIV	New International Version
NRSV	New Revised Standard Version
RSV	Revised Standard Version

General:

ET English Translation
KGA Schleiermacher, Friedrich. Kritische Gesamtausgabe. Berlin/New York: Walter de Gruyter, 1980–2011; Berlin/Boston: Walter de Gruyter, since 2011.
trans. Translated

Introduction

In his seminal new work, *Auch eine Geschichte der Philosophie*, Jürgen Habermas reconstructs the origins and the development of occidental philosophy from the Axial Age onwards through the guideline of the relationship between "faith" and "knowledge". Chapters II and III of Volume One discuss the key terms and exemplify Karl Jaspers's thesis with studies of the transitions in the world religions from mythos to logos, for example, in worked-out accounts of divine or cosmic laws. Chapters IV, V, and VI examine major turning points in European thinking from Antiquity to Early Modernity as stages on the way to a postmetaphysical mode of philosophy. For the first time in his publications treating religion, Habermas offers a detailed investigation of the role that biblical monotheism and Christian theology have played in the development of key concepts of modern self-understandings and of structures of political governance. He investigates the origins of biblical monotheism in Israel and its specific development of Torah as the law of the one unique God in the midst of cultures marked by polytheism. The profession of faith in Christ as Son of God and Redeemer is presented as resulting from the theology of Paul and followed up in its mission to the Gentiles in the Roman Empire. The Patristic era is discussed in the shape bestowed on it by Augustine as an author spanning distinct eras from late Antiquity to the Reformation and to an independent modern philosophy that are no longer part of a theological project of "faith seeking understanding". The Middle Ages are identified as the turning point to Modernity, due to the development of a philosophical natural law by Thomas Aquinas and to the intellectual breakthrough to an autonomous foundation of law by John Duns Scotus. Since Ockham's step to Nominalism, a bifurcation marks philosophy as either analytical and empirical, or realist and subject-oriented. In Ockham's approach, the previously held link between faith and reason is replaced by their separation. Volume Two takes the reconstruction of European philosophy from the Reformation to the beginning of the twentieth century. The two alternative paths which had been charted by Ockham and Duns Scotus are epitomised by Hume and Kant. The striking discovery that the two currents of European thinking following either an empirical or a transcendental method of enquiry can be traced back to the late Middle Ages is a key point of Habermas's elaboration of its contingent origins and turns. The decisive changes of direction in theological reflection examined across two millennia also constitute *"A History of Philosophy"* by which new paths were forged and alternative courses of thought opened up. How the two origins identified by Karl Jaspers, the philosophical systems conceived in Greece, and biblical monotheism as part of the world religions, have intersected, is thus made the subject of a genealogical exercise of self-enlightenment undertaken by reason.

In order to discuss the clear-cut trajectories mapped out in the two learned, wide-ranging volumes entitled *The Occidental Constellation of Faith and Knowledge*, and *Rational Liberty: Traces of the Discourse on Faith and Knowledge*, a range of disciplines is required. In view of the impressive sequence of learning processes charted by Habermas, it will be necessary to draw on research in Second Temple Judaism and Early Christianity, Patristics, the High Middle Ages, Voluntarism and Nominalism before engaging with current debates on the contributions of the mutually critical approaches in Modernity. My aim in taking up the key stages reconstructed by Habermas is to examine debates in the disciplines of biblical studies, theology and philosophy that are relevant to his findings. The ongoing theological exchange of arguments on the innovations and legacies of the first to the 13th centuries will throw a light on some of the terms which Habermas presents as key to the major shifts in this development: "incarnation" and "atonement", "original sin" and "grace", "sacrifice" and "salvation", "two kingdoms" and religious "interiority".

Before embarking on analyses on the momentous steps taken in different epochs, a question relevant for any turn to historical roots of current intellectual streams must be addressed: How can the past be accessed? The first chapter deals with contemporary understandings of what degree of "objectivity" can be achieved and applies this to the questions arising from the New Testament. The wider background of Christian origins and the Patristic era, outlined in Chapters Two to Five, serves to contextualise the concept of "Pauline Christianity" as well as the role of Augustine which are emphasised throughout the two volumes. This is done in order to complement and relativise Habermas's reconstruction of the Christian tradition as focused on human sin, on the interpretation of Christ's work in terms of atonement and of Christian agency as uniquely owed to God's grace. While this position has had a significant history of reception in both main churches in Western Christianity, it has never been left uncontested in any of its eras. They are not the only sources that have marked the Christian tradition as a whole. The variety of approaches developed by theologians in the patristic and the medieval eras could not be understood if not all of the foundational documents of Christianity had been available to them: that is, above all the Gospels in their narrative form, as distinct from Paul's theology. A more complex process of tradition must be assumed of which the Pauline mission was one part. The plurality of communities in their geographically, culturally and linguistically distinct and intellectually changing contexts draws on different elements of the whole heritage, as also the two main lines of Christological thinking – Alexandrian and Antiochian – in the fourth and fifth centuries show. As Chapters Two to Four investigate some key debates on the development of Christian self-understanding which place Paul into a wider context, so does Chapter Five with Augustine. The new approaches in the Middle Ages, anchored in the theologies of Aquinas and of Duns Scotus which Habermas analyses with great erudition and acuity both in their own time and regarding the relevance of their histories of effect for subsequent eras, are set into a wider theological background in Chapter Six. By elucidating their innovations from contemporary debates, the theological commitments that carry them are made clearer.

When discussing the periods prior to the era of Modernity in which my own research is located, I substantially draw on enquiries by English- and German-speaking scholars in biblical and theological studies. The aspects and differentiated conclusions they add provide a different platform from which to consider the new trajectories of theology and philosophy in Modernity. The question posed by Hans Blumenberg on the continuity or rupture of this era with the Middle Ages is the entry point to Chapter Seven which then discusses Habermas's reception and critique of Kant regarding the transcendental method, morality, faith and knowledge. Chapter Eight treats the linguistic turn away from a philosophy of the subject, attributed to Herder, Schleiermacher and Humboldt, as well as the interpretation of Schleiermacher's Dogmatics as a reconciliation of theology with Modernity that champions a pious inwardness. Chapter Nine enquires into the resulting loss of an internal connection of religion to reason that leads to locating its difference as consisting in "ritual", and identifies the problems raised by this theory decision made from a sociological perspective.

The "bold arcs of salvation history" which Habermas identifies in the Christian worldview as spanning the whole of history from the beginning to the end of the world, can be elucidated with different accentuations, as the history of Christian thinking shows regarding each of the three pillars he names: Adam's Fall, Christ's atoning death, and the Last Judgement.[1]

I conclude that the challenge theology faced and accepted in the post-biblical eras to relate "faith" and "reason" remains. Today, this task includes the need to question the erosion of the distinction between "autonomous" and "secular" also by Habermas.[2] This critique puts forward a different account of the counterpart to "faith": a concept of reason (*Vernunft*) that is not split into the "intelligible" and the "empirical" as if they were "two kingdoms", but that retains the transcendental level as the "invisible" premise of its concrete performances.

---

1 Habermas, Vol. I, 513, "die kühnen Bögen der Heilsgeschichte".
2 In one of many cases, Habermas formulates in Vol. II, 208: "Unlike Hume, Kant does not reject (*schlägt ... aus*) the heritage of Christian philosophy but transforms it from the view (*Sicht*) of secular thinking."

The human subject's world relation and recognition of other subjects can only be made its own if it is not already constituted by intersubjectivity. Both language and religion are to be accessed from the subjective pole, not that of the system, as Humboldt's and Schleiermacher's theories show. Reconstructing religion from a sociological or historical observer's perspective as "ritual" will not be able to take account of the internal understandings and motivations of believers. Also within the church communities, liturgical practice will open up "sources of solidarity" only if their theological interpretation is not caught in a vicious circle.[3] Instead of moving forth to given contexts of prior mediation – be they the prelinguistic origins of ritual, the structures of language, or intersubjectivity and the lifeworld – a move back to Kant's critical epistemology is called for. At the level of practical reason, this includes taking seriously his philosophical outline of faith in God as a perspective of hope from a person's own agency. It offers an answer to the "defeatism lurking in reason",[4] without being an unshakeable, fideist certitude that would constitute an intrinsic difference to every other autonomous human. In the alternative futures Habermas charts for philosophy, insisting on its capacity to reflect on what new insights in knowledge of the objective world "mean for us",[5] it would be important to include the "relation to oneself" into the argument against naturalism. It is a foundational capacity of subjectivity, shared by religious and secular persons, as the contingent origins and intricate turns of European thinking, elucidated so impressively in the two volumes, demonstrate convincingly.

---

[3] See below, Chapters Five and Nine, on the shift to infant baptism in the context of the controversial doctrinal innovation of an "original sin" inherited at conception.
[4] Habermas, Vol. II, e.g., 299, 305, 353, 367, 370.
[5] Habermas, Vol. I, 12.

1 Recent Philosophical Debates on the Hermeneutics of Past Events and Their Relevance for Biblical Research

The task of identifying the origins and following up the typical features of a historical tradition is confronted with a range of questions that have been debated in a number of disciplines: history, sociology and theory of culture, epistemology of history and philosophical approaches to temporality as part of the human condition, as well as biblical studies, history of religions, and theology for the Christian tradition. These disciplines exemplify relevant avenues for a hermeneutics of the past. Yet a more encompassing question concerning the understanding of the "objectivity" that can be attained through all the disciplines must be examined first (1.1), before the more specific challenges arising for research into history can be explored through their key terms: "memory" – individual, communicative, collective, cultural –, "objectivity", and "history of effects" that links a past event to the present and the future. Here, the contributions of "testimony" and "eyewitness", and of "interpretation" from a subsequent era are matters of debate, raising the fundamental question of the concluded or ongoing nature of both the historical past and of the processes of establishing its meaning (1.2). New issues arise with the Bible's reference to God as an agent in history, posing the question of the limits of what historical enquiry can deliver (1.3). The historical aspects of the early Christian mission to be explored in Chapters Two, Three, and Four are identified in conclusion (1.4).

1.1 Debates on the "objectivity" achievable in research

The question about "objectivity" throws up fundamental philosophical problems about how to theorise the human subject's access to the "world", about the approaches that capture this reality – for example, as one of "objects" or "*res extensae*", or as a "lifeworld" prior to the subject-object division – and about the methods devised, such as transcendental versus empirical. While some of these alternatives will be followed up more closely in Chapters Seven and Eight on Habermas's reception and critique of Kant in the light of the linguistic turn, the point to be examined here is the claim attached to scientific enquiries both in the natural sciences and the humanities. Since the positivism debate in which Habermas was involved in the late 1960s, renewed efforts have gone into elaborating in greater detail the steps required for establishing "objectivity" to a degree that can be justified. Three terms indicate the positions refuted and the agreements obtained: first, against the claim of "scientism" to deliver definitive, objective findings, the insight into the *situated* and provisional *status of knowledge*; second, against the disappearance of the enquiring subject, the uncovering of the link between the designing and structuring activity of research and the underlying "interests"; and third, against the ideal of "value-free" science, the insistence that research, too, as a human activity, must satisfy the standards of morality that have been achieved in historical struggles and institutionalised in governance systems based on equal human rights. Thus, an explication of moral criteria – such as non-discrimination and transparency – is required as part of the pursuit of a project. In consequence, "objectivity" is not relinquished as a claim, but redefined as requiring intersubjective confirmation by a community of researchers which exposes it to diverse standpoints.

Regarding the first specification, Habermas has consistently underlined the "fallible" nature of research processes and their results.[6] This awareness does not, however, lead to a diminished view of academic enquiry, as the discussion shows. Endorsing the increasingly self-critical understanding of scientific activity, Herta Nagl-Docekal argues against a relativist position which would undermine the standard of rationality itself. It is important not to exaggerate in either direction: neither does scientific endeavour lead to once-and-for-all results, nor does the insight into the time-conditioned character of the structured examinations of world aspects require the abandonment of the concept of reason. Rather, since "the situatedness of thinking formerly ignored is now reflected, objectivity has been increased."[7]

The *first* insight – that scientism is oblivious of the roles of paradigms, guiding hypotheses, experimental design and the possibility of alternative ap-

---

[6] Habermas, "Philosophy as Stand-In and Interpreter", in *Moral Consciousness and Communicative Action*, trans. Christian Lenhardt and Shierry Weber Nicholsen (Cambridge, MA: MIT Press, 1991): 1–20. In his article on this text, "Stand-In and Interpreter", *The Habermas Handbook*, ed. Hauke Brunkhorst, Cristina Lafont and Regina Kreide (New York: Columbia University Press, 2017): 349–359, 350, Hauke Brunkhorst marks it as "one – if not *the* – key to his work as a whole."

[7] Herta Nagl-Docekal, *Feminist Philosophy*, trans. Katharina Vester (Boulder, CO and London: Westview Press, 2004), 103, as a conclusion avoiding both scientism and relativism: "First, there is no way back to the idea that it is the aim of scholarship to discover truths that are valid once and for all. In the face of the strong evidence of the situatedness of research, any attempts to renew the concept of objectivity in the rigid sense of a scientistic program would fail [...] The question is how to define the claim of science if, on the one hand, the inevitable contextuality is taken into account, and on the other, an epistemological relativism is to be avoided."

proaches – leads to the *second:* not only do the premises which the enquirers bring with them belong to the task of critical analysis; also the link between the pursuit of specific directions of knowledge and human interests can be further specified. For example, it can be classified according to disciplines and their methods, as Habermas proposed in 1968 regarding object-related, hermeneutical and social sciences with their interests in scientific truth, historical self-understanding, and emancipation.[8] From 1981 onwards, he has highlighted the integrative and critical roles of philosophy with its universalising capacity and its mediating function for the lifeworld. In its revised roles, philosophy is given the tasks of orienting research and of translating between expert cultures and citizens in the lifeworld. Habermas develops these two functions as overdue replacements of a previous self-perception of philosophy as "queen of the sciences" and "usher", linked by him to Kant,[9] thus critiquing not only science but also his own subject for having an over-inflated view of itself. These two tasks can be justified even if philosophy retains a method of its own and is not assimilated to the methods of the individual sciences.[10]

Thirdly, the designation of "value-free" in order to rule out bias has been questioned for similar reasons: Ricoeur sees this classification by Max Weber as a misunderstanding since ultimately, research has to do with human agency and for this reason must take into account its link to the subject's own reflection.[11] In view of the missing normative dimension, Nagl-Docekal characterises it as mistaken to understand objectivity as only attainable on the basis of "value-free" premises:

> The idea "of value-free research [...] is not only unredeemable but counterproductive [...] If one considers the interest background of the sciences (first aspect of situatedness) it be-

---

8 For an overview of the background, the theses and reception of *Knowledge and Human Interests* (original 1968), cf. William Rehg, "Critique of Knowledge as Social Theory", and "Cognitive Interests", in *Habermas Handbook*, 271–287 and 489–493.
9 Habermas, "Philosophy as Stand-In", 2.
10 Karl-Otto Apel and Dieter Henrich argued for this point in the debate on this proposal of 1981. I have treated the discussion in *Habermas and Theology* (London and New York: T & T Clark International, 2011), 67–80.
11 In "Bouretz on Weber", in *Reflections on the Just*, trans. D. Pellauer (Chicago: University of Chicago Press, 2007): 149–155, 152, Ricoeur asks: "How are we to hold together the *wertfrei* posture, claimed by Weber, with having to make recourse to the meanings experienced by social actors in the identification of the object of the social sciences?" His enquiry into "The Fundamental Categories of Max Weber's Sociology" (133–148, 148, in the same volume) ended with the judgement: "What we might have to give up in the process is the axiological neutrality so proudly claimed by the theory of fundamental sociological categories presented in *Economy and Society.*"

comes clear that research topics do not emerge from our need for information alone but also derive from our present problems of practical orientation, [...] current conflicts and upcoming practical decisions. Searching for value-free theories means ignoring an essential task of research. We have to acknowledge that normative disagreement forms a regular element of scientific discourse and that a comprehensive theory of science must take this fact into account."[12]

A more complex, methodologically conscious and circumspect understanding of scientific enquiry is gained which also includes reflection on criteria of justifiability:

"Concepts such as knowledge, science, and research are based on the principle that theories must be well founded and accessible to an intersubjective examination. A thesis can be considered valid only if it has been checked, as far as possible, by the available methods and confronted with an extensive series of objections. Alternative approaches to the object in question do not remain unconsidered but are, on the contrary, specifically acknowledged [...] Thus plurality in an epistemological context has value as a precondition for research, not as an aim. Therefore diverse approaches and opinions (arising in different social contexts [...]) are not, from an epistemological perspective, the final word but are always individual statements that must be related to each other and put to test in the community of investigators."[13]

The shift towards accounting for the situatedness of expertise provided by researchers and its testing against other reconstructions puts the growing realisation of the history-dependent character of cognition since the 19th century to fruitful use within the processes of enquiry. They also receive a practical orientation through the idea of a "world concept" of philosophy put forward by Kant beyond its discipline-internal use. All human endeavour is assigned a direction towards a more enlightened and self-determined future of human subjects in a peace-oriented political cooperation of federal states. Their efforts are oriented towards the ultimate purpose (*Endzweck*) of human existence where their "interest" is to come true that the moral action and the happiness of the individual agents will be connected.[14]

---

12 Nagl-Docekal, *Feminist Philosophy*, 105–106, concluding: "If we recognize that the idea of value-free scholarship is not redeemable and its validation is not desirable, then we see that controversies evolving around normative language concerning, for instance, the social position of women, gender relations, and so on, are genuine elements of historical research."
13 Nagl-Docekal, *Feminist Philosophy*, 102–103.
14 Kant characterises the "world concept of philosophy" to which he refers at the end of the *Critique of Pure Reason*, trans. Norman Kemp Smith (New York: St Martin's Press and Toronto: Macmillan, 1929), 658, as relating to "that in which everyone necessarily has an interest" (B 868a). The cosmological, moral and religious dimensions of this "world concept" are analysed

At the same time, in what ways research can be justified as contributing to more enlightenment and liberation, less oppression and misrecognition must itself be worked out based on criteria. How historical traditions may have fostered this orientation and how they may continue to do so will be followed up regarding biblical sources. The next step, however, is to discover in what way historiography partakes in the provisional and non-completable character of knowledge, and which key terms are used to indicate the specific dimensions of enquiry in this field.

1.2 Key terms in the study of history

The failure to take into account the unavoidable input of the researcher also into the set-up of experimentation in the natural sciences was the reason for the problematic understanding of "objectivity" in positivism. Regarding the exploration of history, a variety of approaches and methods has been developed: searching for oral traditions and archaeological clues, accounting for microhistory as well as actions by known protagonists, studying turning points as well as long-term trends, and linking up with other individual disciplines such as economy, sociology and geography. Three concepts indicative of ongoing debates will be examined for the role they accord to the enquiring agent: "memory" (1.2.1), the "interpretation" resulting from the combination of critically examined sources with a structure justified by reasons (1.2.2), and the relationship between past and future to which attention is drawn by the hermeneutical concept of a "history of effects" (1.2.3).

1.2.1 "Memory" – individual, communicative, collective, cultural?

The career of the concept of "memory" towards a lead category over the past few decades is multifaceted. On the one hand, its different dimensions have been elaborated in a way that aims to constitute a new basis for the humanities as such. On the other hand, with such resonance across disciplines, it is all the more important to distinguish different levels in the use of "memory" and "remembering" and to determine more closely the basic dimension that is to be taken as the epistemological avenue to justify its findings. While historiography

---

by Jürgen Stolzenberg, "Kants Weltbegriff der Philosophie", in *Kantovskii Sbornik/Kantian Journal* 36 (April 2017), http://www.kant-online.ru/en/?p=841 (accessed April 7, 2021).

has developed concepts to deal with other relevant aspects, such as long-term duration, or structural factors that cannot be traced back to memory as a human capacity, the strength of this concept is to identify the problem of accessing the past, rather than presuppose the givenness of events and processes, decisions and turning points as plain, undisputed facts. What is needed is a critical delineation of the boundaries of seemingly self-explanatory conceptions, including "collective memory", or "cultural memory", which is a task for philosophy.

Having highlighted the recognition of "remembering" (*Erinnerung*) as the "central area of enquiry of the humanities and an intensely debated theme of public discourses", the philosopher Dieter Teichert on the one hand points out its integrative capacity: it increasingly constitutes "a new paradigm of cultural studies that allows to see different cultural phenomena and fields – art and literature, politics and society, religion and law – in a new connection".[15] At the same time, its use as an overarching category runs the danger of overlooking mutually exclusive positions competing within it. It is in *Memory, History, Forgetting* that Paul Ricoeur, while "clearly articulating the aporias and paradoxes",[16] succeeds in untying some of the knots of seemingly "incompatible" avenues: He "demonstrates through a differentiated treatment [...] that a careful distinction of contexts of theory formation is able to present many of the conceptions as compatible – since they have been devised at distinct levels and for different functions – on the one side. On the other, no concluding definition of the concept of memory is in view."[17]

A theory decision is needed on where to anchor this concept. Ricoeur opts for memory as based in the individual's cognitive capability, while recognising the significance of forms of collective memory. They include "theory of science aspects of historical remembering, the ethical-political problems of remembering and concealing by non-disclosure/forgetting (*Erinnerung und des Verschweigens/Vergessens*), and its anthropological relevance as a defining element of being human."[18]

---

15 Dieter Teichert, "Erinnerte Einbildungen und eingebildete Erinnerungen. Erinnerung und Imagination in epistemologischer Perspektive", in *Erinnerungsarbeit. Zu Paul Ricoeurs Philosophie von Gedächtnis, Geschichte und Vergessen*, ed. Andris Breitling and Stefan Orth (Berlin: Berliner Wissenschafts-Verlag, 2004): 89–100, 89, with reference to Jan Assmann as one of the key theorists of "cultural memory".
16 Dieter Teichert, "Erinnerte Einbildungen", 90, with reference to Paul Ricoeur, *Memory, History, Forgetting*, trans. Kathleen Blamey and David Pellauer (Chicago: University of Chicago Press, 2004) [French original 2000].
17 Teichert, "Erinnerte Einbildungen", 89.
18 Teichert, "Erinnerte Einbildungen", 90.

In view of the varied and at times opposing implications examined by Ricoeur and Teichert, specifying in each case the discipline from which the field is being ordered helps to avoid equivocal applications. It is instructive to compare a structuring proposal from an empirical cultural studies perspective with that of a philosophy of subjectivity which spells out the concepts associated with memory in relation to human thinking and agency.

From their work in sociology and literary studies, Egyptology and Ancient Near Eastern studies, Aleida and Jan Assmann have devised useful distinctions to the existing term of "collective memory", introduced by Maurice Halbwachs in the 1920s. For them, collective memory is made up of two factors: "cultural", and "communicative" memory. The first is to cover components of culture and identity which Halbwachs had originally left out, and is divided into the institutional forms of "canon" and "archive"; the second investigates the social dimension of being linked to persons and relates to the memory worlds of three or four interacting generations, covering a past spanning around eighty to one hundred years. The "archive", which is located as the root of the "canon" as the outcome of selections, is designated on the one hand as a "meta-memory [...] of second order"; on the other, it is judged as an "achievement" of civil society, on a par with the recognition of human rights.[19] They point out the stabilising function of memory for individual and collective identities, and criticise exclusions, resulting, for example, from elitist "canon" decisions or political interests. Jan Assmann states clearly also what this descriptive approach cannot provide:

> In the contexts of cultural memory, the distinction between myth and history vanishes. Not the past as such, as it is investigated and reconstructed by archaeologists and historians, counts for the cultural memory, but only the past as it is remembered [...] Whereas knowledge has a universalist perspective [...], memory, even cultural memory, is local, egocentric, and specific to a group and its values.[20]

However, in order to be able to criticise the power to decide what is to count as normative and as a culture's "canon", and to actually refute distorting accounts of history, it seems to me that a separate theoretical approach is required which distinguishes currency (*Geltung*) from validity (*Gültigkeit*). From a sociological perspective, what is "given" and real, is cultural memory as such, in its active and passive forms as "canon" and "archive", "working memory" and "reference

---

19 Aleida Assmann, "Canon and Archive", in *Cultural Memory Studies: An International and Interdisciplinary Handbook*, ed. Astrid Erll and Ansgar Nünning (Berlin/New York: De Gruyter, 2008): 97–107, 104–106.
20 Jan Assmann, "Communicative and Cultural Memory", in *Cultural Memory Studies*, 109–118, 113.

memory".²¹ In the truth orientation of philosophy, however, what is "given" is the past, and the task is to name the conditions of an accurate reconstruction, as Jan Assmann demands it from historians. The "archive" in Ricoeur's use of the term is part of this historiographical effort. Thus, the lacunae and open questions left at the level of describing cultural and collective memory can be filled by a philosophical account. It analyses the enquiring subject both in its quest for truth and its fragility and propensity for ideological self-affirmation, assesses the distinctive contents of cultural memory, and is able to identify sources of renewal, not just of fluctuation or "reshuffling" between "canon" and "archive". The social scientific division of the field of cultural memory into these two terms, explicated from a power perspective, needs to be embedded in a critical theoretical account of the human subject's capability to "remember", to represent faithfully something that is past. The "storehouse" of the "archive" must be linked to history itself, not to a floating and admittedly often self-serving cultural memory, in order to be able to judge on the truth of a past that is independent of the agent's thinking.²² Finally, instead of a process of "reshuffling" which can be noted by an observer without analysing the material transmitted, a *content-specific* perspective needs to be taken that is able to distinguish factual developments from the potentialities of the original history that did not come to pass.²³ This factor which provides the basis for renewals will be further explored in 1.2.3 under "history of effects" in which latent elements come to fruition and also the hopes of the original participants may find a future fulfilment.

1.2.2 "Interpretation" through forging a "plot" out of critically ascertained sources

From the two uses of "archive" just compared, the conclusion can be drawn that in all reconstructions of history, the key concepts must allow for the subjective

---

21 Aleida Assmann, "Canon and Archive", 106.
22 With Aristotle, Paul Ricoeur insists that memory refers to the past, to something that really happened and has not been invented. For Ricoeur, "archive" denotes the historiographical institution and activity of documenting the past. Without it, and without clarifying the epistemic centre of reconstructing what happened, one cannot decide what is a true or a false memory, a "just" memory or a biased, manipulated one.
23 I have provided a more detailed comparison of the approaches of Aleida and Jan Assmann to Paul Ricoeur's in "Poetics of Culture and Christian Memory. The Relevance of Ricoeur's Thinking for Christian Ethics", in *Paul Ricoeur: Poetics and Religion*, ed. Joseph Verheyden, Theo L. Hettema and Pieter Vandecasteele (Leuven: Peeters, 2011): 37–66.

component of the process of enquiry to be named in order to become more controllable. Its orientation towards truth is unrelinquishable, the "distinction between myth and history" cannot be permitted to "vanish".[24] At the same time, access to the past is constitutively indirect and mediated. Documents and archaeological data do not reinstitute the events as such, much less the intentions behind them. The decisive role of "interpretation" must be acknowledged as the active organisation of the material traces at work from the gathering of data to the constitution of a horizon of understanding. This constructive component has been named as devising a "plot" which throws a net of cohesion over disparate, not intrinsically related material. The tension between the critical and the constructive parts, between "documentation" and "narration", is a constant companion of the task to give an account of historical processes by proposing a consistent outline of what happened and why. Counterviews must be treated to corroborate the version one deems to be the most accurate. The tasks posed have often been captured by oppositional terms, such as "explanation" and "understanding", as distinguished by Johann Gustav Droysen and Wilhelm Dilthey.[25] Instead of privileging one of them, as Dilthey does with the latter, seen as the key method for the humanities, Ricoeur has proposed to relate the two as alternating aspects of the one project of investigation.[26] This turns the dichotomy into a "dialectical relationship", as the philosopher Friedrich von Petersdorff qualifies Ricoeur's treatment of the interlocked steps of historiography. In giving the material a structure and proposing a sequence, both elements are at work: "the understanding of others is also given in the historical-critical method of the critique of documents [...] Understanding goes along with attempts to explain."[27] Rather than restrict the methodologies a priori, the real accomplishment will consist in bringing together the evidence of, for example, philological, archaeological and documentary sources and their reflection in different research paradigms.

---

24 J. Assmann, "Communicative and Cultural Memory", 113.
25 Concise comparisons of their approaches are provided by Georg Essen in *Historische Vernunft und Auferweckung Jesu* (Mainz: Grünewald, 1995), 175–195.
26 See, for example, Ricoeur, "What is a text? Explanation and understanding", in *Hermeneutics and the Human Sciences*, ed. and trans. John B. Thompson (Cambridge: CUP, 1981): 145–164.
27 Friedrich von Petersdorff, "Verstehen und historische Erklärung bei Ricoeur", in *Erinnerungsarbeit*, ed. Breitling and Orth, 127–140, 134. He includes articles and books prior to *Memory, History, Forgetting* from Ricoeur's discussion of the work of the historian also in relation to Arthur Danto's position in "Expliquer et comprendre", *Revue philosophique de Louvain* 75 (1977): 126–147, and of French approaches (Raymond Aron, Henri-Irénée Marrou, Paul Veyne) in "La recherche et la preuve documentaire" (1994), as well as Maurice Halbwachs, Michel de Certeau and Pierre Nora again in 2000.

Yet even if a distanciated elucidation of factors in the act of "explaining" is recognised as part of historical research, the activity of forging a "plot" undeniably draws on the capacity of imagination. The contingency of historical changes can only be grasped by devising and checking possible alternative causes, processes, and effects. The horizon of possibility of the era itself is to be accounted for, in order for the "plot" not to be discredited by anachronistic expectations – as examples to be treated below will show in relation to the New Testament. In view of the longstanding debates about the element of "fiction" consisting in each historian's assembly of data in a coherent framework supplied by them, not by the past, Ricoeur's statement can stand as a summary of the active input of the researcher: "The choice of plot (*Intrige*) is at the same time the choice of what counts as an event (*Ereignis*)."[28]

1.2.3 "History of effects" as the awareness of the incompleteness of the past

As unexpected renaissances show – in philosophy, the return of virtue ethics and of Nietzsche could be seen as such reappearances to contemporary resonance – what is "past" can produce unforeseen renewals. These show that what is history is not necessarily concluded; it contains undercurrents the resurgence of which shows that both the historical past and the process of establishing its meaning are still live matters. Thus, not only is there a history of reception; it also makes the insight unavoidable that equally, the processes of understanding are "in principle incompletable".[29] This awareness, however, has been spelt out in different models. The way in which the origins of a tradition and the "pre-understandings" shaped also by the effective cultural history of the "classics" impacts on the present has been disputed, for example, between Hans-Georg Gadamer and Habermas in the late 1960s and early 1970s.[30] Both in literature and in his-

---

28 Ricoeur, *Zufall und Vernunft in der Geschichte*, 13, quoted by von Petersdorff, "Verstehen und historische Erklärung bei Ricoeur", 136. For an in-depth discussion of several of the authors treated – Danto, Hayden White – on the relation between "*res gestae*" and "*res fictae*", on the background of the approaches of Hans-Michael Baumgartner and Jörn Rüsen, see Georg Essen, *Historische Vernunft und Auferweckung Jesu*, for example, 267–277.
29 Stefan Orth, "Kriteriologie des Göttlichen – Hermeneutik der Zeugnisse. Paul Ricoeur, Jean Nabert und die fundamentaltheologische Diskussion", in *Unbedingtes Verstehen? Fundamentaltheologie zwischen Erstphilosophie und Hermeneutik*, ed. Joachim Valentin and Saskia Wendel (Regensburg: Pustet, 2001): 81–91, 89.
30 Habermas, "The Hermeneutic Claim to Universality" in *The Hermeneutic Tradition: From Ast to Ricoeur*, ed. Gayle L. Ormiston and Alan D. Schrift (Albany: SUNY Press, 1990): 245–272.

tory, there are moments that take on an unprecedented relevance at a later time, bringing hidden, but nevertheless latent elements to the surface. They have the power to move the tradition in a different direction from its previous paths and syntheses. One of Ricoeur's key contributions to this seminal discussion is that "distanciation" from a tradition is a necessary step and functions as a condition for new appropriations.[31] A key point for the consciousness of history to be retained from the different proposals is that all writing about it is penultimate, inherently destined to be surpassed and thus challenged to take its own premature character into account. Von Petersdorff explains Ricoeur's distinction of the three positions involved in relation to time: "1., the time of the event described, 2., the time of the event in relation to which the first is being described, 3., the time of the narrator. An earlier event is described in the light of a subsequent one."[32] An example of this, to be treated in the next subsection, is the death of Jesus Christ as the earlier event, narrated in the light of a later event, namely the experience of his resurrection. The upshot of the insight into the three different time zones in their interconnection is that "history does not only have to be written anew because additional sources appear, different questions are being posed, or a new generation is growing up, but mainly because the truth of historiography, due to the three time positions identified, has a temporal limit." Von Petersdorff concludes with the point that the "necessarily new interpretations that an event will undergo raise the question to what extent historiography is obliged or is able to reflect on its limited validity."[33]

1.3 Memory, plot, and history of effects in biblical interpretation and the premise of God as acting in history

Before discussing the feature of biblical texts that is at odds with accounts of the past in history writing, namely the belief in a God who acts in history, I want to apply the three terms just analysed to the field of biblical studies. It is clear by now that the concepts of "memory" and "testimony" and the analysis of accounts for their creditability or ideological strategy are instruments of any research into history, not just in theological contexts. These shared features are im-

---

[31] Ricoeur, "The Hermeneutical Function of Distanciation", in *Hermeneutics and the Human Sciences*, 131–144.
[32] Von Petersdorff, "Verstehen und historische Erklärung bei Ricoeur", 132.
[33] Von Petersdorff, "Verstehen und historische Erklärung bei Ricoeur", 139–140.

portant to make it clear that religious content does not *eo ipso* fall under the verdict of "myth". The ongoing effort of biblical and theological scholars has been to distinguish in the theologised histories provided in the four Gospels between possible facts and the authorial intentions of the evangelists. So how do the concepts of "memory" (1.3.1), "plot" (1.3.2), its exemplification in one exegetical debate (1.3.3), and the framework of origin and possibility that is contained in the "history of effects" (1.3.4) elucidate research into the New Testament writings?

1.3.1 Attempting to constitute facts from memory, testimony, and eyewitness accounts

The reason for endorsing the prerogative of philosophy over sociology or cultural studies was its ability to analyse the status of truth claims, following up the connection of a statement of fact to the memory of an individual agent. In view of the problematisation of how "facts" are constituted, that it depends on the framework or "plot" of the interpreter what counts as a relevant event, however, it is also necessary to employ a wide range of methods in researching the elements of history recounted in the New Testament. The new stages of the quest of the historical Jesus have drawn on social sciences, literary studies and further comparative methods. They have produced new backdrops for reconstructing Jesus' life and death, e. g. the genre of ancient biographies, or the proposal of subsuming his message into a general "Mediterranean" model of wisdom teaching.[34] The renewed quests are showing that much more historical detail can be established than Rudolf Bultmann assumed, though the methods employed remain contested.[35]

Agreeing with Ricoeur's defence of distinct operations within "interpretation", the key question is when "understanding" and when "explaining" are the appropriate modes in studying the New Testament. Clearly, "understanding"

---

[34] John Dominic Crossan, *The Historical Jesus: The Life of a Mediterranean Jewish Peasant* (New York: HarperSan Francisco, 1991).
[35] Bultmann's conclusion that only "the That not the What" of Jesus' life and death could be investigated was put into question by the New Testament scholar Ernst Käsemann in 1953 and the systematic theological starting point of Wolfhart Pannenberg and others with "Revelation as History". Existential analysis as the philosophical backdrop of Bultmann's position was questioned by these new movements in the 1950s and 1960s. For a recent discussion, see Martin Laube, "'Der Kampf muss ausgefochten werden'. Überlegungen zur historischen Jesusfrage mit einem Verweis auf Ernst Troeltsch", in *Dogmatische Christologie in der Moderne. Problemkonstellationen gegenwärtiger Forschung*, ed. Christian Danz and Georg Essen (Regensburg: Pustet, 2019): 133–152.

applies when what is described in a text seems accessible from one's own contemporary background, while the need to move to the different level of "explanation" only seems to occur when obstacles put this seemingly shared backdrop into question.[36] Bultmann's call for "demythologisation" belongs to the level of "explaining", where the rift between antique religious and modern assumptions signals a problem. But the risk of misinterpretation is even greater where differences in the use of key terms are not obvious and the distinct cultural settings of seemingly universal anthropological terms like "friendship", or "love" are not taken into account; significant differences can then be missed.[37]

The key challenge of the Gospels, however, is the status of accounts that are mainly presented as the testimonies of Jesus followers. Controversies between biblical scholars include a polarity between contemporary defenders of the ongoing value of form criticism – despite its drawback of possibly atomising texts into sections traced back to different sources[38] – and the classification of these texts as basically trustworthy reports by "eyewitnesses";[39] they were transmitted by oral tradition and then given permanence in the Gospel accounts composed from 70 CE, in an era which the second position deems as partly overlapping with the first generation of the Jesus movement. By tracing back the Gospels to the original "eyewitnesses", the historical gap assumed by other exegetes is minimised. What should be kept in mind, however, is that not only in biblical texts, "facts" are only accessible together with their interpretation as carrying a specific significance. Those reporting are active interpreters and not merely passive recipients of unequivocal events. This insight enlarges the task of the scholars to also reconstruct the frameworks of interpretation that were part of the intellectual streams of the era. What it does not imply, as will be outlined in the next subsection under the concept of "plot", is that fact and interpretation

---

36 In "Verstehen und historische Erklärung bei Ricoeur", 137, von Petersdorff elucidates Ricoeur's analysis of 1977 in the context of secular history writing, that the "task of explaining [...] is in order to be able to continue following the historical narrative when the given understanding is not sufficient. Ricoeur's answer is that superimposing (*Überlagerung*) explanation to understanding adds a narrative element" that in turn allows to "follow (*nachvollziehen*) the sequence and unexpected turns".
37 Cf. Tom Deidun, "The Bible and Christian Ethics," in *Christian Ethics. An Introduction*, ed. Bernard Hoose (London: Cassell, 1998), 3–46, 16.
38 Cf. Hans-Josef Klauck, "'Ein Wort, das in der ganzen Welt erschallt': Traditions- und Identitätsbildung durch Evangelien", in *Die Anfänge des Christentums*, ed. Friedrich W. Graf and Klaus Wiegand (Frankfurt: Fischer, 2009): 57–89, 66–67.
39 Richard Bauckham, *Jesus and the Eyewitnesses: The Gospels as Eyewitness Testimony* (Grand Rapids, MI: Eerdmans, 2nd edn 2017).

are so intertwined that it no longer makes sense to distinguish a real event from its interpreted form.

1.3.2 A "plot" that does justice to the context of the past

Before one of the vigorous debates in biblical studies is treated in 1.3.3, involving questions of the standing, the limits, and the combination of the critical methods developed over more than two centuries, a dispute in philosophical hermeneutics needs to be recalled. The finding that all history-writing is dependent on the contributions of "testimonies" has been radicalised by a specific philosophical approach into the position that looking for exterior facts constitutes a problematic "naturalisation"; interpretive processes are seen instead as only taking place in the recipients' heads, and cannot face the possible resistance of external facts. The counterargument to this view is that it gives up on understanding what is "other". Ricoeur has defended the second position with a nuanced reconstruction. As the systematic theologian Hermann-Josef Pottmeyer sums up, already the first, historical level of the different meanings of "testimony" (*Zeugnis*) distinguished by Ricoeur is called "quasi-empirical" since it "comprises the dual function of the eyewitness and the interpreter who understands and spells out (*auslegt*) history."[40] Thus, a real event is being referred to, though "testimony" comprises more than the empirical fact. The first position denying that there is an event distinct from its interpretation is exemplified by Rainer Adolphi's philosophical critique of Ricoeur. According to him, Ricoeur's insistence on such a foothold in history downplays the consciousness that there is no original event to be ascertained.[41] For Adolphi, the only thing available is what has already been understood, thus collapsing the distinction between the already interpreted content of the testimony, and the reality to which it relates. His critique perceptively mentions the difference between Kant's and Hegel's approaches as a backdrop to his disagreement with Ricoeur's position – Ricoeur takes the critical view of Kant, Adolphi is close to Hegel. What in this critique is relevant for biblical studies?

---

[40] Hermann J. Pottmeyer, "Zeichen und Kriterien der Glaubwürdigkeit des Christentums", in *Handbuch der Fundamentaltheologie*, ed. Walter Kern, Hermann J. Pottmeyer and Max Seckler (Freiburg: Herder, 1988): Vol. IV, 373–413, 400–401.
[41] Rainer Adolphi, "Das Verschwinden der wissenschaftlichen Erklärung. Über eine Problematik der Theoriebildung in Paul Ricoeurs Hermeneutik des historischen Bewußtseins", in *Erinnerungsarbeit*, 141–171, 165–168.

On the one hand, Adolphi's reminder that the pure facts are not attainable is correct. All that can be achieved in historical research are degrees of objectivity, for which intersubjective agreement must be sought. Yet, it continues to be necessary to retain the concept of "fact" in the sense of an occurrence that is distinct from its interpretation. This is not a "naturalist" but, in line with Kant, a criticist account of an entity in external reality. The real event to which the interpretation refers, and of which new takes are possible, cannot be dissolved into the way in which it is currently being understood. What follows from this for biblical scholars is that their task includes uncovering the past horizon in which an event had its original meaning. This is the proximate benchmark for its most adequate understanding also today. The event has meaning in the context that is most immediate to it, and the subsequent interpretations – even within the period of the 27 writings of the New Testament – find their measure in it.

This rule of interpretation has consequences for judging subsequent theological and doctrinal developments. The history of the person of Jesus remains the benchmark for all "plots", even if it is true that access to it is only available in mediated form in the shape of the Gospel narratives, in what the New Testament retains of the oral tradition, the Letters, and the independent evidence found in sources like Josephus and Tacitus. With knowledge of the intellectual and religious movements of the time having much increased, for example, by the findings of the Dead Sea Scrolls and of early Christian Gnostic writings at Nag Hammadi, the task for biblical studies is to reconstruct the world in which Jesus carried out his ministry and the cultures in which his followers undertook their mission.

1.3.3 A case study of "plots": Jesus as a Cynic wisdom teacher?

An example for divergent methods and conclusions regarding these parameters can be found in the classification of Jesus' message and lifestyle as a case of Cynic teaching in Hellenised urban settings. The question which procedures and proposals give a more adequate interpretation includes the task of scanning for elements of twentieth-century culture that are transported in the horizon of understanding used for a decisively different ancient context. Is it adequate to read Jesus' proclamation on the lines of coping with everyday contingencies, promoting the attitude of a philosopher-king,[42] and fitting into one of the coun-

---

[42] In *Galilee and Gospel* (WUNT 125) (Tübingen: Mohr Siebeck, 2000): 208–229, 203, Seán Freyne objects that "Jesus was remembered [...] for his outspoken criticism of the standards

ter-cultural movements around the Mediterranean? Or does this "plot" ignore key elements of Jesus' self-understanding, such as responding to the Creator God of Jewish monotheism? Notions of human kingship and domination have been severely critiqued by parts of this tradition. Jesus is portrayed as gathering the twelve tribes of Israel and preparing a banquet that welcomes also the Gentiles as part of the promise to Abraham.[43] Does the figure of an ancient Greek frugal wisdom teacher addressing individuals in a city offer the most convincing mould to interpret Jesus and his movement?[44] Crucially, by which methods has this horizon been reached as the most likely backdrop to account for Jesus' teaching and lifestyle?

The more one insists on the need to research what can be historically ascertained about Jesus, the more instructive is the debate between the two positions. Is it possible, regarding a tradition of oral transmission between the first Letter to the final Gospel and the final Letter of the New Testament, to reach its very first layer, as John Dominic Crossan aspires to? Is the criterion of two independent places of quotation adequate, also in view of the narrow textual basis resulting from this condition, for which not even the Gospel of Mark qualifies? Are the stark revisions of datings of early Christian texts convincing, even in relation to the highly esteemed archaeological findings? Without going into the detail of these objections, it should be clear that a gulf opens up between the two meth-

---

of royal power and privilege [...] There is here no idealisation of Kingship in terms of the philosopher-king of the Cynic-Stoic world view."

43 In *Jesus a Jewish Galilean: A New Reading of the Jesus Story* (Edinburgh: T & T Clark, 2004), 157, Freyne interprets references to Abraham and quotes from Isaiah as indicative of Jesus' understanding regarding the "place of the gentiles in the eschatological community that he believed was being inaugurated by his own ministry". Jesus' act of turning over the tables of the money lenders gives an insight into his view of the Temple. Agreeing with E. P. Sanders that "Jesus' attack was [...] against the sacrificial system itself insofar as the trade that was required for it to function was being abolished" (158), Freyne sees a different vision of God's presence expressed. Against Sanders, he thinks it possible that the "eschatological temple" was to be "transformed from a place of sacrifice to one of prayer, as suggested by the Markan citation of Isaiah 56.7 [...] direct access to the divine was possible independently of the temple and its religious practices" (162). The conflicts on rituals will be returned to, also in the final chapter, regarding Habermas's emphasis on ritual as the distinctive feature of religion.

44 It is important to distinguish which understanding of "wisdom" is being used: that of Greek philosophical sages, that of a professional class, such as Jesus ben Sira in the Hebrew Bible, or an evocative, everyday wisdom as expressed in aphorisms and in the parables Jesus told, combined with an expectation of imminent change: "The way of wisdom provided one element of an appropriate response in the present, since God's wisdom could be discerned from his creation. Yet the radical element of newness was provided by the apocalyptic belief that a fundamental change was occurring now in and through his own actions". Freyne, *Jesus a Jewish Galilean*, 143.

ods: an enquiry that is hoped to deliver conclusive evidence at least on minimal elements which can be taken as certified, and an approach that reckons with a long period of oral tradition, justifies which milieu is more likely to have been the location of a Gospel – Rome or Syria in the case of its prototype, the Gospel of Mark – and needs to include the history of reception. In each case, the criterion of seeking intersubjective validation in the community of researchers applies. But is the procedure of validation in the Jesus Seminar (to which the authors of the Cynic wisdom thesis belong) to cast votes and propose the view to which most have given their assent the best way of operationalising this demand? Or does it constitute heteronomy when individual scholars' positions, elaborated in debate with opposed views and divergent reconstructions, are asked to subordinate their critique of specific conclusions to a position deemed superior because it is held by a relative majority?

Thus, standards of precision which prove to be unreachable regarding the first layer, a discounting of the four cohesive narratives that exist, a questionable procedure for agreeing on a truth claim, and, finally, also some visible indebtedness to late twentieth-century cultural and economic predilections for "innovation" are the methodical reasons for rejecting the adequacy of the argumentation. Regarding content, it ends up minimising Jesus' own tradition of Jewish monotheism. The historical question is whether the context in which his ministry took place was that of "an urbanised and Hellenised Galilee" as the "proponents of the Cynic-hypothesis [...] call for". Or does the New Testament's silence on nearby, newly founded urban centres like Sepphoris indicate Jesus' conscious priority for the villages of Galilee and the area of the "Greater Israel" as a counter-vision to the erosion of biblical prophetic motifs by the new values of the Roman occupying forces and those benefitting from their economic links? The following series of questions suggests a different possibility:

> What if we let Galilee take its place in the Greco-Roman world? What if the people of Galilee were not isolated from the cultural mix that stimulated thought and produced social experimentation in response to the times? What if the Galileans were fully aware of the cultural forces surging through the Levant? What if we thought that the Galileans were capable of entertaining novel notions of social identity? What then? Why then we would be ready for the story of the people of Q.[45]

Do these questions regarding those who gathered sayings of Jesus into "Q" – the *Quelle* or source that is assumed to have been available to Matthew and Luke –

---

[45] Burton Mack, *The Lost Gospel. The Book of Q and Christian Origins*, 68, quoted in Freyne, *Galilee and Gospel*, 1.

illuminate the horizon of the past, or of a certain Western present? There is a clear difference between seeing Jesus as inspired by a general and "atopical", that is geographically, culturally and religiously unspecific, lifestyle of social withdrawal, and by the biblical traditions of Genesis and the prophets:

> it was with an essentially Jewish understanding of history and from a decidedly Jewish hope of restoration and renewal that Jesus and his movement mounted their critique of both value systems, Herodian and theocratic alike. I do not believe that what began as a set of insights for coping with life, which is what Cynicism of a popular kind essentially was, could have been transformed into an apocalyptically inspired renewal movement with a radical social agenda [...] and with only the memory of a discredited wisdom teacher to inspire it.[46]

As distinct as the early Christian understandings of Jesus that can be found in the Gospels are, a modernising starting point will be unable to account for them. With the faith in the resurrection of the discredited, crucified "Son of Man", however, history writing encounters a definite limit which it cannot encompass from today's presuppositions: that an event deemed outside of all parameters of historical understanding is part of the story portrayed.

1.3.4 A framework of the possible, resurrection included?

Since an unforeseeable future dimension is part of historical events as such, it has become clear that their meaning cannot be defined conclusively; it is always open to a range of unpredictable possibilities. Yet the key difference of biblical texts goes beyond this awareness. They refer to a hidden but present agency of God as the creator and sustainer of the world and its inhabitants. This is the element that remains foreign to a framework of thinking in which the only admissible causes and factors must be able to be accounted for on immanent terms. Any other approach would seem to throw open the gates to all kinds of "magic" explanations that do not pass the test of intersubjectively justifiable intellectual standards. So how is the "possible" that belongs to the history of effects of developments and events in history to be defined in a way that remains compatible with these modern standards? The New Testament's claim is that the story it tells of the life, death and resurrection of Jesus Christ relates to an event which has an ultimate, universal meaning relevant for all human beings. This requires the elaboration of criteria of meaning. These differ between specific phil-

---

[46] Freyne, *Galilee and Gospel*, 203–204.

osophical approaches, such as Kant's, Kierkegaard's and Hegel's. The task is to compare and identify which expectation of meaning is being proposed from which perspective, and to judge them, having laid open one's criteria.

It is possible to argue for the relevance of belief in the resurrection in relation to human agency. The solution to the antinomy of practical reason analysed by Kant is his postulate of the existence of a God who is able to fulfil what individuals aim for in their best intentions. It allows agency to be oriented by reasonable hope. Such an agency-sustaining concept of meaning can be used to critique an idea of reason that remains self-enclosed. In his comparison of approaches to history writing, Georg Essen makes it clear that a concept of reason which rules out what according to Kant can be "thought", though it cannot be "known", restricts the conception of reality to an immanent framework. It is so tied to a currently given thought form marked by the decision to go without and refute the conceivable assumption of a God that it needs a critique which theology can and should provide.[47] It cannot be regarded as a foregone conclusion that the premise of the possibility of faith in a God who can rescue must be ruled out as a justifiable orientation for contemporary humans. It needs to be highlighted that "openness to future new interpretations" as part of historical events is being extended from an entirely immanent understanding to a faith position that can at least not be ruled out. It is reasonable to argue that the claim of the New Testament texts does not have to be dismissed as "traditional" and belonging to a bygone era but can be allowed into the universe of actual options of life for today's fellow citizens. These texts can then be heard in their otherness without subduing them immediately to the constraints of a particular view of what is compatible with modern assumptions. However, the criteria of an option for meaning in this emphatic sense must be outlined. Such an expectation of ultimate meaning, though it was deemed reasonable by Kant, is no longer part of a generally shared horizon. Yet, despite Habermas's view that only an answer based on a "secular" justification conforms to reason,[48] the question of absolute meaning cannot be dismissed and needs to be kept open.

---

47 Cf. Essen, *Historische Vernunft und Auferweckung Jesu*, 316–321.
48 For example, in Vol. II, 348, Habermas could have identified an "autonomous" instead of a "secular" answer as being in agreement with reason. When treating Kant's theory of morality and his doctrine of the postulates of practical reason, he states regarding the "doubt about the absolute priority of morality *as such*" which arises from an "anthropologically deeper lying (*tieferliegende*) level" that it "requires an answer that is justified on rational, thus secular terms (*vernünftig, also säkular begründete Antwort*)".

1.4 Questions to pursue in Chapters Two, Three and Four

Exegetical debates on New Testament texts in the diversity of the basic conceptions they provide will be examined next. It accords with the rule that interpretation has to do justice to the context of origin that the variety of the earliest communities and their images of Jesus are examined for clues to the details of the history of the movement and its founder. One of these trajectories is Paul's interpretation of which there is unmatched evidence through the Letters he wrote to the Christian centres he founded, or visited, such as Rome. The religious background shared by Jesus, Paul and the Gospel writers is Second Temple Judaism in a long-standing period of Hellenisation. The Greek cultural presence is evident, for example, in the Septuagint, the translation of the Hebrew Bible into Greek that began around 250 BCE in Alexandria with its well-established Jewish community. When tracing the contingent origins of the Western intellectual heritage that has led to postmetaphysical thinking, as Habermas intends to, it is important to identify the constituent traditions in a differentiated way so that key steps in their encounters and exchanges can be identified correctly. He sketches the origins and the expansion of Christianity with many perceptive and thought-provoking comparisons and interpretations. Among the premises that guide his enquiry, however, there are at least three which need to be exposed to a greater range of views. Crucial assumptions of his need to be examined since no consensus by scholars in the fallible process just described exists: one, the alleged dependence of the Gospels on Paul, and the thesis that "post-Easter Christianity was from the start (*von Haus aus*) a formation of spirit that was marked by Hellenism" (*hellenistisch geprägte Gestalt des Geistes*),[49] to be treated in Chapter Two. Secondly, the judgement that Jesus did not have a self-understanding other than that of a prophet, proclaiming "the kingdom of God but not himself". This view results in the "sobering insight that he had no Christology" which is seen as arising as an unprecedented post-Easter reflection and to be entirely the work of his followers.[50] Different theses on the origins of the worship of Christ will be examined in Chapter Three. In the light of these debates, thirdly, Habermas's assumption will be judged that Paul's interpretation became dominant in the mission to the Gentiles and thus for subsequent Christian thinking. To find out what belonged to the most basic shared understanding, the question of how Paul relates to the oral tradition will be assessed in Chapter Four, which concludes with a final evaluation of these premises. Further issues

---

[49] Habermas, vol. I, 515.
[50] Habermas, vol. I, 496.

that would have required detailed treatment include the overemphasis in the two volumes on the role of "law" for Judaism and the contrast between "grace" and "sin", "faith" and "works", in view of the plurality found in the New Testament that counterbalances any one use of these concepts.

My aim in the following chapters is to present key controversies between exegetes which will, first, help contextualise the person and message of Jesus within the different strands of the Jewish tradition; they will, secondly, show the methods used by biblical scholarship in their application, and thirdly, identify ongoing enquiries. Seemingly unequivocal concepts such as "Jewish" in contrast to "Gentile" will have to be defined in more specific terms within an ongoing history of Hellenisation. Their application to writings in the New Testament will give surprising insights into some open questions. For example, in relation to a passage quoted by Habermas, is "*Kyrios*" in the hymn in Philippians 2 taken from its Jewish use, referring to God as Lord, or from a Roman imperial understanding? Habermas connects it with the forgiveness of sins, but does this theme appear in the famous verses on "self-emptying" in Philippians 2?[51] And staying with this text, is "being in the form of God" equivalent to being called the "Son of God", or does it point to Adam, made in the image of God (Gen 1:26–27)?

The aim in outlining these problems is not to make systematic statements impossible by pointing to unresolved debates between biblical scholars but to correct simplifications and anachronistic readings. They obscure the sources from which a plurality of understandings emerged on which subsequent eras could draw. Equally, they risk misrepresenting the backdrop from which subsequent developments can be explained as continuations in new cultural horizons, as reactions, transformations, or disappearances. A crucial question in the patristic era will be the concept of "*Erbsünde*", inherited original sin, which Habermas already attributes to Paul.[52] Depending on how its effect on human freedom and agency is envisioned, the critical transformation of doctrines in later periods, especially Modernity, could fall under the verdict that it does not deliver on the seriousness of the message of Christianity. The basic understanding of its core that is established in the portrayal of its origins will be decisive for judging whether in its engagement with "reason" or "knowledge", the "faith" side is reneging on essential elements only it can provide.

Regarding the three problematic assumptions, conclusions will be reached in Chapter Four, after portraying the questions arising for exegetes from these

---

[51] Habermas, vol. I, 495: "that God would have carried out the *act of the forgiveness of sins* not through divine sovereignty (*Vollmacht*), but by way of becoming human, thus through a self-humiliating incarnation."
[52] Habermas, vol. I, 566. 625.

texts and from other archaeological and written sources of the era. As brief indications, however, the answers will turn out to be, one, that Paul and the Gospels are separate strands with distinct and not overlapping theologies; two, that Jesus' symbolic actions and his presentation of God point to a Messianic self-understanding that the Gospels relate in different ways; three, that Paul's use of the cultic term of "atonement" for Jesus' death contrasts with a different Jewish conception chosen by the Gospels: the death of a just person.[53] They present the new act of God to raise him from the dead as the vindication of his life spent on putting into practice his understanding of God and God's reign. Without the content of Jesus' proclamation, and based uniquely on Paul's contraction of the term "Gospel" to comprise only Jesus' death and resurrection, it is hard to imagine any long-term resonance especially with Gentiles and thus for subsequent Christian inculturations.

---

53 In vol. I, 503–504, Habermas refers to the difference between Paul and Luke: "For Jesus' execution, Paul does not use, as Luke does, the interpretive scheme of the unjustly suffering prophet, known from the Bible"; but he does not follow up the resulting view of the "theological challenge of the Easter event" as the divine vindication of the historical life of Jesus that marks the Gospels' understanding in contrast to Paul's.

2 Reconstructing the Position of Paul in Early Christianity

As the debate treated in 1.3.3 on the allocation of typical motifs in Jesus' teaching and lifestyle to an overarching "Mediterranean" horizon exemplifies, one focus of enquiry is on how marked a contrast between Jewish monotheism and Graeco-Roman polytheism, schools of philosophy and Roman emperor cult can be assumed. This field of study is relevant for locating both the person of Jesus, whether Cynic, or marked by a specific combination of traditions in the Hebrew scriptures,[54] and Paul. It helps clarify the selection of key themes in interpreting the salvific role of Jesus Christ that the early Christian mission carried into Gentile cities. What Jürgen Habermas sums up as "Pauline Christianity" – assuming this to be the dominant tradition that shaped the Western part of the Christian heritage – needs to be examined historically. Thus, the first subsection deals with the different self-understandings identified indirectly through research into the sources (2.1), the second with Paul's theological approach in comparison to them (2.2). Approaches to Christolatry as the origin of the doctrine of Christ will follow in Chapter Three, and exegetical analyses of the types of connection that can be found from Paul's Letters to the oral tradition in Chapter Four. Only then, informed by these exegetical exchanges, can the three premises on which Habermas's enquiry is based be assessed in conclusion.

2.1 Enquiring into Christian origins: Contested issues

In view of the noted variations between texts that relate to the same historical facts, the enquiry must start with the exegetical task of assessing the sources (2.1.1). From the evidence of the conflicts that can be discovered, an overview of early Christian self-understandings has identified four groupings (2.1.2). A third point will be the attempt to infer from the narratives of the Gospels if and how a mission to the Gentiles can already be connected to the outlook of Jesus himself. This will be done by attending to the religious symbolism implied in his actions, preaching and travels (2.1.3).

---

54 In *Galilee and Gospel*, 185, Freyne notes that John D. Crossan also stresses the need to locate Jesus in the Jewish tradition without, however, investigating the specific accentuations Jesus gives to different strands within it: "His Jesus is a Mediterranean Jewish peasant, but when one analyses the data base on which this picture of Jesus is constructed, very little of the distinctively Jewish concerns of the Jesus tradition as a whole is considered to be relevant."

2.1.1 The exegetical task of assessing the sources

Which view one adopts of Christianity in the first hundred years of its expansion, depends to some extent on whether the companion volume to Luke's Gospel, Acts of the Apostles, is treated primarily as a historical or as an ecclesiological-theological document. In the latter case, careful distinctions must be made between normative and historical-empirical statements. The narrator's perspective will be analysed for the overall orientation it seeks to convey: the development is portrayed as a Spirit-led, successful mission beyond Israel to the Gentiles. It does not conclude with Paul's violent death two years after his arrival as a prisoner in Rome, but with Paul "proclaiming the kingdom of God and teaching the facts about the Lord Jesus Christ quite openly and without hindrance" (Acts 28:31). It will matter which links between the two parts of the diptych are identified, and how aspects in Luke's Gospel are assessed in relation to the portrait of the primitive church provided in Acts. Luke's silence on events known to him raises the question of what the term "Gospel" signifies, and secondly, the status of historical information. What methods are involved in arriving at them, how are sources compared, and what paradigms guide their interpretation? There seems to be no way of avoiding the circularity inherent in any of these argumentations.[55] To know what Jesus said and did, all that scholars have are the Gospels written forty to perhaps eighty years later with their own angles. What factors explain the move to a narrative portrait from the existing short credal formulas and Paul's use of the term "Gospel" only for the salvific death and resurrection of Jesus Christ?

At a literary level, it must be decided how the narrative outlines of the four Gospels are to be treated: as a coherent story, based on events in the past but unified by an underlying interpretation of the meaning of the recounted events? Or as a loose framework within which existing material – events, sayings, miniature scenes – is put into a sequence? While the New Testament scholar Hans-Josef Klauck defends the method of form criticism that has been put into question by readings of the Gospels as "eyewitness" accounts, he equally points out

---

55 Regarding the circularity which scholars are aware of, cf. Freyne, "The Jesus-Paul debate revisited and re-imagining Christian origins", in *Christian Origins: Worship, Belief, and Society*, ed. Kieran J. O'Mahoney (Sheffield: Sheffield Academic Press, 2003): 143–162, 153. Also Annette Merz points out in "Der historische Jesus – faszinierend und unverzichtbar", in *Die Anfänge des Christentums*, 23–56, 54, that "any historical presentation of Jesus is a scientific construct, attained in view of the sources that have been evaluated as knowledgeably and conscientiously as possible, while in the process of weighing up [...] also the presuppositions of the historian with their individual imprint and the literature received by him/her have a bearing."

its shortcomings: unlike a "mosaic", a Gospel is a coherent, elaborated story that is marked by the tension between the whole and its parts.[56] Individual events have a function regarding the ending, they foreshadow subsequent parts of the plot. The story in its entirety conveys impressions that one scene alone could not transmit. His example is the view of the disciples in Mark who are often depicted as failing to understand Jesus' teaching, actions and intentions.[57] So if an adequate assessment of a Gospel needs to consider it as a whole from which its parts depend, form critical "atomism" does not help in this task, even if it allows to identify breaks and junctures between separate units. Thus, "Gospels" must be approached as integrated compositions, not only as a framework for separate items. What are the reasons for Mark's creation of the first Gospel which was to have such an extraordinary history of effects, first by leading to further such accounts being composed, thus, becoming "tradition-forming to the highest degree"? Klauck names "four partial reasons",[58] which he derives from both external and internal causes. I will treat them in reverse order, beginning with the fourth: *bioi* or *vitae* were popular in the ancient world, and Christianity needed to make itself known since for many, it was barely distinguishable from Judaism. Philo had written a two-volume *Life of Moses* in the 50s CE, and the Hebrew Bible contained "ideal biographies of the prophet or of the suffering just person".[59] A further external reason was, three, a crisis situation marked by the succession of three emperors in one year leading up to the destruction of the Temple. It called for the composition of a counterview to Flavian governance, based on alternative values. Second, as reflected in Jan Assmann's theory of memory, the limit of the first generation had been reached, with Peter, James and Paul having been killed in the early 60s CE, and a different, stable basis for handing on the memory of Jesus had to be provided. The first reason

---

[56] Klauck, "'Ein Wort'", 66–68. He locates the possibility of "eyewitness" testimonies at the level of the oral tradition, showing that "the gospels themselves are the result of a formation of tradition" (67).

[57] Thus, at least the first gospel does not seem to validate Annette Merz's view that a "collective Messiahship" was shared by "competent" disciples ("Der historische Jesus", 55). The impression of the disciples as trustworthy friends is rather what John's Gospel puts forward. Klauck and Freyne point out how Mark emphasizses their failures. Klauck, "'Ein Wort'", 67: "only the combination (*Zusammenstellung*) in the Gospel allows to draw a profile of the disciples which, moreover, proves to be very unfavourable for them in the Gospel of Mark". Cf. Freyne, "In Search of Identity: Narrativity, Discipleship and Moral Agency", in *Moral Language in the New Testament*, ed. Ruben Zimmermann, J. Van der Watt, in cooperation with Susanne Luther (Tübingen: Mohr Siebeck, 2010), 75–76.

[58] Klauck, "'Ein Wort'", 72.

[59] Klauck, "'Ein Wort'", 69.

given, however, is an internal one relating to what can count as a "Gospel": "The Pauline and pre-Pauline credal formulas, also called 'Gospel', were brief and colourless. It was an obvious step to render them more imaginable and vivid through additional narrative traditions (*Erzählgut*)." Thus, the "rudimentary narrative structures" given already in what Paul professes to have received, that "Jesus died, was buried, was resurrected and appeared to the Twelve" (1 Cor 15:1–5) are "extended backwards", in other words, into the life of Jesus.[60]

The need for this to happen is evident: to put on a basis of writing what the oral tradition about Jesus had been transmitting to the newly founded communities. The hermeneutical challenge posed by the loss of connection to the memory of the original members of the movement after they had died could not have been bridged by the restriction of the term "Gospel" to "Jesus' death and resurrection".[61] It left it unclear how his crucifixion had come about and how God's new act was connected to Jesus' proclamation. This could only be done in a narrative of his life, of the passion and death in which it ended, and of a new beginning attributed to God's intervention, interpreted as a vindication of the understanding of God that Jesus had preached and practised.

2.1.2 An overview of early Christian self-understandings: Four groupings

In order to understand the progress of the Christian mission in the time before the first biographical account of Jesus was written, the religious and cultural backgrounds of the different Christian centres that had been founded prior to Paul's conversion must be taken into account. Asking about the groupings and self-understandings present in them constitutes a shift of method to the historical and social sciences, away from a purely systematic theological interest in tracing points of doctrine that are still under debate to the earliest stages of articulation. Christian theology in the twentieth century owes a debt to biblical studies for having upturned previous assumptions about mono-linear developments of motifs; one of these resulted in the restriction of salvation to the idea of "atonement", based on a straight line from Paul to the present. Before discussing this theme as part of the history of effects of Paul's theology in section 2.2, investigations of Christian origins must go back to the stage prior to

---

[60] Klauck, "'Ein Wort'", 60, 61.
[61] While the closing words of Acts describe Paul as speaking of the "kingdom" and of the "facts about the Lord Jesus Christ" (Acts 28:30–31), which seems to indicate a content connected with Jesus' ministry, and not merely his death, this view of the author of Acts does not find confirmation in Paul's Letters themselves.

Paul's Letters, to the oral tradition that was later taken up in the Gospels. The New Testament scholar Heinz Schürmann spelt out its significance for Roman Catholic fundamental theology and dogmatics in the 1980s: "The proclamation of salvation can only be proclaimed as 'Gospel' when Pauline soteriology [...] is filled in critically with the Gospels' material of speeches and narratives. Without it, the proclamation not only lacks its anchorage in history (the 'fundamental theological' aspect) but also the 'incarnational' counterpoint (the 'dogmatic' aspect)."[62] I read the point Schürmann is making in relation to the two systematic theological disciplines as underlining, first, that without the life of Jesus, his crucifixion cannot be understood, and that the contemporary credibility which fundamental theology is concerned with remains a task to be delivered; it cannot be short-circuited by only providing the Christian confession that Jesus' death was followed by his resurrection. Secondly, also the doctrinal understanding of Jesus Christ is underdetermined if the New Testament references to his unique status which include stories on the beginning of his life are left out. A soteriology must reflect that God became human in the person of Jesus who revealed God's essence through his life. Speaking of the incarnation as the "counterpoint" indicates the tension contained in the concept of salvation between an incarnational and a staurocentric soteriology which will become relevant in the history of Christian thinking.[63]

It remains contested among biblical scholars which key themes can be found in Paul's writings themselves, and which are owed to subsequent theological positions; this includes the concept of "original sin" that will be discussed in Chapter Five in the context of Augustine's doctrinal innovations in the patristic era. But it should be clear that the formulas quoted by Paul and taken as the basis of his soteriology lack a crucial element. In their condensed form, "he died, was buried, rose again and appeared", they take Jesus' specific proclamation for granted when dating salvation from his death. Margaret Mitchell spells out the decisive difference that the gospel accounts made for subsequent communities of believers: "Mark transformed the narrative potentials of bare-bones pre-Pauline missionary kerygma (1 Cor 15.3f) [...] into a work which offered his read-

---

62 Heinz Schürmann, *Gottes Reich – Jesu Geschick. Jesu ureigener Tod im Licht seiner Basileia-Verkündigung* (Freiburg: Herder, 1983), 248–249, quoted by Thomas Pröpper, *Erlösungsglaube und Freiheitsgeschichte. Eine Skizze zur Soteriologie* (München: Kösel, 3rd edn 1991), 228.
63 Cf. Pröpper, *Erlösungsglaube und Freiheitsgeschichte*, 69–88.

ers [...] a chance to stand on an equal footing with the original disciples of Jesus. It was this hermeneutical act that won the day".[64]

In order to access the communities out of which the gospels were written, the question is what can be ascertained historically about these foundations for which the oral tradition was the basis of their belief in Christ. Which groupings were active in mission in those cities? A first insight of research since the 1980s has been that the context was more complex than a simple Jewish/Gentile contrast allows for. The first major centre outside of Jerusalem was Antioch, with the Christian mission linked to the *hellenistai* who had to flee after their member Stephen had been killed. Both in Antioch and in Rome, founded a decade later, the mission was to Diaspora Jews. Practical questions had arisen for Jews due to this location, such as keeping the Sabbath as a day of rest and Torah reading,[65] instead of conforming to the Gentiles' working weeks that were only interrupted by occasional festivals or civic feast days.[66] New matters arose when the first Gentiles wished to join the Christian community: food laws, marriage laws, and circumcision. Here, different understandings appeared that had already been voiced in the critique in Jerusalem of Peter's decision to fulfil Cornelius's request for baptism without imposing the Mosaic law.[67] Behind the controversy was the theological question of how Gentiles qualified for being included into God's covenant with Israel.[68]

Once it becomes clear that not just two positions need to be distinguished, a more nuanced assessment emerges of where the three leaders Peter, James and Paul stood, how their perspectives changed and what was at stake. Raymond Brown identifies four groupings. On completely opposite sides were those who

---

[64] Margaret M. Mitchell, "Patristic Counter-Evidence to the Claim that 'The Gospels were Written for all Christians'", in *New Testament Studies* 51 (2005) 36–79, 79, quoted by Klauck, "'Ein Wort'", 73, n. 31.
[65] Cf. Margaret Daly-Denton, "Instilling the Word", *Worship* 95 (2021): 196–203, especially 197–198.
[66] Cf. Habermas 2019, Vol. I, 494, on the difference Jews instituted in the Babylonian exile from the "continuous flow of time of their pagan environment through a caesura otherwise unknown in Antiquity, namely a *weekly* holiday (*Feiertag*) dedicated to the reverence (*Anbetung*) of the Lord".
[67] Cf. Brown, "Rome", in Raymond Brown and John Meier, *Antioch and Rome: New Testament Cradles of Catholic Christianity* (London: Chapman, 1982), 125: "According to Acts 11:2–3, after Peter baptized Cornelius (in the late 30s?) they criticized him in Jerusalem on his openness to Gentiles."
[68] Freyne, *The Jesus Movement and its Expansion. Meaning and Mission* (Grand Rapids, MI: Eerdmans, 2014), 226: The "deeper issue was theological, namely, on what conditions could the Gentiles share in the messianic blessings?"

insisted on all features of the Torah, including circumcision, and those whose Temple critique was so fundamental that no links to the religious centre and the traditions of Judaism were to be upheld. The second and the third positions agreed that for Gentiles, circumcision was not required to join the community. They differed on the requirement to keep to the food laws, the Sabbath and the Jewish festivals. John Meier who otherwise describes Barnabas's split from Paul in terms of his "capitulation to Peter and James and his desertion of Paul" states that in Acts, James, the brother of Jesus who joined the circle of the Apostles after the Easter events and became leader of the Jerusalem church, was "the chief and climactic spokesman for the circumcision-free mission".[69] The judgements of the exegetes differ especially on James. Meier speaks of the "ascendancy of the James party, which Peter had not been able to resist and Paul had not been able to defeat" and of the "circumcision-free mission [...] hobbled for a while by the strict policies imposed by the James party from Jerusalem".[70] In the same co-authored book, Brown offers a discerning explanation: that the first grouping for whom Torah observance was to be imposed without exception eventually gathered under the name of James,[71] even though his actual position differed from theirs. Seán Freyne points out the minimal attention given in Luke-Acts to James despite the fact that

> in less than a decade after Jesus' death, James the brother of the Lord was clearly in a leadership role in Jerusalem, side by side with Peter, the leader of the Twelve [...] we hear remarkably little about him in the New Testament, especially in Acts [...] James was not wholly written out of the official version of Christian origins, but only because those who were responsible for that version, including Luke, could not have omitted him and remained credible.[72]

While Luke-Acts plays down the conflict between Paul and the original disciples, at the same time, a nuanced difference can be noted in that Luke does not use the term "apostle" for Paul, as he himself does: "Yet in subtle ways, such as the absence of his own favorite self-designation 'apostle', which Luke reserves for the Twelve, he is made subservient to them and to the Jerusalem church".[73]

---

[69] John Meier, "Antioch", in Raymond Brown and John Meier, *Antioch and Rome*, 34, 36.
[70] Meier, "Antioch", 44. 22.
[71] Brown, "Rome", 132, n. 279: "The name of James and the memory of Jerusalem were co-opted by the more extreme Jewish Christians (Group One, Introduction) who insisted on circumcision".
[72] Freyne, *Expansion*, 223–224.
[73] Freyne, *Expansion*, 189. "Luke's main purpose was to present a unified picture of the movement as it progressed on its mission of witnessing about Jesus from Jerusalem to Rome. In doing

For Freyne, the important role of James "for all the different branches of the emerging Jesus movement" lies in "keeping alive the issue of Jewish participation in the universal plan of God". From this perspective, he sees in Acts a choice of direction that comes at the expense of the connection to the prophet of the Exile period who was most significant for Jesus, namely Isaiah: "part of the 'success' of Luke's account is that it so emphasizsed the Jerusalem–Rome axis that the other axis one might describe as the Jerusalem–Babylon axis was largely forgotten or ignored".[74]

Among the conflicted items that separated Group Two from Group Three in Raymond Brown's distinction were the food laws. The significance of one key aspect is explained by Philip Esler, namely the question whether it was permitted to eat meat sacrificed to idols. In his view, it acquired a game-changing status because more than the question of availing of the opportunity of low sales prices was involved. It owed its importance to a core principle of the Jewish conception of God: the prohibition of idolatry. Meat sacrificed to statues of gods and wine that could have been converted into an offering for a Gentile's god breached this prohibition.[75] It was therefore a matter of principle and not one that could be resolved pragmatically.

Thus, the differences between those who insisted on the ongoing relevance of specific Jewish laws as reflecting not just a dietary regulation, but their essential view of God, and those for whom Christ's death and resurrection had put an end to "the Law" were based on matters of principal importance. They are misrepresented if they are merely portrayed as the inability of the "Judaizers" to understand the implications of their new faith orientation. Before investigating Paul's position on what was at issue theologically, how the Covenant could include Gentiles, it must be examined how Jesus' position towards them can be determined. Is Paul's focus on mission to the Gentiles an inherently new departure, as Habermas seems to assume?[76]

---

so, he smoothed over various divergences and conflicts that occurred, especially with regard to Paul" (227).

[74] Freyne, *Expansion*, 241.

[75] This is the view Philip Esler arrives at on this question from his use of literary and social sciences in biblical studies. Philip F. Esler, *Galatians* (London: Routledge, 1998), 104–108, in Chapter 4 on "The problem of mixed table-fellowship", 93–116.

[76] In Vol. I, 502–503, Habermas agrees that the "question if Jesus radicalised Jewish teaching also in the sense of a universalisation of God's commandments beyond Israel to all of humanity, is not quite easy to answer [...] Jesus subordinates the separating purity and ritual commandments to the commandment of love and reconciliation. Yet [...] the strictly universalist interpretation of the divine law is only established as a result of the mission to the Gentiles for which Paul had to request the agreement of Peter and James in the primitive church of Jerusalem."

2.1.3 Uncovering the religious symbolism of Jesus' actions, travels and preaching

The decisions made in the primitive church at the "Council of Jerusalem" (portrayed as having the standing of a Council in Acts, but not in Paul's Letters) need to be compared to Jesus' own practice. They included the resolution not to impose all of the Torah requirements on Gentiles, to divide up the next steps of the Christian mission between preaching to the Gentiles (who were to be addressed by Paul), and "the circumcised" in the Diaspora (to whom Peter was sent), and to come to joint agreements.

In Jesus' own ministry, a key difference emerges: on the one hand, his inclusion also of the non-Jews into God's salvific will, based on Isaiah's vision of the Gentiles as offering their prayers and even their sacrifices at the Jerusalem Temple; on the other hand, the priority of the House of Israel in his own mission. The early Christian outreach towards the Gentiles can be seen as a consequence of Jesus' endorsement of Isaiah's image of an eschatological "banquet with the patriarchs", including all of humanity, due to God's promise of descendants to Abraham. Following Annette Merz's pointer to the "power of symbol-political actions",[77] I will highlight exegetical research on four themes from Jesus' proclamation and public action: first, the symbolic function of selecting the Twelve; second, the political relevance of the announcement of the Kingdom of God already begun in his actions; third, the implications of his Temple critique for access to the forgiveness of a merciful God; fourth, the mixture of wisdom and apocalyptic thinking in his parables and prayers.

2.1.3.1 The symbolism of the Twelve
The selection of the Twelve, symbolising the twelve sons of Jacob, standing for Israel, indicates a specific conception of the renewal of Israel by reaching back to the pre-monarchic tradition. Annette Merz sees a marked contrast between the Twelve installed as "judges" and constituting "an exile government of twelve persons hailing from the ordinary people", and the "members of the Jewish elite who collaborated with the Romans".[78] While agreeing that the "restoration of the twelve tribes was a regular motif in Second Temple restoration literature", Freyne interprets also Jesus' journeys as symbolic, extending to the "boundaries of the Promised Land" by going beyond the territory of the "political Galilee of

---

77 Merz, "Der historische Jesus", 51–53.
78 Merz, "Der historische Jesus", 52–53.

his day".⁷⁹ Declining at the same time the existing understanding of the role of Messiah in political terms, the directions in which Jesus proclaims the arrival of the Kingdom of God relate to the gathering of the lost tribes; it cannot be confused with the military territorial aspirations pursued by the contemporary movement of the Zealots. Instead, the backdrop is Isaiah's announcement of a peaceful future which is introduced by the "oracle of salvation for the north that mentions the Galilean tribes (Isa 8:23 [9:1])." It contains the "joyful poem" that "celebrates the arrival of the Messiah king in the form of a child whose birth signals an end to war, whose names include the titles of Wonderful Counselor and Prince of Peace, and who will rule with justice and integrity (9:2–6)". Thus, a "strong messianic subtext" can be detected in the "election of the Twelve".⁸⁰ The symbolism of their number and of the destinations of Jesus' mission travels endorses the primacy of announcing the Kingdom of God to the greater Israel, including the lands of the northern tribes.

2.1.3.2 The Kingdom of God as a counter-vision to existing oppressive powers

While Jesus refuses a direct answer to the question, transmitted in Q, of the disciples of John whether he is the Messiah, the lines he quotes from Isaiah constitute an indirect claim: "the blind receive their sight, the lame walk, lepers are cleansed, the deaf hear, the dead are raised, and the poor have good news preached to them" (Q Luke 7:18–23; Matt 11:2–6). Healings were part of the expectations to this figure.⁸¹ By explaining the backdrop of the Roman occupation and the growing economic hardship especially for the rural population resulting from the construction of cities and imperial building projects, Theissen, Merz, and Freyne highlight the political dimension of the "values revolution" inaugurated by Jesus.⁸² The link to John the Baptist is itself a politically risky statement:

---

79 Freyne, *Expansion*, 141. He points out that "Luke omits these forays into the Gentile territory" and connects this to his interest in portraying "mission as expanding from Jerusalem" in Acts, not from Galilee (*Expansion*, 143, n. 17). The other three evangelists record that the disciples went back to Galilee after Jesus' death, while Luke reports them as gathering in Jerusalem.
80 Freyne, *Expansion*, 142.
81 Freyne describes "Jesus' exorcisms/healings" with reference to Isaiah as "an important aspect of his messianic claims". The response to John the Baptist "combines several discrete references from Isaiah: Isa 26:19, 29:18–19, 35:5–6" (*Expansion*, 155).
82 Gerd Theissen, "Die Jesus-Bewegung als charismatische Wertrevolution", in *New Testament Studies* 35 (1989): 343–360, quoted by Freyne, *Expansion*, 162. In "Der historische Jesus", 49, Merz refers to the "eminently political dimension" of the "statement that the 'Kingdom of

"By aligning himself so emphatically with John in the Q passage [...], Jesus was inevitably placing himself in the public eye also [...] The fact that his opening declaration was couched in a highly political statement about the imminent arrival of God's *basileia* or kingly rule leaves the matter in no doubt". In contrast to John's preaching in remote locations, Jesus went to the villages, "engaging with the people of Galilee. By traveling among them, healing their sick, and instructing them in the values of God's *basileia* through his own action and lifestyle, Jesus was directly but subtly challenging the values that Rome and its collaborators were espousing."[83]

Merz sees a connection between the heightening of "universal ethical norms and the relativising of cultural norms [...] It was consistent (*stimmig*) with this to transfer the dynamic of reintegrating marginalised persons towards an opening for non-Jews".[84] It needs to be asked, however, whether the question of the inclusion of Gentiles is not distinct from the problem of social justice and recognition within Israel. For Freyne, the roots of the "universal" horizon are to be found in Jesus' selection of sources within Jewish monotheism, especially the God of Genesis, and the prophets, above all, Isaiah and Jeremiah. The increasing discrepancy between the Temple and the city of Jerusalem that depended on it, and the rural experience of debt and servitude, are countered with the biblical norms of justice and the designation of the land as belonging to all.[85] The growth parables convey the earth's impressive fertility with enough resources to feed everyone. Two further particular features from Jesus' heritage need to be illuminated before conclusions can be drawn regarding the extension of God's promises to Israel also to the Gentiles.

2.1.3.3 Temple critique as a religious and political challenge

A shared element appearing across the different renewal movements in Second Temple Judaism was a critique of the Temple practices. At stake was the understanding and the accessibility of God's forgiveness for which pilgrims to the Jerusalem Temple offered the sacrifice of animals bought in its precincts. Two aspects are noteworthy: the threat posed by such a critique, and the theology behind it, as evident in the linking of Jesus' cleaning of the Temple of money lenders to the prophets Jeremiah and Isaiah in Mark's Gospel.

God is near' or even 'already there' in a country occupied by the Romans respectively governed by their puppet princes (*Marionettenfürsten*)".
83 Freyne, *Expansion*, 138–139.
84 Merz, "Der historische Jesus", 55.
85 Cf. Freyne, *Expansion*, 159.

The alternative sites of worship – not in Jerusalem but in the desert – chosen by the Essenes and by John the Baptist and his rite of baptism highlight the degree to which rituals include struggles with authority about the core inspiration of a religious tradition. The more "dysfunctional" the Jerusalem Temple had become "in terms of its primary responsibility as the seat of the divine presence for all Israel because of the power alliances [...] with the officers of Roman rule",[86] the more important was it to be able to relate to the heritage of the prophets. Gerd Theissen points out the rural origins also of the previous critics: Micah, Uriah, Jeremiah, "the prophets before Jesus who challenged Jerusalem were also from the country".[87] Merz invokes the "power of the prophetic destabilisation of the status quo" and concludes from it the "death-bringing enmity of the temple aristocracy towards Jesus [...] A movement that turned against the temple as the main source of income of the priestly aristocracy could not hope for tolerance".[88] Quoting the Hebrew Scriptures constituted a challenge to the core of their basis of legitimation. Precisely with regard to "the temple and the land, the cornerstone on which the temple based its claims and depended for its maintenance [...], it offered a different interpretation of those symbols in terms of God's original design for all Israel."[89]

It should be clear from the ritual context as elucidated by these exegetes that it was the constellation of Roman occupiers, Sadducean keepers of the Temple and Jesus' symbolic actions that led to Jesus' violent end. They constitute the circumstances that determine the interpretation of his death; they cannot be left behind as contingent conditions that do not have a bearing on the understanding

---

86 Freyne, *Expansion*, 150.
87 Freyne, *Expansion*, 179, with reference to Theissen, "Die Tempelweissagung Jesu. Prophetie im Spannungsfeld zwischen Tempel und Land", in *Theologische Zeitung* 32 (1976): 144–158.
88 Merz, "Der historische Jesus", 47.
89 Freyne, *Expansion*, 180. In *Galilee and Gospel*, 205, he refers to the "downwards spiral of options – from landowning to leasing, to day-labouring, to slavery or banditry [...] Jesus' vision of shared goods and rejection of the normal securities, including money [...] though utopian in its intention, did provide an alternative vision, operating within a genuinely prophetic framework". As Freyne outlines in *Jesus, a Jewish Galilean*, 47, the sayings collected in the Beatitudes of the Sermon on the Mount (Matthew) or on the Plain (Luke) appeal to God's original design for Israel. They "seek to reassure people who have to face the prospect of being reduced to conditions of impoverishment, hunger and mourning, and who felt the right to rail against such conditions in the light of the promise of 'a land flowing with milk and honey'. The promise that had been made to their ancestors was now being enjoyed by outsiders – veterans of Herod the Great's armies and other pro-Herodian favourites who had been given shares in the best land of the country as a reward for their loyalty [...] Jesus' call for unconditional trust in the heavenly Father in the face of deep anxieties about food, drink and clothing – the very basics of human life – was indeed a strange demand".

of his message. By combining Jeremiah's accusation for the Temple, "you have turned it into a den of thieves" (Jer 7:11),[90] with its designation by Isaiah as a "house of prayer for all nations" (Isa 56:7), Jesus establishes a different understanding of worship, making God's forgiveness available in all settings.

2.1.3.4 A unique combination of apocalyptic thinking and wisdom

A further source of symbolism, to be examined in conclusion, is the presence of two genres in Jesus' teaching: apocalypse, and wisdom – neither scribal nor Cynic, but in the Jewish tradition of *mashal*, as evident in the parables. Both are marked by poetic language and an imaginative appeal to the hearers. With its portrayal of political powers as dangerous animals, dreams containing visions of God's final judgement on the perpetrators of evil and of a "new world", apocalyptic thought, too, makes use of indirect communication. Their social locations, the Lord's Prayer as a case in which both genres are joined, and a key distinction from a Greek ethos in the underlying understanding of agency will be the three aspects treated.

As a first characterisation, apocalyptic groupings had a justice concern at their core which was outlined in cosmic dimensions. For Merz it is clear that for "the Sadducees, all apocalyptic movements which regarded the existing order as one to be overcome were a thorn in their eye as potential troublemakers (*Unruhestifter*)".[91] Regarding the shared social and political situation with Jesus' mentor John the Baptist, Freyne sums up Judean society as "divided between allegiance to the central symbol system and its guardians and concern about the social deprivation and distance from the power structures that the populace at large was experiencing [...] both aspects – the apocalyptic worldview and the passion for social justice – are hallmarks of Jesus' public ministry also".[92]

Yet how does a worldview that has "strong resonances in the context of oppression and social exclusion"[93] relate to wisdom which has been classified as opposite with its acceptance of natural processes, its proverbial anchorage in everyday experiences, and its distance from sudden upheavals? Freyne argues that

---

90 In *Expansion*, 179, Freyne points out the parallel to Jeremiah's breaking of a ceramic jug as a symbol of what Yahweh will do with the people practising syncretism (Jer 19:1–11). The threat present in such an announcement which can also be found in Psalm 2:9, is audible in Händel's *Messiah*, in the air, "Thou shalt dash them in pieces like a potter's vessel", just before the Hallelujah chorus.
91 Merz, "Der historische Jesus", 47.
92 Freyne, *Expansion*, 138.
93 Freyne, *Expansion*, 151.

positioning the two at polar ends is misleading; he points to an area of overlap for the specific strand of wisdom that is separate from the "court adviser" and the privileged position of scribes as secure civil servants in the capital's administration. In contrast, peasant wisdom was located in settings where its bearers were thoroughly occupied to meet the most basic needs. What both strands share is a "visionary" element. Also the parables contain "qualities of the enigmatic, the unexpected, and the subversive", an "element of exaggeration and surprise", calling for people's individual insight to "reappraise their own assessments". Thus, "apocalyptic and wisdom play off each other to reveal the hidden mysterious nature of God's involvement in the everyday".[94] Wisdom, as practised in Jesus' sayings and parables, confirms the listeners in their perceptiveness, enabling them to discover new aspects themselves. It not only "sublimates the observations and language of the ordinary people" but also moves to "privileging their lives and their world as a locus of revelation in terms of God's care for the whole creation".[95]

An example of both backgrounds being drawn on can, secondly, be seen in the Lord's Prayer, the earliest version of which is found in Luke. Freyne interprets the request, "May your kingdom come", as apocalyptic, and for "daily bread" and delivery from debt as a reminder of key stories and institutions in the Hebrew Bible:

> The first and last petitions refer to God's coming kingdom and the judgment that will ensue, while the middle two deal with the everyday needs of humans – bread and debt-relief [...] on the basis that the suppliants also forgive their debtors. Both reflect a social situation of mere subsistence and indebtedness [...] the petitions also recall two separate biblical images [...] The notion of daily bread recalls the gift of manna in the desert [...] The forgiveness of debt was part of the Jubilee legislation [...] intended to maintain equitable land ownership [...], since the land really belonged to Yahweh and Israelites shared in it as leaseholders only.[96]

This final point evokes the Jewish understanding of creation and of the implications of having been led out of slavery to their own land: it protects the land from

---

[94] Freyne, *Expansion*, 161. 160. In her treatment of the "poetic power of parables" in "Der historische Jesus", 54, Merz also points out the "poetic freedom" and "scope" (*Spielraum*) given to the hearers, contrasting, in her view, with "judgement sermons or the Beatitudes" which "allocate the hearers their places very accurately". Yet with their "counterfactual status ascriptions" (50), can the Beatitudes not equally be seen as conveying the element of surprise, of overturning oppressive situations and norms? Even preaching on the Last Judgement can be seen to share in the "power to restructure perceptions and to learn to see the present anew" highlighted by Merz.
[95] Freyne, *Expansion*, 162.
[96] Freyne, *Expansion*, 158–159, with references to Q Lk 11:2–4/Matt 6:9–13, and to Lev 25:8–17.

individual claims and delegitimises any collusion with the occupying Roman forces which allowed them to build edifices with decorations which contravened the prohibition of images.

The third insight relates to the different understandings of self and God, world and history between the Jewish and the Greek traditions that will pose tasks of translation for centuries to come.[97] The view of agency differs as a result: the will-based ethics of biblical monotheism contrasts with a cognition-based Greek view of striving for a flourishing life that assumes humans to be part of a natural teleology. Jesus' proclamation draws on each individual's ability to repent and to begin anew and evokes imaginative responses to situations of tension and coercion. His commandment to "love your enemy" should not be mistaken for quietism.[98] The promise to the "meek", to those "thirsting for justice" and "the peacemakers" in the Beatitudes that they will be the ones to "inherit the land", "be filled" and "be called the children of God" (Mt 5:5 – 6.9)[99] has been interpreted as charting a "third way" of nonviolent resistance between

---

[97] The fact that the key ethical concepts and directions in Western thinking have been shaped by the encounter with biblical monotheism was already highlighted in Habermas's response to Johann Baptist Metz in "Jerusalem or Athens? Where does anamnestic reason belong? J. B. Metz on unity amidst multicultural plurality", in Habermas, *Religion and Rationality. Essays on Reason, God and Modernity* (Cambridge: Polity, 2002), 129 – 138.

[98] Habermas's judgement of early Christian ethics as "quietist" may owe more to Paul than to Jesus who challenged the religious and political powers with his own vision "for an alternative social arrangement in which all Israel would share equally in the land" (Freyne, *Expansion*, 159). Habermas refers to the "decoupling of personal salvation (*Heil*) from the rescue of the people [...] The peace commandment has an outstanding rank in Christian ethics. A quietist submission to the sword of worldly government was the preferred option. Despite the persecutions of Christians also in the Roman Empire they behaved in a conformist (*angepasst*) way" (Vol. I, 489). He subsequently points out the different priorities they chose: "The commandment of love of neighbour known already from the Old Testament is not only renewed but radicalised by giving it a new standing: "You have heard that it was said, 'Love your neighbour and hate your enemy.' But I tell you, love your enemies and pray for those who persecute you" (Mt 5:43 – 44) [...] *Ethics of law* is now *subordinated* (*nachgeordnet*) to the *commandment to love*. Love of neighbour is proven (*bewährt sich*) in the willingness to forgive by those who have themselves become guilty towards their debtors. Indeed, God's forgiveness is dependent on the willingness of humans to forgive one another (Mt 6:14 – 15). In this sense, 'true justice' is fulfilled in love of neighbour. The latter is not tailored (*zugeschnitten*) towards the just solution of conflicts of action under the *existing* societal conditions but towards a *reconciliatory* conduct of life beyond mere justice which is to disrupt the *dynamics of human relationships of violence*" (Vol. I, 500).

[99] Merz, "Der historische Jesus", 50, emphasises that they constitute "counterfactual status ascriptions".

"fight and flight".¹⁰⁰ Also the answer Jesus gives to a question designed to trap him, whether Jews are required to pay tax to the Romans, exemplifies an artful way of resolving tensions peacefully. As Merz points out, by asking the questioner to identify the image of the Emperor on the coin, he made him aware of equally being "implicated in the imperial economic processes: Jesus' rejection of violence [...] does not by any means demonstrate an unpolitical attitude. The same is true of his diplomatic answer, 'Give to Caesar what is Caesar's, but to God what is God's'". In a situation in which "any refusal to pay tax would have resulted in an immediate military intervention by the Romans [...] he successfully de-escalates the conflict while maintaining his own religious identity".¹⁰¹ The biblical awareness of evil is matched by the conviction that there is no cosmic force on a par with God, the creator and judge. Hope based on Israel's historical experiences of rescue by Yahweh is available to all. Healings of embodied humans – not disembodied souls – are one of the signs of the Kingdom of God, who is the only legitimate holder of the title of king.

Each of the four features just treated show the importance of locating Jesus' ministry in the symbolic understandings of lived Jewish monotheism. But how can the message be translated into the intellectual and practice-shaping contexts of the polytheistic cultures of a Greek or Roman majority? This is where the different models of Christian mission need to be examined.

2.2 Paul's theological approach

Regarding its relationship to the Gentiles, the early Christian community could base its understanding on the book of Isaiah in its three eras, written before, in and after the Babylonian exile. It professed God as creator and redeemer in the most encompassing terms and envisaged the ultimate inclusion of all of humanity into Yahweh's universal salvific will. There were other strands, including Ezekiel, that had drawn exclusivist consequences from the experiences of conquest and occupation,¹⁰² which Jesus did not align himself with in his symbolic practices and references. Isaiah's model was one of the nations coming as pilgrims to Mount Zion and joining with Israel in its worship at the Temple. The

---

100 In Chapter 2 of *Jesus and Nonviolence. A Third Way* (Minneapolis: Fortress Press, 2003), Walter Wink explains that "turning the other cheek" in the context of the existing cultural rules was not submissive but an actual challenge, as was the offer to carry a Roman soldier's bag for two miles, instead of the one mile permitted for the occupying forces.
101 Merz, "Der historische Jesus", 47.
102 Freyne, "The Jesus-Paul Debate Revisited", 153.

decision already by the primitive church in Jerusalem to engage in mission after the killing of Stephen led to new constellations. The communities founded in Syria and Samaria were Jewish Christian, just like the one in Rome, which emerged a decade later from the same strong connection between Jerusalem and the Jewish Diaspora. Yet the horizons were changed by Diaspora settings in which there were Gentiles already sympathetic to Jewish monotheism. With men and women from this group being attracted by the missionaries' message of the crucified and risen Lord Jesus Christ to these gatherings, unprecedented questions arose. What was the content of this faith, and which standing did the history of Israel as elected by God retain in it? Which rites of admission and expression of the connection to its founder, as well as shared measures of conduct did the community develop? These issues become all the more substantial when the new faith orientation is no longer spread by the original disciples whose proclamation draws on their shared experience of Jesus' ministry but by new preachers who cannot avail of this background, such as Paul. From the ongoing discussions among scholars in Second Temple Judaism and Early Christianity, as well as theologians and philosophers,[103] three issues will be selected; they will illuminate the complex situation of early Christian mission within which Paul's theology constitutes one strand. What is his conception of the message of salvation that he transmits without the benefit of having been part of the movement during the lifetime of its founder (2.2.1)? Which are the practical consequences of being a Christian that he outlines to the communities he established (2.2.2)? And how does he solve the problem of the relationship between faith in Christ as saviour of all humankind and in a God who elected and made promises to Israel (2.2.3)?

2.2.1 A soteriology of atonement

Before comparing Paul's interpretation of Jesus' death – which Habermas regards as dominant in the history of Christianity – to the New Testament narratives, the question about the role of Jesus' life in Paul's proclamation must be mentioned. By using "Jesus Christ" as a proper name, he takes already for granted what the Gospels will work out as a contested claim: the status of Jesus as the Messiah, the anointed one or "Christ". The issues of whether features of his pub-

---

[103] See, for example, Paul Ricoeur's contribution and the interpretations of Alain Badiou and Giorgio Agamben discussed in *Esprit* no. 292, February 2003, on "L'événement saint Paul: juif, grec, roman, chrétien", 64–124.

lic activity belonged to the messianic expectations, Jesus' own reticence regarding this title and his redefinition of its meaning as well as its link to the official justification for his crucifixion as "King of the Jews" remain out of sight. The question why Jesus' own ministry does not appear in Paul's writings has exercised scholarly debate. For James Dunn, the background is that Jesus' life could be assumed to have been known, and that Paul's theology took off from interpreting his death on the backdrop of this shared common knowledge.[104] Jerome Murphy-O'Connor envisages the theme of the first meeting between Peter and Paul three years after his conversion to have been exactly about Jesus' life.[105] While the content of their meetings over a fortnight is not a possible item for research, it shows that Pauline and New Testament scholars wonder whether Paul had any interest in the details of Jesus' actual practice and proclamation: "Even after his Damascus Road experience it is noteworthy how Paul [...] shows little interest in memories of the historical Jesus for developing his own theological synthesis."[106]

Jesus' significance is explicated instead with a cultic term, a category taken from the Jewish Temple sacrifice, when Paul states that "God presented Christ as a *hilastērion*" (Rom 3:25).[107] It refers to the mercy seat in the Temple that was sprinkled with blood on the Day of Atonement, in accordance with Lev 16:13–15. What is the difference between this interpretation and the presentations given in the Gospels and Acts: that Jesus' death was due to the political and religious powers colluding in their interest in a Passover season without disturbances, and that God vindicated his person and message by resurrecting him?

> The crucifixion and subsequent resurrection are central to all these accounts, but unlike Paul's and later theology, where Jesus' death is understood as an "atoning sacrifice for sin" (Rom 3:24–25; Heb 10:12; Acts 13:38–38), the emphasis of the early speeches is on the fact of the Judean leaders' complicity in the unjust handing over of Jesus to Pilate and his subsequent vindication by God. It is this latter experience, not Jesus' death, that was crucial to these first preachers.[108]

---

104 James D. G. Dunn, *The Theology of Paul the Apostle* (Grand Rapids, MI: Eerdmans, 1998), 185.
105 Jerome Murphy-O'Connor, *Paul. His Story* (Oxford: Oxford University Press, 2006), 1–37.
106 Freyne, *Expansion*, 222, Fn. 54, states that "only four actual sayings of Jesus have been identified": on marriage, divorce, support for missionaries, and the Lord's Supper.
107 A differentiated exegetical treatment of the term "*hilastērion*", generally translated as "atonement", is offered by Christopher M. Tuckett in "Atonement in the NT", in *The Anchor Bible Dictionary* (New York: Doubleday, 1992), Vol. 1, 518–522.
108 Freyne, *Expansion*, 198–199. His comparison of the different understandings of his death in Paul and in Acts goes on: "As Luke presents it, God's plan, foretold in the prophets, has been wonderfully realized [...] Peter's speech in the house of the Roman centurion Cornelius is the

It seems that when Jesus' death and resurrection are disconnected from his life, these terms become theological contents in their own right. They can be further interpreted without having to check their particular imprint against what can be sought to be ascertained at least indirectly about Jesus' proclamation. Yet like every other theological concept, "atonement" must be put to the test of whatever consensus is achievable on the historical knowledge about Jesus. How his death is understood sets the course for different views of God and the human person, of agency, history, and eschatology. From Q, which shows no interest in Jesus' death,[109] to Paul, for whom it is the key point of Jesus' historical existence, and to the Gospels which reconstruct its factors from the perspectives of their situations in the first and the early second centuries, exegetes and theologians have put forward divergent positions. These exemplify the problem that was laid out in Chapter One: that the "brute facts" of historical events are never accessible and that the facts of Jesus' life and proclamation are only available in interpreted form. At the same time, it is crucial to distinguish from these already interpreted forms the prior events that gave rise to them, and to compare different interpretations in relation to them. Thus, it is possible and necessary to compare Paul's presentation of the death of Jesus as "*hilastērion*" (Rom 3:25) to the other New Testament accounts which draw on a different understanding of God, for example, in Luke's version of the crucifixion. According to Luke, it is Jesus who asks for his executioners, "Father, forgive them, for they do not know what they are doing" (Lk 23:34). Exegetically, these two sources can be allowed to stand as distinct, equally original traditions. Yet in theology, also in view of the effects on the spirituality and practices of the believing communities, such a parallel status would be insufficient and would make a coherent presentation impossible. The event behind the interpretations matters, even if it escapes a definitive reconstruction. While the claim to present history "as it was" is untenable, it is still possible to argue from the different interpretations given in the New Testament and make a case for or against a specific reading. Paul's reference to Christ

---

most detailed in terms of a description of Jesus' ministry [...] Far from being a criminal deserving of death by crucifixion, Jesus is in fact God's anointed one, fulfilling his destiny as this had been foretold in the Scriptures" which "could now be mined for suitable epithets: he is *mare'* (Lord) and *Mashiah* (Christ); he is the Holy and Righteous one; he is the rejected stone that has become the Cornerstone, as announced in Ps 118:22 with regard to the new temple; or, finally, he is the savior of all."

109 In his comparison with the oral tradition, Freyne points out: "Certainly there is no mention of an 'atoning death' as elaborated by Paul in either Q or the *Gospel of Thomas*", nor in "the Didache's account of the eucharistic celebrations". Freyne, *Expansion*, 259, with reference to *Didache* 9–10.

"whom God put forward as a *hilastērion* through faith in his blood" remains an elliptic verse with divergent translations and interpretations already at the exegetical level.[110] Since Paul also draws on other conceptions,[111] systematic theology is well advised not to attribute a unitary understanding even to Paul and much less, to use this term as the core foundation of the universal salvific significance of Jesus.

Each of these guiding preconceptions is fallible and can be challenged; but it does make sense to elaborate an integrated view and subject it to the process of intersubjective validation; it remains true, however, that only degrees of objectivity in interpretation can be achieved. What needs to be examined next are the implications of Paul's theology for human agency and the social world it relates to.

2.2.2 An ethics structured by the distinction of gospel and grace from law

A consistent feature of Paul's theology is its structuring by antitheses which comprise complex counterparts that are condensed into one concept: Law-Gospel, Adam-Christ, sin-grace, death-resurrection. How does a map like this prefigure the conceptions of God's salvific action in relation to human agency and to the Kingdom of God? Did it affect features and structures of the nascent Christian communities gathered around a "Gospel" identified by these polarities?

---

110 The word "sacrifice" does not appear in the Greek. "A sacrifice of atonement" is the NRSV and NIV attempt at translation of *hilastērion*, while the RSV and the NAB translate it as "an expiation". The CSB, ESV and NIV also interpret "faith" as referring to the Christian believers even if it could also refer to Christ when it renders the Greek as "a sacrifice of atonement, through the shedding of his blood—to be received by faith". Such additions to the literal wording provided by the translations arise from the subsequent traditions of reception. I am grateful to Dr Margaret Daly-Denton for offering careful clarifications and enriching new perspectives of interpretation.
111 In "Atonement in the NT", Tuckett summarises: "Certainly Paul uses a variety of metaphors. Jesus' death can be seen variously as new Passover sacrifice (1 Cor 5:7), a new covenant sacrifice (1 Cor 11:25), perhaps as a sin-offering (Rom 8:3, though the precise interpretation is disputed), perhaps as the sin-offering of the Day of Atonement (cf. *hilastērion* in Rom 3:25: again the precise reference is disputed [...])" (*The Anchor Bible Dictionary*, Vol. 1, 519). Tuckett judges on the one hand that "Paul's use of this tradition presumably implies a measure of agreement with it, and one should perhaps accept a rich variety in Paul's interpretation of the atonement" (520). On the other hand, he notes: "It is also striking that Paul is evidently not bound by any one language of atonement in that he can describe the effects of Jesus' death in heavily cultic and forensic language in Rom 5:8–9, only to follow with a parallel statement in Rom 5:10 using the quite different categories of personal relationships, an initial state of 'enmity' being ended by God's act of 'reconciliation'" (521).

The key term under which the new life of Christians is comprised is that of "grace", and the process by which it is made happen is by God's "justification" of the sinner. How this generic term for humans in their concrete existences is developed into an ontological statement by Augustine will be one of the themes of Christian theology to be pursued in the fifth chapter. But the basic equality between humans denoted by both concepts – their actual sin, and the new life of grace bestowed on them through God's action in response to Jesus Christ's atoning death – is played out in a non-hierarchical conception of structures in Paul's communities.

The counterpart to sin and death, "grace", is a term to be located first in the original cultural setting where its use in Paul can be specified by comparing it to the antique framework of clients and gifts.[112] Regarding "justification by faith", James Dunn makes the case that this theological conception "was Paul's answer to the question: How is it that Gentiles can be equally acceptable to God as Jews?"[113] This originating context will have to be kept in mind. Yet also for Paul's ethics, a feature linked to his dialectical way of thinking needs to be highlighted against the impression given by Habermas's two volumes that the content of Western Christianity is mainly owed to Paul's and Augustine's theologies. From the perspective of theological anthropology and ethics, the question arises whether Paul's account is at risk of putting a concept of agency out of reach that is recognised in the Gospels: the call to *metanoia* by Jesus which manifested an unqualified regard for a person's own ability to repent, to change course and to respond to God's continuous love from the spontaneity of their freedom. It is a strength typical of the Gospels' narrative form over Paul's conceptual reflection (in which the activity is completely allocated to God) that the underlying biographical continuity is maintained in which changes are recognised as one's own. The portrayal of the individual's insight and capacity for action, for example, of the Prodigal Son, is not retained in the mode of conceptual contrasts,[114] such as sin and grace. How the continuity of the person can be safeguarded in

---

112 This backdrop has been highlighted by John Barclay, together with the generosity and reciprocity identified as the responses expected from believers in Christ, in *Paul and the Gift* (Grand Rapids, MI: Eerdmans, 2015), Vol. 2.
113 Dunn, *Theology of Paul the Apostle*, 340.
114 In *An Awareness of What is Missing. Faith and Reason in a Postsecular Age,* ed. Habermas et al., trans. Ciaran Cronin (Cambridge: Polity Press, 2010): 50–57, Friedo Ricken explains in his response to Habermas the advantage that a narrative, for example of the Fall, gives to religion, while philosophy abstracts a concept, such as that of freedom, from reflecting on the experience of having been able to act differently. In "Postmetaphysical Reason and Religion", 52–53, Ricken uncovers "translation" as the opposite move to "genealogy", of going back to the original experience of the human person in front of God.

her own realisation of her shortcomings and her request for forgiveness, remains unclear. The legacy of this pointed change from the trust recorded of Jesus in the sinner's own awareness of a need for healing and new beginnings will be evident in the centuries to come. It will be heightened by additional factors, such as Gnostic dualism, as the backdrop against which early patristic analyses sought to highlight freedom as a human capacity.

A further difference to the Gospels' account of Jesus' proclamation and practice is the concept of "Kingdom of God". For Jesus, this was the positive alternative to the current reign of evil powers, especially in the apocalyptic hope in God's action of liberation from the oppressive forces of the present. The invitation was to turn one's life towards it and contribute to the growth of something hidden that God had already begun. In Paul, commentators have seen the announcement of the "Kingdom of God" as being replaced by the "Spirit" who is present in the community and in each believer. Is this new focus in danger of privatising what needs the support of each individual for advancing it also as a communal project? At the same time, Paul distinguishes between two reigns: the political reign of the legitimate power of governance, to which obedience is demanded, and the reign of God. So what are the house churches called to do in their Gentile cultures? When human agency is not accredited directly with an original validity, and "law" discredited as overcome, what view of the world outside of the Christian centres is implied? Is there a place where the goodness of God's creation and the resources in human life to initiate change, transmitted in Jesus' parables, can take root? With such a dialectical mapping of redeemed versus sinful existence, the apocalyptic longing for liberation is kept alive. While the call to "put on Christ" and the designation to be "in Christ" presuppose such a possibility of conscious change in humans, they do not spell it out in a narrative way which is interested in the connection between self-reflection and action. The focus is on God's deed, the triumph over evil that makes the resurrection relevant for all of humanity. With the idea of "justification" connected to the problem of how Gentiles could be included into the Covenant, how does this concept relate to the Jewish path of salvation, living according to the Law?

2.2.3 The role of Abraham as the model of faith for Jews and Gentiles

In Dunn's interpretation of Paul's framework, "justification by faith" is the answer to the question of how also the Gentiles can become beneficiaries of salvation, made to be as acceptable to God as the Jews who fulfil the Law in response to the Covenant. In view of the polemic against a position held by some members of the Galatian community that forms the background to his statements in this letter, Paul's attempt to work out an answer has given rise to the question what role it envisaged for the Jews as the people of God. The position arrived at in Romans some years later argues with God's plan for history (2.2.3.1). Despite the evident differences between Paul's proclamation and that of Jesus, as discernible from the Synoptics, a common horizon between the two can be identified: an Abrahamic view of God's salvific plan for humanity, and destinations of Paul's missionary journeys that correspond to a map drawn from Jewish restoration models (2.2.3.2).

2.2.3.1 From Galatians to Romans

Also the Letter to the Galatians regards the Jesus believers as part of the "Israel of God" (Gal 6:16).[115] Yet it contains a rhetoric that is aimed at Jewish Christians who belonged to the first of the groups distinguished by Raymond Brown, which deemed circumcision as mandatory for the male Gentile converts. In Paul's polemics against their stance, the Sinai covenant is portrayed as "one of slavery" (Gal 4:24), a "denigration"[116] that serves as the backdrop to the elevation of Christ. The rank of the Law is radically questioned (Gal 3:6–14) and a singular focus on faith in Christ advocated.

Despite the existential anguish expressed about not being able to fulfil the demands of the Law, Paul's tone has changed and his theological position has been refined by the time of writing the Letter to the Romans. It was designated as an introduction to the Jewish Christian community in Rome. The Letter tries to clarify Paul's position and offers a perspective in which both the ongoing calling of the Jews and the person of Jesus Christ are given their places in God's salvific plan. In Romans 15:7–12, he demonstrates from Scripture quotations how evident it is that God wants the Gentiles to be included: "Christ became a servant to the circumcised to show God's truthfulness, in order to confirm the promises given to the patriarchs, and in order that the Gentiles might glorify God for his mercy." The four quotations from Romans 15:9–15:12, are taken from 2 Samuel 22:50 and Psalm 18:49 (Rom 15:9), Deuteronomy 32:43 (Rom 15:10), Psalm 117:1

---

[115] In *Paul* (Oxford: Oxford University Press, 1991), 2, E. P. Sanders characterises the self-understanding of Paul as being "the one who would fulfil the expectations of the prophets and perhaps of Jesus himself: he would bring the Gentiles to worship the God of Israel."
[116] Brown, "Rome", 112. On p. 111, he quotes Ulrich Wilckens, "Zur Entwicklung des paulinischen Gesetzesverständnisses", in *New Testament Studies* 28 (1982): 154–191, 180: "On the whole, the position in Romans is a revision of the polemical position of Philippians and Galatians", with reference in Fn. 232 also to J. C. Beker and R. B. Ward.

(Rom 15:11), and Isaiah 11:10 (Rom 15:12). The addition of the Gentiles in their glorification of God is based on what Rom 9–11 has elaborated. Freyne points out the specific foundation chosen:

> it is the triumph of God, manifested in the death and resurrection of Jesus, that provides the controlling metaphor for his thinking [...] it is noteworthy that when he does come to develop his hopes for Israel's future within that context (Rom 9–11), he does not draw on the messianic ideal or base an argument on the messianic status of Jesus, but pins his hopes rather on the final plan or *mysterion* of God for history that has begun to unfold in the career of Jesus.[117]

Comparing Paul's Letter to the Romans to Matthew's Gospel, Freyne uncovers a remarkable contrast. While Paul disconnects the Christian life of discipleship in principle from the Law, he provides a metaphor which expresses the prior and lasting role of Israel: the "rootstock" onto which the Gentile Christians are "grafted": Instead of the Jews recognising Jesus as the Christ,

> the Gentiles had come flocking in [...] Romans 9–11 was his pained and often contorted way of trying to reconcile the facts with the scriptures [...] he repeatedly turns on the gentile converts, admonishing them not to boast at their new found status. In the end he can only resort to God's ability to do the seemingly impossible – to graft on to the one root that is Israel both the Gentiles and the Jews, so that the messianic ideal can be achieved.[118]

Matthew on the one hand underlines both the fulfilment of the messianic hopes in Jesus with quotations from the Hebrew Bible, and the radicalisation, but not the replacement of the Law which his call entails; on the other, he expresses the consequences of not recognising Jesus as Messiah in threatening terms:

> Unlike Paul who is desperately concerned to get everyone included under the one umbrella, Matthew's is a much tougher, and in the end, a more judgemental stance. He has the representatives of this Jewish opponents declare "his blood be on us and our children" at the trial before Pilate, and this can only mean that in refusing to accept Jesus as the Messiah and the Matthean community as the true Israel, they are drawing down a curse rather than a blessing on themselves (Matthew 27:25). Yet the Matthean Jesus remains thoroughly Jewish: He has come not to destroy the law and the prophets but to fulfil them (Matthew 5:17), as a new Moses-like figure. As the various instructions of the Sermon on the Mount (Mat-

---

117 Freyne, "The Early Christians and Jewish Messianic Ideas", in *Messianism Through History*, ed. Wim Beuken, Seán Freyne and Anton Weiler, *Concilium* (London: SCM Press, 1993): 30–41, 33.The "context" Freyne refers to is that of mission to the Gentiles.
118 Freyne, "How the Early Christians Read the Hebrew Scriptures", in *Reading the Sacred Scriptures. From Oral Tradition to Written Documents and their Reception*, ed. Fiachra Long and Siobhán Dowling Long (London: Routledge, 2018): 66–78, 72.

thew 5–7) are discussed – "you have heard that it was said to them of old, and (not but) I say to you" – Jesus is not abolishing the old but placing a more radical ideal still for the new Israel.[119]

While Matthew portrays the arrival of Jesus as the Messiah, for example in the infancy stories, by drawing on comparisons with Moses, Paul invokes another figure that stands for a universal understanding of God's promise: Abraham.

2.3.3.2 Shared by Jesus and Paul: An Abrahamic view

While Romans opens up a fruitful direction for reflection on the "covenants" entered into by God in the Hebrew Bible and the New Testament, one may ask about the implications of the resolution for theological anthropology. The level which Jews and believers in Christ share seems to be that of sinner. Does reaching for God's plan really resolve the problem of mediating between the "two poles [...] the universality of Adam and the particularity of Moses" on which the "success of the Pauline mission to the Gentiles" depended?[120] In this case, universal Adam in both particularities, Mosaic and Christian, has been reduced to sin. All agency is allocated to God, and Jesus Christ's role is not revelatory of God's essence, but principally determined by the contrast to Adam's disobedience. It is in this situation of polar opposites which does not allow for any mediating element between God and humans that the figure of Abraham provides symbolic resources for both issues: his example offers a starting point that claims more than sinfulness for humanity, namely a faith that hopes against the odds; and a shared platform for Jews and believers in Christ.[121] The opposition of concepts abstracted from experiences in history is refitted into their original settings and reinterpreted from this foundation; in this way, a hermeneutical process of exchanging and comparing key events of salvation can begin. As Wayne Meeks and Freyne show, it is misleading to identify Paul completely

---

119 Freyne, "How the Early Christians", 72–73.
120 Freyne, *Expansion*, 204.
121 In "The Origins of Paul's Christology: From Thessalonians to Galatians", 113–142, 132, Jerome Murphy-O'Connor points out the relevance of this motif in Paul's dispute with the first group, Christian Jews who insisted on all matters of the Law to be kept by the new Christian community. Paul establishes Abraham's "faith" as the key point, more important than the requirement for circumcision in the ensuing Covenant with God: "'he believed the Lord, and the Lord reckoned it to him as righteousness' (Gen. 15.1,6 = Gal 3.6). The righteousness of Abraham, therefore, *antedated* the covenant of circumcision, and it was rooted in faith. In consequence, it was not really circumcision, but faith, that made humans descendants of Abraham (Gal 3.7)."

with a Gentile perspective: "The promise to Abraham that in his offspring 'all the nations [...] would bless themselves' is then the correct background for Paul's self-designation as 'apostle of the nations'".[122] This role turns out to be anchored in Gen 26: 3–5, including "all the nations of the earth".

Wayne Meeks has noted the long-term effect which the Hegel-inspired view of the nineteenth-century church historian Ferdinand Christian Baur has had on a problem that defies a neat division into two poles: "the adjectives 'Jewish' and 'Hellenistic' are practically no help at all in sorting out that variety. Like the other varieties of Judaism, the earliest Christian groups were simultaneously Jewish and Hellenistic." Thus, "more particular questions" must be asked:

> Which parts of the Jewish tradition were being assumed and reinterpreted by this or that group of early Christians? Which institutions were continued, which discarded? [...] The more broadly we cast our nets, the more interpretive fish we bring up [...] The parade example, of course, is the apostle Paul, key player on the Hellenistic team for the Tübingen school and center of controversy in modern scholarship as in ancient polemics. [...] Paul was more aware of the specific philosophical school discussions of his day than we had previously guessed. Yet it is impossible to ignore the fact that frequently he also employs interpretive strategies and traditions of reading the Jewish scriptures that are strikingly like those that are found in earlier and later Jewish interpretations, both sectarian and rabbinic. Impossible, too, to erase the typically apocalyptic scenario.[123]

In Freyne's assessment, "shared ideas of restoration" are "what shaped the imagination and motivation of both Jesus and Paul". While noting that it is "remarkable how little the 'restoration of Israel' seems to have concerned him until quite late (Rom 9–11)", he judges that "Paul's preference for Abraham over Moses [...] in both Galatians and Romans [...] would conform well" with this background. A change of perspective is required since we have "become so accustomed to identifying Luke's portrayal of 'the apostle of the gentiles' with the modern construct of Paul, the convert from Judaism to Hellenism, that it proves difficult to see him in a different light in which his Jewish map of the world might have played an important role in the way in which he understood his tasks".[124] Examining Paul's previous missionary travels and the one to Spain that he was planning to embark on at the time he was arrested and brought to Rome, Freyne recognises both a correspondence to Abraham's journey as his preferred point of refer-

---

122 Freyne, "The Jesus–Paul Debate Revisited", 158–159.
123 Wayne A. Meeks, "Judaism, Hellenism and the Birth of Christianity", in *Paul Beyond the Judaism/Hellenism Divide*, ed. Troels Engberg-Pedersen (Louisville: Westminster John Knox Press, 2001), 17–27, 26–27.
124 Freyne, "The Jesus–Paul Debate Revisited", 153. 157.

ence over Moses, and a symbolic map covering the territories of Shem, Ham and Japheth: "he is operating with a mental map akin to that of the list of nations in Jubilees 8–9, Jerusalem as the centre of the world with the nations around in a circle (cf. Ezek 5.5; 38.12)."[125] Freyne concludes with a perspective that regards both Jesus and Paul as

> interpreters of a shared tradition about Israel's destiny and the nations' role within the divine plan for history, as this was anticipated for the coming messianic age [...] each saw themselves as having special roles to play in inaugurating and bringing to completion the divine plan as this was to be found in the Hebrew Scriptures [...] Jesus emerges as the restorer of Israel [...] but in an inclusive rather than exclusive way [...] Jewish ethnographic maps [...] guided Paul in how he was to fulfil the tasks which he felt called on to accomplish as the apostle of Jesus Christ, being Jew to the Jew and Greek to the Greeks.[126]

The Lukan apologetic history of the earliest Christian community shows lacunae in relation to centres in Galilee, to the mission in the Diaspora already begun by the Gentile Christian members of the Jerusalem community as well as Peter and John, and to Paul's own more complex message drawing both from a Second Temple and from a Greek intellectual background. The designation in Acts of Paul as "missionary to the Gentiles" that has impressed itself on the reception history together with the Jerusalem-Rome axis preferred by Luke simplifies and reduces a far more intricate web of connections. More specific details of the *content* preached to the increasingly Gentile converts beyond Israel-Palestine and Jews in the diaspora must be ascertained. Therefore, exegetical scholarship on the worship of Jesus Christ as *"Kyrios"* as a new liturgical practice in the post-Easter movement will be examined in Chapter Three. Chapter Four returns to the relation between Paul and the understandings of Jesus' ministry and destiny in the subsequent Gospels. Going back from Paul's own Christological perspective to the practice of the earliest Christian communities, as it is reflected in the formulae quoted in his Letters and in other sources, will help to address a gap that has been noted between research on Paul's theology and on Jesus' proclamation: "a lack of scholarly concern with establishing a relationship of the various construals of his ministry with Paul's account of what constituted Christian faith."[127]

---

125 Freyne, "The Jesus–Paul Debate Revisited", 158–159, with reference to Martin Hengel and Anna Maria Schwemer, *Paul Between Antioch and Damascus. The Unknown Years* (London: SCM Press, 1997), 106–126.
126 Freyne, "The Jesus–Paul Debate Revisited", 159–160.
127 Freyne, "The Jesus–Paul Debate Revisited", 149.

3 Tracing the Origins of the Doctrine of Christ

The portrayal of post-Easter Christianity by Habermas as both "Pauline" and as "a formation of spirit inherently marked by Hellenism" poses the task of researching possible links between Paul's understanding of the core of the Christian message of salvation and the Gospel portrayals of Jesus. The first step is to investigate evidence for worship of Christ at the stage prior to the Letters (3.1). The use of the Psalter provides a key area of investigation, giving access to a level of symbolic expression and to the method of intertextual reading between the two Testaments. In this case, "Hellenism" is not the crucial background for the origins of Christology; a communal use of the Hebrew Bible is. The Psalms feature in different settings: they were sung in the Temple before its destruction in 70 CE, in domestic rituals such as the Passover meal, heard in synagogue readings, and were a resource and model for the composition of new prayers (3.2.1).[128] Like the Psalms, also the poetic passage in the second chapter of the Letter to the Philippians, which may be a quotation from an early Christian hymn or Paul's own composition, refers to the *Kyrios*. Is the transition to understanding Jesus as *Kyrios* to be placed in a Hebrew religious or a Greek and Roman political context (3.2.2)? The exchange of arguments on these issues will show that the idea of a clear-cut departure of Christianity from its Jewish origins to a Greek framework is incorrect and that new understandings emerge less by way of discursive categories than from a reservoir of symbols.

3.1 Christolatry as the origin of Christology?

Two positions regarding Christolatry as the origin of the doctrine of Christ will be compared, one arguing for his worship beginning at a very early stage (3.1.1), the other as a later, gradual development (3.1.2).

3.1.1 Cultic worship of Christ based on a revelatory experience: Larry Hurtado's thesis

For Larry Hurtado, a significant area has been left out in researching the development of early Christianity regarding the singular status of Jesus Christ: the

---

[128] Cf. Margaret Daly-Denton, *Psalm-Shaped Prayerfulness. A Guide to the Christian Reception of the Psalms* (Collegeville, MN: Liturgical Press, 2011), 114–127.

practice of the communities. To be able to answer both historical and normative-conceptual questions, enquiries need to be directed into their liturgical practice, and into how it originated. Despite recognising some parallels in the Hebrew Bible which is marked by the concern to worship solely the one God, Hurtado sees a principally new departure within monotheism that requires explanation: a "binitarian" form of worship.[129] The first point to be established is one of datings: is the worship of Christ an early or a late phenomenon? By attempting to demonstrate that it belongs to the earliest phase, he can equally make the case that it does not constitute a continuation of existing factors. Breaking down "worship" into six features, he defends the claim that no "analogy" can be found in Jewish religious practice "for the full *pattern* of devotional phenomena focused on Jesus".[130] After outlining his assessment of the six traits compared (3.1.1.1), the three decisive elements he identifies in a subsequent chapter will be analysed: the portrayal of Jesus on the lines of a "principal agent" of God, like Moses or David in the Jewish Scriptures (3.1.1.2); the polarisation which resulted from Jesus' ministry (3.1.1.3); and a new, revelatory religious experience as the cause of including Christ into the worship of God (3.1.1.4).[131]

3.1.1.1 "Without analogy": Six factors in the worship of Jesus Christ
In Hurtado's analysis, it is a combination of six factors which justifies the conclusion that Jesus was worshipped, in distinction from other human figures in Jewish monotheism: "prayer" which continued to be "offered to God" but for which it was "equally characteristic" that it was "offered 'through' Jesus (Rom 1:8)"; secondly, "invocation and confession" in which "Jesus is addressed ritually (and probably collectively) as the 'Lord'", with "no known parallel in any other group tied to the Jewish religious matrix".[132] Regarding the level of rituals, there was, thirdly, "baptism" that "involved invocation of Jesus' name" (200), and fourthly, the "Lord's Supper", a joint meal; there seems to be "no analogy for

---

129 Larry W. Hurtado, "The Binitarian Shape of Early Christian Worship", in *The Jewish Roots of Christological Monotheism. Papers from the St. Andrews Conference on the Historical Origins of the Worship of Jesus*, ed. Carey C. Newman, James R. Davila and Gladys S. Lewis (Leiden: Brill, 1999): 187–214.
130 Hurtado, "The Binitarian Shape", 193.
131 Cf. Hurtado, "The Origin and Development of Christ-Devotion: Forces and Factors", in *Christian Origins: Worship, Belief and Society*, ed. Kieran J. O'Mahoney): 52–82, with reference to his book, *One God, One Lord: Early Christian Devotion and Ancient Jewish Monotheism* (Edinburgh: T & T Clark, 2nd edn 1998).
132 Hurtado, "The Binitarian Shape", 197. Further page numbers in the text.

such a cultic role for any figure other than God in Jewish religious circles of the Second Temple period" (203).¹³³ Two more cultic features are examined: fifth, hymns, and sixth, prophesying. The latter indicates "oracles delivered as revelatory speech [...] presented as inspired by Jesus", with the "claim to be speaking under direct divine revelation" (208). Regarding hymns, a key question examined also by James Dunn and Margaret Daly-Denton is whether they were sung "about" or "to" Jesus, as the practice described by Pliny in his letter to Trajan written in the early second century indicates, and whether verses 6–11 of Philippians 2 represent a poem or hymn which Paul quoted. For Hurtado, it is not the "contents, the christological ideas and beliefs reflected in these passages" (204) that interest him, but the singing itself "as a feature of devotional *practice*", to be classified as "an important feature of the binitarian worship pattern in which Jesus figures so very prominently" (205). Based on the assumption that Second Temple Judaism used the Psalter as a hymnbook, he states "that a great part of earliest Christian 'hymnody' involved the chanting of OT psalms, interpreted christologically" (205). The key question then is whether stages of development can be distinguished. Here Hurtado opts for interpreting them as a "component of the cultic practices of earliest Christian groups" (205). He rejects the "transition" assumed by James Dunn since it "implies a movement from one worship practice to another", over against the "intensity of devotion to Jesus" (208) he sees as resulting in these factors appearing simultaneously at the earliest stage.¹³⁴ While the meanings of "cultic", "worship", and "christological" need to be specified, as the subsequent exchanges will show, it is already evident that Hurtado anchors the new self-understanding of the Christian community in a practice that cannot be derived from existing patterns. A history of religions approach that seeks precedents and brings an evolutionary pre-understanding to its enquiries is critiqued as inadequate.¹³⁵ So how does he argue in an area where precedents and analogies abound, viewing the person of Jesus in the Jewish framework of a "principal agent" of God?

---

133 The question of analogies with meals in polytheistic settings is examined by Adela Yarbro Collins, "The Worship of Jesus and the Imperial Cult", in *The Jewish Roots of Christological Monotheism*, 234–257.
134 Hurtado, "The Binitarian Shape", 208, with reference to James Dunn, *The Theology of Paul the Apostle*, 260.
135 Cf., for example, Hurtado, *How on Earth Did Jesus Become a God?* (Grand Rapids, MI: Eerdmans, 2005), 16–18, for a brief summary of his critique of Wilhelm Bousset.

3.1.1.2 Jesus as God's "principal agent"

On the one hand, the idea that there are human beings whom God invests with special authority and who enjoy a close relationship to God is taken by Hurtado as a suitable model: "Christ functions as God's principal agent, Christ's revelatory and redemptive actions consistently portrayed as done on God's authority, as expressions of God's will, and as serving God's purposes and glory."[136] It also fits the Christian believers' understanding that Jesus is worshipped together with God, and not as a different deity: "the inclusion of Christ as recipient of religious devotion was not intended by early Christians as recognising another god [...] 'di-theism'[...] does not seem to represent their own views of their devotional pattern." The "characteristic 'two-ishness' of their devotional practice [...] links Christ with God in ways that seem intended to maintain an exclusivist 'monotheistic' stance".[137] This "binitarian direction" is not an abandonment of monotheism but a new form of it, if the alternative is "the direction of an apotheosis of Jesus as a new deity in his own right after the pagan pattern."[138]

On the other hand, the relativising implications of God selecting a plurality of "principal agents" are not taken over. Jesus is the final fulfilment of this role, indicating that the model is first accepted and then made exclusive to Christ: "Jesus is incorporated into an exclusivistic devotion in which there is room only for *one God and one Lord* (e.g., 1 Cor 8:5–6).[139] Thus, in distinction from a model that emphasises precedents – Enoch and Elijah are mentioned as well as Moses and David[140] – and leaves room for analogies also in the future, Hurtado interprets it as accomplished in Christ. The Jewish and Greek religious contexts serve to highlight the uniqueness of the Christian saviour: In comparison with a "new deity", that is, with the polytheistic possibility of a god or goddess with her own cult, Jesus' status is subordinated to that of God, but in comparison with Jewish Scriptures, an unprecedented closeness to God is emphasised.

This procedure throws up questions of hermeneutical method. By arguing from the believers' convictions which would not be represented either by a Greek or Roman figure of apotheosis, nor by a unitary monotheism without a cultic worship of Christ, Hurtado adopts a perspective in which the difference between a historical and a normative approach is diminished. What is referred to

---

136 Hurtado, "The Origin and Development of Christ-Devotion", 62.
137 Hurtado, "The Binitarian Shape", 191.
138 Hurtado, "The Origin and Development of Christ-Devotion", 78.
139 Hurtado, "The Binitarian Shape", 212.
140 Cf. Yarbro Collins, "The Worship of Jesus", 246–247, and Dunn, *Theology of Paul the Apostle*, 252.

as a mere description of the early Christian consciousness, is quite indistinguishable from a systematic theological statement. The historical search for a possible range of different post-Easter understandings of Jesus Christ is replaced by one standard. Yet the question of how to interpret Jesus adequately in the sequence of the life, death and resurrection reported of him remains, and cannot be regarded as answered by the faith of the community. After all, already Paul's Letters show a practice of correcting the interpretations, pursuits and structures of the Christian centres they were sent to. The issue remains open how to determine the innovation which the Christian specification of Jewish monotheism represents. The consciousness of a local church cannot be the ultimate datum. It needs to be judged itself against what can be established historically about Jesus' understanding of himself as a "principal agent" of God, even if this is only accessible through the evidences of the communities. The key epistemological role which Hurtado accords to the faith position of the Christian centres will surface again in the groundbreaking religious experience he attributes to them, to be analysed in 3.1.1.4. But also the second decisive cause oscillates between a factor that can be traced back to Jesus' own proclamation and one that arises in the self-understanding of early Christian circles.

3.1.1.3 A ministry with polarising effect

Hurtado observes a remarkable feature of Jesus' activity that will require further attention: the "polarising effect or outcome of Jesus' ministry is thus a second force/factor to include in an adequate theory of the origin and formation of Christ-devotion."[141] It is not clear, however, whether this "outcome" refers to Jesus' lifetime or to the earliest communities. It is important to locate the "polarising" elements accurately in order not to succumb to a *petitio principii* in which factors that will only result from subsequent developments are assumed as foundational breaks. Some points of difference identified by Hurtado have been questioned in exegetical discussion.

One example of attributing a function to Jesus which other New Testament scholars reserve for God is related to the "Holy Spirit". Hurtado makes it clear that the full trinitarian account only emerges at a later date.[142] But he links "the Spirit" to the raised Christ who disposes over its activity, and interprets

---

141 Hurtado, "The Origin and Development of Christ-Devotion", 65.
142 Hurtado, "The Binitarian Shape", 200, Fn. 38: "It is commonly accepted that the 'trinitarian' baptismal formula of Matt 28:19 and *Did* 7:1 (but cf. 9:5!) is probably a somewhat later expression and that earliest practice is the 'in/into the name of Jesus' formula."

this as a further feature of discontinuity with practices shared in Second Temple Judaism: "Through God's exaltation of him, Jesus is now able to bestow the Holy Spirit (Acts 2:36), the manifestations of which enable various ministries of his church of Jesus the Lord, which are at the same time 'activities' of God (1 Cor 12:4–6)."[143]

What is considered to be polarising includes features taken from post-Easter interpretation. Closely examined, Hurtado's second factor does not refer to the earthly Jesus but to his reception in early Christian circles, and only indirectly to his own ministry, which will thus have to be evaluated separately. The key thesis towards which his interpretation is driving is that the analogy-defying newness claimed for the church's message is due to a new, revelatory act of God. While it is named "religious creativity", it is referred back to God as its author in some formulations; thus, this "creativity" is not a human feature of Christian believers but an innovation owed to God's action. Again the question appears – to be explored in section 4.2 of the next chapter – whether the locus of radical newness has been selected adequately. For Hurtado, the innovation that marks the Christian faith in Jesus as the crucified but resurrected Messiah refers to a new revelation of God to the community. But other points of reference are possible, such as an unprecedented action of God as omnipotent creator against the finality of death, confirming Jesus' proclamation.

3.1.1.4 Religious experience as the cause of a "binitarian mutation" of Jewish monotheism

The alternative to the evolutionary model of the history of religions approach is seen in a definitive new beginning which is located in "religious experience". This is a term frequently used in religious studies, but which requires an analysis of its constitutive premises. It stands for a dimension that has been neglected, in his view, and that is distinct from other aspects: "Even in more recent studies of the social and cultural characteristics of early churches, there is a tendency to focus on other aspects and questions, such as the economic levels of early Christians, the roles exercised by women, or the organizational structures, or rituals."[144] What such enquiries cannot capture is the quality of the believers' experience which has the force of a "volcanic eruption".[145] In the face of such phenomena, it is a task of historical enquiry to clarify its conditions: "I contend

---

143 Hurtado, "The Binitarian Shape", 212.
144 Hurtado, "The Origin and Development of Christ-Devotion", 67.
145 Hurtado, *How on Earth*, 25.

that we need to allow for the *causative* significance of revelatory experiences in the religious innovations that took place in these circles [...] an adequate historical understanding of early Christianity requires us to grant significant attention to the religious experiences that obviously formed such a major part of the early Christian ethos."[146]

This task for historical enquiry does not extend to judging on the "validity" of such impressions. It is sufficient to recognise their "efficacy":

> I propose that the most plausible factor is the effect of powerful religious experiences in early Christian circles, experiences that struck the recipients [...] as having revelatory validity and force, sufficient to demand such a significant re-configuring of monotheistic practice [...] It is not necessary for my theory that we, however, grant the religious *validity* of these [...] experiences. All that is necessary is for us to recognize: (1) the demonstrable *efficacy* of such experiences in generating significant innovations in various religious traditions; and (2) the likelihood that this efficacy is to be granted in the case of early Christianity as well.[147]

At the same time, a theological premise seems to appear when the "generative role" is specified as belonging to "revelatory religious experience".[148] Maurice Casey, who argues for a late date in leaving behind Jewish monotheism, beginning only with the Gospel of John in a Gentile context, points out a circularity in Hurtado's and other Christian interpretations: "He has isolated a few points in early Christian treatment of Jesus which are analogous to normal treatment of deities, and has fitted them into his own pattern, rather than into the cultural environment to which they originally belonged." His own research in Second Temple Judaism shows that "there was no bar against taking over features of God". Instead of judging it in its most immediate context, "Hurtado has mistaken the significance of unique features of Christological development by forming one of the hermeneutical circles which are such a major feature of New Testament scholarship [...] He has consequently exaggerated the importance of worship of Jesus in the first century."[149]

Casey's warning against building assumptions on "an apparently raw experiential category" can be endorsed from a philosophical perspective. It is true that "religious experience" is only "apparently raw", and is actually an already

---

146 Hurtado, "The Origin and Development of Christ-Devotion", 67.
147 Hurtado, "The Origin and Development of Christ-Devotion", 66.
148 Hurtado, "The Origin and Development of Christ-Devotion", 74.
149 Maurice Casey, "Christology and the Legitimating Use of the Old Testament in the New Testament", in *The Old Testament in the New Testament. Essays in Honour of J. L. North*, ed. Steve Moyise (Sheffield: Sheffield Academic Press, 2000): 42–64, 54.

processed datum, inseparable from the symbolic resources of the religious tradition in which it is situated:

> Religious experience does not occur prior to the religions but always belongs to them already and is shaped by their contents since experience is never pure and immediate but is always already interpreted and conceptually or linguistically mediated in the interplay of receptivity and spontaneity. This is why it can neither be claimed as the reason (*Grund*) for the appearance (*Aufkommens*) of religion nor can it serve as an authority of justification (*Rechtfertigungsinstanz*) of religious convictions, since it is already determined by these convictions.[150]

But it can also be asked in view of ideology-critical reductions of religion whether the attempt to locate the foundation of a distinct tradition in "religious experience" does not turn out to be susceptible to Feuerbach's projection theory. Can it be protected against the suspicion that humans are prone to wishful thinking and to personifying their own best features? The alternative to treating "religious experience" as an inescapable event that profoundly marks its recipients is to relate the content of the faith professed to an account of the human person who is open for such experiences of ultimate meaning. Its definition and status can still be interrogated; but anchoring them in a worked-out anthropology is distinct from setting the foundation in the claimed experience itself. The practical option for a faith commitment can be justified as a stance taken in existential reflection rather than stated as an occurrence at the level of a seemingly indubitable feeling. For these reasons, Hurtado's thesis that historical research shows the need to "posit powerful revelatory experiences" which lead to a "novel and significant pattern that signals Jesus' divine status"[151] must be questioned and compared with other argumentations.

---

150 The systematic theologian Saskia Wendel has made this philosophical point in the context of her discussion of Habermas in "Die religiöse Selbst- und Weltdeutung des bewussten Daseins und ihre Bedeutung für eine 'moderne Religion'. Was der 'Postmetaphysiker' Habermas über Religion nicht zu denken wagt", in *Moderne Religion? Theologische und religionsphilosophische Reaktionen auf Jürgen Habermas*, ed. Thomas Schmidt and Knut Wenzel (Freiburg: Herder, 2009): 225–265, 246, Fn. 35. In "The Worship of Jesus", 241, Yarbro Collins makes this point in dialogue with Hurtado: "I agree with Hurtado that such experiences were not simply products of prior christological convictions, but were also the generative cause of christological convictions […] But […] I would argue that the prior cultural experiences of those who experienced Jesus as risen played a significant role in the shaping and interpreting of the experiences of the risen Lord themselves."
151 Hurtado, *How on Earth*, 30. 27.

3.1.2 Prayer *to* God *through* Christ: James Dunn's analysis

As also Hurtado points out, instead of a di-theism in which two distinct gods were addressed, the Christian liturgical praxis was to "pray *to* God *through* Christ". For James Dunn, however, this indicates a different position than the "binitarian" view identified by Hurtado. Dunn explains divine worship in terms of places, times, meals and persons being attributed as belonging to God and then examines which of these can be judged to apply to the first-century Christian movement (3.1.2.1). A category he singles out as definitive for the worship of deities in Antiquity is "sacrifice". This is where a decisive crossroad opens up in the Christian understanding of God and of Jesus' mission of redemption, especially if the concept of divinity gets tied to "sacrifice" as an inherent element of human interaction with God. While Dunn accepts this paradigm, he draws conclusions which effectively question its applicability (3.1.2.2).

3.1.2.1 The sacredness of places, times, meals, and people in Judaism and early Christianity

While agreeing with Hurtado's comment that "prayer to Christ is to be framed by the sovereignty of the one God", Dunn concludes that private prayer could have been addressed to Christ, but public, "collective prayer to God".[152] Regarding the singing to Christ which was one of the six features Hurtado deemed to be early practices, Dunn thinks it possible "that the psalms sung by early Christians were addressed to Christ" (38); however, he regards it as "not clear [...] whether the hymns evident in the Pauline letters provide evidence that Pliny's description of early second century worship would have been appropriate fifty years earlier" (42). Thus, it is not obvious whether these early circles were already singing "hymns to Christ as to a God". In view of poetic New Testament expressions of praise and gratitude that were clearly directed to God, such as in the Lukan infancy story the *Magnificat*, the *Gloria* (Lk 2:14), and the *Nunc dimittis*, these are not to Christ as God, but "canticles in praise of God, not Christ, through Christ" (40). The same is true, in his view, of the possible "hymns" in Phil 2:5–11 and Col 1:15–20, which he regards as "properly Christ hymns, not, however, hymns *to* Christ" (41). The question of the worship of Christ needs to be ar-

---

[152] Dunn, *Did the First Christians Worship Jesus?* (London: SPCK, 2010), 37, Fn. 29, with reference to Hurtado, *At the Origins of Christian Worship. The Context and Character of the Earliest Christian Devotion* (Grand Rapids, MI: Eerdmans, 1999). Further page numbers in the text.

gued much more cautiously and to do so, he investigates four elements that can be turned from ordinary into divine significations.

Under "sacred spaces", it is the Jerusalem Temple which fulfils this criterion completely in Jewish religious practice. For the beginnings of Christianity, the positions of Jesus, Stephen, Paul and the Letter to the Hebrews are compared. How is Jesus' cleansing of the Temple from the money lenders and merchants to be interpreted – as intending to end the offering of sacrifices as such? But he did not question the Temple tax which went into its upkeep. Rather than assuming that "by preventing the business transactions on which the offering of sacrifice depended [...] Jesus was rejecting the practise of sacrifice as such [...] it is more likely that the criticism implied in this action was a criticism of abuse; the Temple had become 'a den of robbers' (Mk 11.17)". The counterimage for its intended use is that it is a "house of prayer", even "for all nations (Isa 56:7)" (43).

As for Jesus, also for Stephen, the Jewish critique of the Temple cult is the tradition they draw on. No function is left for the Temple by Stephen according to the speech recollected in Acts in which he quotes Isaiah 66:1–2: "the Most High does not live in houses made by human hands. As the prophet says: 'Heaven is my throne, and the earth is my footstool'" (7:48–49). Dunn interprets this critique as indicating that for "Stephen, to think of God as available through the Temple ritual was in effect to treat the Temple as an idol" (44). Paul who continued to attend the Temple festivals is summarised as offering an alternative to the Temple: "Paul rejoiced that Christians now had immediate access to the divine grace, that is, without having to go to, and receive it by means of, the Temple (Rom. 5.2)" (45). Instead, each believer's body is declared a "temple of the Holy Spirit in you". While earliest Christian worship took place "in the temple (ironically)", for Paul, "Christ himself functions in effect as the Christian sacred space", as the frequent term, "in Christ" testifies (47).[153]

One perspective on this development is that it proposes a radical privatisation of the encounter with God, losing the communal and public dimensions, the dialogical and polyphonic practice that the shared space allows for. It can equally be seen as an emancipation and radical departure from a symbolic system that had been defended against colonisers and been able to reorient itself when it was challenged. The destruction of the Temple in 70 CE could not be foreseen by Paul but the final document examined, the Letter to the Hebrews, just like the Gospels, was written after this cataclysmic event. Dunn comments on Chap-

---

[153] Dunn has expanded on this "locative meaning" also in his *Theology of Paul the Apostle*, 396–401.

ters 8–10 that for its author, in "fact, the Jerusalem Temple is passé, its job now done, its ritual obsolete [...] With such theology, the understanding of the sacred space has been transformed. The place where God and humans can meet is no longer restricted to a physical holy place" (46). If it now is Christ who "functions as the Christian sacred space", does this mean he is worshipped as God? Dunn does not draw this conclusion and goes on to compare specific times dedicated to God in the Jewish tradition, in Jesus' practice, and in the post-Easter circles. Here he sees evidence, as in the following point, that with inaugurating Sunday as the "Lord's day [...] worship was offered through him and to him" (49). First, he points out with reference to Josephus how remarkable it was that the Jewish tradition had given a structure to the week: "Indeed the unusualness of such a regular day of rest (every seven days) not only marked out the distinctiveness of Judaism but also made it religiously very attractive to other nationalities" (48). In Jesus' conflicts with the Pharisees, it was "more a question of *how* the Sabbath should be observed, not *whether* the Sabbath should be observed. At the same time, Jesus [...] honoured the pilgrims feasts, most notably the feast of the Passover" (48). The Jesus followers confirmed the model but changed the day and content: Sunday was "seen as a weekly celebration of Easter" (49).

Also regarding sacred meals, Dunn judges the Lord's Supper to be a "devotion that is not far from worship" (51). As far as the designation of specific persons as "holy" was concerned, he discusses the diminished importance of Temple priests when there is a different, unmediated way of attaining forgiveness. With reference to Mt 17:24–27, he highlights a contrast: "Jesus accepted temple tax, to pay for morning and evening sacrifice. But he also pronounced sins forgiven, without priest or [...] offering" (54). The question about God's forgiveness and about how and through whom it takes place has been fundamental in the history of Christian thinking and not least of its ritual practice.[154]

Even if there are examples that come close to worship, Dunn is hesitant to concede that the liturgical practice allows for the conclusion that Christ was worshipped as God. Since Paul's Christology is "theocentric",[155] it is difficult to draw a line where Jesus is addressed on his own. He recommends "Paul's reserve which was soon lost to sight" in the following century.[156]

---

[154] In view of the different understandings proposed in the course of the centuries, Chapter Nine will recall the crucial link between rituals or sacraments and the interpretations that accompany them.
[155] Dunn, *Theology of Paul the Apostle*, 255.
[156] Dunn, *Theology of Paul the Apostle*, 260, with reference to "John 20.28; Pliny, Epistles 10.97.7" in Fn. 142.

3.1.2.2 Jesus' death as sacrifice – an inevitable interpretation?

On the one hand, Dunn makes a case in the strongest possible terms for one specific understanding of Jesus' death. It is put forward as a historical statement, extending not just to Paul but to "the first Christians" in general, and underlined as the one exceptionless possibility available in this era. On the backdrop of the Jewish tradition in which the "(s)acrificial death" of animals is explained as a religious custom practised in "Israel for centuries", he concludes that "the first Christians should inevitably understand Jesus' death as sacrifice".[157] Yet does the observation quoted by him that for religions in general, sacrifice is "the ultimate criterion of deity",[158] provide an adequate summary for a tradition that has been marked by the most rigorous prophetic critique of exactly this mode of worship? God's warning that "Your sacrifices are abominable to me" (Amos 5:22) marks Jewish monotheism no less than the cultic tradition of animal slaughter at the Jerusalem Temple. If there are already reasons to doubt an unquestioned link between the God of Israel and types of worship that involve sacrifice, this is even more the case with classifying Jesus' death as belonging within this paradigm. From his research into the Historical Jesus, Seán Freyne, as we have seen, rejects this interpretation. It marks the earliest stage as much as can be ascertained from the Gospels and the documents that give insight into the oral tradition: Jesus' death was understood as resulting from the collusion of the dominant political and religious forces; it was portrayed as an increasingly likely risk that Jesus warned his followers about in the midst of the conflicts caused by his message and practices of inclusion in the Roman-occupied territories of Greater Israel.[159] While the mould of "atonement" is the one adopted by Paul, even the "Lamb of God" metaphor used in John's Gospel has been traced to different backgrounds.[160] Both the "Q" group that is credited with hav-

---

157 Dunn, *Did the First Christians Worship Jesus?*, 52.56.
158 Dunn, *Did the First Christians Worship Jesus?*, 53, with reference to J. Lionel North, "Jesus and Worship", 200.
159 These warnings are either not considered in Habermas's judgement or possibly left out, assuming them to belong to the post-Easter portrayals with no basis in Jesus' lifetime: "Of course the Evangelists are convinced of Jesus being the Son of God (cf. Mt 17:5); but even these accounts do not convey (*erkennen lassen*) that the Historical Jesus would have anticipated his violent death on the cross and interpreted it as an unheard-of (*unerhörten*) act of the atoning *self-sacrifice of God* (*Selbstaufopferung Gottes*)" (Vol. I, 494).
160 In *John: An Earth Bible Commentary. Supposing Him to Be the Gardener* (London: Bloomsbury, 2017), 50–52, Margaret Daly-Denton outlines a variety of backgrounds and notes that deriving the "symbolic meaning" from "the lamb provided by God instead of Isaac (Gen. 22,8, 13), the paschal lamb (Exod. 12), the servant depicted as a lamb led to slaughter (Isa 53.7), [...] jar somewhat with the distinctively Johannine view of Jesus' death as glorification" (50).

ing collected the available oral tradition in a source from which both Matthew and Luke are assumed to have drawn, and the *Didache* are not concerned with Jesus' death. The Synoptics narrate the events of the Passion as the unjust end of the one sinless human person, and Jesus' resurrection as God's vindication of his person and message by the power of the Creator over death. It is one specific dogmatic pre-understanding that has focused on the terms of "sacrifice" and "atonement" by New Testament authors despite the overwhelming critique of this practice centuries before Jesus and in his own proclamation.

On the other hand, also in Dunn's wording and in the conclusions he draws, a more differentiated handling of the concept is evident. In his initial explanation of the features of "cultic devotion [...], prayer, hymns, space set aside", the "sacrifice of animals" is an example of the "surrender of material goods".[161] It is thus related to anything that exacts a cost from the believer. Clearly, this opens up a whole range of possibilities; for example, Jesus' response to the rich young man, "Go, sell all your possessions, give the money to the poor and then come and follow me" (Mt 19:21 and Lk 18:22) would fall under "sacrifice" as giving up prized possessions.

Another observation of Dunn's could offer a guiding perspective out of the unitary focus on sacrifice. He emphasises the "interiority" of the relationship to God that did not need mediation by priests for first century Christians: "the first Christians had no need of priests. They did not need anyone to mediate between them and God or the Lord Christ [...] for the first Christians, the existential experience of knowing God immediately, without any mediation other than that of Jesus, was too real and too precious to be quickly lost to sight".[162]

He concludes from Rom 3:25 that the "logic runs counter to the rationale of sacrifice as offered to God [...] God is on both sides of the transaction."[163] With this interpretation, the paradigm of atonement is stretched so far that one can see it as being invalidated. If God is "on both sides of the transaction", the basic assumption that God needs to be assuaged for human sin and disobedience is undermined. God is no longer a deity who must be placated in the face of human transgressions. It may be an instructive feature of early and subsequent Christian worship that "Christ was never understood as the one to whom sacrifice was offered". Even Hebrews where Christ is at the same time "sacrificing High priest and sacrificial victim"[164] could be seen as offering a paradoxical reflection; so much that the inadequacy of the metaphor taken from the Temple

---

[161] Dunn, *Did the First Christians Worship Jesus?*, 30.
[162] Dunn, *Did the First Christians Worship Jesus?*, 51–52.
[163] Dunn, *Did the First Christians Worship Jesus?*, 56.
[164] Dunn, *Did the First Christians Worship Jesus?*, 56.

cult to express the meaning of his death signals the end of this mode of thinking about God. Nowhere in the Gospels, including John, is there a notion that God had to be appeased by the death of his Son. The key text for the early Christian understanding of Jesus' ministry and the violent end of his life was Isaiah's poem of the "Suffering Servant of God" (Isa 53). It offers an interpretation of his suffering as vicarious for the real sinners who maltreated and despised him. God turns his fate to a salvific end, yet there is no indication that this sacrifice was demanded by God.

The interpretations produced by the antithetical pattern of Paul's theologising replace the real-life political factors operative in the conflictual setting that Jesus shared with his contemporaries, including Paul. The dichotomy of death and resurrection is abstract as long as it lacks the link to Jesus' life and what he stood for: the announcement of the reign of God and an interpretation of God's prevenient forgiveness. What marked Jesus' teaching and symbolic action, a trust in the agency of women and men that enabled them to reflect and take stock, repent and change their ways is replaced by Paul with God's "grace". There is a link between this theological concept which minimises human agency with its possibility of a free response to God's offer, and the notion of "sacrifice" which is then externally applied to the sinners as the cause of their justification, irrespective of an internal reflection. Yet the paradoxical terms of Hebrews as well as Dunn's own statements relativise the concept of sacrifice. He offers a more cautious account than Hurtado's of the point in time when the worship of Christ began to be expressed in concepts that would become the basis of Christology. A more extended backdrop to be explored in its relevance for an emerging Christology is the Psalter in the Hebrew Scriptures.

3.2 The role of the Psalms in enabling a transition to Christology and the question of the "*Kyrios*"

Although Dunn does not share the early dating of Hurtado for a "binitarian mutation" of Jewish monotheism and positions the "singing to Christ as to a God" at the turn to the second century, he does see "hymns" as an important vehicle of expression of the early Christian communities. The role of quotations from the Psalms for the turn to a Christology that became the basis of Christianity as a new religion separate from Judaism is analysed by Margaret Daly-Denton (3.2.1). The Psalms are addressed to the "*Kyrios*", a title that can be enlarged to include Christ as "Lord". But the term is also used in a Gentile context. Thus, a further question arises that will be investigated in relation to a much-quoted text which cannot be counted among the possible hymns addressed to

Jesus Christ, since it is written in the third person: Philippians 2.[165] But it expresses a three-stage theory of Christ from being "in the form of God", to human life and death, and to exaltation by God. It offers a case study for divergent interpretations that are instructive since they outline alternative backgrounds for contextualisation according to which the meaning of the title "*Kyrios*" changes, as Adela Yarbro Collins shows (3.2.2).

3.2.1 The Psalms as a locus of Christological reinterpretation: Margaret Daly-Denton's analysis

Among the hymns sung about or to Christ were the Psalms. They provided a reservoir for new attributions. Exploring them brings to attention the indirect ways in which the new consciousness grew: through the transfer of images much more than through concepts (3.2.1.1). A much-used term in this field that requires clarification is "intertextuality" (3.2.1.2).

3.2.1.1 A transfer at the level of images

Encountering the prayers of hope, despair and praise that are collected in the Psalter and recognising their resonances in the Letters of Paul and in the Gospels brings the distinctiveness of the biblical experience of God's loyalty into focus. It makes it obvious that the language used is poetic, imaginative and metaphorical, and that the systematic task of reflecting on the implications of the interaction of humans with God – the anthropological premises of the believer and the understanding of God's attributes and actions – is a separate one. While systematic and ethical conclusions can be drawn with conceptual accuracy and coherence, the danger of approaching these documents with the intention of mining them for preconceived clues is "'norm reductionism'".[166] A further danger lies in a purely terminological approach, as, for example, in selecting "*Theos*" as the relevant idea to be harvested from the text as proof for the status of Christ. This procedure, which has also been pursued in ethics, loses the field of meaning that constitutes the range of the sought-for concept out of sight. For example,

---

[165] Margaret Daly-Denton, "Singing Hymns to Christ as to a God (Cf. Pliny *Ep.* X, 96)," in *The Jewish Roots of Christological Monotheism*, 277–292, 278.

[166] Tom Deidun, "The Bible and Christian Ethics", 23. He states this danger in the context of appropriations of the Bible by theological ethics, but the "norms" can equally stem from systematic theology. The solution is to clearly distinguish between "exegesis" and "appropriation" as two steps (20).

in ethics searching only for "dignity" will yield many combinations that are irrelevant from a normative perspective, while adjectives like "inviolable" or "inalienable" are indispensable to mark out the contours of that enquiry. Similarly, in the investigation of a nascent Christology, to single out *"theos"* as the key referent reveals itself as a positivistic and superficial approach that risks to be insensitive to the subtle hermeneutical shifts that can be detected through a different procedure.

One of these is a study of "intertextuality" in which existing texts, in this case the Psalms, are discovered in quotes and allusions within writings of a subsequent era, with a different audience and constellation of religious, intellectual, and social factors. The earlier texts thus become the locus of continuity and discontinuity, of a new practice and self-understanding that still attaches itself to the given tradition's expressions. To allow for such processes of reinterpretation requires a different ability to grasp correspondences than the well-thought-out doctrines and treatises that will be studied in Chapters Five and Six on the patristic and the medieval stages of Christian thinking. These authors will also interpret the images and symbolic stories of the Bible. But the enquiry into the origins of Christology in Christolatry looks for expressions used in the act of worship itself and traces their sources. It exemplifies the two-way connection between language and experience highlighted by Saskia Wendel in her critique of a generic concept of religious experience when Daly-Denton observes, "one cannot but wonder to what extent the cultic practice is fuelling the Christology."[167]

Thus, without directly using the term "God", the account of Jesus walking on water across the lake draws on the depiction of God in the Exodus as master over the sea which was parted to allow Israel to escape from its life as slaves in Egypt. In a similarly symbolic way, the Psalms are read as pointing to Jesus with a "transfer to Jesus of prerogatives which the Psalter reserves for God" (284). An example is the use of Psalm 68 in 2 Thess which "applies the psalm's theophanic imagery to the day when 'the Lord Jesus is revealed from heaven with his mighty angels in flaming fire' (2 Thess 1:7). Again, allusion to the psalms tips the balance in favor of a reference to Jesus as θεός" (284). Besides employing the title of *"theos"* in only three places (281), the NT privileges a different form of articulation: Its "writers had at their disposal, however, another and perhaps more effective, technique for conveying Jesus' divine status – symbolic expression. It was the Psalter which provided them with their most favoured symbolic expression for the exalted Jesus' divine status – the concept of royal enthronement at God's right hand as found in Psalm 110" (285). A *"relecture"* of this

---

[167] Daly-Denton, "Singing Hymns to Christ as to a God", 281. Further page numbers in the text.

Psalm had already taken place: from the throne on which the king was installed by God, to two thrones, and, by "the NT period [...] a messianic reading" (285–286). The perspective changes in three stages:

> We might think of three levels of interpretation – the Jewish reading where David speaks in the psalms, the Christian reading where Jesus is the prophetically foretold prayer of the psalms, the Christological reading where Jesus is the Lord described or addressed in the psalms. It is at this third level that the Johannine reception of the psalms approaches Pliny's *carmen Christo quasi deo*. (288)

The Psalms as prayers or hymns to God provide the bridge towards addressing Jesus Christ as "Lord", *Kyrios*, the Greek translation of *Adonai*. Compared to the concept of *"theos"* or later dogmatic specifications like *"homoousios"* (of one being, the Council of Nicaea's term for Jesus Christ's equal standing with God), one can read the symbolism used as an understated, but figuratively all the more effective way of invoking an equivalent status of Jesus to God.

3.2.1.2 The model of "intertextuality"

What is the theoretical model used in this linking of earlier and later texts of the Bible, as explored by Margaret Daly-Denton regarding the resonance of the Psalms of the Hebrew Bible in New Testament authors? As Steve Moyise describes in his Introduction, intertextual references are inherently plural, which is an attractive feature for contemporary culture. He distinguishes three approaches connected to this "umbrella term" that was originally coined by Julia Kristeva in 1966, indicating "dialogical relationships between 'texts', broadly understood as a system of codes or signs [...] such relationships are more like an 'intersection of textual surfaces rather than a point (a fixed meaning)'".[168]

At first sight, this description seems to abstract from the speaking and understanding of human agents and to hypostasise "texts" as entities with an agency of their own. Yet, the readers play a role at each of the three levels distinguished: "The first (category) I call Intertextual Echo [...] it aims to show that a particular allusion or echo can sometimes be more important than its 'volume' might suggest."[169] This model of intertextuality appears as asymmetric in that it is not itself reinterpreted; its pervasive influence is unidirectional. By contrast,

---

168 Steve Moyise, "Intertextuality and the Study of the Old Testament in the New Testament", in *The Old Testament in the New Testament*, 14–41, 17. 14, with reference to Julia Kristeva, "Word, Dialogue and Novel" (1966), in *The Kristeva Reader*, ed. T. Moi (New York: Columbia University Press, 1986), 36.
169 Moyise, "Intertextuality", 17.

a "second category" is proposed, "called Dialogical Intertextuality [...] where the interaction between text and subtext is seen to operate in both directions". An example of this is that "on the one hand, the early church wants to claim that Jesus' life and death is a fulfilment of Scripture (1 Cor 15.3–54). On the other hand, it wants to claim that it is only in Christ that Scripture finds its true meaning (2 Cor 3.15)." The interpreters, one could say, depend on the matrix of the existing Scriptures but they qualify them in turn through their specific perspective. It is a two-way impression, even if its qualification as "dialogical" by Moyise may underestimate that it is the appropriation of a tradition without a space for agreement or contestation from the original body of texts. His third use is called "Postmodern Intertextuality" which "shows how this process is inherently unstable [...] a reader always brings texts they know to every reading [...] meaning can only result if some interactions are privileged and others are silenced."[170] This third use subordinates the "meaning" of the readings to the contingent array of texts that have played a role for each specific interpreter. There is no counterpart against which the adequacy of the individual interpretations could be judged. His quote of a comment makes this shift in the meaning of "text" clear: "First [...] the phenomenon text has been redefined. It has become a network of references to other texts (intertexts). Secondly [...] more attention is to be given to text as a process of production and not to the sources and their influences [...] thirdly [...] the role of the reader is not to be neglected in this approach".[171]

A potential disregard of the intertextuality approach for the *Sitz im Leben* that can be researched not primarily with literary but with social scientific and historical methods is a risk, but it is not unavoidable. A study of the early Christian reception of the Psalms is not forced to subscribe to a model that sees texts as communicating with each other, rather than between readers, writers, and re-interpreting communities. This is relevant for an enquiry, to be portrayed in conclusion, that does connect with the social and political environment in which their key terms play a role. The processes of rereading and creating a new understanding from the existing psalms and composing new ones are a main avenue for the development of Christology. How the term "*Kyrios*", the contrast between the first two states and the concluding call for a universal worship of Jesus Christ have been interpreted are questions in the debate on the second chapter of Paul's Letter to the Philippians.

---

170 Moyise, "Intertextuality", 18.
171 Moyise, "Intertextuality", 15, with reference to W. Vorster, "Intertextuality and *Redaktionsgeschichte*", in *Intertextuality in Biblical Writings* (Festschrift B. van Iersel), ed. S. Draisma (Kampen: Kok, 1989), 21.

3.2.2 Philippians 2 as a case study of addressing Christ as *Kyrios*

The poem or hymn in Phil 2:6–11, assumed to have been quoted by Paul and not composed by him,[172] describes a sequence of three states: "being in the form of God", exchanging this for a human life that extends to "death on the cross", and an exaltation by God by which Christ is made the recipient of universal worship. The initiative taken by Christ to "humble himself" has had a multiple history of effects, including the motivation for Ambrose's ministry to the poor in fourth-century Milan, and philosophical receptions and parallels of the idea of "self-emptying" in Neoplatonism and as far as Hegel. The questions to be treated here concern the direct context: first, the resonances and significance of the term "Lord" being used at such an early stage for Jesus (3.2.2.1); secondly, the interpretation of his being "in the form (*morphe*) of God". Should this be taken as immediately signifying his divine status, or as belonging to a contrast constituted between him and "Adam", made in the image (*eikon*) of God (3.2.2.2)?

3.2.2.1 Which background for *Kyrios*?

Adela Yarbro Collins has made a case for reading "worship" (*latria*) and "*Kyrios*" also as a polemic against the Roman ruler. "Every knee shall bow" for Christ, not for the Roman emperor, who is not a worthy recipient of the worship demanded for him, a human person, against the monotheistic conviction of Judaism. Jesus Christ is put forward by God as the only one about whom "every tongue shall confess that he is Lord" (Phil 2:10–11). Thus, its immediate context is practical, a question of choices to be made in a lifeworld of already plural religious traditions in which a colonising power had imposed its civil religion as a replacement against the resistance of Jewish believers in the one God. It arises in the first place not as a theoretical statement about Jesus Christ as God but as a counter-practice, refusing to accept the pagan political theology of the apotheosis of Roman emperors at their death into the ranks of gods.[173]

---

[172] Morna D. Hooker, however, does not adopt this position, as the end of her chapter, "Adam Redivivus: Philippians 2 once more", in *The Old Testament in the New Testament*, 220–234, 234, Fn. 20, shows: "Those who regard Phil 2.6–11 as a pre-Pauline 'hymn' have no need to wrestle with these problems!"

[173] In "The Worship of Jesus and the Imperial Cult", in *The Jewish Roots of Christological Monotheism*, 248, Yarbro Collins draws attention to this existing pattern of divinisation: The "strongest parallels to the worship of an exalted human being after death are found once again in Greek and Roman religion."

Hurtado reads the same lines and their ending in Phil 2:10 – 11 as an "utterly remarkable allusion to Isa 45.23 finding a reference to Christ as *Kyrios* as well as God in what is perhaps the most stridently monotheistic passage in the OT!"[174] In the face of these distinct interpretations, it becomes clear that the referent of "*Kyrios*" is not without alternatives; to understand it as the Greek equivalent of *Adonai*, the name by which God is addressed, is only one possibility. At the same time, it is not a question of ruling out certain readings, but of keeping the different constellations in mind that illuminate the horizons of that era. Yarbro Collins judges: "The veneration and acclamation here may be read in a political sense (Jesus is Messiah or King in God's stead) or in a religious sense (Jesus is cosmic Lord in God's stead). Both connotations were probably intended and perceived in the first century C.E."[175] The exegetical question about the period from which onwards a worship of Christ can be assumed can thus be left open, but taking the hymn as evidence of such worship even before Paul's Letter overstates what can be established.

3.2.2.2 "Self-emptying" as implying pre-existence?

The second issue for analysis relates to the first stage attributed to Jesus Christ, before the initiative to share a vulnerable human existence. While "the precise mode of existence or being is left unspecified", his being "in the form of God" is the starting point to which the second stage constitutes "a change in being as well as in status".[176] Morna Hooker argues for relating the key contrasts in this passage to the Genesis account of the creation of the human person "in the image of God" (Gen 1.26 – 27). In this comparison, Adam's "disobedience" contrasts with Christ's "obedience", which is, however, a self-chosen action: "Whereas Adam was stripped of his privileges, Christ deliberately emptied himself, becoming what Adam had become – a slave, subject to death". Hooker recognises an "Adamic influence not only in the phrase 'in the form of God' in v. 6 which *may* be reminiscent of Gen 1.26, but in the implicit contrast between Adam, who grasped at equality with God, and Christ, who did not grasp at/cling to/exploit that equality".[177] Since Hooker regards the text as Pauline, not as a hymn quoted by him, in view of the crucial Adam-Christ typology, she compares his use of the key term *morphe* here to *eikon*, the "image of God" in Genesis. Regarding the semantic differentiation between "*eikon*", "*morphe*", and

---

[174] Hurtado, "The Origin and Development of Christ-Devotion", 73.
[175] Yarbro Collins, "The Worship of Jesus", 247, Fn. 56.
[176] Yarbro Collins, "The Worship of Jesus", 244.
[177] Hooker, "Adam Redivivus", 220.

"*doxa*" (appearance), she points out, on the one hand, that while they are "not synonyms", this "does not mean they do not belong together".¹⁷⁸ On the other hand, "*morphe*" is seen as more encompassing and foundational: "Paul may well have used the phrase *en morphe theou* precisely because the theme of the contrast with Adam is fundamental to the argument" in order to "express both that contrast and the superiority of the one who was and who remained, even during his humiliation, 'in the form of God'".¹⁷⁹

What speaks for this reading is that the Adam-Christ comparison is a key motif of Paul's; Rom 5:14 and 1 Cor 15:22.45 show the same contrast as found in Phil 2. Hooker does not understand these verses as proposing a Christology of pre-existence. Such a reading may be considered a conclusion owed to applying a Johannine perspective already to Paul. Regarding a similar contrast made in 2 Cor, that "though he was rich, yet for your sake he became poor" (2 Cor 8:9), it is possible to interpret this verse as referring to a decision of the earthly Jesus to leave the security of his family context behind. It is this practical option which Paul takes as a model for his own life after Damascus:

> Paul alludes to the precariousness of his lifestyle, his financial poverty and homelessness in 2 Cor 6.10. In 6.10 he describes himself as "poor, yet making many rich", and in 8.9 he makes a similar statement about the Lord Jesus Christ himself, noting that "though he was rich, yet for our sakes he became poor, so that by his poverty you might become rich". The juxtaposition of these two statements probably indicates that Paul saw himself following in the tradition of Jesus by living the life of poverty and humility that he did.¹⁸⁰

---

178 Hooker, "Adam Redivivus", 221. Relevant for the understanding of the equality between men and women, she points out the discrepancy to Paul's statement in Galatians 3:28 that there "is neither Jew nor Gentile, neither slave nor free, nor is there male and female, for you are all one in Christ Jesus". This equality, however, is not maintained in the details of Paul's reception of Gen 1:26 which specifies in 1 Cor 11:7 that "man (but not woman!) is the image and glory of God", using "the biblical material to support a sexist hierarchy that conflicts with [...] Gal 3.28 [...] he has tried to combine what is said in Genesis 1 (where both male and female are created in the image of God) with a justification for social convention based on Genesis 2 (where the woman is subordinate to the man). By interpreting Genesis 1 in light of Genesis 2, he is able to argue for an important *difference* between male and female, for although he does not in fact deny that woman is 'the image of God' , his argument clearly depends on the denial that she is the *glory* of God." She proposes for 1 Cor 11: "What Paul *ought* to be saying in v. 7 is that it is the *head* of man (= Christ) who is the image and glory of God."
179 Hooker, "Adam Redivivus", 234.
180 Larry Kreitzer, *2 Corinthians*. New Testament Guides (Sheffield: Sheffield Academic Press, 1996), 17. I owe the clarification of these alternative readings to Margaret Daly-Denton.

This would match Paul's clearest statement of his understanding of Jesus' divine status at the beginning of Romans: he has been set apart for "the gospel of God [...] concerning his Son who was descended from David according to the flesh and was declared to be Son of God with power according to the spirit of holiness by resurrection from the dead" (Rom 1:3–4). There is no reference to a pre-existence with God but to the royal enthronement of Christ as "Son of God" through his resurrection.

Assuming the hymn to predate Paul's Letter and reading "in the form of God" as probably referring to a divine level and not to Adam, Yarbro Collins compares Jewish and pagan parallels: "The plot or *Gestalt* of the hymn (or poem) in Philippians 2 [...] on the one hand, expresses a strikingly novel perspective in the context of the history of religions. On the other hand, certain features of both Jewish and non-Jewish tradition illuminate the meaning of this innovative composition in its cultural context".[181] Figures who can be seen as precedents in the Hebrew Bible for the third stage of exaltation – Elijah, Enoch – did not die, Moses was not exalted, and the idea of transformation into a human being is different also from a "partial manifestation", such as the Wisdom of Solomon where "'in every generation Wisdom passes into holy souls'".[182] The pagan paradigm for the transition from stage one to stage two, a god or goddess becoming human, such as Demeter, did so only for a period of time, before they regained their divine realm. That a "god takes on human form is common in Greek literature;[183] but what is "distinctive of the Christian passage" in the "laying aside of glory and the taking on of a humble appearance and status [...] is the idea that the transformation lasts for the entire lifetime of the human being. Even more striking is the idea that the transformation is so real and so complete that it involves death."[184] The background to the third stage is the Creator God who has brought the world into being: "The high exaltation of the third and final stage means a restoration of the mode of existence as a heavenly being. It is now explicit that this mode of being involves also the status of 'Lord' over all creation".[185]

The universal acclamation in which every tongue confesses him as Lord clearly fulfils the criteria of divine "worship". But is this a "literary" text, or is

---

181 Yarbro Collins, "The Worship of Jesus", 243.
182 Yarbro Collins, "The Worship of Jesus", 244.
183 Yarbro Collins, "The Worship of Jesus", 245, with a reference also to the warning in the Odyssey that the stranger may be a god.
184 Yarbro Collins, "The Worship of Jesus", 246.
185 Yarbro Collins, "The Worship of Jesus", 244.

it based on actual practice?[186] Does it leave behind the oneness of God in Jewish monotheism, or is an interpretation of "being in the form of God" as indicating a divine level still in line with other hypostases of God? For Yarbro Collins, the opening provided by not specifying "the precise mode of existence or being" means that "this gap could be filled by imagining a principal angel; a hypostasis of God, such as the Logos or Wisdom; or, less likely, the noetic Adam, still possessing the glory of God as the image of God."[187]

It should be clear from the array of possibilities explored by biblical scholars also for this hymn or new Christian psalm quoted by Paul that nailing down one specific interpretation may not be an approach that is adequate to poetic texts. It is more fruitful to assume a connection between the practice of worship and conceptual interpretation, while respecting the figurative quality, the images and the translatability of the texts into emerging religious and cultural horizons. The next step was the appearance of accounts on the person of Jesus that did specify his "precise mode of existence" by putting together stories and sayings from his life, providing a narrative progression from his calling, his birth, or his pre-existence as Logos, to his ministry, his passion and his resurrection. The contours of "Pauline Christianity" as one strand of interpretation will be further outlined by following up on the question of Paul's links to the oral tradition from which the different models given in the four Gospels drew. Habermas's second assumption, that Christology only begins with the post-Easter conclusions of the first disciples and does not have a basis in Jesus' self-conception will thus be submitted to further historical enquiry. Chapter Four will equally address the question of how the confession shared by the Gospels and Paul, of Jesus' resurrection, stands in relation to modern historical consciousness. It will also offer an assessment on whether Habermas's third claim, based itself on the separation of the post-Easter from the pre-Easter message, can be upheld: that the interpretation of Jesus' death as atonement has turned out to be as least as significant as the history of reception of his proclamation and ethics.

---

[186] Yarbro Collins, "The Worship of Jesus", 250.
[187] Yarbro Collins, "The Worship of Jesus", 243–244.

4 Assessing the Pauline Strand: Exegetical, Methodological and Theological Disputes and Conclusions

A test case for the continued assessment of Paul's proclamation in comparison with the subsequent Gospels is his relation to accounts of Jesus' life gathered in the oral tradition (4.1). The independence of his approach raises the question of the methods used in dealing with the history of tradition and what they consider to be their referent – history itself, or its tradition (4.2)? In view of the clash, already alluded to in Chapter One, between accounts of a historical person who is claimed to have been resurrected, and the research methods accepted in history as a discipline, a methodological question about the principle of analogy in historiography arises (4.3). In conclusion, the three premises identified in Habermas's interpretation of the New Testament will be evaluated (4.4).

4.1 Paul, the oral tradition, and the Gospels

The comparison of different interpretations of the earliest phase of the post-Easter Jesus movement has shown that in summarising the soteriological significance of Jesus Christ in the formula of his salvific "death and resurrection", Paul only rarely sees the need to refer to his life. For some Pauline scholars, such as James Dunn and Jerome Murphy-O'Connor, this link is presupposed as known and shared with the Jerusalem community and the new Christian centres in Syria, Asia Minor, Greece, and Rome. Those in Antioch, northern Asia Minor, and Rome had been founded by groups of followers who had known Jesus or his disciples and who must have built their mission on accounts of the whole nexus of meaning expressed in Jesus' life, death and resurrection. Regarding the communities founded by Paul in other parts of Asia Minor and in Greece, what clues are there of him knowing elements of Jesus' ministry (4.1.1)? And how do the written accounts of Jesus' life, the Gospels, transmit the past in their distinct understandings (4.1.2)?

4.1.1 An enquiry into the references in Paul's Letters to the tradition about Jesus: Christine Jacobi's reconstruction

Viewed from the perspective of the Gospels which have shaped Christian and European cultural imagination, Paul offers a theological interpretation of his own that can be linked back to what is known about Jesus' conduct and destiny; it does not, however, complement or correct aspects in the written accounts of his ministry. At the same time, there are principal conflicts addressed in his Letters to local churches like Corinth which can be assumed to be motivated by an awareness of decisive practices of Jesus, such as his inclusion of the poor. Then the leaders of the community in Corinth would have been so strongly rebuked for their arrangements in celebrating the Lord's Supper – a problem put on the agenda of its founder Paul not by their own letter to him but by observers[188] – because it ran counter to Jesus' own practice. Paul's admonishing may include reasons of ethics and of ecclesial unity, but the judgement itself reflects a memory of what was typical for Jesus himself. With this unspoken backdrop, New Testament scholars have identified key themes of Paul's that take up core points which will be later expanded on in Mark's, Matthew's, Luke's and John's Gospels, such as love of enemy and engagement in reconciliation.

In her study of possible links between Paul and the oral tradition, Christine Jacobi combines methodological and historical insights. The findings of her structural comparisons and in-depth analyses of shared themes include that Paul's theology barely overlaps with any of the sayings collected of Jesus, so that one can only speak of "analogies" (4.1.1.1); that Paul draws on his own authority when making decisions in conflicts, a further sign that his approach constitutes an "autonomous appropriation"[189] (4.1.1.2). Its designation by Freyne as "quasi-mystical" is highlighted in conclusion (4.1.1.3).

4.1.1.1 No direct links, just "analogies"

Jacobi distinguishes three types of reference: Paul's use of identifiable Jesus *logia* prefaced with an introduction; recognisable but unmarked elements in his argumentations; and "references to the Kyrios without a synoptic parallel".[190] This

---

[188] Attention is drawn to this discrepancy, for example, by Dunn, *Theology of Paul the Apostle*, 611.
[189] Christine Jacobi, *Jesusüberlieferung bei Paulus? Analogien zwischen den echten Paulusbriefen und den synoptischen Evangelien* (Berlin/Boston: De Gruyter, 2015), 37.
[190] Cf. Jacobi, *Jesusüberlieferung bei Paulus?*, 42–46, 45. Examples for the first use, paraphrases or quotes of Jesus sayings, are 1 Cor 7:10–11; 9:14; 11:23–25 (Last Supper); for the second, the

includes his much-interpreted designation "in Christ" (for example, in Rom 14:14) which, as mentioned before, James Dunn has taken to be a Christian concretisation of "sacred places": "Christ himself functions in effect as the Christian sacred space."[191] She also examines to what effect the verbal references to Jesus sayings are dealt with, whether as the "climax" of an argumentation, thus endorsing it, or as possibly diverging from his own view. What legitimating power do distinctive traits of Jesus' proclamation have, for example, regarding the treatment of enemies? It is instructive that in this context Paul quotes the Hebrew Bible (Deut 32:35 and Prov. 25:21–22) to legitimate his statement, or his reinterpretation, in Rom 12:19–20: "Do not take revenge, my dear friends, but leave room for God's wrath, for it is written: 'It is mine to avenge; I will repay,' says the Lord. On the contrary: 'If your enemy is hungry, feed him; if he is thirsty, give him something to drink. In doing this, you will heap burning coals on his head.'" Jacobi interprets this passage as indicating that there is no reference to the Jesus tradition in this case while assuming that love of enemy is part of the context before as well as in the New Testament.[192] For readers who are not biblical scholars it is illuminating how experts in Second Temple Judaism and Early Christianity are able to interpret statements on the backdrop of alternatives that would have been available to them. Paul could probably have drawn directly on Jesus sayings, such as those in the Q collection that Matthew brought together in the Sermon on the Mount, but chooses to argue a slightly different point by combining two quotes from the common background of the Hebrew Scriptures. Jacobi's overall judgement is that elements which have parallels or allusions in the synoptic gospels are only rarely traced back to Jesus. Thus, she concludes that "as founder of the tradition and as teacher, Jesus is not relevant for Paul".[193] She adds that "for Paul, the *Kyrios* has more weight as the foundation of faith than as founder of the tradition".[194]

4.1.1.2 Making decisions in conflicts: How does Paul justify them?

The practical sphere of settling conflicts in the community by making decisions offers a further example of Paul's use of authority. Jacobi bases her conclusion

---

anonymous use, Rom 12:14–21; 1Thess 5:1–11; and for the third, 1 Cor 14:37; 1 Thess 4:15; 1 Thess 4:2, and examples of "in Christ", such as Rom 14:14.
191 Dunn, *Did the First Christians Worship Jesus?*, 45.
192 Jacobi, *Jesusüberlieferung bei Paulus?*, 103.
193 Jacobi, *Jesusüberlieferung bei Paulus?*, 392 ("*dass Jesus als Traditionsurheber und als Lehrer für Paulus nicht relevant ist*").
194 Jacobi, *Jesusüberlieferung bei Paulus?*, 394.

on the patterns she identifies in Pauline argumentation. Even key contents, which are marked as sayings of the Lord, are relativised from a "Christological perspective".[195] Her observation throws a light on the internal heterogeneity of the New Testament Christologies. It will have to be asked how far the Synoptic Gospels and John go in rectifying the inherited oral tradition, not simply rereading it from their own locations forty to eighty years after Jesus's ministry and death. Paul takes a remarkable liberty in interpreting the earliest, unwritten accounts in line with his privileging of the antithesis of crucifixion and resurrection, which constitutes his summary of Jesus' significance as the salvific turning point in the history of humanity since its creation. Subsequent periods of theological thought will have to be checked for similarly inventive creations of tradition. But at this originating stage of Christian mission, the relevance of not subordinating himself to serving the memory of Jesus's own proclamation of God's kingdom has an even greater impact. This is reflected in the practical decisions Paul takes in matters of conflict, such as divorce and food, where he draws on his own authority. On the problem of divorce, Paul supplies a quote from the Lord (1 Cor 7:10) but offers his own argumentation from Genesis.[196] Also in resolving conflicts on the purity issue of food laws, Jesus' own practice plays no role as a factor in decision-making, in the absence of unambiguous statements of his to be taken into account.[197]

Based on a self-understanding as directly commissioned by the exalted Lord Jesus Christ, Paul not only calls himself "Apostle" and comments critically on the Jerusalem church leaders as "so-called pillars".[198] He also takes elements which appear in the oral tradition as a touchstone that can be relativised, ironically, for Christological reasons. As Jacobi shows, Jesus' own proclamation is called upon only in specific cases and reinterpreted in Paul's own framework. It is, as she anticipates in the first chapter, an "autonomous appropriation".[199]

---

195 Jacobi, *Jesusüberlieferung bei Paulus?*, 394, with reference to the Jesus sayings mentioned expressly in 1 Cor 7:10–11 and 9:14, as examples of Paul's Christological relativisation.
196 Cf. Jacobi, *Jesusüberlieferung bei Paulus?*, 252–260.
197 Jacobi treats this theme also in comparison to Mark, Matthew and Acts in her seventh chapter, 300–386.
198 Cf., among others, Brown, *Antioch and Rome*, 3, and Freyne, *Expansion*, 224, on Paul's reference to "those who were supposed to be leaders; what they are makes no difference to me" (Gal 2:9).
199 Cf. Jacobi, *Jesusüberlieferung bei Paulus?*, 37.

4.1.1.3 "In Christ": Paul's "quasi-mystical" appropriation

The hermeneutically decisive term "appropriation" denotes a process in which the past and the present are interlinked in the interpreter's vision of the core content, and it applies equally to the Gospels. While "Q", the sayings source, also lacks a narrative structure, it documents the interest in Jesus' teachings as the basis of the revelation it recognises him to be. Paul draws on other resources, especially the Hebrew Bible, for his interpretation of Jesus Christ and the lifestyle that follows from becoming part of those who have "turned from idols to serve a living and true God and to wait for his Son" (1 Thess 1:9–10). The separate authority claimed by Paul also appears in his exhortations to his communities to take him as their model. "Imitate me, as I imitate Christ" (1 Cor 1:11), is a mediated form of practical faith, including, as we saw, his voluntary poverty. Yet for the Gospels with their narrative structure, the model that followers can emulate directly is that of Jesus. Even if the extant Letters only date from the 50s CE onwards, Paul's foundation of communities began after his conversion in the later 30s CE, and three years before he went back to Jerusalem to encounter the immediate group of followers who had been with Jesus. How is this lack of more specific connections to be assessed since it seems clear for Paul himself that nothing is missing? Freyne identifies his approach as "quasi-mystical" and spells out the contrast in the ethical understanding of what type of Christian life to strive for:

> his own radical shift of horizons from the centrality of Torah to the centrality of Christ meant that he viewed the goal of Christian moral living as conforming to the death and resurrection of Jesus, understood as the eschatological event [...] The "in Christ" model suggests a quasi-mystical transformation of the self so that one's own ego is replaced by that of Christ: "I live, now not I, but Christ lives in me" (Gal 2:20), or, "Let this mind be in you which was also in Christ Jesus" (Phil 2:5), are typical expressions of this understanding. True, Paul does introduce a biographical dimension into his understanding of the moral life when he points to his own life as a mimesis of that of Christ, and therefore, an example to be followed by the Corinthians (1 Cor 11:1). Yet it is clear from his paraenetic instructions that he has in mind the death/resurrection paradigm of the Easter faith, rather than drawing on the Jesus-biography in any substantial way.[200]

How the Gospels compare on this point with Paul's independent, self-reliant appropriation, is to be assessed briefly in conclusion.

---

[200] Freyne, "In Search of Identity: Narrativity, Discipleship and Moral Agency", in *Moral Language in the New Testament*, ed. Ruben Zimmermann and J. Van der Watt, in cooperation with Susanne Luther (Tübingen: Mohr Siebeck, 2010): 67–85, 67–68.

4.1.2 Before and beyond Paul: Understandings of Jesus' life and of discipleship

What Paul devises at a cosmic and world historical scale – the alternative between Adam and Christ, sin and grace, death and salvation[201] – finds a counterpart in the Gospels' call for the decision to follow Jesus. The difference is that the attitudes and agency demanded and encouraged are concretised by narratives that record exemplary situations and speak to the imagination of the early Christians in their different cultural settings. They illustrate "values and norms (in which) the disciples might discover a totally new set of human dispositions that they could appropriate and internalise".[202] While the dispositions are new, it is their own moral capability that is being appealed to which can be re-oriented by the model of Christ's life who had called people at the margins and sinners to follow him.

The way in which "discipleship" is portrayed in the Gospels and whom it includes varies considerably. Freyne compares Mark's and John's descriptions by employing the distinction Paul Ricoeur makes between "*idem*" and "*ipse*" in his theory of self. John stands for the "*ipse*" and the self-constancy manifested in keeping one's promise, resulting in the portrayal of the disciples as unfailing friends. Mark represents the pole of "*idem*" or sameness, reporting critically on the failure of the Twelve to understand Jesus' parables, his values and mission: Tied to their existing self-conceptions, the "*Idem* [...] created almost insurmountable obstacles for the disciples", while in John, it "has already been left behind"[203] when they join Jesus.

---

[201] In *Jesus Symbol of God* (Maryknoll: Orbis, 2000), 156–157, Roger Haight begins his brief comparison of the five NT soteriologies (155–178) with an outline of Paul's Last Adam Christology: "The point of the correspondence is that they are both one person in whom the destiny of all has been determined [...] one should consider [...] the sheer scope of the vision it contains, the breadth of the context in which Jesus Christ is considered [...] the framework for understanding him includes all creation and the whole of human history. All of human history is divided into two parts, the period of sin up to Jesus Christ and the history after it until the future end [...] In him, in effect a new race of human beings has begun. [...] The contrast is a classic description of salvation, a reversal of an evil and desperate situation by the power of God working through the agency of Jesus Christ."
[202] Freyne, "Identity", 77.
[203] Freyne, "Identity", 78.

Despite the fact that in John, time is not treated in a sequential way but as suspending narrative progression by the simultaneity of the present with past and future eras,[204] all four gospels point

> to the remembered life of Jesus as a model for Christian living [...] the discipleship model is based on the memory of a physical accompanying of Jesus as prophet, moral guide and teacher. As we shall see it involves a radical re-orientation of the self under the direction and inspiration of the master, but without the immediacy of the self-emptying dimension in the Pauline understanding. While discipleship does indeed involve a process of "losing one's life," "taking up one's cross," or "becoming the least of all and the servant of all," there is a more marked temporal dimension to its full actualisation that is not as clearly articulated in the Pauline ethical system. Thus, Jesus reminds the disciples that "they are the ones who have endured/persevered [...] with him in his trials" (Luke 22:28), indicating perseverance, commitment and sharing as important aspects of faithful following. Paul on the other hand envisages a transformation of the self with immediate ethical consequences through the mystical experience of dying and rising with Christ in the baptismal ritual (Rom 6:1–11).[205]

Like Paul, the Gospels offer different appropriations, as is evident in their divergent treatments of discipleship, but equally in their different accentuations throughout their accounts of the life and destiny of Jesus. They provide a variety of portraits that has animated distinct trajectories of understanding and community structures in the history of reception: "It is characteristic for primitive Christianity (*Urchristentum*) that it attempted to describe the normative beginning in a juxtaposition (*Nebeneinander*) of *different images* of Jesus."[206]

Through the narrative structure that marks the Gospels, some of the antitheses that structure Paul's theology are replaced by the real conflicts that marked Jesus' lifetime. The "polarizing effect or outcome of Jesus' ministry" that Hurtado had identified as "a second force/factor to include in an adequate theory of the origin and formation of Christ-devotion"[207] can thus be understood as a constant backdrop, a reaction that accompanied his proclamation of the kingdom of God as beginning with his actions. The controversy it created ultimately led to his execution by the Romans but equally to the claim of his followers that his violent death was not the end. How the claim that Jesus was raised from the dead can be assessed in comparison with existing paradigms in theories of historiography will be investigated in subsection 4.3, after outlining a theory dispute on biblical

---

204 Freyne, "Identity", 77: "Past and future are repeatedly collapsed into the present of Jesus' hour."
205 Freyne, "Identity", 68.
206 Merz, "Der historische Jesus", 56.
207 Hurtado, "The Origin and Development of Christ Devotion", 65.

methods that is relevant for the general status of exegetical enquiries in relation to history.

First, however, taking stock of the course of enquiry so far, the following conclusions must be drawn, although they remain preliminary in the sense that further refinements are needed: The title "Pauline Christianity" has turned out to be an insufficient label for the complex processes of expansion of the Christian movement into different cultural and linguistic regions; it also does not reflect the variety of its internal composition, including procedures and results of attempting to resolve conflicts. The New Testament as a whole, established in its basic shape already around 200 CE, two centuries before the canon formation was completed, must count as the basis that made possible the next stage of the legacy of the life and destiny of Jesus: bringing forward a multi-faceted plurality of models to be elaborated in the intellectual and institutional settings of Greek and Latin cultures, philosophies and law. It was to this range of understandings of the core Christian message that Paul contributed his specific vision. It needs to be reconstructed in a hermeneutics of early Christianity that takes all the New Testament sources with their diverse Jewish and Gentile backgrounds into account. The different accentuations of Paul and the other authors of Letters and of the four canonical evangelists in the early Christian proclamation of Jesus as the Messiah offer a wellspring of insights into the context of Jesus' proclamation. Their significance for interpreting his message can be assessed with discursively justifiable arguments.[208] Thus, Bultmann's conclusion that enquiries into the founder of the pre-Easter movement need to be abandoned is no longer shared, though there are different starting points based on programmatic reasons, as will become evident in the following debate.

4.2 A dispute on methods

Exchanges about methods among biblical scholars and classicists have been referred to before in the context of arguments for a "Cynic" understanding of Jesus,

---

[208] For example, the proposal to read the Fourth Gospel with the claim of the "Son" to do the will of the "Father" on the backdrop of the juridical concept of "agency" of the Jewish *halakha*, as Théo Preiss did in 1954 and Peder Borgen in 1968. It offers striking insights into the idea of representation, authority and accountability of the one who has been sent and in turn sends out new agents as ambassadors of his own mission. Cf. Peder Borgen, "God's Agent in the Fourth Gospel" (1968), in *The Interpretation of John*, edited with an Introduction by John Ashton (Issues in Religion and Theology 9) (Philadelphia: Fortress Press and London: SPCK, 1986): 67–78. I am grateful to Margaret Daly-Denton for this reference.

in line with urban wisdom teachers around the Mediterranean. Apart from the question of an adequate framework, it has also become clear that competing timelines as well as discrepancies on material questions between the Gospels are resolved in different ways by exegetical schools. We have seen, for example, how Luke-Acts differs from Mark, Matthew and John on the location of the disciples after Jesus' death – Jerusalem or Galilee, and on the origin and directions of their mission. Such internal divergences are a matter for New Testament Studies and the methods employed.

Against the suspicion that the Gospels are not even to be regarded as theologised history but as compositions of myths, a new approach, not satisfied with mainly literary and history of religion analyses, has been elaborated that investigates especially the synoptic Gospels as based on "eyewitness" accounts. This position, developed with different accentuations[209], minimises the gap between the past reality and the scope of interpretation that the New Testament writers engaged in. They are accepted as keeping as closely as they could to the reports they had received from the oral tradition constituted by sayings remembered by witnesses who had been contemporaries of Jesus. Among those who disagree with taking the Synoptics as directly reporting from memories of Jesus' history are biblical scholars who draw a specific conclusion from the insight that each Gospel offers a "plot" designed by the individual or group of authors responsible for its composition: they restrict the task of enquiry to investigating traditions in process, and their "contexts", but leave the question undecided how these refer to the past reality. The view discussed also by Christine Jacobi is whether the "quest" or "enquiry back to Jesus" has been superseded, and whether new approaches to the concept of memory must be taken on board.[210] One can detect a shifting of the burden of proof to those biblical scholars who claim that the four Gospels point to a factual core the details of which can be investigated. The charge is that this can amount to a "rather positivistic view of the past constructed in the Gospels".[211] Especially one methodological limit is seen to have been transgressed: instead of keeping the two questions distinct, "Byrskog following Dunn's work, *Jesus Remembered*, draws together the history of the Jesus tradition with the historical enquiry back to Jesus: '[...] the

---

[209] Authors include Samuel Byrskog, Richard Bauckham, James Dunn and Dale Allison.
[210] Jacobi, *Jesusüberlieferung bei Paulus?*, 11, in relation to Dale Allison, *Constructing Jesus. Memory, Imagination, and History* (Grand Rapids, NI: Eerdmans, 2010).
[211] Jacobi, *Jesusüberlieferung bei Paulus?*, 38, Fn. 117.

documents which we employ as sources betray a use of traditional material and […] this material presents the avenue from the gospels back to Jesus'".²¹²

The counterposition, developed by Jens Schröter and shared by Jacobi, does not claim "that the picture (*Bild*) painted by the Gospels of the beginnings of the tradition (*Überlieferungsanfänge*) with Jesus and his circle of disciples does not correspond to 'historical facts', but it distinguishes critically between the two – against an equation (*Gleichsetzung*) of what the Gospels state as the origin of early Christian tradition with the actual (*tatsächlichen*) beginnings of the tradition."²¹³

How can these two polar opposites – the premise of maximal accuracy to historical reality, and a factual bracketing of this parameter – be responded to? It would require a worked-out theory of historical reason based on a philosophical analysis of the human historical condition to settle this dispute. The "eyewitness" theory would have to accept that the very action of isolating "historical facts" from the flow of time constitutes a selective, interpretive act within a framework that itself needs justification. What is regarded as relevant in temporal processes with many factors and "effects" is not evident but is arrived at in a process of synthesis.²¹⁴ The conviction of being able to access "history as it was" is untenable. Reconstructing the past reality through memories presupposes numerous, momentous decisions on what is credible. They need to be accounted for in the intersubjective dialogue on "objectivity" that was discussed in Chapter One. But also the opposite view which at first appears more critical and sophisticated needs to be questioned. It is equally taking a position by remaining within the complex of tradition and by not including an extra-textual referent. By foregoing judgement on them, it just passes on the torch of interpretation but does not examine, or think it possible to examine, their anchoring in history. This theory decision is commented on in one of the reviews of Jacobi's groundbreaking work:

> Those who view the problem from the perspective of the synoptic Gospels, may get nervous: Is there thus no longer a reliable bridge back to Jesus' action (*Wirken*)? Do we not even need it? Whoever wants to retain a continuity – however it is outlined – between the words of the

---

212 Jacobi, *Jesusüberlieferung bei Paulus?*, 38, Fn. 117, with reference to Samuel Byrskog, "The Transmission of the Jesus Tradition", in *Handbook for the Study of the Historical Jesus*, vol. 2, ed. T. Holmén and S.E. Porter (Leiden: Brill, 2011): 1465–1494, 1465.
213 Jacobi, *Jesusüberlieferung bei Paulus?*, 38, Fn. 117
214 Essen, *Historische Vernunft*, 264–286.

earthly Jesus and the synoptic tradition must explain why Paul put so little store by it (*so wenig Wert auf sie legte*).²¹⁵

Jens Schröter confines the "contact to the historical events" to understanding "the conceptions of the Gospels as 'reactions to Jesus' action (*Wirken*)'".²¹⁶ In a further contribution to the debate with the "eyewitness" position he outlines the two poles of history and memory: "Aristotle's well-known distinction between the poet and the historian is therefore too schematic and should be replaced by what Paul Ricoeur has called the "interweaving" (*croisement*) of history and narrative." While "the *goal* of a historical or narrative has to be distinguished from that of a novel and also from legend or fiction, [...] there is no clear-cut distinction between the historical and a fictional narrative." Schröter concludes: "the distinction between 'history proper' and 'mnemohistory' as well as of 'factuality' and 'actuality' have to be called into question."²¹⁷ He justifies his approach by referring to Paul Ricoeur's analyses in the three volumes of *Time and Narrative* published in the 1980s, and to an article of 1994.²¹⁸ This would back his position, summarised in the abstract of Schröter's article: "Because the past is always perceived from the perspective of the present, historical reconstruction and reception of the past are per se intertwined. Thus, there is no 'real' past behind the sources. Instead, our view of events and figures from the past is a result of the remains from the past interpreted from the perspective of the present."²¹⁹

This conclusion, that "there is no 'real' past behind the sources" is an unwarranted step, and regarding Ricoeur as endorsing this view is questionable. In his monumental study that appeared in 2000, *Memory, History, Forgetting*, Ricoeur corrected his earlier position and insisted on the importance of the extra-textual referent of the reconstruction: the past in its independence.²²⁰ It is a different

---

215 Hildegard Scherer, Review of C. Jacobi, *Jesusüberlieferung bei Paulus?*, in *Biblische Zeitschrift* 61/2 (2017): 279–280, 280.
216 Jacobi, *Jesusüberlieferung bei Paulus?*, 12, with reference to Schröter, *Erinnerung an Jesu Worte. Studien zur Rezeption der Logienüberlieferung in Markus, Q und Thomas* (Neukirchen-Vluyn: Neukirchener Verlag, 1997), 484.
217 Jens Schröter, "Memory, Theories of History, and the Reception of Jesus", *Journal for the Study of the Historical Jesus* 16 (2018): 85–107, 98.
218 Schröter, "Memory, Theories of History, and the Reception of Jesus", 96, Fn. 32, with the reference to Ricoeur, "Philosophies critiques de l'histoire. Recherche, explication, écriture", in *Philosophical Problems Today*, Vol. I, ed. G. Fløistad (Dordrecht: Kluwer, 1994): 139–201.
219 Schröter, "Memory, Theories of History, and the Reception of Jesus", 85.
220 Ricoeur, *Memory, History, Forgetting*, trans. Kathleen Blamey and David Pellauer (Chicago: University of Chicago Press, 2004) (French original 2000), 109: "My approach to Husserl in the

question that is being pursued through a concept of memory that cannot be replaced by "cultural" or "collective" memory: to account for the distance which separates us from the past in its independence from consciousness.[221]

Thus, regarding the New Testament, the answer to the problem of never being able to access the "event" in question directly is not to retreat into the web of traditions and restrict claims to intra-traditional discourse about previous discourses which might be inventions. It is to persevere with the previously accepted and still defensible task of searching and assessing all available clues into the life of Jesus: literary and historical, archaeological and philological, as well as inferences from the history of reception of the New Testament. Even if the actual person who walked Galilee is not accessible, the scholarly construct of the "Historical Jesus" requires expert debate on new theses and avenues regarding their greater or lesser adequacy. The plots designed by the gospel writers continue to call for reconstruction in two directions: the history they convey of Jesus, and the present of their own political and ecclesial contexts. We must "evaluate how they rendered their debt to the past of Jesus and his world", as they saw it in the light of their present.[222] The objection to the "eyewitness" approach made by Jacobi can be taken as mainly accepted, that "also the Gospels provide their own picture on the beginning of the Jesus tradition and thus interpret the present".[223] In relation to the biblical application of the different approaches to historiography, Schröter does conclude his article with a more carefully worded assessment: the Gospels "refer to an actual past that is framed and interpreted with fictional elements. Therefore, they provide the basis for a portrait of Jesus from a historical-critical perspective."[224]

---

present context differs noticeably from that proposed in *Time and Narrative*, where the constitution of time was the principal issue." See also the discussion by Wayne Coppins, "Richard Bauckham, Jens Schröter, and Paul Ricoeur on Memory and its Errors", in https://germanforneutestamentler.com/tag/schroterposts/ (last accessed April 21, 2021).

221 In "Memory and Forgetting in Paul Ricoeur's Theory of the Capable Self", in *Handbook of Cultural Memory Studies*, 203–211, I have outlined his position, as developed in his seminal work of 2000.

222 Freyne, *Galilee and Gospel*, 212.

223 Jacobi, *Jesusüberlieferung bei Paulus?*, 38, Fn. 117.

224 Schröter, "Memory, Theories of History, and the Reception of Jesus", 99. In "Der 'erinnerte Jesus': Erinnerung als geschichtshermeneutisches Paradigma der Jesusforschung", in *Jesus Handbuch*, ed. Jens Schröter and Christine Jacobi, with cooperation by Lena Nogossek (Tübingen: Mohr Siebeck, 2017): 112–124, he refers to research on processes of oral tradition which have found that it is not "one 'original' that is varied again and again but that each presentation is itself an 'original'" (116). He sums up that these "contours are themselves a specific mode of Jesus remembrance and not a path to the past 'behind' the texts. Rather, the 'historical Jesus' appears from this perspective as a form of Jesus remembrance on a historical-critical basis

The danger for subsequent generations of readers is to miss clues which would have been familiar to the original communities: the allusions to the story of Moses, for example, in the infancy narrative of Matthew. The alleged killing of infant boys by Herod lacks a counterpart in Luke, and is not reported by any historical sources. Thus, the slaughter of the innocents is a literary, figurative, narrative unit designed to convey the significance of Jesus in comparison with Moses. The problem with reading the Gospels as completely factual accounts ignores the plot around which each of them is structured, the cultural and religious contexts (in which two of the New Testament authors decided to extend the story of Jesus to his birth), and the conflicts their communities were facing at the time. Investigating these traces is the alternative to both literalism and a suspension of all claims to historical truth.

4.3 The principle of analogy in history and the claim of Jesus' resurrection

A question of "method" and premises at a different level is posed by the incommensurability of the claim of Jesus' resurrection with the methodological insistence of the historical sciences on the principle of analogy. Before the communicability of "resurrection" to a contemporary consciousness can be treated (4.3.3), it is necessary to discuss the role of the "possible" (4.3.2), after clarifying the two biblical directions of interpreting this divine intervention into history (4.3.1).

4.3.1 Jesus' death and resurrection in terms of sacrifice, or of vindication?

The earliest written testimony that Jesus was resurrected by God is found in the pre-Pauline formula quoted in 1 Cor 15: Jesus who had died redemptively for sins was "raised on the third day according to the Scriptures" (v. 4). The witnesses to whom the resurrected Jesus had appeared are referred to, though Jesus' appearances to his women followers who had remained with him at the cross are not mentioned specifically.

Before dealing with the question of the epistemological or hermeneutical status of such claims, the two key interpretations of this statement need to be

---

which is not to be identified with the 'real Jesus' behind the texts" (124). While the second part of the sentence is correct, the conclusion that historical-critical research itself is a form of Jesus remembrance cuts off the connection of memory to the past that Ricoeur insists on in his work of 2000.

recalled: for Paul, Jesus' death is a sacrifice accepted by God to which God responded by raising him; for the Synoptics, it is a vindication by God of Jesus as the "Son" and "Messiah" who had claimed to be acting in God's will and was crucified for his proclamation in critique of existing powers. The polarised response which Hurtado sees as a key to the origin of the devotion to Jesus is indeed a crucial historical factor. The conduct and claim Jesus put forward publicly did call for justification.[225] Despite the obvious differences between the Evangelists' accounts, their portrayal of Jesus' resurrection is that of a just person suffering who is vindicated by God. This is also the position put forward by Christine Jacobi:

> This specificity (*Besonderheit*) is closely connected to the action (*Wirken*) of the earthly Jesus. This is shown implicitly and explicitly in the Easter stories (*Ostererzählungen*) of the four Gospels. Jesus' proclamation, linked to the more recent Israelite-Jewish conviction of the power of God over life and death and of the implementation (*Durchsetzung*) of God's justice beyond the limits of death, ultimately created the presuppositions for the disciples' testimony that Jesus had been raised from the dead; in return, the conviction that Jesus had been resurrected by God confirmed his pre-Easter message. It is common to the Gospels that became canonical that they do not state a rupture between Jesus and the one who was resurrected but let Jesus be confirmed by the resurrection as the one he has been (*ist*) basically from the beginning.[226]

What then about the dimension of "sacrifice" which has been tradition-forming since Paul's message? As outlined before, it is necessary to exercise skills of differentiation and nuance in coming to a consistent interpretation based on the concept of God proclaimed by Jesus in which forgiveness is a constant feature. It can also be shown at various turning points in the New Testament's history of reception that the metaphor of "sacrifice", used as a comprehensive term for Jesus' salvific significance, has been subjected to literalising readings. The meaning of "resurrection" is affected when it is conceived as a divine reward for undergoing the passion required by the same God to atone for humanity's sins. It is understood differently when it appears as an act of rescue by the power of the Creator God as the one "who gives life to the dead and calls

---

[225] In *Theologische Anthropologie* (Freiburg: Herder, 2011), 2 Vols., Vol. II, 1301–1303, Pröpper points out that Jesus' proclamation required justification already due to its content, claiming that God was present in his own actions, which led to the challenge of blasphemy (cf. Mk 2:7).
[226] Christine Jacobi, "II. Auferstehung, Erscheinungen, Weisungen des Auferstandenen", in *Jesus Handbuch*, 490–504, 503–504, with reference to Ulrich Luz, *Das Evangelium nach Matthäus (Mt 26–28)*, EKK I/4 (Zürich: Benziger, 2002), under "Section E. Early Traces of Effects and Receptions of Jesus", 487–561.

non-existent things into existence" (Rom 4:17) and who is "making everything new" (Rev 21:5).[227] This is an alternative that also affects the debate with secular fellow citizens and scholars on the concept of history, if this concept is to include a dimension of meaning which is relevant for practical self-understandings.

4.3.2 A horizon of the "possible", not the "plausible": Elisabeth Schüssler Fiorenza's call for a shift in criteria

While the Easter faith of the disciples is a historical fact, the claim of theologians to contemporary cultures of knowledge goes further than giving an explanation for their drive to found Christian communities and missionise also in Gentile cities. The challenge to secular fellow scholars is the request not to rule out "resurrection" as a conceivable reality, as a possibility that is at least "thinkable", following Kant's distinction between what can be "known" and what can be "thought". A first query needs to be addressed to the concept of "plausibility" which operates at a level of accepted but not really tested probabilities and existing conventions. The feminist biblical scholar Elisabeth Schüssler Fiorenza has critiqued the attitude of restricting research to likely settings and has called for greater stringency, redefining the remit of historians who are requested to ask about power relations: "then history/historiography, in contrast to the prevailing view, is not simply an objective science but a critical social practice."[228] A scope for new perspectives beyond the existing consensus is demanded by her as a matter of academic rigour:

> I suggest that the "common sense" criterion of "plausibility" must be replaced with the criterion of "possibility" [...] Instead of asking, "Is it likely or plausible that wo/men shaped the Jesus-traditions?" one must ask, "Is it historically possible and thinkable that they did so?" This shift requires scholars to prove that such a possibility did not exist at the time. Such an argument would presuppose that scholars have studied not only hegemonic historical formations but also the emancipatory elements in Greco-Roman and Jewish societies. In using the criterion of possibility one must, however, be careful not to turn around and answer it again with reference to what is deemed "plausible" and "common sense" truism.[229]

---

227 Cf. Pröpper, *Der Jesus der Philosophen und der Jesus des Glaubens. Ein theologisches Gespräch mit Jaspers – Bloch – Kolakowski – Gardavsky – Machovec – Fromm – Ben-Chorin* (Mainz: Grünewald, 1976), 129.
228 Elisabeth Schüssler Fiorenza, "Re-visioning Christian Origins: *In Memory of Her* Revisited", in *Christian Origins: Worship, Belief and Society*, 225–250, 225.
229 Elisabeth Schüssler Fiorenza, "Re-visioning Christian Origins", 244–245.

Enquiring about what is "possible" opens up a further dimension that belongs to the conditions of living as a historical being. It is the overall horizon of possibility that is a question for human agency as such: How does the way in which I envisage what is possible influence my projects and actions? Which intentions can be achieved in a present marked by the legacy of historical struggles and by the currently coexisting agents? In Kant's analysis of practical reason which comprises both morality and the justified desire for happiness or meaning, the horizon of the possible is linked to the basis of hope on which agency depends.[230] This orientation is taken up in two contemporary proposals. In view of different conceptions of historical enquiry, the critique of the merely "plausible", outlined above by Elisabeth Schüssler Fiorenza, is also prominent in Georg Essen's argument in favour of resisting a reduction of "possibility" to a framework of habitual and calculable probability. This could only be maintained at the cost of a serious diminution of the scope of intention and action, and of underestimating the very contingency of what comes to pass in history. What has in fact happened needs to be reconstructed on the background of what could have happened.[231] The hermeneutical philosopher Ricoeur has brought this insight to fruition also in his social ethical writings. He draws from it the conclusion that history is moved by new attempts to realise what previous generations could not complete. The *movens* of agency is the consciousness of "betrayed" or "unfulfilled promises" in which the "*ipse*" of the agent is engaged, wishing to convert the unrealised promises of a tradition into reality.[232] Without a dialectical awareness of what was intended but failed to be realised, it is not possible to write history. There is always more than what has ma-

---

[230] Habermas discusses the problem of "motivation" and of the "defeatism of reason" as an observable trend, but objects to the foundational significance of "meaning" which according to Kant's analysis of the "antinomy of practical reason" is threatened and requires nothing less than the postulate of the existence of God. Kant's argumentation shows the relevance of faith in a God who rescues, especially in relation to the victims of violence. While Habermas's interpretation of Kant will be treated mainly in Chapter Seven, Kant's inclusion of the question of meaning also into his "world concept of philosophy" in connection with the "public use of reason" should already be noted here. Cf. Kant, "An Answer to the Question: 'What is Enlightenment?'", in *Kant's Political Writings*, edited with an Introduction, and Notes by Hans Reiss, trans. H.B. Nisbet (Cambridge: CUP, 1970), 54–60. Among the philosophers who have analysed the implications of the "world concept" of philosophy is Jürgen Stolzenberg in "'Was jedermann notwendig interessiert'. Kants Weltbegriff der Philosophie", in *Protestantismus zwischen Aufklärung und Moderne (FS Ulrich Barth)*, ed. Roderich Barth, Claus-Dieter Osthövener and Arnulf von Scheliha (Frankfurt: P. Lang, 2005): 83–94.
[231] Essen, *Historische Vernunft*, 214–225.
[232] Ricoeur, *Reflections on the Just*, trans. D. Pellauer (Chicago: University of Chicago Press, 2007), 105.

terialised empirically, and even determining these "facts" is a complex endeavour that needs to declare its criteria. Thus, without the horizon of the "possible", one cannot state what is real, what is a historical outcome, and what tendencies it harbours for the future.

4.3.3 Resurrection as a practical claim of meaning

The above analysis should be acceptable to historians as a description of their intellectual operations in naming factors from a horizon of possibilities that have contributed to a development. It is one step further to include an event without analogy and claim that it cannot be dismissed a priori as irrational. Thinking about history reaches a different level when the question of the horizon for action and of meaning is posed. It involves the issue of elementary self-understanding not at a cognitive-theoretical, but at a practical level, where diverse answers can be expected. The "polarising" effect of Jesus' claim of authority shows up the ineradicable, fundamental nature of a response with multiple options. It will remain controversial and "ambivalent".[233] However, conceding that "resurrection" does not have to be classified as impossible is a big step in self-limitation for theorists: it means accepting the changing paradigms and fallibility of cultural knowledge that become evident in hermeneutical reflections on the spirit of different eras. These range from theory- and contemplation-oriented, to mystical, and from empirical, and naturalising, to praxis-directed attitudes. Each of them can benefit from an exercise of questioning their parameters to detect their self-limitations. However, to be able to include "resurrection" into the realm of the possible, its epistemological status must be clarified.

On the one hand, it is clear that the resurrection of Jesus does not fall under the criteria for historical events "since it does not have a spatial-temporal terminus. It was not an object of intuition by the senses and principally eludes empirical ascertainability [...] Thus, the category of 'historical event' cannot be applied to the resurrection of Jesus".[234] Yet it does have "a reference to history". On the other hand, even if "it cannot belong to the field of objects of history (*Gegen-*

---

[233] Magnus Lerch, *Selbstmitteilung Gottes. Herausforderungen einer freiheitstheoretischen Offenbarungstheologie* (Regensburg: Pustet, 2015), 193.
[234] Essen, *Historische Vernunft*, 379–380. 381. Lerch, *Selbstmitteilung Gottes* 215, summarises that the category of "historical event" cannot be applied "since the action of resurrection does not possess a material-empirical substrate and thus the moment of a spatially and temporally definable facticity that is indispensable for this category" is not given.

standsbereich)",²³⁵ this does not make it unthinkable, and keeping open its possibility serves as a critique of closing horizons prematurely. It puts forward a diagnosis of cultural options that are unduly restricting themselves to current plausibilities, constituting a preconception of reality which is, in fact, limiting: These "factually generate a preconception (*Vorbegriff*)" which "is taken as the principled condition of possibility of the historical object".²³⁶ Essen contrasts the principle of analogy which remains "indispensable" with a separate requirement for history writing, namely a "frame of reference in which something new can be experienced as new". This shows that is must be possible to go beyond specific horizons since each of these is "empirically posited", and therefore "not compelling".²³⁷ Lerch sees the significance of Essen's conclusion that God's act of resurrection is "without analogy" in that "it explodes a thought form which grasps 'reality' only in the framework of what is 'humanly possible'".²³⁸

Thus, the interest of reason in the practical outcome of our actions underlined by Kant reappears in the context of judging what is historically possible. The New Testament scholar Karl Kertelge framed a previous return to the quest of the historical Jesus in these terms, of history under the perspective of the human orientation towards meaning: "the renewed actuality of the discussion on the historical Jesus cannot be narrowed down to the tracing of historical rudiments of Jesus' life but is related to the question of methods and to the question of meaning (*Sinnhaftigkeit*) of historical enquiry in general".²³⁹

4.4 Conclusions on the three premises of Habermas's New Testament interpretation

Instructed by actual exegetical controversies with their different approaches and evaluations of evidence, it is time to return to Habermas's assessment of the New Testament. His three premises are the basis of more specific judgements on the major factors and stages in the history of Western thinking. Is the Christian tradition a predominantly Hellenistic formation of the spirit (4.3.1), and is Christol-

---

[235] Cf. Essen, *Historische Vernunft*, 381, agreeing with Wolfhart Pannenberg that being "an event without analogy [...] does not allow in any way to deny its historicity a priori".
[236] Essen, *Historische Vernunft*, 398.
[237] Cf. Lerch's summary of Essen's argumentation in *Selbstmitteilung Gottes*, 216–217, with reference to the conception of "thought form (*Denkform*)", in Essen, *Historische Vernunft*, 394–403.
[238] Lerch, *Selbstmitteilung Gottes*, 217, with reference to Essen, *Historische Vernunft*, 398. 400.
[239] Karl Kertelge,"Einführung", in Kertelge (ed.), *Rückfrage nach Jesus* (Quaestiones disputatae 63) (Freiburg: Herder, 1974): 7–10, 10.

ogy as the doctrine of Jesus' divinity a post-Easter development without a basis in Jesus' own self-conception (4.3.2)? How dominant was Paul's understanding of Jesus' death as itself salvific in its atonement for human sin in comparison with other key contents, such as Jesus' own message of salvation, or the Sermon on the Mount, for the history of effects of the New Testament (4.3.3)?

4.4.1 Post-Easter Christianity – a formation of spirit inherently marked by Hellenism?

The label under which Habermas subsumes at least the tradition's Western development, "Pauline Christianity", is based on the judgement that some of the Gospels take over from Paul the title of "Son of God" for Jesus[240] and are thus dependent on him for their Christologies. In his view, from its inception, "post-Easter Christianity was inherently (*von Haus aus*) a formation of spirit that was marked by Hellenism" (*hellenistisch geprägte Gestalt des Geistes*).[241] From the earliest available written documents, Paul's Letters, onwards, the content of the Christian faith is determined in this direction. Having examined debates between biblical scholars, however, this is a premise that must be questioned: For one, already Jesus, and not only Paul, selected the universalist strands of the Hebrew Bible in which the Gentiles are seen as pilgrims to Zion. Habermas mentions this theme, but still attributes the move to the nations to Paul's vision. Exegetically decisive is that Jesus, not Paul, subordinated the Sinai tradition, Moses and Exodus to a conception inspired by Genesis, by the promise to Abraham and Isaiah's inclusion of all of humanity into God's salvific will. This points to an internal Jewish diversity of motifs, and not to a division between Jesus' own calling to restore Israel, and the allegedly entirely different decision of Paul's to missionise among the Gentiles. Also the purported dependence of two Gospels on Paul is not borne out by debates between biblical experts. In addition, the over-reliance on Acts that marked research in the 1980s has since been questioned. If Acts were to be attributed to "a student of Paul's",[242] why does it deny him the title of Apostle? Its charting of the direction of mission from Jerusalem to Rome has been rejected for historical reasons and identified as a theological construction. The reasons for situating the prototype

---

240 As quoted before, at the conclusion of Chapter One, Habermas resumes: "Certainly the evangelists, above all John and Luke, draw on (*zehren von*) Pauline theology and recognise in the historical Jesus the 'Son of God'" (Vol. I, 496).
241 Habermas, Vol. I, 515.
242 Habermas, Vol. I, 495.

of the new genre of Gospel – Mark – in Rome, have been challenged with pointers to an origin in Syria, more precisely the first Christian centre founded on Gentile ground, the city of Antioch. It simplifies and diminishes the variety of locations and understandings which shaped the history of reception to only acknowledge Paul as the decisive multiplicator. This comes at the expense of the history of effects of the different Gospels and of the ongoing Jewish-Christian centres which continued the original Jerusalem community's conception under the leadership of James, that discontinued circumcision but not worship at the Temple. The dispute Paul recognised and submitted to the decision of the Apostles' Council on the question of circumcision was a decisive new departure. Yet the Gospels portray encounters of Jesus with Gentiles, and Acts reports Peter's baptism of Cornelius, thus legitimising this move as congruent with Jesus' own decisions of healing also Gentiles (such as the daughter of the Syro-Phoenician woman), accepting them as followers, and of proclaiming a Samaritan, that is, a member of an alienated Israelite group, as an ethical model. Even if these examples are written in the light of post-Easter community formation outside the borders of the original movement, they feature exchanges that throw a light on Jesus' extending his own position to include them into his mission.

4.4.2 Christology from post-Easter conclusions with no basis in Jesus' self-understanding?

In his judgement that the "transformation (*Gestaltwandel*) from prophet to Redeemer is a response to the death on the cross by Pauline theology that is as productive as it is momentous",[243] Habermas draws on some current exegetical interpretations. However, in comparison with the positions of the biblical scholars I have treated, it seems to me that they do not account sufficiently for the literary and symbolic expressions of Jesus' self-conception. Limiting it categorically to the title of "prophet" underplays the implicit backgrounds and resonances which cannot be subsumed under one single concept. The Gospels differ in their descriptions and key designations. A crucial first phase, predating the Gospels and their specific Christological titles, seems to be the practice of praying to Jesus. As we have seen in Margaret Daly-Denton's research, the Psalms were an existing genre that accommodated the evolving understanding of Jesus' person: as the Messiah predicted by David, as the *Kyrios* to whom prayers and hymns were addressed, and finally, in conceptual Christologies. It would ignore the

---

[243] Habermas, Vol. I, 490.

multivalence of literary writings to look for a doctrinal Christology proclaimed by Jesus of himself, a method of terminological proof which is as inadequate as the "norm-hunting" to which Christian ethicists have at times subjected the New Testament.[244] It is misleading to repeat the verdict of an allegedly unbridgeable gap between Jesus in his proclamation of the Kingdom of God and the Jesus proclaimed[245] as Messiah, Son of God or Logos. A path that turns out to be more productive, open-minded and instructive is to explore key themes in the New Testament accounts of his ministry that link the Historical Jesus with his understanding in the early Christian circles: Messiahship, openness to Gentiles, and the role of wisdom teacher and personification of wisdom, as in Q and in the highest Christology in the New Testament, John's Gospel. Its Prologue with the hymn in which the Logos becomes "flesh" (*sarx*) draws on the role of personified "Wisdom" who accompanies God's creation.[246] Anchored in the Historical Jesus, these three themes have shaped subsequent Christologies which can therefore not be regarded as new and independent developments of a subsequent era disconnected from Jesus' own symbolic actions, words, and self-understanding.

4.4.3 The interpretation of Jesus' death as atonement – as significant in the history of reception as his proclamation and ethics?

This third assumption focuses on the first part of the antithesis of Paul's interpretation of Jesus' death and resurrection, supposedly marking the history of effects of Christianity as profoundly as his actual proclamation: "the writings that originated after Jesus' death [...], especially the Letters of Paul and Acts [...], construct a theology of the death on the cross that has determined the history of reception of Christianity at least as much as Jesus' actualisation of the Jewish message of salvation and his radical ethics, condensed in the Sermon on the Mount."[247] This judgement of Habermas's is a challenge that requires a careful weighing in view of the history of reception of Paul.

It is true that the Latin tradition has been characterised as "staurocentric" in distinction from the emphasis of the Orthodox and Oriental churches on the in-

---

244 Tom Deidun's warning in "The Bible and Christian Ethics", 23, should be recalled that Christian ethicists who ignore the "whole vision of salvation" expressed in parables, aphorisms, and macarisms will end up with "norm reductionism".
245 Cf. Habermas, Vol. I, 495–496.
246 Cf. Freyne, "The Galilean Jesus and a Contemporary Christology", *Theological Studies* 70 (2009): 281–297.
247 Habermas, Vol. I, 495.

carnation in its timeless constitution. The Western focus, however, in principle included attention to the historical details also of Jesus' life which led to his death, counteracting both an orientation of salvation towards a divine atemporality and an isolated contemplation of Jesus' death as salvific on its own. Habermas's summary does not mention the Easter faith, but only the historically verifiable elements: Jesus' aim of restoring Israel, a demanding ethics, and his death. Similarly, the "three pillars over which the bold arcs of salvation history extend" (*drei Pfeiler, über die sich die kühnen Bögen der Heilsgeschichte spannen*) are seen to consist in "Adam's Fall, Christ's atoning death (*Sühnetod*), and the Last Judgement".[248] It may imply but does not identify the vindication by God of Jesus' practice of the kingdom in God's name by resurrecting him. We have seen that the Adam-Christ connection not only appears in Paul's Second-Adam-Christology but may also lie behind being "obedient" and "not grasping" or exploiting the "likeness with God" predicated in the verses quoted by Paul in Philippians 2. Yet the "three pillars" named are at best incomplete, if they refer to Paul, since they leave out the resurrection as the counterpart of the "atoning death", and they are certainly not representative for the Gospels either individually or in their combination. Habermas's summary of the "altogether (*ganz und gar*) original grace-based conception (*Gnadenkonzeption*) of faith in Christ's atoning death", while true of Paul, does not cover all of the New Testament: the "groundbreaking (*bahnbrechende*) idea that God prevenes through the vicarious sacrifice of God's Son the active, yet inherently (*aus eigener Kraft*) powerless repentance of a sinful humanity".[249]

Habermas notes that this understanding cannot be assumed to have been that of Jesus himself: "even these accounts do not convey that Jesus anticipated his violent death on the cross and interpreted it as the extraordinary act of *God's* atoning *self-sacrifice* (*unerhörten Akt der entsühnenden* Selbstaufopferung Gottes)." It is true that a gulf exists between the understanding of God recorded of Jesus in the Gospels – as Abba, as the Creator of an abundantly productive earth, as merciful, loyal, and indeed prevenient, with God's essence being love – and reverting, as Habermas himself points out, to the myth of sacrifice through which God is assuaged. That Jesus did not offer explanations of his death in these terms is correct. The earliest formula of the Last Supper in 1 Cor 11:25 contains no link to the forgiveness of sins. But the judgement that "these accounts do not relay (*erkennen lassen*) that he did not anticipate his vi-

---

248 Habermas, Vol. I, 513.
249 Habermas, vol. I, 506, with reference to Rom 5:8, "that Christ died for us when we were still sinners".

olent death on the cross"²⁵⁰ is questionable in view of the conflicts with his disciples on the theme of his likely death in Jerusalem. The fact that he did not avoid the potentially lethal conflict with the Romans and the Temple aristocracy can be expressed in different terms than the cultic one of "atonement". The transactional model implicit in it of a good – in this case his life – offered up for God's granting of forgiveness, grace, or eternal life, binds the divine-human relationship into a legal logic of equivalence. It would be instructive to follow the histories of reception both of this Pauline interpretation with its risks of engendering an equally dialectical concept of God, in contrast to the model of divine rehabilitation put forward in the differently accentuated frameworks of each of the four Gospels.

For the next stages of development in the changing cultural contexts from the second century onwards, Habermas identifies as important factors the "apologetics against Gnostic tendencies" and the "impulse to clarify their own teachings", especially in relation to its parent, the Jewish faith tradition. Themes include the "complex of the consciousness of sin, grace and free will as well as the new relevance of time consciousness and generally, the sphere of interiority".²⁵¹ The following two chapters deal with the patristic and the medieval receptions in their encounters with other intellectual streams in view of their significance for the transition to the modern era.

---

250 Habermas, vol. I, 494.
251 Habermas, vol. I, 491.

5 The Patristic Era as Setting the Course for Relating Religion to Reason

Chapters Two to Four have shown that also the theology of the philosophically and rhetorically learned Paul still belongs to Second Temple Judaism. Even in its contrasts, such as "Law" and "Gospel", it unfolds its vision of the content of the Christian faith in the symbolic universe of the Hebrew Bible. Chapter Five is dedicated to sketching key theory decisions in the period that followed the composition of the New Testament. The patristic era, beginning barely forty years after the Fourth Gospel with the writings of Justin and Theophilus, bishop of Antioch, constitutes a watershed for the conceptions in which the significance of the person of Jesus for all of human history is developed. Its authors draw on the New Testament and its use of the Jewish Scriptures but now express the standing of Christ and its consequences for theological anthropology and the concept of God in the terms of Greek ontology. In his discussion of this new step on the road towards postmetaphysical thinking, Habermas refers to the divergent assessments of the merits or losses posed by the "Hellenisation" of the Christian view of salvation by twentieth-century theologians: Adolf von Harnack, Joseph Ratzinger and Johann Baptist Metz.[252]

When treating the patristic era, one is faced from the start with an observation that will pose a major alternative for its presentation: Augustine's era-transcending significance calls for an early decision on how the inaugurating thinkers of this period will be configured. Are they stepping stones to the foundations created by Augustine, or are they representatives of quite distinct directions? Does his theology signal a "crisis"[253] of the first patristic reception and explication of the Gospel message in terms of Platonic, Aristotelian and Stoic philosophies, or its continuation and perfection? This question arises also in view of the often divergent readings of Anglophone and German-speaking theologians. If Augustine's final position is seen as a break with the earlier Greek and Latin authors, how is this contrast to be assessed? Does it invalidate the work of thinkers like Justin, Irenaeus, Clement of Alexandria, Origen, and the Cappadocians? They have their own histories of reception beyond the patristic era: in the Middle Ages, the Renaissance, in Cambridge Platonism (or "Origenism")[254], the Enlightenment and the new theological departures in the context of German Idealism,

---

252 The compatibilities and the barriers that are weighed up in this debate are outlined by Habermas in Vol. I, 525–545.
253 Pröpper, *Theologische Anthropologie*, Vol. II, 983.
254 Theo Kobusch, *Selbstwerdung und Personalität* (Tübingen: Mohr Siebeck, 2018), 219.

including the Catholic Tübingen School which traced its concept of freedom back to these church fathers, and in *la nouvelle théologie* from the 1930s. If theology after the anthropological turn can find forerunners in the patristic age, it testifies to the polycentric and internally diverse character of this era. It began its appropriation of the New Testament message against the emerging intellectual stream of Gnosticism with a decisive step: it began to explicate the incarnation of God in Jesus Christ and the standing of the human person as made in God's image in terms of freedom. Thus, prior to discussing Augustine's theology and its legacy (5.5), the following themes that produced groundbreaking turns will be discussed first: the decision not to connect the Christian message to "religion" in the various polytheistic cults of Gentile cultures, but to philosophy as the general consciousness of truth (5.1); the new differentiations that became possible by rediscovering the "inner person" in her freedom – affected, but not destroyed by Adam's Fall (5.2); the development of soteriology into a conceptual Christology (5.3); and the language philosophy inaugurated by Gregory of Nyssa from his interpretation of the creation story in Genesis as a further explication of the divine gift of human self-determination (5.4).

5.1 Correspondences and points of conflict between the Christian message of salvation and philosophy

In his portrayal of the contrasting assessments of the patristic move into the world of philosophy by Joseph Ratzinger and Johann Baptist Metz, Habermas identifies some of the theological themes under dispute. What Benedict XVI regards as a "successful (*geglückte*) synthesis of reason and faith, worldly wisdom and hope in redemption" was challenged by Metz as a "metaphysical disfiguration (*Entstellung*) of the promise of rescue in the theology of Covenant and the hollowing out of the core (*Aushöhlung des Kerns*) of the primitive Christian experience of the coming kingdom of God".[255] In the late 1980s, Habermas had countered Metz's critique of the replacement of the narrative and practical biblical core of Jewish and Christian monotheisms by metaphysics with nuanced questions. He specified how diverse schools and concepts of philosophical self-understanding had undergone a profound reinterpretation since Antiquity, producing counterproposals to the idealism and substance-ontological thinking of Plato

---

255 Habermas, Vol. I, 538.

and Aristotle.²⁵⁶ In his new two-volume work, the steps of this transition as part of the contingent origins of Western thought are followed up in greater detail within their social and political contexts, and perceptive points are made on the compatibility of the two translation partners.

In what follows, I will highlight the prior decision of the patristic authors to link up with philosophy's truth claim and judge their syntheses from biblical and theological perspectives. Regarding the cultural background of monotheism at that time, the patristic fathers were not more Hellenised than, for example, the Jewish philosopher Philo, who interpreted Genesis and the human position of being made in the image of God in Platonic concepts. But it is evident from the directions they embarked on that a merely internal elucidation of the Christian writings was not seen as sufficient and that other possibilities of translation and mission were regarded as less compelling. Their choice of dialogue partner did come at a price: for example, the neglect of the embodiment constitutive of the human person and recognised in biblical thinking, now ranked as secondary to rationality. Yet, it "set in motion the discourse on faith and knowledge [...] In hindsight, in late Antiquity, the cultural programme that was decisive (*maßgebende*) for Europe is formed." After the "downfall of the Roman Empire the cultural knowledge preserved in monasteries and orders, received and vitally developed further in universities, safeguarded across the ruptures of political and economic development a strong continuity in the Occident's understanding of self and world".²⁵⁷ Habermas rightly points out the era's "catalysing function"²⁵⁸ which defined the "basic concepts of practical philosophy that are decisive until today." It "uprooted Greek cosmology" and ultimately "transferred the semantic contents of biblical origin into the basic concepts of postmetaphysical thinking".²⁵⁹ Such transformations were made possible, as the philosopher Theo Kobusch notes, because the exchange was sought with fellow philosophers in Antiquity who shared the practical understanding of philosophy as a life form.²⁶⁰

---

256 Cf. Habermas, "Jerusalem or Athens: Where does Anamnestic Reason Belong?" in *Religion and Rationality. Essays on Reason, God and Modernity*, ed. and intro. Eduardo Mendieta (Cambridge: Polity, 2002): 129–138. Cf. Vol. I, 15, Fn. 8. 538, Fn. 68.
257 Habermas, Vol. I, 489–490.
258 Habermas, Vol. I, 538.
259 Habermas, Vol. I, 15.
260 Kobusch, *Christliche Philosophie. Die Entdeckung der Subjektivität* (Darmstadt: Wissenschaftliche Buchgesellschaft, 2006) 22. 34–40. 155, Fn. 23, with reference to Pierre Hadot, *Exercices spirituelles et philosophie antique* (Paris: Albin Michel, 2014, 1ˢᵗ edn 1981).

At the same time, there were also incompatibilities, resulting in tensions and inconsistencies. A case where the need for "shifts and corrections"²⁶¹ arose is outlined by Pröpper: the discrepancy in Stoic thinking between their "consciousness of the primordiality (*Ursprünglichkeit*) of human freedom which was the most developed in antiquity", and their fatalistic framework. For the patristic authors the latter was an element that was

> impossible to follow. Stoic thought had pursued in an exemplary way the conflict between the self-determination of humans and their inclusion into the logos-filled cosmos to the point where freedom was absorbed completely into total providence. On the one hand, it seemed that with the ability to give assent, the true centre of spontaneity of the human person had been found and her disposition over her own acts seemed secured. On the other hand, the idea of providence only allowed the recommendation to bring one's own will into agreement with the world logos and to make the world plan one's own through assent. The objection of quietism was countered by the Stoics with the point that also cooperation had been destined and precisely through it, fate was set to realise itself – a response which qualified all consciousness of freedom as a merely subjective appearance.²⁶²

In view of such a system-related discrepancy even in a rather congenial approach like the Stoa, the church fathers were challenged to develop from their biblical sources the internal components of an anthropology of freedom. These will be outlined in the subsection on language as a human property and as indicator of the constitutive diversity of humanity (5.4), and in the foundational concept to be treated next: the analysis of the "inner person" which for Kobusch is the crucial legacy of this early Christian thinking.

5.2 The "inner person" in her freedom

Scholarly assessments have pointed out repeatedly that the different strands of Gnosis which serve as the backdrop of the patristic development of their alternative position are only obliquely reflected in their critiques.²⁶³ Yet even if the volumes written "against the heretics" are markedly polemical, they do give evi-

---

261 Pröpper, *Theologische Anthropologie*, Vol. I, 203.
262 Pröpper, *Theologische Anthropologie*, Vol. I, 206, Fn. 219. He concludes that it "is true that the later Stoa – in subordinating the speculative to the practical interest – weakened the antinomy between freedom and fate and attempted to preserve an inner order of life by distinguishing carefully between what is one's own and what is alien."
263 Cf., for example, Christoph Markschies, *Die Gnosis* (München: C. H. Beck, 4th edn 2018), 37–46.

dence of the principled alliance sought by Christian theology with a platform of freedom which will then attain its own validity and set off its history of effects. It is remarkable how Irenaeus outlines a first theology of history which is not merely restorative, with salvation explained as God's action that goes far beyond just making up for the Fall.[264] The backdrop for responding to several components of Platonism, such as the doctrine of *metempsychosis*, the wandering of souls, was the biblical view of the non-substitutability of each person in her own response to God. Gregory of Nyssa rejects this Platonic conception in the name of the human freedom of the believers in their singularity. Habermas's explicit recognition of the achievements of these authors will be further illustrated with their emphases on the general accessibility of such insights, not restricted to an educated elite, and on praxis. The consequences for the individual's self-relationship, as they appear, for example, in moral feelings and attitudes, imply a reflective continuity and a renewed capability for action that is opened up by forgiveness.[265] To use the distinction made by Ricoeur, as introduced in the discussion of discipleship in Mark and John by Freyne, this deepened sense of self safeguards the lived connection of the "*idem*" to the "*ipse*". It explicates a self-aware avenue of understanding, as distinct from postulating an abrupt break effected by divine grace with no anchorage in the moral subject's own ability to reflect on herself and act accordingly.[266]

Habermas depicts the new "universes of discourse" opened up by the "dimension of a history of salvation and the idea of the incarnation of God" as "alien to Greek thinking, indeed to the cosmological thought of the Asian world religions in general. With both themes – the experience of the absolute in history and the temporalising incarnation of the Spirit – they explode the ontological conceptuality of metaphysics".[267]

As the basis of these changes, the momentous character of the patristic choice of "freedom" as the organising centre of theological anthropology and doctrine of God has been pointed out by Pröpper. It is expressed in Irenaeus's

---

264 Cf. Pröpper, *Theologische Anthropologie*, Vol. I, 216.
265 On the new validation of moral feelings like remorse and of actions like forgiveness, cf. Kobusch, *Selbstwerdung und Personalität*, 224–248, and *Christliche Philosophie*, 112–130.
266 This is clearly the danger in the stark polarities between which Christians must choose, according to Paul: sin or grace, death or life. In his discussion of the role of revelation, Habermas sees Paul as taking "natural reason also to be an organ for understanding divine revelation (Rom 1:20) [...] Pauline theology energetically maintains a communicative access to God; but by reorienting (*Umpolung*) the path of salvation from 'obedience to the law' to 'faith', the harsh opposition between contemplation and revelation is attenuated". Habermas, Vol. I, 530.
267 Habermas, Vol. I, 539.

prioritising of the "free will" of humans, "just like God, after whose image they have been created, has a free will".[268] It was because "the church fathers defined the relation between God and humans so decidedly as fundamentally a relationship of freedoms [...] and connected human freedom so indissolubly to their understanding of being made in the image of God" that the jarring inconsistency in Stoic thinking was discovered: its idea of "consciousness was rendered ontologically aporetic through fatalistic consequences."[269] Kobusch endorses the transformations initiated by these thinkers with quotes that highlight an inherently practical understanding of the "inner person" and a social and religious inclusivity: They "always distanced themselves from the elitist attitude of Plato. According to Origen, the Christian preacher must 'cook for the multitudes'", it is "not a truth for specialists but a truth of the lifeworld, for lay people".[270] An egalitarian conviction in the multi-religious setting of antique societies becomes evident in the inclusive view of natural morality: "God provided for shared (*gemeinsame*) basic ethical intuitions in the human race [...] in order to give them all the same chance regarding the Last Judgement".[271]

Drawing from Plato's *Politeia*[272] and the Stoic reception of this concept, as well as from its use by and after Paul in 2 Corinthians and Ephesians 3, the inner world of the person is now made foundational in its "irreducibility":

> Western and Eastern patristics all agreed that the inner person is the true (*eigentlich*) person [...] The independence (*Eigenständigkeit*) of the world of the phenomena of the internal life [...] relies on a specific relationship to oneself. Without the inner human being, there is none. This original idea of the foundational function of the inner human being is at the basis of all talk about her external behaviour.[273]

---

268 Pröpper, *Theologische Anthropologie*, Vol. I, 204, with reference to Irenaeus, *Haer.* IV, 37,6.4.
269 Pröpper, *Theologische Anthropologie*, Vol. I, 206. For a thought-through elaboration of a theology of freedom, both he and Kobusch refer to Origen who is the first to identify the will as the determining principle, as opposed to a pre-given "essence" or "nature" defining the human being. In *Die Gnosis*, 41, Markschies characterises Origen as the "first really highly educated Christian theologian and universal *savant*".
270 Kobusch, *Christliche Philosophie*, 46, with reference to Origen, *Contra Cels.* VII 58–59.
271 Kobusch, *Christliche Philosophie*, 41.
272 In *Christliche Philosophie*, 64, Kobusch points out that the "practical core" of this concept can be seen in the ninth book of Plato's *Politeia* which refers to the "reason-endowed part of the soul" that together with courage can "domesticate the many-headed animal of desire' (*Politeia* 589)". It is "through justice that the inner human being experiences the benefit of the soul."
273 Kobusch, *Christliche Philosophie*, 18. 21. 96. The patristic discovery of the "inner person" in its link to freedom elaborated by Kobusch provides a long-term perspective for the "normative accounts of the human person" that are one of the four sources of Theological Ethics. I have ar-

It is evident that by connecting with and internally transforming this thinking, extrinsicism in the conception of God's salvific encounter with humans is avoided. But where does the high regard for human freedom leave the message of Jesus Christ as Redeemer?

5.3 Developing soteriology into a conceptual Christology

It is remarkable that in the Deutero-Pauline Letter to the Ephesians it is exactly the "inner person" also of the Gentiles where "Christ can make his home" (Eph 3:17).[274] In the following three centuries, the church fathers brought this concept to prominence, keen to underline the compatibility of the Christian faith with philosophical explications of truth. If already Socrates "lived with the Logos" according to Justin Martyr and if the church does not begin with Christ but has already existed as an *"ecclesia ab Abel"* comprising "all who are of good will",[275] does this play down the uniqueness of Christ?

It seems that being open to the general consciousness of truth was not suspected as moving away from the core of the Christian message which was, instead, defended as the "true philosophy" that was, moreover, directed towards "all".[276] The doctrinal struggles took place in philosophical terminology and in newly forged conceptions that sought to express the standing of Jesus Christ in relation to God. Oriented by New Testament accounts and quotations, the effort was to secure an understanding that would not place the Saviour in an inferior or functionalised position. Three aspects will be analysed: first, Habermas's assessment of the changeover to the language of the Christological councils (5.3.1). It will be contrasted, secondly, with a different reconstruction of the position Arius came to, judging the use of the language available to have been relatively successful (5.3.2). Thirdly, the starting point of Habermas's assessment of Christology, the Pauline restriction of his salvific significance to his death and resurrection, by which the achievement or failure of the Nicaean and Chalcedonian doctrinal decisions are judged, will be questioned (5.3.3).

---

gued for the foundational relevance of this focus on the origins of subjectivity in *Approaches to Theological Ethics. Sources – Traditions – Visions* (London: T & T Clark, 2019), 55–58.
274 Kobusch, *Christliche Philosophie*, 97.
275 Kobusch, *Christliche Philosophie*, 45, and *Selbstwerdung und Personalität*, 46.
276 Kobusch, *Selbstwerdung und Personalität*, 26.

5.3.1 Substance ontology as a "trap"

Habermas describes the difference between the New Testament and the fourth and fifth century Christological debates in terms of the distance between two "language games" and two "epistemological dispositions": "meditative" versus "communicative". He seems to side with Johann Baptist Metz against the metaphysical turn of what the Bible expressed as personal encounters:

> The effort to express the core of the Gospel message about the "Son of Man" in the concepts of Greek metaphysics issues (*mündet*) [...] in the paradoxical statement of the Council of Chalcedon that in his person two different "unmixed" natures are joined "indivisibly" to each other. The attempt to determine the "nature" of the person of Jesus, introduced narratively, and involved (*verwickelten*) in a historical event of salvation, in a language the Platonic-Aristotelian basic concepts of which had been developed in an ontological presentation of the cosmos, draws attention to a difference between language games. They go back to distinct epistemological dispositions (*Einstellungen*).[277]

He then traces the two divergent attitudes back to the fundamental conceptions of world and self which constitute alternatives:

> The *contemplative* or *meditative access* to the absolute suggests a different disposition than the *communicative access* of the faithful to the divine Logos. What is encountered by the *wise person* in the objectivising disposition of a third person towards the cosmos, or by the meditating monk in the reflexive attitude of the first person towards his own interiority is an object made present in spiritual intuition (*geistiger Anschauung*): the world as the absolute One and All. What is encountered, however, by the *faithful person* (*Gläubigen*) in the performative attitude of a participant in the communication with the totally Other (*dem ganz Anderen*) is not primarily the world but the counterpart (*Gegenüber*) of a second person, even if elevated above all other persons – that of the God who intervenes in history.[278]

The contrast he states is an accurate depiction of the gulf that separates a cosmological, atemporal system from a framework able to express contingency and free historical action. However, in view of the achievements it could nevertheless claim, is Habermas's evaluation convincing that the "substance metaphysical speculation on the connection of opposite 'natures' was a trap"? Is the Platonic system judged to be equally self-sufficient as the Aristotelian, despite the transcendence and outreach towards the idea of the good which offers a more meaning-oriented concept of the human person than, for example, an "Aristotelian

---

277 Habermas, Vol. I, 152–153.
278 Habermas, Vol. I, 153.

metaphysics oriented towards the area of things of nature"?[279] Does the attraction of Plato for Stoic thinkers not show an internal range that cannot be merely summed up as "substance-ontological"? Some of Habermas's long-term critiques of the factors he identifies in metaphysics, that is, its "identity thinking", its "idealism", its "strong conception of theory", first articulated in his critique in the 1980s,[280] reappear in his highly perceptive comparison of biblical and patristic "language games". But did their philosophical terms not protect with the best linguistic means available the integrity of the person of Jesus in his both human and divine standing? It ruled out monophysitism and Docetism and also an understanding of Jesus in line with the prophets, purely and abidingly human without a unique, unmatched closeness to God. So while agreeing with his view that the philosophical terminology employed needed to be transformed and changed into a person-oriented, freedom-based reconstruction, the concepts used were successful in excluding one-sided interpretations and in indicating that language was reaching its limits. It could not relay the internal dimension of the "Son's" relationship to the "Father", and also failed to offer an expression to which the faithful could relate.[281] The corrective, limiting function of the metaphysical concepts is evident in the negative attributes of Chalcedon quoted by Habermas, designed to block the "fusion" theory of Eutyches[282] while still preserving the unity of the person. The paradox they formulate – not without precedent in philosophy of religion – is an invitation to develop more adequate thought forms. Interpretive precision, on the other hand, can be studied in the theological agreement of Nicaea against Arius, well before a conceptual frame-

---

[279] Kobusch, *Christliche Philosophie*, 15.

[280] Habermas, "Themes in Postmetaphysical Thinking", in *Postmetaphysical Thinking. Philosophical Essays*, trans. W. M. Hohengarten (Cambridge, MA: MIT Press, 1992): 28–53. The dissatisfaction with the legacy of this thinking lies at the origin of the project of "postmetaphysical thinking" advocated and defended in controversies about metaphysics and modernity since the 1980s.

[281] This is what Schleiermacher saw as the greatest deficit of the two-natures Christology, replacing its aporetic substance ontological terms with the "total impression" Jesus made and makes on his disciples then and subsequently. Schleiermacher's analysis of the essence of religion in the second edition of *The Christian Faith* (1830/31) will be treated in Chapter Eight after discussing his position in the turn to language in Habermas's outline of the steps towards postmetaphysical thinking.

[282] The famous image proposed by Eutyches was that Jesus' humanity was like a drop of honey in the ocean of divinity, against which the Council insisted on their "unmixed" simultaneity. For a portrait of the competing theological positions that also includes the church political background, cf. Dirk Ansorge, *Kleine Geschichte der christlichen Theologie. Epochen, Denker, Weichenstellungen* (Regensburg: Pustet, 2017), 93–96.

work became possible in which not nature but Jesus' freedom would constitute the key to his relationship to God and his work of salvation.

5.3.2 Countering Arius's Neoplatonic interpretation of "Logos" as the instrument of creation

Habermas's warning that "substance metaphysical speculation" could not deliver a message that required communicative, performative terms for it to be expressed adequately, is to be heeded because it brings in a standard that presupposes, first, the context of monotheism. With its personal relationship between God and the human creature, called to respond to God and to fellow humans at the level set by being made in the image of God, it includes as a practical consequence the prohibition to spill the blood of the other, who is a fellow image of God (Gen 9:6). The "communicative" rather than cosmological direction, secondly, also implicitly draws on the Gospel accounts of Jesus' proclamation, encounters and exchanges with their symbolic richness. Yet instead of judging the fourth-century controversies as deficient by this standard, the first point to be recognised is that they were motivated by soteriological concerns. Since, however, the salvific role of Jesus Christ was the starting point, the question about the internal being of this figure could not be avoided. His "work" had to be grounded in his "person". The alternative was to insist on a fideistic stance, as some groups did.[283] They remained indifferent to the danger of a growing discrepancy between the work of salvation attributed to Jesus Christ and the reasons specific to his person that enabled him to do so. The ways in which the standing of his person was configured, however, could be more or less adequate. Nicaea is an example of excluding a reconstruction that is identified as a misleading account due to its terms of Neoplatonic provenance, thus speculative and not suitable for Christ. It is exactly this interpretive precision that uncovers in Arius's statement about the Logos – the bridge term between John's Gospel and Greek philosophy – a use that limits the significance of Christ to a given cultural horizon without transforming it. The result is evident in Arius's explanation of the Logos as the instrument of creation, as in Neoplatonism, that his role is instrumental, tied to being the required mediator of creation, and losing his relevance after having delivered this function on behalf of humanity.[284] Instead of the sub-

---

[283] Cf. Kobusch, *Selbstwerdung und Personalität*, 117–118.
[284] Cf. for example, Walter Kasper, *Jesus the Christ* (London: Burns & Oates and New York: Paulist Press, 1976), 176.

sidiary role of a "second God" allocated by this framework, Nicaea defined Jesus to be "of one being with the Father", as *homoousios*, not as *homoiousios*, that is, merely "similar" to God. The Councils after 325, Constantinople in 381 and Chalcedon in 451, followed this prototype of coming to a decision after shared theological reflection, argued-out disputes and a communal commitment to respect the existing liturgical confessions of faith. It made it possible to further define the relationship of the "Spirit" to God and Christ, and of the natures within the person of Christ. It is true that the crucial terms are used inconsistently between the doctrines of the Trinity and Christology, compelling subsequent eras to deepen their conceptual reflection.[285] But despite the long dawn of a new departure in terms of historical thinking and categories of freedom, the benefits of using and of pushing the concepts available include their relevance to the contemporary possibilities of understanding; they put forward a principled recognition of the validity of each side, divine and human. Patristic reflections on this distinction extended to spelling out the consequences of the "two natures" of Christ for the church-state relationship, confirming their independence.[286] Expressed in metaphysical and not in narrative language, it nonetheless established a distinction which the Middle Ages could take up again and the modern era regard as being without alternative. The political contexts of the theologians who were the first to draw these conceptual conclusions on the irreducibility of the human and the divine in Christ, leading to an accepted autonomy of the world, however, were dependence on the emperors, and even theocratic systems. The interest of these rulers in an empire that was not split by confessional disputes is evident already in Nicaea; but the doctrinal decisions made by the Council succeeded in drawing a theological line between adequate and inadequate philosophical conceptions to express the standing of Jesus as the "Son" to the "Father". Habermas recognises the significance of the "continued theological attempts to clarify dogmatic contents discursively" which "in turn also *infiltrated, reshaped and extended philosophical conceptual language* through the semantics

---

[285] Cf. Karl-Heinz Menke, *Jesus ist Gott der Sohn. Denkformen und Brennpunkte der Christologie* (Regensburg: Pustet, 2008), 342–343. The inconsistency of using "nature" in different senses incurs the risk of inadvertently representing each of the three "persons" of the Trinity as finite. This equivocal use is one of Schleiermacher's arguments in *The Christian Faith* for opting to replace the refined conceptual apparatus of late antique Christology with a different paradigm in which Jesus' effect on the consciousness of believers in their freedom is the epistemological starting point.

[286] Cf. Georg Essen, "Autonomer Geltungssinn und religiöser Begründungszusammenhang. Papst Gelasius I. († 496) als Fallstudie zur religionspolitischen Differenzsemantik", *Archiv für Rechts- und Sozialphilosophie* 99 (2013): 1–10.

of their faith experiences. Since theology insisted on a clarification of concepts of faith, it gave the impetus for overcoming the narrowing of philosophy to questions of an ontology that had been designated as the basic science."[287]

5.3.3 The premise of Habermas's critique: the "incarnation of God in the crucified Jesus"

Habermas's diagnosis of the discrepancies between Platonic and biblical thinking and especially of the failure of concepts taken from a substance ontology to convey an eminently intersubjective content is accurate. He perceptively follows up the corrections pioneered by theological approaches in the late Middle Ages, as the next chapter will show. By the same token, adequacy to intersubjective processes, the theorist of communicative action has also critiqued modern thinkers like Max Weber as well as the "philosophy of consciousness". A more specific reason, however, for his assessment of the patristic engagement with the philosophical approaches of their time as problematic can be found in his point of departure in interpreting the New Testament. Also subsequent theological approaches will be evaluated by this measure: the normative criterion for adequacy is taken to be the "incarnation of God in the crucified Jesus". From this premise of what is seen to constitute the core of Christianity by its own standards, an "ontological explanation" must appear not only as surpassable by historically conscious and interaction-oriented terms, but as in itself "falsifying (*verfälschend*)".[288] Two points must be made here that will be spelt out further in the context of discussing his assessment of Schleiermacher in Chapter Eight. First, one can see in his formula a telescoping of two different soteriologies into one amalgamated figure: of the Eastern incarnational with the Latin staurocentric soteriology. Second, a specific interpretation of Paul's soteriology, which itself, as Chapters Two to Four have tried to show, cannot count as a generally accepted summary of the New Testament's message of salvation. Having explained the theological background questions to Nicaea, Habermas articulates his objection, "Why should the incarnation of God in the crucified Jesus Christ need a circuitous-falsifying (*umwegig-verfälschende*), namely ontological explanation?", in the following terms:

> "Understood as a symbol, the crucifixion of the Son of Man has the meaning of a revolutionary act of atonement (*Entsühnung*) of humanity which is performed (*ausgeführt*) by the

---

[287] Habermas Vol. I, 545.
[288] Habermas, Vol. I, 539–545, 544.

God who has become human himself (*menschgewordenen Gott selbst*). According to this, the suffering of Christ embodies God's own action – it is God's Spirit which has been embodied in Christ on the cross" (*sich in Christus am Kreuz verkörpert hat*).[289]

As already outlined, this description narrows the salvific significance of Jesus from his symbolic practice of the kingdom of God to his death, and risks replacing his own voluntary acceptance of the risk of being killed as the outcome of his proclamation of God with "God's Spirit". Yet the variety of motifs appearing in the writings of the New Testament must be remembered. These motifs are not identical and each has played a role in the history of reception. Privileging the Pauline sin-grace, death-resurrection antithesis risks a different "falsifying" effect: It incorrectly sidelines direct references to Jesus in his earthly ministry, his evocative parables and provocative practices. It also risks misrepresenting the God proclaimed by Jesus. While his unjust, violent death was interpreted through Isaiah's figure of the suffering servant, neither Isaiah nor Jesus present a God who demands suffering. Jesus' message about God is unequivocal: a God of love and forgiveness. Also in Philippians 2, the different readings of which have been sketched in Chapter Three, the language of "self-emptying" and subsequently, of God's "raising" him to the new position of universal worship, permits a variety of interpretations. It does not imply that God demanded the suffering and death of a possibly pre-existent figure as a condition for a salvific return to the divine level. Much less does this text allow for the conclusion that "God died on the cross". The God professed is still distinct from the one "in the form of God", whose *kenosis* was his own initiative. The key meaning attributed to "humiliating himself" is solidarity with humans in their vocation and their finitude, extending "even to death on the cross". The endpoint of the hymn about Christ is the praise of God's "glory" (Phil 2:11); it represents a contraction of the three-phase movement it outlines as well as a confusion of the acting subjects to attribute death on the cross to "God".

Thus, also if this early poem is read as referring to the "incarnation of God" on the lines of the much later Prologue to John's Gospel, it includes a statement about Jesus' life. It would be barely conceivable for a history of reception of the New Testament to have begun from an account which excludes the life in which this specific understanding of God was concretised. Two more aspects will be outlined before turning to the Middle Ages: the patristic foundation of a distinctive philosophy of language, and the "crisis" of its capability-oriented view of humanity in Augustine's return to and radicalisation of Paul.

---

[289] Habermas, vol. I, 544.

5.4 The human freedom of naming in Gregory of Nyssa's reading of Genesis

The context of Gregory's philosophy of language written in critique of Eunomius, a follower of Arius, in 380–383 are the ongoing divisions about Nicaea. The first Council had lacked the concepts for differentiating between a general and an individually specific level, using "*ousia*" and "*hypostasis*" as synonyms for the being of God. Eunomius took the concept of "*agennesis*", of not having become, as the defining statement about God. From that view, "the Logos/Son and the Spirit are essentially unequal to God the Father."[290] Gregory's brother Basil applied a distinction of two levels taken over from the Stoics to the emerging Christological and Trinitarian concepts: "*ousia* as something general" denoting the shared being of God, and "*hypostasis* [...] as the concrete individual embodiment of this common being". This opened up the possibility of identifying their specificity without destroying the unity of God: not having been born (the '*agennesis*' of Eunomius) is true of the *hypostasis* or 'way of being' of God the Father, being generated by the Father is the way of being of the Son, and that of the Spirit is its 'procession'. This differentiation achieved clarification in two respects: "Since the distinction of the three persons is based on the three hypostases, a modalistic misunderstanding is fended off; the essence shared by the three hypostases excludes a subordinationist misunderstanding."[291]

The relevance of these precise and subtle developments of conceptions for a philosophy of subjectivity should be evident: it becomes possible to think singularity while maintaining the shared human "*ousia*"; individuals are not merely exemplars, they are unrepeatable existences. For the "ways of existence", the *hypostases*, their uniqueness is owed to their coming "into being as complexes of *idiomata*, i.e., individualising characteristics. These *idiomata* are here understood not as accidents but as constitutive elements of the concrete existent".[292] The theological interest to secure the equality of the Son and the Spirit instead of their subordination to the Father led to a distinction that could avert both dangers, tritheism and modalism, that is, only a semblance of differences between the three.

---

[290] Wolf-Dieter Hauschild, "*Kata Eunomiou*", in *Lexikon der theologischen Werke*, ed. Michael Eckert, Eilert Herms, Hans-Jochen Hilberath and Eberhard Jüngel (Stutttgart: Kröner, 2003): 425.
[291] Ansorge, *Kleine Geschichte*, 75–76.
[292] Kasper, *The God of Jesus Christ*, trans. Matthew J. O'Connell (New York: Crossroad, 1984), 259.

Having defended the "incomprehensibility" of God by the human intellect against the claim of the Arians,[293] Gregory clarifies the human power of language as well as its limits. Against the "discreditation of human consciousness" as only capable of producing "false, deceptive and fictional" results that are the opposite of truth, he establishes the constitutive function of *epinoia* "by presenting it as a creative, linguistically gifted, methodically disciplined capacity of reason".[294] For Eunomius, God, not Adam, had named the animals: "The first humans would have 'lived together irrationally and speechless' if God had not taught them the names of things." In contrast, the Cappadocian thinker insists that God is not a "schoolmaster", and that language is a God-given "power" (*exousia*) through which humans are free to name their world, and change those names, reconceptualising them, if needed. "God is the creator of things, not of language. This is what God left to human reason itself [...] It was completely 'conceived by ourselves' [...] No era is conceivable in which humans existed without language, reason, or culture."[295]

Apart from the Genesis account in which naming is presented as the task of the human creature, an argument from reason is proposed: the variety of languages which is taken as a sign that humans, not God, are its authors. "Since what is reasonable is in all humans, also the differences of names, that is, of languages, need to be considered according to the differences between peoples. The plurality of languages is no longer seen as the fall away from an original language but as the expression of a God-given freedom."[296]

Thus, while error and falsity are features of the human use of language, this does not invalidate its original ability to instal a rational order in the world by *epinoia*, human consciousness. Two elements mark Gregory's approach to language: the creative human power, and its limits, most obvious in relation to the divine, which cannot be grasped by human efforts. This awareness does not, however, rule out trying to apply precise concepts even to the Trinity, distinguished between immanent and economic. With conceptual clarity, human thinking is also able to refute a secondary status for Christ who shares (like the Spirit) in the divine *ousia*, even if God the Father's specific way of being,

---

293 Kasper, *The God of Jesus Christ*, 126.
294 Kobusch, *Christliche Philosophie*, 77–78.
295 Kobusch, *Christliche Philosophie*, 81–82, with reference to Gregory of Nyssa, *Contra Eunomium* II 246; GNO I, p. 298,10 et seq.
296 Kobusch, *Christliche Philosophie*, 83. He concludes: "One has to take note (*sich vergegenwärtigen*) of what is happening here, in the wonderful texts of a great spirit of the fourth century. For the first time, human speaking and thinking, consciousness as such, is identified *expressis verbis* as a matter of freedom" (83), and this by a contemporary of Augustine.

not having been generated and born, remains unique to the first person of the Trinity.

5.5 Creation ending in damnation? The ambiguous theological heritage left by Augustine

While the intellectual weight of Augustine's work across epochs in Western Christianity is evident, the key question to its assessment by Habermas is: Can it be treated as the summit and most thought-through version of the patristic attempt to account for the Christian faith in dialogue with philosophy? Or does it represent a counterposition to the intentions and achievements of the earlier church fathers? This conclusion would reveal a polarity in the history of reception of the New Testament in the intellectual exchanges of this era. Habermas takes the confident style and impact of Augustine's theology also as reflecting the new political context of Christianity in its recently gained status as the Roman Empire's state religion. The historian Robert Markus, on the other hand, has linked the contrast drawn by Augustine between the *civitas Dei* and the *civitas terrena* to the need to work out a Christian profile against the normalisation of Christianity: its new legal status which might induce a habitual following without deeper commitment.[297] The decline of the Western Roman Empire after invasions and the sack of Rome by Alaric in 410 can also count as a factor in the emerging crisis consciousness with its scepticism about human capacities.[298] In the era of patristic theology, the predominant style of immanent critiques and transformations of Platonic, Stoic and Aristotelian thinking in the fight against Gnosticism from Justin to the Cappadocians was replaced by Augustine's principled dualisms. A further difference from these Greek thinkers lies in the markedly juridical and institutional interest of Latin theology: it conceives of church far more in terms of membership duties and hierarchical competences, and of the God-human relationship under the lens of what is owed, violated, and to be compensated for[299] – a contrast that will be returned to in the following chapter on the Middle Ages. The question is whether the accentuations that mark Augustine's work should be seen as continuations, or as decisive correc-

---

[297] Cf. Robert A. Markus, *Christianity and the Secular* (South Bend, IN: Notre Dame University Press, 2006).
[298] One of its ecclesial effects was that it brought Christian refugees like Pelagius and his School to North Africa where two synods were convened to condemn their writings. Cf. Ansorge, *Kleine Geschichte*, 118.
[299] Cf. Ansorge, *Kleine Geschichte*, 107.

tions and reversals: his analysis of interiority (5.5.1), his innovation, the concept of an inherited "original sin" (5.5.2), and his eschatology (5.5.3). The observation that the patristic age developed different uses of Platonism, and that Augustine's late work may be seen as departing from this heritage will conclude the chapter.

5.5.1 An era-transcending legacy: Augustine's analysis of interiority

A new style of theology based on biographical experience is inaugurated by Augustine. While it develops the Platonic idea of the "inner person", which already appears in Pauline Letters, it pushes the patristic connection to philosophy as the consciousness of truth into a scrutiny of the self. Since it uncovers that the self evades analysis and remains hidden in its depth, Kobusch can interpret it as an anticipation of the renowned post-Kantian insight of Johann Gottlieb Fichte into the aporetics of self-reflection: "the inner self is the subject of remembering (*Erinnerung*) and at the same time its object [...] the self owned itself (*hatte sich*), but it has lost itself. This is why it is searching for itself in order to find itself".[300] The way it does this is by form of narration:

> In Book 10 of the *Confessiones*, Augustine wants to narrate what the I is. It is the story of the interior of the I. In the form of a confession Augustine wants to reveal it to God and to humans [...] In front of God who knows the 'abyss of human consciousness' (Conf. X 2,2), it is a confession of sin, and of praise. In front of humans who want to know 'what I am in my interior self' (Conf. X 3,4), it is the revelation of someone unknown.[301]

Yet this is also the problem for the subject himself: "there is something inscrutable (*Unergründliches*) in *memoria* since 'I do not grasp completely what I am'".[302] There is a limit to self-knowledge. At the same time, it is evident that insight into one's subjectivity cannot be reached by self-objectivisation. Completely transparent insight is only given to God.

This conclusion, however, reached in the *Confessiones* written around 400 CE, could in principle have been elaborated in different directions. In the course of developing his anthropological theory, different positions were taken by Augustine, as the critics of his post-397 stance remind him: the self's inscrutability could be allowed to stand, in the knowledge of God's encouraging grace and of

---

[300] In *Christliche Philosophie*, 88, Kobusch summarises: "*Memoria*, that is the inner person, the *homo absconditus*".
[301] Kobusch, *Christliche Philosophie*, 87, noting two references in the Memoria-treatise to the "Platonic-Pauline concept of the inner person".
[302] Kobusch, *Christliche Philosophie*, 88.

the model of Christ, as stated in *De libero arbitrio* of 387/88;[303] ten years later, he had become convinced that the self is committed to evil, sinning with necessity, and – still inscrutable – not being aware of its state of being utterly lost and deserving damnation. The "interiority" narrated so movingly by Augustine ultimately reveals itself as that of a radical rejection of God, the highest good, by turning towards itself and finite causes including equally sinful fellow human beings. Thus the awareness of living as a confirmed sinner in front of God is taken as the essence of the human person.

How is this analysis to be judged in relation to the biblical view of the human creature as an image of God? What has been lost by Adam's Fall is *libertas*, basic human freedom; *liberum arbitrium*, however, is deemed as still existing in order to be able to attribute the invariably evil choices to the human agent himself. At least verbally, Augustine maintains a notion of free choice for the human self which he has examined in the depths of its inner life.[304] The core of interiority, then, is already entangled in an incapacity that comes with the human condition since Adam's history-changing act of disobedience. What is the function of the doctrine of sin which Augustine spells out, based on selected biblical quotes?[305] The interpretations I will present next access the era-transcending heritage of his thinking from a systematic account that identifies his idea of an inherited "original sin" as the bridging theory between two anchor points: theodicy, and the defence of God's justice. It provides the link in his lifelong quest for an answer to the problem of the origin of evil that will succeed in solving the theodicy question and justify God,[306] and the need to defend God's

---

[303] Pröpper in *Theologische Anthropologie*, Vol. II, 1003–1009, and Ansorge in *Gerechtigkeit und Barmherzigkeit Gottes. Die Dramatik von Vergebung und Versöhnung in bibeltheologischer, theologiegeschichtlicher und philosophiegeschichtlicher Perspektive* (Freiburg: Herder, 2009), 237–243, point out this change.

[304] The merely "verbal" role of human freedom is key in Flasch's reconstruction in *Logik des Schreckens. Augustinus von Hippo: Die Gnadenlehre von 387* (lateinisch/deutsch) (Exzerpta classica 8) (Mainz: Dieterich'sche Verlagsbuchhandlung, 2nd edn 1993).

[305] Paul's quote of the prophet Malachi's statement that "God hated Esau and loved Jacob" (Rom 9:13) is taken over by Augustine and directed towards God's hatred of "sin". References in the Synoptics (Mark, Matthew) to risking punishment in hell are taken as literal and final. In "The Restoration of All Things", in *The Coming of God: Christian Eschatology* (London: SCM, 1996), 235–255, Jürgen Moltmann has shown in a comparison of four theological approaches to the Last Judgement how these lines have had a history of effects of their own.

[306] In Vol. I, 564, Habermas notes the theodicy function of his doctrine of sin and includes some quotes of Kurt Flasch's analyses of the theory moves of the later Augustine. Flasch's historical and philological work on Augustine has also been discussed by theologians, whose reconstruction had come to similar assessments, such as Hermann Häring's *Die Macht des Bösen. Das Erbe Augustins* (Zürich/Köln/Gütersloh: Benziger/Gütersloher Verlagshaus, 1979).

justice in view of the consequence of damnation for those not predestined for election: "The universal attribution of guilt from Adam's sin now functions as the bridging element between the doctrine of predestination that had become inevitable, and the still intended theodicy. [...] The theory of original sin is thus a supporting hypothesis (*Hilfshypothese*) of the doctrine of predestination which is itself a consequence of the doctrine of sin and grace".[307] Those not elected "perish for their own guilt", it is not God who is to be blamed for this outcome of the history of created humanity.

5.5.2 Inherited "original sin": A doctrinal innovation based on a misreading of Paul

As undisputed as Augustine's pioneering work on the analysis of self-consciousness is, as controversial is his determination of human interiority by his doctrine of sin. Since innovations in dogmatic theology need to be justified by recourse to the original content – God's revelation – which they seek to transmit, they must be measured against the biblical accounts and their history of reception. If the new concept of an inherited "original sin" turns out to be "invented", this affects its status. The number and the tone of debates between theologians, synods and Councils dealing with this heritage over more than one and a half millennia reveal by themselves that this doctrine and the concepts of the human person, of God and of history implied in it have continued to exercise and divide Christian thinking. First to be examined is its link to the New Testament author whom Augustine quotes for this conclusion – Paul; second, the systematic question posed by the double appearance of sin both as a "power" over humans, and as a "deed" for which the individual agent is accountable.[308]

Current research agrees that a mistranslation from the Greek text of the New Testament into Latin is to be blamed for the far-reaching conclusions drawn by Augustine. In Romans, Paul in his Adam–Christ comparison argued that "be-

---

Häring and Pröpper point out that it is not sufficient to focus merely on the elements comprised in his concept of sin but that its function as a pillar in the architecture of Augustine's later work must be elucidated in order to grasp the internal logic of his theological approach.
307 Cf. Pröpper's summary of the internal logic in *Theologische Anthropologie*, Vol. II, 1016– 1025, 118, with reference to Häring and Greshake as well as to Flasch.
308 In Aaron Langenfeld and Magnus Lerch, *Theologische Anthropologie* (Paderborn: Schöningh, 2018), 200–204, Lerch elaborates the contrast between sin as "power" (*Macht*) and as "deed" (*Tat*). In *Theologische Anthropologie*, Vol. II, 1024, Pröpper identifies the "task that is posed from *Paul*" as attending to the "dialectic of sin as fate (*Verhängnis*) and guilt (*Schuld*)".

cause all have sinned", they were in need of redemption by Christ. The translation by Ambrosiaster in 370 turns the "*eph ho*" in this reference to Adam into a relative clause: it is now Adam "in whom all sinned" (*in quo omnes peccaverunt*), which Augustine took as a proof that historically, each human person delivers and is guilty of Adam's failure. The insight into this philological error is owed to Erasmus. His correction in 1525 is crucial for understanding the difference between Paul and Augustine on how each individual is to be seen in relation to humanity's implication in the guilt of Adam. Yet, it remains true, as Dirk Ansorge comments, that reception history is a different matter: The mistranslation carried the day in Western Christianity, based on Augustine's authority, even if Paul's statement is different from the elaboration it received by him. The descriptions Paul offers in Romans leave two elements side by side: sin as an already established power which affects the conditions of action for all of humanity, and the question of individual sin that could always have been avoided. In recent exegetical debates, two further aspects have been clarified: Paul's context of reflection is the church's mission to non-monotheistic cultures; his focus is not on individual confession, as the "New Perspective on Paul" debate has shown. Furthermore, he is misinterpreted if an understanding of sin as fate is attributed to him. Thus, what Augustine asserts is unprecedented in the New Testament and in patristic authors: Adam's sin not only co-inhabits, weakens and confuses human agency but corrupts it completely. The distinctions elaborated between inherited mortality, sin, and personal guilt, on the basis of a God-given possible orientation towards enacting good choices are overruled. The construct of an inevitable, naturally engendered personal sin replaces the previous biblical and theological anthropologies worked out exactly against Gnostic conclusions of complete incapacity in order to counteract and transform, not just escape from an irretrievably fallen world.

Thus, once it is clear that the distinction between sin as "power" and as culpable "deed" must be maintained, instead of collapsed, the systematic task remains to determine the balance between the two aspects. While Paul left it unresolved, Augustine has taken a stance that minimises the chance for human action. In addition, he explains the unbroken line to Adam in naturalising terms: original sin is "inherited" by children from their parents, linking, as Ricoeur has analysed, a "quasi-biological" to a "quasi-juridical" concept".[309] One is as external as the other, and their combination amounts to a near-Manichean view of human beings as delivered over to the forces of evil they have no chance

---

309 Ricoeur, "Original Sin: A Study in Meaning" (1960), trans. Peter McCormick, in *The Conflict of Interpretations* (Evanston: Northwestern University Press, 1974): 269–286, 270.

to resist. Grace must come from outside to liberate human agents who are so entangled in the prior history of sin, both structural and personal, that their own capacities for acting otherwise are inaccessible. The question this diagnosis poses is: which conception of history does the disappearance of any concept of human agency in the absolute priority of God's grace lead to?

5.5.3 The outcome of the history of a humanity created by God

The dogmatic theologians I have drawn on so far reconstruct Augustine's thesis of a naturally transmitted, unavoidably inherited original sin as the connection he needed to provide the justification of God against evil: human action is so damnable that justice compels God to punish and show God's mercy only by exempting a few from the just desert of sin as their own deed. The pessimism of this anthropology is recognised.[310]

At the same time, he is still being credited with offering a serious counter-position to antique cosmological fatalism where the laws of the cosmos trump human efforts. Ludger Honnefelder makes the case for Augustine's *De civitate Dei* as defending a Christian view of salvation history which, against the lack of a consciousness of history in Greek cosmological thinking, is presented as "open-ended".[311] But can it count as an open history, if, apart from God, the key actor is Adam, and humans after him have their hands tied and no longer possess regular alternative directions for action? Pröpper concludes that the

---

[310] In Vol. I, 569, also Habermas notes Augustine's "anthropological pessimism", but recognises his insistence on the "darkest" truths of the Christian tradition: "On the other hand, he does not want to [...] take away the provocative positivity, seemingly inaccessible to reason, from the biblical tradition and the Christian message of salvation. Precisely this motif, to take the faith seriously in its darkest theologoumena at the same time as reconciling it with the Platonic conceptual world led Augustine to his most momentous philosophical innovations" (Vol. I, 558).
[311] Honnefelder, "Das Rätsel der Geschichte: Eine philosophische Betrachtung der theologischen Geschichtsdeutung Augustins", in *Woher kommen wir?*, 251–271. By putting human history under the perspective of the totality anchored in God, "interpretations of meaning and the critique of history become possible, providing orientation for action." He adds, however, that "Augustine's interest in a theology of grace does not allow the conception of such a history to be unfolded, while presupposing it as such" (270). Thus the disabling definition of human agency and freedom and its subsumption to or replacement by divine grace criticised by systematic theologians and by Flasch may be recognisable behind the comment on the limiting effect of his doctrine of grace.

only human freedom of action that ever existed belonged to Adam and that "history was over before it had really begun".³¹²

A further reason to find human historical action underrepresented is linked to an undoubted breakthrough of Augustine's, his exploration of interiority. But by locating God's grace almost exclusively in the human soul, a path is chosen by the most influential theologian of Antiquity that Habermas will later criticise in the Romantic era, especially in Schleiermacher's "turning away from the world" to one's own interior "feeling".³¹³ In Augustine, it happens at the expense of the role of Christ and of fellow humans: exterior causes which mediate grace are radically devalued, other human beings are given a strictly secondary place to the overarching goal to love God, and the necessary link to love of neighbour is sidelined.³¹⁴ The reason for this subordination of other humans as possible carriers of grace has been identified as lying in Augustine's Neoplatonism: if God is the highest good, there is no revelatory role of Christ regarding God's essence;³¹⁵ intersubjectivity is ruled out as a level where grace can be experienced. It remains internal in the highly personal relationship of the individual believer to God.

What conception of God is ultimately embraced, despite the incomparably evocative addresses to God as "closer to me than myself" (*interior intimo meo*) and as the Whence and destination in whom our heart will ultimately find "rest" (*requiescat in te*)? How can such complete trust in a benevolent God be

---

312 Pröpper, *Theologische Anthropologie*, Vol. II, 1023.
313 Cf. Habermas, "The Boundary between Faith and Knowledge: On the Reception and Contemporary Importance of Kant's Philosophy of Religion", in *Between Naturalism and Religion. Philosophical Essays*, trans. Ciaran Cronin (Cambridge: Polity, 2008): 209–247, 233.
314 Not only is the relation to others secondary to love of God, setting both into an unnecessary competition. In Vol. I, 614, Habermas correctly points out the anticipation of a "Hobbesian" view of humans and their intersubjectivity, and the onerous effects it had on the political concepts of authority and participation. A principally negative depiction of the role of political authority permits movements like Radical Orthodoxy to insert a massive ecclesiology to counteract the allegedly irretrievable violence of governance. In *Kleine Geschichte*. 114, Ansorge makes the historical point that church-emperor relations remained ambivalent, used as support for church measures on the one hand and resisted, on the other, when bishops refused to abide by imperial decrees. Also Habermas notes Augustine's use of state power and the forced exile of bishops who defended Pelagius, like Julian of Eclanum (Vol I, 614, Fn. 140).
315 Rainer Gottschalg, *"Was nützt die Liebe in Gedanken?" Ekklesiologische Orientierungen zwischen Gnade und Freiheit* (Paderborn: Brill/Schöningh, 2020), 30. He points out the "levelling of the relevance of the figure of Jesus Christ. The turn away from history as the place of revelation extends into Christology, as the ontology of the scheme of orientation moves the glance from the incarnated to the pre-existent Son. Christ as God and as human is not compatible with the system of emanation and Augustine's concern."

squared with the same God's pronouncement of judgement on the *massa damnata?* Alternative conceptions were available: for example, Irenaeus's early theology of history linking creation in its goodness to an ultimate return to God, against Gnostic views of perdition; Origen for whom only a complete reconciliation, an *apokatastasis panton,* could count as fulfilling God's intention of creation;[316] and Ambrose of Milan who had baptised Augustine, in his own era.[317]

The concept of predestination presents a divisive solution for a self-inflicted problem of his later thinking: the sovereignty of God's grace is so absolute that it not only marks the beginning of God's outreach to the human creature but absorbs the entire relationship and is supposed to replace the addressee's own response. As especially the positions examined in Habermas's second volume show, the possibility of contributing one's own "Yes/No stance" constitutes a criterion by which theory proposals are judged as sufficient or deficient. Do they have the conceptual tools to establish the basis for this irreplaceable personal agreement or refusal?[318] Augustine does not even leave the human response to God's gracious call to human agency, but attributes it to the Spirit. If the human agent is completely passive, then the reason for judging her cannot be her own action. Instead, it is due to how God has predestined her. This logic is compelling and allows for no gaps. But the immense desire to free God from culpability for the evil committed by the human creatures from the first-ever person onwards backfires by undermining the credibility of God as a merciful Creator. Justice in the sense of punishing the sinner prevails over grace. The Greek idea of divine perfection coerces the theologian of grace not only to renounce human freedom but also any thought of "change" in God as a response to humans in their need, the torn state of their freedom, and their hope in God's promise. In view of these consequences, the judgement that this is the model of a failed reconciliation between justice and mercy can hardly be refuted.[319]

The next stage of consequences of Augustine's work will appear in the Middle Ages. On the one hand, Habermas is right that Augustine belongs to the

---

316 Kobusch, *Christliche Philosophie*, 23, points out how "Augustine's thinking became discredited exactly because of his doctrine of grace" and quotes from a letter of Erasmus in 1518 to Eck: "A single page of Origen teaches me more than ten by Augustine [...] let's say five".
317 On Ambrose, cf. Ansorge, *Gerechtigkeit und Barmherzigkeit Gottes*, 249–251.
318 In Vol. II, 237–238, in his treatment of empiricism as a strand of subject philosophy, Habermas assesses Hume's approach as "removing from consciousness the relation to the Ego *(Ich-Bezug)* and spontaneity" and as "deleting from the concept of subjectivity any trace *(Anklang)* of capacity for action *(Handlungsfähigkeit)*".
319 Ansorge, *Gerechtigkeit und Barmherzigkeit Gottes*, 255.

"Christian transformation of Platonism".[320] But his decisive corrections and revocations of key conclusions of earlier representatives of Platonism in patristic thinking demonstrate that this is by no means a unified school. The Bishop of Hippo does not share comparable lines of interpretation on the understanding of God, the role of Christ, the human person and the Last Judgement on world history with his predecessors or with his contemporaries. While it was the unified concept of God as the Highest Good that attracted Augustine from Manicheism to the Platonic system, it has been argued that his later thinking constitutes a return to the dualism of the Manichean worldview.[321] The irresolvable dialectic in which human agency was caught for Paul is replaced by an exclusive emphasis on the destructive effect of Adam's Fall on human freedom. Both the property of being made in the image of God and human *libertas* have been lost for good. How did the Middle Ages deal with this legacy?

---

320 This is the heading under which Habermas treats the period of "Plotinus and Augustine" with its theological culmination in Augustine (Vol, I, 546).
321 Ansorge, *Gerechtigkeit und Barmherzigkeit Gottes*, 248, quotes Wilhelm Geerlings on the "Manichean mood" of his theology that "imposed a heavy burden on the Western church", in Geerlings, "Art. Augustinus", in *Lexikon der antiken christlichen Literatur*, ed. Siegmar Döpp, Wilhelm Geerlings et al. (Freiburg: Herder, 2nd edn 1999), 83.

6 The Origins of Modernity in the Late Middle Ages

While it is true that the knowledge of Augustine's thought was limited to the West, there were nevertheless ecumenical Councils at which doctrinal decisions were made for the whole church, Greek- and Latin-speaking. There was a major intellectual breakthrough in the Christological disputes following the Chalcedonian confirmation of Jesus Christ as sharing equally in human and divine "natures" that provides a stepping stone towards more adequate categories: the distinction introduced by Maximus Confessor of two levels of the will. It paved the way towards elucidating Jesus' historical human agency, as distinct from his eternal status as the Logos. The shifting grounds found by medieval theologians in a new intellectual era of rediscovering Aristotle, Islamic science and philosophy of religion thus already contained the seeds of a different view of human freedom, drawing on the New Testament accounts of Jesus (6.1). The distinct soteriological argumentations of Anselm and Thomas Aquinas will be examined subsequently in order to contextualise Habermas's perceptive analysis of the new philosophical moves of medieval theologians (6.2 and 6.3). The turning point to categories of thinking that inaugurate modernity is found in Duns Scotus. Habermas charts the contexts and theological, philosophical and legal texts of the High and Late Middle Ages with great erudition. He elucidates especially the argumentations that justify a law that applies to all, Gentiles and the adherents of the different monotheisms, princes and citizens. While he offers a striking reconstruction of the medieval foundation of an independent civic legal sphere, reconceiving Roman law into individualised basic rights, my focus will be on the theological underpinnings of such turning points. As the foundation of this universalist view, the theological programme developed by Duns Scotus will be outlined in its distinction from the disputed stances transmitted from the later Augustine (6.4). A comparison of Scotist voluntarism with William of Ockham's nominalism (6.5) will lead to a conclusion that takes stock of crucial changes in categories since Late Antiquity (6.6).

6.1 Taking substance ontology to its limits: Maximus Confessor on the will as capacity and as concrete decision

From the Council of Nicaea in 325 onwards, a search for suitable categories to encompass the givenness of a unique historical existence in which divinity and humanity were united has been conducted in public theological debate. A crucial distinction not only of terms but of levels is introduced by Maximus Confessor in the seventh century. The person of Jesus is now further defined regarding the implications of the statement that he is "equal in being" to humans. This clarification is required by the need to link the Christological doctrines back to the New Testament. Especially the portrayals of his passion serve Maximus Confessor as a touchstone for judging theological movements, such as the adherents of the monophysitism defeated by Chalcedon's insistence on the "unmixed" continuity of both natures in Christ. It is significant that the debate now moves on to the will, a key biblical theme, over against the Greek privileging of cognition also in ethics and philosophy of religion. The "unity" of the person of the Redeemer, the old Alexandrian theme against the more biblically oriented Antiochians[322] with their emphasis on equal parity between the divine and the human, was proposed to be secured in the "one will" of Christ which was divine. But if Jesus' human will was absorbed into disappearance by the divine Logos, how could his prayer at Gethsemane be understood – that God should spare him, that the cup should pass, yet ending in the decision to listen and follow "your will, not mine"? Only Jesus in his human willing could have agreed to let God's will prevail, showing until the end a human will that "had determined itself unreservedly to allow itself to be led by the will of God".[323] This implied a distinction between the human will as a foundational capacity, and its concrete decisions. Thus, the decree by the Emperor Heraclius that elevated the monotheletic position into the ultimate doctrine in order to unify Christianity as the state religion called forth the protest of Maximus in 638. His argument against "the renewed attempt to amputate the human nature of Jesus"[324] was: For salvation to be effected, a status essential for human conscious life must be "assumed": that of being a centre of reflection and action. It is therefore decisive not to undermine the integrity of the human will by replacing it with the divine will of the second person of the Trinity. A new level of thinking is opened up by drawing an

---

322 Ansorge, *Kleine Geschichte*, 88.
323 Ansorge, *Kleine Geschichte*, 103, with reference to Mk 14:36.
324 Ansorge, *Kleine Geschichte*, 102.

internal distinction within the will of humans, between the faculty and its effective power (*Wirkkraft*) as "*potentia*", and its actualisation.³²⁵ "*Thelesis*" (the will as a natural capacity) is distinguished from "*thelema*" (the concrete enactment of the will): "In principle, Jesus *could* have sinned but in reality, he did not *want* to sin at any point in time." It was his free will "which Jesus determined unconditionally for the good."³²⁶ Ansorge draws far-reaching conclusions from this insight, confirmed at the Third Council of Constantinople in 680/81, regarding its validity for the future development of the inherited antique thought forms. Not only does it "specify (*präzisiert*) the doctrine of Chalcedon [...] The Council opens up a new access to the historical nature of the life and death of Jesus. From then onwards, Christ's human nature was no longer conceived in a static-ontological manner but dynamically as exercising (*Vollzug*) human freedom [...] Only now is 'being human' no longer thought in substantial-ontological categories but in categories of freedom".³²⁷

Georg Essen identifies the turn which Maximus Confessor initiated in more guarded terms, under the same criterion of moving from general ontological concepts to ones able to express Jesus' freedom in proclaiming and serving the will of God. For him, Maximus has achieved an understanding of *hypostasis* (the "person" uniting the two "natures") that relates to willing, so that one can even speak of an "action-theoretical understanding",³²⁸ rather than one in terms of two substances existing side by side. This becomes possible by using "*hypostasis*" as a completely formal category, as the unifying but undetermined ground of existence. For the Confessor, in Jesus the actualisation of the will which belongs to human nature happens through the divine Logos. Essen states clearly that from a modern understanding of freedom, this would amount to "heteronomy" and still short-change the human commitment and decisions of Jesus throughout his life to reveal God's essence as love.³²⁹ Maximus's achievement is to refute Apollinaris's replacement of Jesus' humanity by the Logos, by devising a distinction between two levels in the crucial practical pursuit of the human person, the exercise of her will. Yet, his argumentation is still tied to the backdrop of a restrictive understanding of the incarnation as being completed with Jesus' conception and birth but leaving out Jesus' life as the incarnation

---

325 Menke, *Jesus ist Gott der Sohn*, 271.
326 Ansorge, *Kleine Geschichte*, 103.
327 Ansorge, *Kleine Geschichte*, 104.
328 Essen, *Die Freiheit Jesu*, 134.
329 Essen, *Die Freiheit Jesu*, 201. Menke agrees to his critique in *Jesus ist Gott der Sohn*, 271, Fn. 554.

of God.³³⁰ The alternative solution for interpreting the unity of God and humanity in Jesus is to argue solely from his relationship to God, not to the Logos, a path which Essen follows by examining Wolfhart Pannenberg's proposal. For him, it is not yet the case in the seventh-century debates that the life of Jesus is regained as the key event in which the self-revelation of God was actualised. By defining the divine *hypostasis* as formal and linking it to the human will, Maximus takes the debate as closely as was possible in the late antique thought form to the threshold of free agency: an understanding of a self that not only recognises the will inherent in human nature but also the self-determination to employ it, leading to the ability to interpret Jesus' life as his free interaction with God. For Essen, it is once again the fear of the Fall resulting in a turn against God that motivates Maximus not to attribute the underlying power of *prohairesis* as a human capability to Jesus but to the Logos.³³¹ The fundamental decision by Jesus in favour of a conscious and free self-determination of his will to agree with another's will, God's, is his own. It realises what humans are oriented towards, unity with God, and thus does not take away but fulfils their humanity.

As also Ansorge points out, after the destructive effects of Adam's Fall on the human will had been emphasised by Augustine two and a half centuries earlier, a different guiding idea of the fourth and fifth centuries in the Christological debates resumes importance: only what has been "assumed" can be "healed": If "the Logos did not accept this will in its need of redemption, [...] it would not be healed". The Bishop of Hippo had distinguished *libertas* from *liberum arbitrium* but the first was deemed lost and the latter was already completely determined in the direction of evil. By returning the capacity of effective will orientation to the human person, Maximus has regained major intellectual space for the future. A framework is called for in which the foundational *libertas* and its concrete determination can be expounded. Maximus's differentiation will leave a mark on the subsequent centuries: on Anselm's argumentation which stresses the voluntary nature of Jesus' acceptance of his death, and on Thomas, Scotus, and Ockham, to be treated in the following sections. While appropriating the substance ontological categories of Aristotle, Aquinas draws on the New Testament in his response to Anselm whose argument for the necessity of the incarnation is explicitly put forward on the grounds of reason. While distinct, their approaches agree in offering a theological alternative to the Augustinian vision of the history of humanity ending overwhelmingly in damnation. For Anselm, "satisfaction" through Jesus' voluntary death is God's merciful alternative. Writ-

---

330 Essen, *Die Freiheit Jesu*, 197.
331 Essen, *Die Freiheit Jesu*, 63.

ing one generation after Thomas's death in 1274, Duns Scotus (1266–1308) inaugurates a new direction which overcomes a theology expressed in terms of natures and their inherent finality to one of freedom both of the Creator and of human beings in their historical agency. Ockham's new departure will again prioritise the absolute freedom of God.

6.2 Anselm of Canterbury's philosophical argument for God's incarnation

In his introduction to the threshold of a new era of self-understanding prepared by "philosophical changes of course (*Weichenstellungen*) towards scientific religious and societal-political Modernity", Habermas contrasts "two tendencies after Anselm's death: the opposition between the intention to justify Christian doctrine from reason alone – *sola ratione* –, and the existential need of faith practice", reassuring itself by recourse to "collections of Sentences and Bible commentaries".[332]

Anselm's apologetic argument in *Cur Deus Homo*, developed in a dialogue with his interlocutor Boso, limits itself to shared points between thinkers from the three monotheistic traditions. With his earlier work, the *Proslogion*, combining philosophical analyses with addressing God in prayer, he thus unites the two tendencies named by Habermas. In *Cur Deus Homo*, the argumentation towards his non-Christian contemporaries is based explicitly on grounds he assumes to be non-controversial. His method raises the question what the adequate starting point for interreligious dialogue can be: philosophy of religion, or the internal faith convictions of each participating tradition. Core objections from the subsequent history of reception are already posed by Anselm, such as the opposing argument from God's mercy put forward by Boso, which is dismissed on the basis of reason.

Anselm's intention to convince the "unbelievers" on the one hand endorses a Pauline atonement Christology but on the other hand highlights the relevance of Jesus' free decision, and the separate step of the faithful agreeing to their redemption and responding of their own accord with a changed life. In this respect, soteriology is linked to an anthropology of capability in the use of freedom. In view of the era-transcending history of effects of his thought model, it is important to portray the junctions precisely. Does it put forward the concept of a God who feels insulted by the sin of the human creature and demands

---

[332] Habermas, Vol. I, 759. 762.

the death of Jesus as satisfaction? Martin Kirschner shows how this misidentifies the problem of human disobedience as affecting God at the psychological level of an "insult". He provides a concise reconstruction of the key concepts "*honor*", "*rectitudo*", "*iustitita*", "*misericordia*", "*satisfactio*", and their ordering.[333] In the context of tracing changes in the relationship between "faith" and "knowledge", I will touch on four themes: the dominant motif of "*rectitudo*"; a different way to conceive of "justice" than as the opposite to mercy; a scrutiny of the goal and the method to establish a "necessity" for God to become incarnate; and a concluding assessment of the value of his separation of philosophical from theological argumentations and of the position he takes to earlier proposals in Christian thinking.

The gaping issue to be addressed is not a psychological hurt, but the human upending of the order of creation. As Ansorge points out, behind the insistence on "*rectitudo*" is the philosophical idea of divine perfection: God "can only ever want the best possible. Yet renouncing to punishment implies that 'something in the kingdom of God remains unordered' [...] God's mercy finds its measure and its limit in the *rectitudo* that is normative for God as for created reality." It is more than an external order, because "God counts as the origin and source of *rectitudo*. This secures not only the legitimacy of the principle of justice that interprets it but also that it is a valid expression of the *summa iustitia* which God is."

There is thus no way for God to turn away from the alternative of "*aut – aut*", either punishment, or satisfaction: "God would contradict God's self by not staying with the order once instituted."[334] Satisfaction can only be delivered by a person who does not require forgiveness herself; thus the sinlessness of Jesus becomes his overarching quality, together with his free willingness to die. His death, however, creates a store of grace of which the sinners in their active relationship to God may avail.

While the concept of God's perfection is philosophical, the thinking employed changes into the juridical, with compensation at its centre. On the one hand, humans are seen as owing God everything and thus starting, one could say, from a position of negative equity that cannot be remedied by their own forces. But on the other hand, once the order has been set right again, they are in a position to cooperate in discipleship, taking Jesus' free act of obedience as the model for their own conduct.

---

[333] Martin Kirschner, *Gott – größer als gedacht. Die Transformation der Vernunft aus der Begegnung mit Gott bei Anselm von Canterbury* (Freiburg: Herder, 2013), 268–288.
[334] Ansorge, *Gerechtigkeit und Barmherzigkeit Gottes*, 270–272.

It testifies to the effects of worldview elements existing also in philosophy that the socio-political plausibilities of the era, such as the vassal–Lord bond, play such a decisive role. Anselm's reasoning has been evaluated as a "successful form of inculturation into Germanic thinking".[335] The success "of the institution of *satisfactio* to resolve conflict and forge peace in the political sphere at the turn of the eleventh to the twelfth century" is pointed out by Ansorge.[336]

One external and one immanent critique of the relationship of "faith" and "knowledge" in Anselm's provision of a stand-alone philosophical line of defence of the incarnation can be raised: "Justice" could equally be conceived as an *internal component* of mercy, not as a simple opposition.[337] And internally, Anselm's own writings could have relativised the position he bequeathed on later centuries. Ansorge concludes that for a thinker who at an earlier stage saw God's sparing of the sinner as an expression of God's perfection, of God's *semper maior*, it is "tragic" that it is overshadowed by his one formal philosophical argument for the incarnation based on "*rectitudo*".[338]

Further tasks for analysis are Anselm's goal and method. A crucial element in Thomas's overcoming of Anselm's staurocentrism is his point that Anselm's aim, to argue for the "necessity" of God becoming human, does not have to be accepted. Theologically, a less ambitious aim is sufficient, as will become clear in Thomas's corrections. On closer examination, it becomes evident that both, in effect, argue from belief in the actual event of God becoming incarnate in Jesus Christ. Anselm abstracts from it in order to show the reasonableness of this faith by outlining the "necessity" of this event. His method turns out to consist of two steps, as Hans Kessler shows in this perceptive reconstruction: "In

---

[335] In *Gott – größer als gedacht*, 187, Fn. 270, Kirschner refers to this assessment of *Cur Deus Homo* by Gisbert Greshake in the 1970s regarding the task to express the relevance of the Gospel message to an era in terms of its own plausibilities.

[336] Ansorge, *Gerechtigkeit und Barmherzigkeit Gottes*, 271–272.

[337] In "Love and Justice", Paul Ricoeur concludes that for each concept, there is an internal need for the other aspect, in order to avert, first, a "*do ut des*" type of ethics which he recognises as a risk in Rawls's argumentation in *Theory of Justice*, because it brings "rational choice" in the sense of self-serving interests into the foundation of ethics; second, to keep "love" from becoming "hyper-ethical" on the verge of the "non-ethical" when each person's equal right to justice is not endorsed. Cf. *Figuring the Sacred, Religion, Narrative and Imagination*, trans. D. Pellauer, ed. M. Walker (Minneapolis: Fortress Press, 1995): 315–329.

[338] Ansorge, *Gerechtigkeit und Barmherzigkeit Gottes*, 279–280. "By concentrating the drama of redemption on Christ's death on the cross [...] without which the *aut – aut* would not be sufficiently provided for, the conception of an abstract demand of justice predominates in *CDH*.[...] God opens up the possibility to the sinner to orient her freedom towards the freedom that God is. The fact that Anselm did not follow up in *CDH* to spell out this thought established in *De veritate* is part of the momentous tragic character (*folgenreichen Tragik*) of this influential work."

terms of logic of argumentation, Anselm first eliminates from a closed theological system the place of Christ; having carried out his programme, it is identified as the vacant location which can only be filled in a necessary and sufficient way through his person and work."[339]

In conclusion, however, Anselm's enterprise can be interpreted as showing that philosophical thought in its independence from divine revelation is recognised not only as the medium of relating to other religions and worldviews; it also serves a conceptually coherent, systematic account of the Christian faith. The alternative would be to base one's theological programme on a selection of biblical quotes that is not articulated and justified in its guiding assumptions. It is therefore an internal necessity for Christian theology to relate to philosophy as the contemporary consciousness of truth and formulate its truth claim for the public of its own era. This is true despite the extent to which Anselm's reasoning is imbued with the unquestioned plausibility of the feudal system of his era. Yet his proposal includes, as Anselm's rejection of "damnation" as a possibility shows, a critical engagement with previous interpretations of the message of the New Testament in the context of God's interactions with humanity, as recounted in the Bible. Unlike his methodologically conscious procedure, what is insufficient also today is to relate biblical quotes directly to the contemporary possibilities for understanding; such immediate connections cut out the previous history of the tradition with its interpretive and problem-spotting potential.[340] Despite the staurocentrism of its reasoning, Anselm's work is a model for covering all the bases. He inserts his own critic, Boso, into the development of the argument and relates to earlier, problematic attempts of connecting in a meaningful framework the key systematic doctrines: God, the creation of humans in the image of God, the experience of the use of their freedom in sinful ways, Jesus Christ as the incarnation of God, and history as marked by salvation.

Subsequent generations have observed in Anselm's as in Augustine's works internal ruptures and conclusions contradicted by their earlier writings. Ansorge contrasts the theological enquiry of the *Proslogion* in which God spares the sinner, subordinating justice to mercy, with the philosophical argument in *Cur Deus Homo* that is centred instead on *rectitudo* and compensation, rather than mercy. Kirschner emphasises the idea of a "different rationality" and "another justice"

---

339 Hans Kessler, *Die theologische Bedeutung des Todes Jesu. Eine traditionsgeschichtliche Untersuchung* (Düsseldorf: Patmos, 1970), 117–157, quoted by Ansorge, *Gerechtigkeit und Barmherzigkeit Gottes*, 270, Fn. 186.
340 Cf. Pröpper and Essen, "Aneignungsprobleme der christologischen Überlieferung. Hermeneutische Vorüberlegungen", in *Gottes ewiger Sohn. Die Präexistenz Christi*, ed. Rudolf Laufen (Paderborn: Schöningh, 1997): 163–178, 167–168.

outside of the antithetical framework.³⁴¹ It is remarkable, however, that the philosophical access used turns out to be actually one of law: The translation Anselm attempts in *Cur Deus Homo* uses law as the anticipated medium and level of universalisation, concluding in the necessity for God to become incarnate if creation is not to end in damnation.

Anselm keeps philosophical and theological reasoning clearly distinguished. How do Thomas and Scotus proceed in relating faith and reason, how do their understandings of human access to knowledge of God compare, and what are the implications for Christology and human agency?

6.3 Thomas Aquinas: Refining the role of reason in theology and ethics

One the one hand, Habermas acknowledges Thomas's "sovereign achievement" of reconceiving and ordering the core doctrines of the Christian faith in a systematic architecture by taking on board the "sharpened conceptions of Aristotelian theory of science".³⁴² On the other hand, he regards the synthesis Thomas elaborated as the approach most impacted by the change of direction effected by the Protestant Reformers, away from the reception of Aristotle, towards the Bible as the revealed knowledge of God.

The breakthroughs are located by Habermas mainly in Thomas's elaboration of the concept of natural law in relation to the *lex aeterna* (the eternal law of God's wisdom governing the cosmos), and the autonomy of the worldly spheres. Yet the subsequent intellectual move away from Aristotelian teleology was to turn Thomas's thorough discursive justifications into a model of relating faith and reason that was to be superseded. How, then, did projects of this era relate philosophical and theological statements to each other, based on which premises? Were they deemed to be separated by a gulf due to their different origins – either in biblical insights, or in a faculty of reason, however much marked by the Fall? Were they considered to be combinable due to human reason being a God-given basis, allowing for "analogical" conclusions from creation to the Creator? Or did they use insights from revelation as a further determination of concepts of reason that were understood to apply to God and humans in a univocal way? The various argumentations developed in the Middle Ages on this point are relevant for the threshold between medieval and modern think-

---

341 Kirschner, *Gott – größer als gedacht*, 394. 415–436.
342 Cf. Habermas, Vol. I, 762.

ing. After outlining Thomas's analogy theory (6.3.1), the differences of his soteriological argumentation from Anselm's will be identified (6.3.2). Finally, I will examine his natural law ethics, analysed in detail by Habermas as a key step in social and legal theory, from an ongoing dispute in theological ethics on the role of reason in a teleological natural order (6.3.3).

6.3.1 Safeguarding accessibility while respecting dissimilarity: "Analogical" talk about God

With a clear appreciation of the requirements of theological thinking, Habermas outlines the task Thomas took on, faced with the Aristotelian concept of God as the "unmoved mover". This Greek conception neither included a relationship to humans nor accounts of historical action, as the Christian understanding of a personal God who creates and redeems demanded:

> When one wants to discover in the anonymous husk of the "unmoved mover" the monotheistic God of creation and redemption, the onto-theological conception of a Primary Being (*Ersten Seienden*) imposes itself as the uniting element (*das Gemeinsame*) by philosophy and theology. It (*Dieses*) formally constitutes the unity-providing point of reference towards which everything that exists in the world (*alles Seiende in der Welt*) is ordered.[343]

Attuned to the theological need for philosophical mediations that are able to convey and not undermine constitutive elements of a faith tradition, Habermas draws attention to the limits of the philosophical concept of God: while it relayed the "originary monotheistic idea of an omnipotent, all-effecting God [...], it needed to be complemented (*Ergänzungsbedürftigkeit*) in soteriological respect, since everything that went beyond the mere existence, the simple being of God, remained closed off."[344] The argument regarding the "five ways" by which God's existence can be found explicitly states that they cannot even establish "whether he is a Who or a What".[345] Habermas sums up the restriction under which Thomas puts the validity of the result of his philosophical search:

> With the aid of our natural reason we can only *infer* indirectly, from the effects which God causes in the world, to God's existence. [...] Thomas chooses two indirect ways on which the human spirit can ascertain (*sich vergewissern*) with metaphysical concepts alone at least a shadow contour (*Schattenriss*) of the divine being – on the one hand the *via negationis* [...];

---

343 Habermas, Vol. I, 695.
344 Habermas, Vol. I, 696.
345 Habermas, Vol. I, 696, Fn. 70, with reference to the *Summa theologiae*, STh I, q. 2, a. 3.

on the other, the *analogia entis*, the path of an analogous understanding (*Auffassung*) of qualities that can be amplified (*steigerungsfähigen*).[346]

In order to estimate the background from which Thomas provides his corrections as well as his applications of Aristotle's thought – followed up in detail through his different works by Habermas – it will be useful to turn to a theological examination of the key intentions that had to be kept in a balance. Comparing Thomas to the efforts of his predecessors, the systematic theologian Magnus Striet outlines the two theological concerns that had to be respected: one, the need to assume a knowability of God at least at the eschatological stage of *visio beatifica*, which ruled out a complete inability of the finite creature's insight into God; two, the insistence on the "ever greater dissimilarity" of all predications, stated by the Fourth Lateran Council in 1215, which was to safeguard the transcendence of God to all human definitions.[347] Thomas's theory of analogy tries to do justice to both intentions, ruling out a univocal understanding of terms, while seeking to avoid equivocal uses. Striet examines the context of the Fourth Lateran Council's statement and compares the two uses of "analogy" by Thomas.

He explains that in 1215, the "ever greater dissimilarity" is emphasised in an argumentation that anchors the priority of "grace" to "nature", aiming to refute the Neoplatonic theory of emanation as a specifically naturalising approach unsuited to the biblical God of creation. For Thomas, "analogy", in a sense that does not refer directly to "qualities but to the way of predication", offers a solution to both interests: Beginning from an understanding of God as supreme goodness (*bonitas*) not just in potency but in fact, it belongs to this Primary Being to "diffuse" itself; its effects in the entities thus created imply "similarity", which enables the creatures to predicate qualities of utmost perfection to God. Without this analogy of attribution, a *visio beatifica* would not be possible after death, since God would remain inaccessible.

In order to do justice to the abiding dissimilarity, however, Thomas draws on a second type of analogy, one of mere "proportion". Aware of the human status as finite, the cautious restriction is not to make direct statements about God but to propose an analogy of relationships as in mathematical proportions: if "100 relates to 50 as 6 to 3", nothing has been claimed of the internal being of the infinite Other. This can only be known through revelation. Striet judges the renewed attempts and different conceptions of analogy as themselves indicating

---

346 Habermas, Vol. I, 696–697.
347 On the following points, I am guided by Magnus Striet, *Offenbares Geheimnis. Zur Kritik der negativen Theologie* (ratio fidei 14) (Regensburg: Pustet, 2003), 94–100.

that the solution was not without problems. Having enquired whether also the analogy of proportion does not imply a shared ontological element, he notes that in the *Summa contra Gentiles* and the *Summa theologiae*, Thomas returns to the analogy of attribution. Although the theological motivation, the biblical promise of seeing God "face to face" (1 Cor 13:12) is a relevant reason, the thought form behind "analogy" is one of participation in a being whose goodness (*bonitas*) is interpreted in the Neoplatonic term of "*diffusio*". This rules out the distinction required both for the *visio beatifica*, and its premise, a divine Creator of a world and of creatures who are different from God and not just ever-connected, dependent emanations. It undermines the ability to specify *creatio ex nihilo* as defining for a God who is the source of all being and as necessary if humans are to be characterised by freedom. An altogether different route will be chosen by Duns Scotus. What Thomas wished to rule out by identifying "analogy" as the best-suited way of speaking of God, is the solution developed one generation after him by Duns Scotus: namely a univocal, completely shared use of concepts for both God and humans proposed for the sake of rational consistency, leaving the framework of analogy and participation behind.

6.3.2 Thomas's soteriology

While Thomas's aim to provide a philosophical justification of the concept of God is carried out by providing the "five ways" (*cinque viae*) of *a posteriori* pointers to God's existence, this does not extend to the incarnation: it is not elaborated on the grounds of human reason. Anselm's attempt to use philosophy of religion to create a shared platform between the three monotheistic traditions is not followed. The soteriology derived from the violation of the order of creation which puts God in a bind of requiring either satisfaction or punishment is replaced by a combination of motives deriving from revelation. For Aquinas, there is no "necessity" for God to become incarnate. Theology takes its starting point in the history of salvation and reflects on its implications and premises after the fact. This includes the thought that God would have been free to have acted differently, which is why "necessity" is a far too ambitious aim of justification. It must attempt to encompass, instead, the whole variety of biblical images in their relevance to human living as intended by God. The insights made possible only through revelation range, as Habermas notes, from "the words of the prophets, the testimonies of the death on the cross, the writings of the Evangelists, the illumination of the Apostle Paul, and the saints". They constitute the "credible signs by which God reveals God's self".[348] It is noteworthy that the route taken by Thomas in his argument from revelation begins from below, with an appeal to what is creditable and worthy of belief; it does not draw on the authority of God's word but on its trustworthiness.[349]

For Thomas, salvation is not achieved simply by Jesus' death, and it assumes the faithful to have the capacity to follow the model of his life. It is a soteriology that is built on encouraging the believers by "awakening faith, strengthening hope, alighting love" and following Christ as the exemplar for right action".[350] While the work of Christ is spelt out in an enriching plurality of biblical images and concepts, the person of Christ is defined mainly by the divinity of the Logos. For Anselm what was paramount was the voluntary nature of Jesus' human decision to offer up his life as the only sinless person who could give recompense for the violation of the order of creation by Adam's sin; yet this was the only place where his life was significant. In contrast, Thomas's Christology elucidates Jesus' life in its revelatory power to a much greater extent than most of his fellow theologians[351] but sees this life as entirely marked by the *visio beatifica* of God.[352]

---

[348] Habermas, Vol. I, 719–720.

[349] This is captured in Habermas's explanation, using a quote from *De veritate*: "The only model by which we can clarify for ourselves the unconditional character of the certainty of faith (*Glaubensgewissheit*) is the *communicative relationship* of one person to another person *worthy of trust* whose shared statements (*Mitteilungen*) she believes [...] 'for example when someone believes the words of a human person because it seems appropriate (*geziemend*) or useful' (De ver. Q. 4, a. 1)". Habermas then goes on to link the element of trust to divine authority: "Perfectionist thinking in terms of *analogia entis* could not find it hard to relate (*zurückzuführen*) the element of trust that stands in (*verbürgt*) for the truth of the propositions communicated to the authority of the divine person. The experience of divine authority is ultimately the verifying (*beglaubigende*) moment that is inscribed into intersubjective relationships and *comes prior to* all individual contents deemed to be true. This experience actualised in prayer is, so-to-speak, prepared by the ontological insight that the human person just like everything that is (*Seiende*) 'is preserved in being (*Sein*) by God'" (Vol. I, 719). While it is true that etymologically, *auctoritas* is linked to *augere*, increase, which can point to a fiduciary relationship, it would be more to the point for Thomas's interweaving of philosophical and biblical elements to relate it to the biblical experience of God's loyalty and steadfastness, basing divine authority on the growth in trust resulting from God's dependable presence and support.

[350] Jan-Heiner Tück, "Jesus Christus – Gottes Heil für uns. Eine dogmatische Skizze", in Gerhard Hotze, Tobias Nicklas, Markus Tomberg, Jan-Heiner Tück, *Jesus begegnen. Zugänge zur Christologie* (Freiburg: Herder, 2009): 119–176, 148.

[351] Menke, *Jesus ist Gott der Sohn*, 479. 484–489. He also refutes the judgement that this position makes Thomas's Christology veer towards a latent monophysitism by specifying in detail his emphasis on the human experience of Jesus.

[352] Cf. Tück, "Gottes Heil für uns", 150, on Thomas's view of Jesus Christ as *simul viator et comprehensor*.

While this view could be derived from the Gospel of John, it risks counteracting the intention in the earlier Christological struggles to reassert the equal standing of Jesus' human nature and will, as developed in Maximus Confessor's distinction between will as capacity and its concrete use. This Christological distinction would have enabled a far greater insistence on specifying human nature as freedom with an emphasis on the human will and would have provided a different starting point for ethics.

So how does Thomas approach the normative dimension of human existence and how does he conceive of the link between anthropology and ethics? On the one hand, it is clear to him that humans can build on their natural virtues while depending on God's grace for the theological virtues of faith, hope and love to be "infused"; on the other hand, this Aristotelian ethics of capability is inscribed into a framework of natural teleology, expressed in "natural inclinations". What roles can human reason and will play in it?

6.3.3 Under dispute: The role of human reason regarding the Natural Law

In view of Habermas's extensive discussion of the merits of the recognition of law that is found in Aquinas's writings, it is helpful to assess his reading against the Neo-Thomist interpretation of this treatise and its critique by post-Vatican II theologians. For nineteenth-century Neo-Thomism and for "classical" natural law, the role of reason consists in reading off human embodied functions what God's plan of creation is: it is evident from the physical structures devised by God's will. For example, procreation as one of the *inclinationes naturales* in this view is seen as a permanently available function that should not be subjected to intervention. By contrast, the "revisionist" Natural Law ethicists point out the historically changing interpretations of human nature with its core inclinations[353] and interpret Thomas's position as stressing the actively legislating function of reason in view of the non-arbitrary givens of the human constitution.[354]

---

353 In his analysis of magisterial documents in "Natural Law Today", in *Natural Law and Theology (Readings in Moral Theology No. 7)*, ed. Charles Curran and Richard McCormick (Mahwah: Paulist Press, 1991): 369–391, Richard Gula finds that also papal encyclicals differ in their interpretation of natural law: in social ethical matters, it is the "order of reason" that is decisive for drawing ethical conclusions; in personal and especially sexual ethics, it is the "order of nature" interpretation. Thus the historical consciousness of modern thought is utilised in matters relating to social, political and international relations; yet it is absent in conjugal ethics as if definitions of the goals and purposes, role attributions and divisions of labour, the legal privileging of

The revisionist view of Thomas's argument and Habermas's reading are compatible with each other. But even with the legislating function of reason, the framework is teleological. The human person seems to come into view as following natural goals but not as setting them herself.[355] In his comparison of Thomas and Duns Scotus, Ludger Honnefelder has outlined in precise comparisons in what way Aquinas refines and corrects Aristotelian definitions as far as was possible within this tradition. He identifies the issues on which both medieval thinkers agree and where Scotus develops shared positions, such as the concept of practical truth and a highest formal principle, in a decisively new direction. Honnefelder's philosophical reconstruction gives independent support to the revisionist reading of Thomas's "natural law" conception. While natural teleology supplies the material to concretise the formal highest principle – to do the good and avoid evil – this is not equivalent to reducing ethics to a biological naturalism. Aquinas is credited with inserting several mediating elements that reduce the danger of taking "Is" for "Ought" in a naturalising ethics. His development away from the early *Commentary on the Nichomachean Ethics* in which "the pre-given nature of the goal is understood in a 'naturalistic' way" is traced to the *Lex* treatise in the *Summa theologiae* I-II which contains two elements of rupture: it distinguishes several levels of practical reason, and offers a "new conception (*Fassung*) of the status of the will in the doctrine of the final end (*Endzweck*)."[356]

For Honnefelder, the result is a distanciation from the pre-set goals of the natural inclinations: they are no longer "immediately normative [...] but only through the *vis ordinativa* of practical reason". Due to the plurality of natural inclinations, practical reason is required to order and decide what priority each of them is to have; it is possible and necessary to distinguish between them by criteria and choose them with reasons, and thus not to simply enact them.[357] Reason is the force (*vis*) that orders them. Honnefelder takes the four *inclinationes* not as a conclusive number, but as "examples" for a "regulatory system that is

---

"heads of households" before equal partnership, not to mention personal understandings of the good of marriage had always remained the same.
354 In *Einführung in die Ethik* (Düsseldorf: Patmos, 1992), 87–97, Arno Anzenbacher elucidates that the *inclinationes naturales* point to "non-arbitrary", constitutive factors of human life (*natural unbeliebige Bestimmungen und Vorgaben des Menschseins*) (97), anthropological givens which to accept does not equate with an essentialist position.
355 Having described the teleological framework in Vol. I, 729–730, Habermas points out the decisive contrast of the approach taken by Scotus and Ockham: "A virtuous *habitus* is not rooted in natural inclinations but in the acts of the will guided by reason" (Vol. I, 829).
356 Cf. Honnefelder, *Woher kommen wir*, 216–217.
357 Honnefelder, *Woher kommen wir*, 226. It is not a case of an "application of the aims of striving of a nature understood in essentialist terms" (216).

not arbitrary but open in its destination (*ein unbeliebiges, aber entwurfsoffenes Regelsystem*)". The "basic strivings (*Grundstrebungen*) that belong to human nature only indicate the framework, as the examples mentioned by Thomas show: the striving for self-preservation, for species preservation, and the relation to communication, truth, and transcendence."[358] Honnefelder even accords a step to Thomas's approach that others find missing in Aristotelian thinking: not merely to follow, but to "set" goals, due to the reflective ordering of partial goals under a supreme one.[359] He also argues against the view that there is one place where the orientation of nature by reason lacks a decisive concept: a link to the inner person and her "*intentio*".[360]

Yet the meaning contained in this term differs between Aquinas and Kant's moral philosophy. One can see the root of the pervasive objectivism of many natural law argumentations, sometimes explicitly distinguished from the "subjectivism" of modern thinking, appearing in the underestimation or even rejection of what is decisive for moral agency: purity of intention. This, however, can be shown to be the point of departure both of deontological ethics and of the internalisation and radicalisation of the Law that is a persistent trait of Jesus' proclamation. Yet without establishing the independent role of "*intentio*" more clearly, and understanding actions as means towards an aspired-to end, can one speak of the difference between the highest formal principle and its concretisation in individual actions which are seen as its historically conscious and "inventive" application?[361] If Thomas's system can be read in this epoch-transcending way, what then does the difference of Scotus's new approach consist in?

---

[358] Honnefelder, *Woher kommen wir*, 288.
[359] Honnefelder, *Woher kommen wir*, 218.
[360] In *Woher kommen wir*, 220, Honnefelder notes in relation to the "introduction of the *intentio* into the interpretation of acting (*Handelns*)" that in "Aristotle and in Thomas's Commentary on the Nichomachean Ethics the remaining naturalism (*Restnaturalismus*) is due to the missing element of *intentio*." It is subsequently corrected in the *Summa*: "The *motives* of the transformation are evident: It is freedom as the faculty of the will (*Willentlichkeit*) which is necessary to preserve human responsibility that leads (*veranlasst*) Thomas to a differentiation of practical reason and to introducing the concept of *intentio*, and Scotus to a clear separation between practical deliberation and decision of the will" (227).
[361] Honnefelder, *Woher kommen wir*, 289–291, in a chapter entitled, "Universale Norm und kontingente Lebensform", 272–304.

6.4 John Duns Scotus as the turning point to Modernity

One generation after the seminal work of Aquinas in developing theology as a justified account or *"scientia"* by incorporating the philosophical framework of Aristotle into its reflection on God, the human person, Christ, and the church, it was easier to identify crucial incompatibilities. The breaking points of the synthesis, as several theological commentators have pointed out, could be perceived more clearly.[362] Since then, also the Neoplatonic sources of Aquinas's philosophical references that shaped his understanding of Aristotle on relevant theological questions have been reconstructed more accurately.[363] The alternative starting point elaborated by Duns Scotus begins with a decisive clarification of its method: his justification of the *univocity* of philosophical and theological concepts, which prohibits an understanding of theology as a discourse based on its own, separately available terms. This would result in an equivocal use of the term "truth", and of subsequent predications, like "freedom" and "love". How are the new departures of Duns Scotus linked: his rejection of the method of analogy (6.4.1), his understanding of the reason for the incarnation and of the difference of Jesus Christ in his supralapsarian Christology (6.4.2), his concept of the human person in her freedom (6.4.3) and of God as opening up a history with humanity that is not determined in advance (6.4.4)?

6.4.1 The univocity of "being" (*ens*) as a category valid for God and for humans

Habermas summarises the distinctive methodological innovation proposed by John Duns Scotus as "disconnecting (*entkoppeln*)" talk about God from a metaphysical knowledge of nature:

---

[362] The determinist framework of the God-world relationship was a serious barrier for a faith tradition that emphasised from its biblical sources God's freedom in creating the world. The latent "necessitarianism" of the Aristotelian system and its Arab and Persian interpretations are commented on by Striet, Pröpper, Honnefelder and Ansorge.

[363] In *Offenbares Geheimnis*, 95, Fn. 94, Striet comments on the Neoplatonic transmission: "Thomas knows Aristotle's concept of proportion only in its Neoplatonic transformation. The unifying 'one' is replaced by 'the One' (Pseudo Dion.), which as the origin of emanation and telos of what emanated is now the foundation (*Grund*) of analogy. For the causality-theoretical foundation (*Grundlegung*) of analogy see already Plato, *Timaios* 3 1 b-c." A conception of God as the world's centre diffusing itself is clearly a counter-factor to Aristotle's "unmoved mover". Yet both Greek ideas share in the assumption of eternal matter, and the insistence by Thomas on creation out of nothing makes him part of a long line of theological critics of Greek cosmology.

The ontological path towards the knowledge of God would only ever lead to general concepts and never to God's self in the essential qualities of the personal divine nature. Thomas, anyway (*immerhin*), had deemed it to be possible to draw inferences by analogy from significant traits of the world order to essential characteristics of its creator. But with his critique of this doctrine of *analogia entis* Duns Scotus then disconnects speaking about God from a metaphysical knowledge of nature. Henceforth, only *transcendental semantic* statements about God as the "First Known (*das Ersterkannte*)" are possible; they can no longer be confused with ontological statements about God as the First Being (*Erstes Seiendes*).[364]

Thus, Scotus's account curtails a previous confidence – tempered, however, by an equal insistence on the ever greater mystery of God – that the human intellect could predicate not only God's existence as the origin of the visible cosmos but possibly also internal divine qualities, such as love, justice and mercy. This comprehensive claim is put under the critical epistemological stricture that all statements are those of a human subject reflecting on what it can and cannot attain through its powers of knowing. If the only way to use language consistently and justifiably as claims to truth is to understand terms as univocal, the search is on for a concept that is true of God and humans. This elementary concept that does not contain significations prejudicial of either divine or human predication is identified by Scotus as the idea of "being as being (*ens inquantum ens*)".[365] On the basis of this formal concept, pairs of antithetical attributes can be specified. The most general idea of God that can be attained is *ens infinitum*. Reflecting on the modalities pertaining to it and to its counterpart, finite being, namely possible versus impossible and necessary versus contingent, the status of the created world and its inhabitants becomes evident: different worlds would have been possible and the one we know is utterly contingent. With a very different method, the abiding mystery of God is thus respected, without dividing human predication up into affirmative, negative or analogous speech about God.[366] The natural

---

364 Habermas, Vol. I, 158–159.
365 Honnefelder and Striet quote the definition gained by recognising the principle of non-contradiction. Striet characterises the result of the justification of God's existence through the transcendental semantic method as a combination "in Kantian terms, of an ontological and a cosmological proof" (*Offenbares Geheimnis*, 140).
366 In *Theologische Anthropologie*, Vol. I, 606, Pröpper explains the alternative to "analogical" talk about God that consists in the further determination of the most basic univocal concept by specifying insights known through God's self-revelation, providing a different avenue to respecting the ongoing mystery of God: "Duns Scotus denied the independence (*Eigenständigkeit*) of analogous predication between univocal and equivocal modes of propositions and insisted on the indispensability of univocal general concepts. Fundamental was the concept of being as the basis of any theological theory formation that determines this concept further in a way

order of the world is rejected as the point of departure of sure knowledge of God and revealed in its constituted, divinely initiated, contingent status; and it is freed from the Aristotelian natural teleology of inbuilt goals and purposes which humans enact, which were then elevated into God's will for the human creatures by the Christian reception of his philosophical system. Instead of being tied into a natural order which allows inferences to its Creator, the human subject and Jesus Christ are given the position of *counterparts* for God's love. Humans can trust in God's continuous support for creation due to an insight not from reason but from revelation: God's omnipotence is an attribute that cannot be concluded from the bare concept of the *ens infinitum*; it draws on biblical sources. These lead to a theological response to a problem that arises when the absolute power of God is analysed. *De potentia Dei absoluta*, God is not bound by anything else; but God's self limits this power by binding its use to the *potentia Dei ordinata*, its dependable actualisation in the ways promised to humans in the biblical narratives. Yet the new realisation of God's unlimited power makes the question why God created anything at all more urgent. This leads to Scotus's account of Christology and through the theme of the incarnation to the relationship to humanity.

6.4.2 A supralapsarian Christology

By allocating divine omnipotence to the insights that are only accessible from revelation, Scotus makes a clear distinction between what philosophical thought can attain, and knowledge that depends on God revealing God's self. Natural reason can reach the concept of a non-contingent being which Scotus determines as the "first known" entity; this designation includes the perspective of human subjectivity into the course of argumentation, instead of stating in an objectivist way the existence of a highest being. By insisting on the univocal use of language, identifying as the most elementary level the term "being" (*ens*), a bifurcation of reason and faith into a truth of reason versus fideism is forestalled. Divine goodness is explicated in a way congruent with freedom as the generative category for God. This is exemplified by the distinctions devised to capture both

---

that is understandable *(einsichtig)* yet never exhausts its theme or conceals the mystery". He refers to Pannenberg, *Systematische Theologie I* (Göttingen: Vandenhoeck & Ruprecht, 1988), 372–373. For a differentiated analysis of the discussion whether the participation model behind Thomas's use of "analogy" leads to a monism, or whether "*actus essendi*" and "*ipsum esse per se subsistens*" are separated, see Lerch's "Exkurs: Zur Univozität des Seins- und Freiheitsbegriffs", in Lerch, *Selbstmitteilung*, 110–120, 114–115, Fn. 193.

the absolute and the ordered power of God: *producere* is the adequate overarching verb referring to the divine initiative of a *creatio ex nihilo*, while the selection from the *creabilia*, possible existences, falls under *creare* and belongs to the *potentia ordinata* of self-restricted divine power.[367]

For what reason then did God resolve to create entities outside of God's self? The answer given to this question involves a supralapsarian Christology which puts forward a conception of the Son of God that is not dependent on human sin. Scotus thus breaks with a soteriology of atonement and demotes "sin" to a clearly secondary position in which it is not a relevant reason for God's incarnation. Though a feature of human action, its rank is too low to be a basis for God's decree.[368]

The reason for God, according to Scotus, to create a free human counterpart was to have "fellow lovers": "*Deus vult condiligentes suis*".[369] The first realisation of this intention is the Eternal Son who responds to God's love. This model is groundbreaking in taking the relationship between God and this first-created counterpart as the unique response of two freedoms to each other. Jesus Christ's uniqueness is captured as his *haecceitas*, his very own specificity. One can see the new focus on his individuality as solving the problem which so many Christological proposals sought to address, in order to give equal weight to the human nature of the Son of God.[370] The problem with the terminology of human nature being taken up or "assumed" by the Logos is summarised by Georg Essen: "The *natura assumpta* would lack any concrete-individual specificity (*Besonderheit*)". The reason for this inability lies in the substantial ontological categories of "nature" and "person": "the difference between *ousia* and *hypostasis* remains tied to a natural ontological level and thus cannot do justice to the genuinely human realisations (*Vollzügen*) of an individual existence."[371]

---

367 In *Offenbares Geheimnis*, 144, Fn. 164 Striet points out how the "doctrine of *creabilia* with its distinction between divine reason and divine will" corrects the necessitarianism of Arabic cosmology.
368 Cf. Ansorge, *Gerechtigkeit und Barmherzigkeit Gottes*, 365: It remains below the level of what is worthy of consideration because divine agency "also in its relation to what is outside of God can have no other measure than God's self".
369 Cf. Ansorge, *Kleine Geschichte*, 169, with reference to Duns Scotus's Paris Commentary on the Sentences, Rep. Par. III 7,4,4. Cf. Pröpper, *Theologische Anthropologie,* Vol. II, 675, with reference to Op. Oxon. III 32, 1, 6.
370 In *Duns Scotus* (Oxford: Oxford University Press, 1999), 118, Richard Cross links him to earlier efforts to avoid both monophysitism and Nestorianism and quotes Scotus's reference to "the authority of John of Damascus: 'The Word assumed a nature in particular (*in atomo*)'".
371 Essen, *Freiheit Jesu*, 129.

By making the factual and individual his point of departure, Scotus arrives at a different understanding of the elements to be related in a Christology. The "humanity" reaffirmed as equal in standing to Christ's divinity in the formula of Chalcedon no longer refers to human nature in general, but to Jesus' unique concretisation of it in his response to God's love.[372]

Christoph Hübenthal has highlighted the relevance of this breakthrough: it offers a principled theological foundation of a world recognised in its secularity and results in conceptions of human and Christian agency that leave the substantial-ontological terms of an Aristotelian natural order behind.[373] With the pre-modern teleological framework "dispatched for good",[374] the path is open to a new framework to reconceive the relationship between nature and grace in terms of freedom.

In Scotus's Christological conception of "absolute incarnation", not only does the idea of atonement change to one of fidelity to God and the obedience of fulfilling his mission even to the point of death; it also means that Christ is not portrayed as "primarily the Redeemer. Rather, he is the personified shape (*Gestalt*), revealed to humans, of the love that God is in God's self", wishing for the response of humans, but "knowing that with the creation of a free being who is able to respond to God's love it is also possible that this free being will close itself off from God." Ansorge comments on the difference to Anselm's argumentation that "God's incarnation does not aim [...] for a work of satisfaction through which an abstract *ordo iustitiae* is restored. Rather, Christ's suffering and his death on the cross are the consequences of Christ's love to the Father under the conditions of the domination of sin".[375]

---

[372] A more detailed analysis of the "order of love (*ordo amoris*)", in which the Son is the first to be offered God's love and redemption is spelt out in terms of divine love is given by Dirk Ansorge in *Gerechtigkeit und Barmherzigkeit Gottes*, 360–375, and in *Kleine Geschichte*, 168–171.
[373] Christoph Hübenthal, "Ethische Begründung aus dem theologischen Grund des Säkularen. Eine katholische Sicht", in *Ökumenische Ethik*, ed. Thomas Weißer (Fribourg: Academic Press/Würzburg: Echter, 2018), 45–63, esp. 55–56.
[374] Hübenthal, *Grundlegung der christlichen Sozialethik. Versuch eines freiheitsanalytisch-handlungsreflexiven Ansatzes* (Münster: Aschendorff, 2006), 369.
[375] Ansorge, *Gerechtigkeit und Barmherzigkeit Gottes*, 366–367. 370. In *Duns Scotus*, 129–131, Cross debates the question whether "satisfaction" is completely replaced by an interpretation of Jesus' death in terms of "merit", and judges his distinction from Anselm as follows: "Most importantly, he disagrees with Anselm that God has to redeem us by Christ's death.[...] Some commentators believe that Scotus's account of the redemption is sufficiently described in terms of merit, and thus that there is no satisfaction component in it at all [...] satisfaction consists in receiving something from God (in this case, the remission of sins). So Christ's satisfaction can be spoken of as a sort of merit [...] We should also note that Scotus differs from Anselm in

It is a view of Jesus' death that is open to verification at the historical level, in line with the Gospels which describe Jesus' struggle with the political and religious authorities as the background to his crucifixion; his resurrection confirms his proclamation of God as love. A different understanding of the Eucharist results from Scotus's new outline of God, creation and incarnation, in a language that replaces the "transubstantiation" of objective elements with "consubstantiation".[376] What are the consequences of a vision of a Christology independent from sin, one which thus goes beyond a restorative function, for the position of human agency?

6.4.3 The human will as a primordial faculty of self-determination

Part of the corrections of Franciscan theology was to replace the Dominicans' priority on God's wisdom with that of love as the most appropriate overarching interpretation of God's essence. In keeping with this praxis orientation in the doctrine of God, the definition of theology is redirected towards its practical destination. This is supported by a reorientation of the notion of "*beatitudo*" from a contemplative *visio* in Aquinas to both a "*visio practica*" and a "*scientia practica*". What role does sin play, if it is not the reason for the incarnation? In which terms is it captured, and how is the ideal form of the relationship between God and humans outlined?

It seems that the resources which the patristic mainstream had developed against Gnosticism by elaborating the "inner person" in her freedom are here coming to fruition. At their best, humans "know that they are able to respond to the divine love [...] due to an enabling and preserving act" of God. It is an encounter that is given the name *amicitia*, friendship.[377] A turn to practical reason is demanded when the idea of an "order of being" is replaced with a contingent world. The competence of theoretical reason consists in the univocal use of concepts. In its relation to philosophy as the general consciousness of truth, theology operates as a further determination of philosophically achievable statements, not as an alternative path, based on analogy. It shares its language, though the source of insight into God's omnipotence, justice and love is God's action, as encountered in the Bible. Faith and reason are neither entwined nor are they separated by a gulf but are seen as pointing to two primary faculties.

---

wanting to see Christ's work as an offering by human nature to the Trinity, and not as an offering by the Son (the second person of the Trinity) to the Father."
376 Ansorge, *Kleine Geschichte*, 132. 211. Cf. Cross, *Duns Scotus*, 139–145.
377 Ansorge, *Gerechtigkeit und Barmherzigkeit Gottes*, 372–374.

In contrast to a natural world order of which humans are part also when they make decisions on the priority of natural inclinations to be realised, in a world that exists through God's contingent decision to create, the primordial faculty is the will both of God and of humans. God's self-limitation in the *potentia ordinata* invites the human counterpart to use their will in an equally self-legislating way. It is not bound by an inbuilt natural teleology but constitutes a foundational practical faculty that originates in the conscious self-relationship of the human being endowed with the capacity for self-reflection. It is thus located at the spiritual and intellectual, not at the natural-biological level. "Freedom" is the key term encompassing God and humans. Magnus Striet sums up the epoch-changing role of Duns Scotus as follows: "The Scotist critique of metaphysics founds the primacy of practical reason over theoretical reason, the primacy of the individual (*des Individuellen*) over what is general (*Allgemeinheit*), and the primacy of contingency over necessity. With this, it is at the same time a metaphysics of freedom, both of God and of the human person."[378]

As in Thomas's outline of natural law, a formal highest principle is assumed yet the concrete conclusions which are also part of Natural Law are reached in a different way, due to the new view of contingency: "The place of the agreement (*Übereinstimmung*) with the broad goals (*Rahmenzielen*) of the *inclinationes naturales* which continues with Thomas despite all the transformations of the Aristotelian approach, is taken by the new criterion of truth of agreeing (*Zusammenstimmens*) (*consonantia*) with the highest principle and with what follows immediately from it, thus by a type of internal consistency (*Stimmigkeit*) or coherence."[379] Yet this criterion of judgement implies that human freedom can also be used adversely, against the highest principle not to commit evil. For Scotus, it is a conflict between two human orientations: the *affectus iustitiae* and the *affectus commodi* with the latter being the winner in the case of sinful acts and intentions.

What view of history is implied in this new constellation of an encounter between two free counterparts in the project begun by God with creation? Here, the doctrine of grace built on the correspondence between human and divine freedom shows its relevance.

---

378 Striet, *Offenbares Geheimnis*, 131.
379 Honnefelder, *Woher kommen wir?*, 224–225.

6.4.4 An open-ended future of creation: God's history with humans and the question of God's "acceptation"

The new rank given to univocity for which the freedom of God draws on the same term as human finite freedom, and to contingency as the status of the existing world, explains the interest in possibility and the future which is to be shaped by the human counterparts. God leaves this space for free decision-making to humans.[380] It is thus an open history in which God risks the negation of the invitation extended to humans who are able to respond freely: either positively as *condiligentes*, or destructively. History as the place of encounter between divine and human freedom is a contingency risked by God. The future is radically open and thus also open to fail. It is a consequence of remodelling the doctrine of grace in terms of freedom: In it, "the *encounter between God and humans* takes the place of a combination of the natural and the supernatural. For that reason, the gracious changing of the essence of the human is replaced by divine acceptance."[381]

Yet, regarding the question of actual acceptance, even in this highest form of mutual response, once again, the freedom of God is emphasised. What are the terms of God's "acceptance"? Pröpper detects a problem in renewing the lynchpin position of God's freedom even at this stage, at the end of a long history of humans in individual cooperation with God's will: In the *potentia Dei absoluta*, God would be free not to forgive, and to discard the lifelong attempts of individuals in their good will in view of their instances of failure. Taken on its own, for Pröpper, this limit reflection is unacceptable: "the 'acceptation theory' which emphasises God's freedom to accept or reject a human person in their quest of forgiveness to God [...] is unbearable", unless one takes into account that this is only stated in relation to God's absolute power, and that the *potentia Dei ordinata* is committed irrevocably to the promise of the Covenant between God and humans.[382]

The priority given to God's freedom over God's love in this contested theory shows how significant the divine self-limitation by the *potentia ordinata* is. It is essential to ward off a conception of God's will not only as an absolute power, in keeping with God's infinity, but as an unbound, arbitrary power. It is, as we shall see, a restriction that Ockham does not wish to uphold. Scotus's shift to categories of interaction from those of an inherent natural teleology gives both sides, divine and human, the ability to self-legislate. Thus the doctrine of grace presup-

---

380 Cf. Honnefelder, *Woher kommen wir?*, 205.
381 Pröpper, *Theologische Anthropologie*, Vol. II, 1281.
382 Cf. Pröpper, *Theologische Anthropologie*, Vol. II, 1057.

poses a "*natura beatificabilis*" which Adam's sin, downgraded already not only in comparison with Augustine and Anselm, but other Christian thinkers, could not destroy. It tries to do justice to two requirements: the spontaneity of human freedom, and its empowerment by God. "Enabled by a gracious natural endowment to fulfil the commandments, to avoid sin and to love God from its own forces [...], the grace of justification empowers humans to engage in actions that were not possible before."[383] The definitive change in how God's power is envisaged is the realisation that it is not diminished by having counterparts who are free, and therefore free also to reject God: "God's omnipotence as distinct from any power that is finite, that remains dependent on opposition and on keeping others dependent [...], appears in bringing forth free beings who can take a stance also to God, and allowing them to be". This new understanding of divine omnipotence concludes in the idea that God allows God's self "to be affected by them and to risk an open history with them".[384]

With William of Ockham, the points of comparison will be, first, how the Scotist move to contingency over against necessitarianism is further developed in the younger Franciscan's radicalisation of the voluntarist framework; secondly, how this results in an opposite outline of the relationship between philosophy and theology.

6.5 William of Ockham's step to Nominalism and its legacy

The directions into which Ockham takes Scotus's new departures lay the ground, as Habermas observes, for the future bifurcation of philosophy into a language-oriented analytical strand and one that continues to enquire about the link between concepts and extra-mental reality.[385] Based on the individual and contingent status of entities as the shared starting point of Scotus and Ockham, the conclusion of Nominalism is that general concepts, the "universals", not only originate in the human intellect but do not express an ontological statement in the sense of relating to an extra-mental given.[386] While Scotus remains a Re-

---

[383] Pröpper, *Theologische Anthropologie*, Vol. II, 1281.
[384] Pröpper, *Theologische Anthropologie*, Vol. I, 608.
[385] Habermas, Vol. I, 764.
[386] The individualisation raises the need for further specifications regarding, for example, the concept of the "human being" as such, as Sigrid Müller explains regarding the statement, "The human being is the most valuable (*wertvollste*) of all bodily existences (*Lebewesen*). What does the term 'human being' stand for if there is no general human nature in extra-mental reality? The proposition was equivocal since according to Ockham one could only understand it as a per-

alist, both agree that concepts do not mirror principles of being in the natural order, instituted by God, as they did for Thomas. The path to knowledge is by empirical, inductive research into singular entities. The knowability of the world is identified as being linked to the processes of human subjectivity. The synthesis of the High Middle Ages connecting God, the natural world and the human creature gives way to an analysis of distinct tasks which affects the relationship between theology and philosophy. Habermas notes that Scotus and Ockham "inadvertently" cause a split between the two disciplines that will be the legacy of late medieval thought for modernity.[387] It is necessary, therefore, to examine what each of them understands as "philosophy" in its distinction from revelation-based theological thinking (6.5.2). Their interpretations are founded in their divergent views of what an emphasis on God's freedom and omnipotence instead of God's wisdom implies (6.5.1).

6.5.1 Voluntarism developed in a Nominalist direction

Scotus had switched to the human will as the effective intellectual capacity since reason in his view had to be counted as passive in the impressions it received from nature. From the idea of the world as the given natural order, the focus moved to how it originated in God's will, underlining a contingency which could also have resulted in a completely different cosmos. Through his distinction between *potentia absoluta* and *potentia ordinata*, Scotus drew the conclusion that the order God gave to the world by the self-limitation of the boundless divine power was fitting and hospitable; it offered reliable structures in which humans could realise the freedom that God had endowed them with in order to have counterparts free to take a stance towards God's love.

The same awareness, however, of divine omnipotence to an unlimited degree, could also lead to a different conclusion, equally motivated by theological

---

sonal supposition for each individual human being. If one did so, however, the proposition was wrong in a literal sense, since one human being could not be more valuable than another human being." Sigrid Müller, *Theologie und Philosophie im Spätmittelalter. Die Anfänge der via moderna und ihre Bedeutung für die Entwicklung der Moraltheologie (1380–1450)* (Münster: Aschendorff, 2018), 64.

387 Habermas, Vol. I, 763: "Duns Scotus and Ockham [...] will, however *inadvertently* (*unbeabsichtigt*) tear a gulf between faith and knowledge that will barely be able to be bridged." It is worth checking, though, whether there may be intrinsic reasons for insisting on a "gulf" to express the difference of God's underivable revelation to human reason and the freedom of God over against necessitarianism. Each time it depends on the counterpart philosophical position.

reasons. As Klaus Bannach argues, Ockham defends the "primacy of the individual to the universal (*Allgemeinen*) in order to secure the status of God's activity of creation in every moment of existence of the real as being without presuppositions".[388] This establishes a link between the starting point of Nominalist epistemology, unconnected individual elements, and voluntarism, in that the existence and the instantaneous preservation of the distinct units are due to God's will. This emphasis on a divine will without presuppositions is reinforced by a further move away from the Scotist conception. As the theological ethicist Sigrid Müller notes both for Ockham and for Luther's Augustinian fellow friar Gregory of Rimini, they "regard also the activities of rationality (*Verstand*) and of the will as arising from a decision and thus as constituting a praxis in the real sense".[389] In contrast, Scotus had bound the will to the insight of the *ratio*, maintaining the will as an intellectual and spiritual capacity.[390] Sigrid Müller specifies: "For Scotus, the free self-determination of the will was closely tied to the rational determination of the good. The object of the will could only be the good in its generality (*Allgemeinheit*) so that the perfection of the object would correspond to the perfection of the capability of the will (*Willensfähigkeit*). Rationality was required for knowing this perfect object."[391]

Ockham's unmooring of Scotus's will-based approach from practical reason can be seen as characteristic of his reconfiguration of initially shared ideas by taking them to their limits. Scotus sought to secure the infinite freedom of God by comparing God's reliable self-binding to the *potentia ordinata* to the extent of the *potentia Dei absoluta*. Ockham relates the two differently and inherits the consequences of basing theoretical reason on the will's decision: disconnected from *ratio*, a dramatic concept of God's will results that is still, even after the biblical revelation of God's saving acts, always on the edge of deciding on the next moment of the future of the world.

"Voluntarism" can thus be spun out in opposing directions: either as practical reason that binds itself to the autonomous commitment to be loyal and respectful of the created other's freedom, or as an approach that endorses an "ab-

---

[388] Klaus Bannach, *Die Lehre von der doppelten Macht Gottes bei Wilhelm von Ockham* (Wiesbaden: F. Steiner, 1975), 200, quoted by Striet, *Offenbares Geheimnis*, 206, Fn. 247.
[389] Müller, *Theologie und Philosophie im Spätmittelalter*, 107.
[390] Honnefelder, *Woher kommen wir?*, 190: "The will and not reason (*Vernunft*) (*intellectus*) is the properly (*eigentlich*) rational faculty."
[391] Müller, *Theologie und Philosophie im Spätmittelalter*, 262.

stract", isolated conception of the will.³⁹² In detailed comparisons, Ludger Honnefelder has refuted the interpretation of Scotus on the lines of Henry of Ghent who developed an "extreme voluntarism".³⁹³ Neither does Scotus share a position, put forward in his time by Roger Marston and Petrus de Falco, which "anticipates Ockham's thesis that everything is by itself singular".³⁹⁴ The less one assumes the world to be of a consistent regularity, the more one depends on the will of its author to support its ongoing functioning.³⁹⁵

6.5.2 Distinctions between Scotus and Ockham on the relationship between philosophy and theology

The question of how the two disciplines relate to each other is solved in opposite directions. For Duns Scotus, the univocity of concepts is a premise required on two grounds: for the unity of reason in order to avoid equivocation in all types of predication, among humans and towards the divine; and for a determinate way of speaking about God. The elementary term, *ens*, is formal, and draws its further specifications from biblical accounts of God's revelation. Thus, theological statements are a further determination of this philosophically attainable concept.

---

392 In *Selbstmitteilung Gottes*, 367, Fn. 212, Lerch speaks of an "abstract concept of omnipotence respectively absolute divine freedom resulting in a slippage (*Gefälle*) in which the essential goodness of God is subordinated to (*unterliegt*) God's contingent decision".
393 Cf. Honnefelder's critique of Thomas Williams's presentation, in *Woher kommen wir?* , 193. He also clarifies that "the goal of Scotus's argumentation in *Ordinatio* and *Lectura* is not the subordination of metaphysics to theology, as has been repeatedly alleged – also unfortunately by Gilson – but the rescue of metaphysics in order to rescue theology" (117).
394 Thamar Rossi Leidi, "Einleitung", in Duns Scotus, *Über das Individuationsprinzip* (Hamburg: Meiner, 2015), VII–LXXXVIII, XLVIII–XLIX.
395 Striet clarifies that "conditioned necessity" includes a regularity that allows humans a "definite freedom of action", for example, to conduct research (*Offenbares Geheimnis*, 131). In her study of Ockham and subsequent 14th- and 15th-century theologians, Müller sums up the critique of Nominalism by John Capreolus who takes a Scotist line on this point: "'The universal is the first-known even when knowing the individual and thus is the unifying moment of any philosophical and theological consideration of the world [...] Nominalists jeopardised (*setzten aufs Spiel*) the unity and comprehensibility of the world'" (*Theologie und Philosophie im Spätmittelalter*, 176).

Also Ockham "assumes as a matter of course that God's existence can be proven".[396] Knowledge of God's essence, however, is attained in a principally separate way, without any link to reason, based entirely on insights from the Bible, such as intervening into the natural course of events by rescuing the three men from the fire oven.[397] The otherness of God is captured in exceptional acts, not in the intention of creating space for human freedom. The empirical and the miraculous exist in parallel worlds. Habermas identifies the danger of falling into a polarity of science versus fideism.[398] From her discipline of moral theology, Sigrid Müller asks about the consequences of constructing an alternative between

> a revealed foundation of faith and natural reason [...] Which model of theology was the force behind the *via moderna*? [...] Is a theology which rejects the knowing of God with the help of natural reason and which trusts only in revelation able to attribute to humans the competence in practical respects to direct their agency adequately with the help of reason? Or is a revealed instruction for morally right action required?[399]

If humans are attributed the capacity for research and for devising general categories, but are otherwise dependent on a distant God, the account appears paradoxical. Yet also the position of the High Middle Ages that natural reason has the ability to assert not only the existence of a divine Creator, but also the benevolence and dependability of this omnipotent source no longer appears convincing; thus, a differentiated conclusion must be sought. The paradox created by the disjunction between knowledge and faith in Ockham's account could be dissolved by distinguishing two perspectives that are open to being combined: first, a theological anthropology of "*gratia supponit naturam*",[400] which does not, however, equate to replacing "grace" with "nature". It indicates the task of exploring the anthropological presuppositions of revelation and specifies "nature" as human "freedom". The second perspective is a conclusion equally pro-

---

396 Striet, 208. He specifies in Fn. 257 that Ockham's proof of the existence of God takes the shape of a "synthesis of the cosmological argument with the question about the *conservatio* of what exists factually."
397 Müller, *Theologie und Philosophie im Spätmittelalter*, 164.
398 Cf. Habermas, Vol. I, 763.
399 Müller, *Theologie und Philosophie im Spätmittelalter*, 23.
400 Striet, *Offenbares Geheimnis*, 211: "From a philosophical perspective [...] if it is to be possible that God comes to be known as God's self in human reason, one must conclude that in a world that has been created *ex nihilo*, God must have founded (*grundgelegt*) the possibility of knowing God. Thus, in line with the classical theological axiom, *gratia supponit naturam*, one may conclude that God pre-posits (*voraussetzt*) human reason as the medium in which the divine will to reveal God's self (*Offenbarwerdenwollen*) was able to arrive".

posed by Scotus, from the doctrine of God, that "the condition of the possibility of the univocal approach is the positive facticity of revelation".[401] The dissolution of the fusion or synthesis of philosophy and theology in the High Middle Ages has led to two opposing models: Scotus distinguishes two levels that are not in competition – the priority given to God's initiative of self-communication does not cancel but invites human freedom. Ockham spells out a different version of theocentrism by reverting to an antithetical configuration of divine and human freedom which portrays an immediacy of God's action similar to Augustine one millennium earlier. Theology deals with an incomprehensible God not in the sense that motivated earlier negative theology, that the language of finite humans is not adequate to God's being, yet whose love was not in doubt. Now, as Striet explains,

> a rudimentary uncertainty (*Restunsicherheit*) remains whether the content of what is believed as having been revealed permits inferences as to the Revealer. It is the low-burning (*schwelende*) Nominalist suspicion that as the reverse side of the rediscovered absolute freedom of God, the *potentia dei absoluta* must throw up the question of the possible wilfulness (*Willkür*) and thus of a hidden essence of God.[402]

These two divergent theological trajectories must be taken into account when the origins of modernity in the Middle Ages are assessed under the guiding perspective of the relationship between knowledge and faith. The two paths they track for the future will now be summarised.

6.6 Two late medieval points of departure for modern thinking

Prepared by decisive moves, especially the early patristic discovery of subjectivity as the "irreducibility" of the inner person[403] and by Maximus Confessor's analysis of the will, the late Middle Ages achieve the decisive move away from substance ontological categories and from the teleological framework taken over from Aristotle. This intellectual horizon which Aquinas had thoroughly and critically appropriated for Christian thinking was left behind for a will-

---

401 Lerch, *Selbstmitteilung Gottes*, 119–120, in his discussion of the sequence between God's freedom and God's love in Striet's outline.
402 Striet, "Unterscheidung der Geister. Negative Theologie in der Kritik", in *Jenseits der Säkularisierung. Religionsphilosophische Studien*, ed. Herta Nagl-Docekal and Friedrich Wolfram (Berlin: Parerga, 2008): 95–107, 99, quoted in Lerch, *Selbstmitteilung Gottes*, 365–366.
403 Kobusch, *Christliche Philosophie*, 18.

based reconstruction of the divine Creator, a creation contingent on God's will, and human initiative in positing goals and determining the intentions of their will. Following Habermas's succinct and perceptive summary of key changes, I shall examine the theological differences between Scotus and Ockham in their significance for the question that will open the following chapter on Kant's anthropological turn: does Modernity owe its rise to the Nominalist insistence on God's absolute power to which it mounts a counterposition, as Hans Blumenberg's much-discussed thesis proposes? Or is there a continuity between the voluntarist transformation of the previously object-oriented medieval thinking and the modern, Kantian prioritising of practical reason? Would this be a place where a revision of the conventional demarcations between the Middle Ages and Modernity is due? With regard to the independent, profane legal framework developed in Thomas's conception of Natural Law, Habermas has illuminated clearly the philosophical continuity to normative modern understandings. Against the hierarchical ordering still valid for Thomas, the Franciscans draw principled conclusions, such as the legal institution of civic participation and a principled critique of slavery. Habermas identifies major innovation in

> the way in which Scotus renews the question of how God can be known from a theologically motivated, but epistemologically transformed point of view. This reflexive fraction (*Brechung*) explains the turn away from the objectifying attitude of the standpoint of God taken by Thomas and the original turn towards a logic-semantic treatment of the ontological paradox [...] Scotus disconnects (*entkoppelt*) knowledge of God from the metaphysical knowledge of nature. This conclusive (*durchschlagende*) critique of the Thomist doctrine of *analogia entis* [...] leads him to the discovery of a transcendental-semantic dimension, in which "quidditative" statements about God are supposed to be possible. Yet they no longer have the sense of ontological statements about God as the First Being but the sense of transcendental statements about the "First Known (*das Ersterkannte*)".[404]

Yet the consequences Habermas draws from this assessment need to be tested on whether they overlook the difference between the characteristics of the theological projects of Scotus and Ockham:

> With theological talk about God renouncing to any speculative claim, the contrast (*Gegensatz*) between theology and philosophy, faith and knowledge is deepened. The growing gap (*Kluft*) also derives from the conception of an omnipotent God and a world that is wholly contingent (*einer im Ganzen kontingenten Welt*). Since nature has been robbed of its inherent reasonableness (*Vernünftigkeit*), the finite spirit encounters contingent objects and factual states (*Sachverhalten*), so that he must deliver an active contribution to the knowledge

---

404 Habermas, Vol. I, 766.

of the natural order [...] A systematic framework is developed for the faculty of knowing which does justice to the new relevance of the particular and the individual.[405]

It must be questioned whether the "gap" or abyss (*Kluft*) between theology and philosophy is the same for Scotus and Ockham. Their theological foundations and motivations differ in crucial ways. Habermas specifies the shared points that mark the paradigm change they inaugurate convincingly: individuality, freedom of the will, the difference to Thomas's natural teleology.[406] But the elements he does not identify mark the alternative between the different paths for theology following on from them: in Scotus, the idea of "absolute incarnation", irrespective of sin, which marks the greatest possible distance from Augustine; the term "predestination" referring in the first instance to the divine decree that results in the Eternal Son as a counterpart to God's love; the rejection of Augustine's anthropology evident in Scotus's assertion of the *liberum arbitrium*; his view of evil as a possible human historical choice in a biblical, not a Manichean or speculative understanding. The clarity with which Scotus dissolves the fusion of theological and philosophical statements is motivated by the interest in honouring God's revelation and in not attributing to human reason what is the action of God.

Habermas mentions the "controversial question in which sense Ockham can count as the 'student' of Duns Scotus in theoretical philosophy." While both their works "shook the foundations of substance ontology, [...] the fact that Ockham radicalised key changes of course (*Weichenstellungen*) of his teacher lends itself to (*verführen*) overlooking the very difference by which both thinkers have introduced opposite (*gegenläufige*) developments."[407]

The opposite directions followed up in the second volume are based on fundamental divergences that are relevant for theology as a discourse on faith, two of which I shall mention: First, Ockham locates the two disciplines in a total disjunction, separated by their contexts, one revelation-based, the other generally human. Scotus regards concepts like God's eternity not as belonging to a different realm but as a further determination of the philosophical concept of *ens*, understandable by everyone due to the consciousness of truth they are endowed with. For a language theory that brings both the general philosophical term and its further Christian determination together, while equally insisting on a univocal use of hermeneutics for both ordinary and biblical texts and on the role of

---

405 Habermas, Vol. I, 767.
406 Habermas, Vol. I, 804.
407 Habermas, Vol. I, 766.

individuality, we shall have to wait for Schleiermacher (Chapter Eight). But for Ockham, theology has an exceptional linguistic status, and its truth claim is directly traced back to revelation which believers are assumed to simply accept in its totality. It is diametrically opposed to Scotus's "univocity".[408] While Habermas notes the danger of fideism, it also seems perfectly set to fulfil his description of religious faith as "exterritorial".

Secondly, what is the consequence of God's absolute freedom for the relation God is assumed to take to the world that owes its existence to divine creation? The "abstract" character of the attribute "absolute" that Lerch criticised and that Striet related to the danger of a principled hiddenness of God offers the temptation to construct a speculative theological edifice on this term; it thereby abstracts from the actual foundation which allows the encounter with God's love in the testimony of Jesus' life. Divine "absolute freedom" lends itself to runaway conclusions untouched by the Gospel accounts of Jesus's proclamation and symbolic practice. In short, the two authors have very different reasons for their stances. For Scotus, the philosophy-theology distinction based on a univocal use of language is made by design, not accidentally or inadvertently, and spells out that the initiative belongs to God's freedom. The form it takes in Ockham's approach anticipates the subsequent bifurcation of theology into a fideism, hailed as the adequate response of trust in God, and a biblically unsupported doctrine of a God of unfettered freedom, not bound by any Covenants God freely concluded with humans. Reason, on the other hand, is reduced to empirical enquiries. In a history of reception marked by opposite views of God as an anchor, or as a menace for human freedom, and of reason examined in its theoretical and practical forms, Modernity will chart a new course.

---

408 Due perhaps to Ockham's historical struggles with the Avignon Popes, leading to his excommunication though not to a papal condemnation of his writings – a subtle difference pointed out by Sigrid Müller in the context of her treatment of John Capreolus (*Theologie und Philosophie im Spätmittelalter*, 166, Fn. 511) – his ecclesiology does not seem to be affected by the separation of the language of theology from philosophy.

7 "Faith" and "Knowledge" after the Copernican Turn in Kant's Critiques of Reason

In his account of the continuities and ruptures between the Middle Ages and Modernity, Habermas regards Kant and German Idealism as part of the history of reception of Duns Scotus: "Hegel, Schelling [...] were already heirs of Duns Scotus who on the path to Kant's transcendental reflection did a first step beyond Thomas's still unbroken ontological thought".[409] The Scotist model of divine and human freedom is presented as an alternative to the latent necessitarianism of Aristotle and its reception in Islamic philosophy of religion. Duns Scotus is thus the clearest advocate of a conception of inner freedom, as it had already begun to be elaborated against Gnosticism from the second century onwards. Both the transcendental method through which Kant achieves the anthropological turn to the subject (7.2), and the priority given to practical reason with its deontological, not teleological profile have the Franciscan theologian as their precursor. In his explanation of what the "Enlightenment" stands for, Kant extends the understanding of philosophy by adding to its role as a discipline its designation towards the "world". It assumes all human beings to be practitioners of reason and includes the question of meaning (7.3). Yet before turning to Kant's anchoring of philosophy in the capability of critical human reflection on its own faculties of reason within the existing world and with fellow humans, an influential controversy that Habermas alludes to will be sketched. It is relevant for his view of the progress in learning since the Axial Age towards a postmetaphysical stage: Hans Blumenberg's defence of the "legitimacy of the modern age",[410] first published in 1966, and his critical reappraisal of the role of the Nominalist concept of God for human freedom in its autonomy (7.1).

7.1 Modernity as grounded in, or as a revolt against, the late Middle Ages? Hans Blumenberg's critique

For Habermas, Blumenberg's repositioning of the Modern Age against a theory of "secularisation" that regards it as an illegitimate rejection of a cultural self-un-

---

409 Habermas, Vol. I, 773.
410 Hans Blumenberg, *The Legitimacy of the Modern Age*, trans. Robert M. Wallace (Cambridge, MA: MIT Press, 1983), ET of the extended and reworked new editions of *Die Legitimität der Neuzeit* (Frankfurt: Suhrkamp, 1973, 1974, 1976).

derstanding unified by belief in an omnipotent God, is a welcome counterposition to the theories of decline he has analysed before: Carl Schmitt, Leo Strauss, Karl Löwith, and Martin Heidegger.[411] In different ways, for each of them the modern age constitutes a turn away from a meaningful ontological, religious, social or legal order and the loss of a comprehensive horizon for human existence and agency.

A genealogy of postmetaphysical thinking, by contrast, is interested in the steps of learning, the successful transformations and institutional innovations. To identify also what is endangered through the processes of modernisation requires a different perspective than one of decline. The "circular" nature of "therapy proposals" from the guiding premise of loss is evident for Habermas, as is a crucial question that is not asked in these evaluations: why developments which they regard as the "causes of the crisis count as achievements".[412] The obvious difference between the outlooks of the two epochs calls for a different response than denying the validity of the new era: a reconstruction of the paths of formation and of the points of origin of principal divergences in subsequent trajectories, so that shifts of focus and the marginalisation of previous questions can be identified. Only then can any specific dynamics with their one-sided consequences be counteracted by the means available to agents in Modernity. In this project, Blumenberg's challenge to those denying the "legitimacy of the modern age" is an important precedent. Yet one can read two remarks as qualifying its place in Habermas's framework: the goal is to provide a "working through by way of remembrance of one's own process of formation (erinnernde *Aufarbeitung des eigenen Bildungsprozesses*)", based on the insight that "even as overcome, one's own past remains a fact full of impact (*prägendes Faktum*) for the present". The aim, therefore, is not marked by a rejection but by elucidating "learning processes which justify themselves, so-to-speak, immanently".[413] Secondly, it is not about "questions of power but of truth (*nicht Machtfragen, sondern Wahrheitsfragen*)".[414] I take this as a clarification that the issues at stake cannot be resolved by a polemic conducted in a situation where a worldview, held to be dominating, needs to be rectified, but only by analytical and comparative enquiries. Thus, it remains possible to identify foundations of Modernity laid in the Middle Ages, and to allow for cultural factors that contributed to its development other than a revolt against the arbitrariness of the absolute power of the Nomi-

---

411 Habermas, Vol. I, 40–63, concluding comparison before turning to Blumenberg, 63–64.
412 Habermas, Vol. I, 64.
413 Habermas, Vol. I, 67. Failing to pursue these contingent turns, may itself lead to a "pathological" relationship to previous periods of self-understanding.
414 Habermas, Vol. I, 67.

nalist God which is key for Blumenberg. I shall reconstruct his thesis and aspects of its long history of reception and critique in five steps: the sequence of epochs as exhibiting a pattern of functional "reoccupation" (*Umbesetzung*) (7.1.1); the Modern Age as a counter-proposal to an unbearable positioning of the human person by medieval theology (7.1.2); his choice of the thread for reconstructing the history of thought from Antiquity to medieval Christianity, namely evil and the problem of theodicy (7.1.3); its questioning by the systematic theologian Wolfhart Pannenberg from his previous examinations of patristic sources and Duns Scotus (7.1.4), followed by a further theological specification of Christian themes that can be recognised as connections and sources for Modernity (7.1.5). Informed by this significant controversy on factors operative in ushering in the new era, Kant's anthropological turn and outline of practical reason, as well as Habermas's assessment of them will be treated in the subsequent sections.

7.1.1 Epochs distinguished by "reoccupations"

Part of Blumenberg's argument for the independent standing of the Modern Era is a methodological point. It is a critique of substantialist premises in judging the beginnings of new cultural periods that is endorsed by Habermas: the "assumed continuity of so-called 'anthropological' basic issues is as questionable as the continuity of answers he rejects".[415] For Blumenberg, it is an important component of countering an understanding of "secularisation" that leads to a rejection of Modernity in its alleged failure to uphold its own intellectual sources. Only if these are regarded as substantial entities, can a claim be posited that they are being negated through the dismissal of premodern thinking. If, however, they are made up by a different type of sequence, the objection loses its foundation. Blumenberg's proposal is to assume a "reoccupation" of positions vacated, left behind by subsequent eras. Thus, it is a significant task of enquiry how a new era faces up to problems that are not its own but that have in some way been inherited: "The continuity of history across the epochal threshold lies not in the permanence of ideal substances but rather in the inheritance of problems, which obliges the heir, in his turn, to know again what was known before".[416] He emphasises the valour of a Modern Age burdened with the pressure to provide a system of world explanation that would be able to encompass these earlier, and in his view, overblown answers. The maximally extended promises of

---

415 Habermas, Vol. I, 66.
416 Blumenberg, *The Legitimacy of the Modern Age*, 48.

meaning proclaimed by Christianity provided a negative starting point since it was impossible to match the answers previously given:

> Modern reason, in the form of philosophy, accepted the challenge of the questions, both the great and the all too great, that were bequeathed to it [...] The pretension of an absolute new beginning suffers from an appearance of illegitimacy on account of the continuity that derives from its inability to shake off inherited questions. The modern age accepted problems as set for it that the Middle Ages had posed and supposedly answered but that had only been posed precisely because people thought they already possessed the "answers". The subsequent epoch [...] cannot simply discharge the unanswered balance of its inherited questions with the admission that it is not a match for them.[417]

At the same time, Blumenberg uncovers the conception of God in the Nominalist framework as a self-inflicted undermining of earlier understandings by isolating the attribute of omnipotence. The resulting extreme position showed how the trust previously invested was undeserved; it called for a complete resetting of foundations. The aim of this change was to safeguard the human subject through "self-assertion" (*Selbstbehauptung*), and to radically reduce the scope of problems to be answered by cutting out those requiring more than human means. The way forward is to "destroy the question itself critically and to undertake amputations on the system of world explanation".[418] The costly "detour" made in the history of human self-understanding through faith in salvation amassed a "volume of expectations and claims – unsatisfied, disappointed and made insistent".[419]

Thus, the sequence from the Middle Ages to Modernity cannot be defined as the latter secularising the earlier eschatological expectations, separating them from their source, namely faith in God; rather, it consists in the legacy of positions that have become vacant and are then reoccupied with less overtaxing assumptions. What are such questions which now reveal themselves as having been too ambitious, needing to be reset to a human scale, and what triggered this new perception?

7.1.2 Modernity as a counterproposal to late medieval theocentrism

One outreach that later appears as simply exorbitant is towards the totality of history. Here an instructive contrast can be noted between Blumenberg's assess-

---

[417] Blumenberg, *The Legitimacy of the Modern Age*, 48.
[418] Blumenberg, *The Legitimacy of the Modern Age*, 66.
[419] Blumenberg, *The Legitimacy of the Modern Age*, 48. 115.

ment of antique philosophical premises in which the cosmos is seen as a reassuring order, and the monotheistic expectation of a Last Judgement. Greek Antiquity's pre-given set of cosmic laws could equally have been judged as being at odds with the realisation of human freedom, rather than as a supportive framework. But for Blumenberg, the human need for a reliable set of conditions is the key aspect. In contrast to such dependable laws, the version of late medieval theocentrism he focuses on is portrayed as a threat. Against the reading of Modernity as "secularisation", he argues that "in any case it would be not secularisation of eschatology but rather secularisation by eschatology".[420] Instead of finding themselves exposed to a God of unlimited power, it was preferable for humans to assert themselves by deconstructing the question. The idea of relating to history as a whole is one of the elements which needed to be taken down to proportions that could be dealt with by human beings on their own.

The reason for no longer setting trust in God lies in becoming aware of the "incidentalness of man in God's dealing with and for Himself". It "eliminated everything that supported the idea that God's creation of man committed Him, in regard to His incarnation, to the choice of human nature as the medium of His appearance in the world", replacing the link between creation and incarnation with "the standard formula of voluntarism, that He could have adopted any other nature and that He adopted this one only because it suited His pure will".[421] The final point reflects the correction of the Scotist position by Ockham: due to God's absolute power, the incarnation could have taken place in any shape; the explanation given by Scotus for God's incarnation in a human person, as wishing to share the life of the human counterparts, is not a valid answer for Ockham. By radicalising the idea of God's limitless freedom also in this regard, Ockham offers a position that Blumenberg interprets as downgrading the worth of human life which had been elevated in the previous history of interpretation of the incarnation.

The more encompassing objection is that already creation was only an exercise in self-interest for God. This pulls the foundations from under the edifice of the Christian faith in God as creator and redeemer. The question also to Scotus's undeniably theocentric approach thus is: does it betray nothing but divine self-interest and a total lack of concern for the creature? Or is God's independence the condition for the freedom to relate? Is a theocentric approach even necessary if the point of the relationship to humans is to create them as fellow lovers? Blumenberg interprets the new insistence on the freedom instead of the wisdom of

---

420 Blumenberg, *The Legitimacy of the Modern Age*, 45.
421 Blumenberg, *The Legitimacy of the Modern Age*, 176–177, and 613, n. 52.

God (as in Aquinas's teleological system) as the attribute of a self-centred God who is no longer bound by the structures instituted at creation. As Wolfhart Pannenberg sums up his argument: "Man had to face the unacceptable arbitrary nature of God – salvation lost its allure. There was little keeping man tied to the church and its absolutist theology. Resulting from this, man began thinking more in terms of science and nature, allowing the progression of a more secular form of thinking which led to the dawn of the modern age."[422]

What is the guiding paradigm for this defence of Modernity as a formation in its own right, offering such a plausible explanation of key motifs for the modern turn to self-assertion? The background for this reconstruction is the thesis that an unresolved problem of an earlier constellation has reappeared in Augustine and in Nominalism: the duality of a bad God of creation and a good God of redemption, as put forward by Gnosticism in the period of Early Christianity.

7.1.3 The problems of evil and of theodicy as the main thread of reconstruction

By including the turn to Nominalism into a much more extended interpretation of the European history of thought, Blumenberg is able to exemplify on the one hand his theory of "reoccupation". Different functional solutions, viewed on the canvas of the problem of evil, replace each other. A problem is seen to resurge that was posed with the late Augustine's theology of history. The summary offered by Pannenberg quoted in the previous subsection begins with the statement: "This absolute assertion of Augustinian predestination is what finally sparked the flame of self-assertion in the late medieval thinkers", before expanding on the "unacceptable arbitrary nature of God".[423] Augustine is classified as offering a solution that will turn out to be a failure since it repeats at the level of God's eschatological judgement on the human creatures' use of their freedom the divisiveness which Gnosticism situates at creation.

In the fifth chapter entitled, "Making History So As to Exonerate God?",[424] the driving motif of Augustine's late work is uncovered as the desire to separate God from any responsibility for the existence of evil in the world. Against the Gnostic answer of positing two equally strong principles, a good and an evil

---

[422] Pannenberg, "Christianity as the Legitimacy of the Modern Age: Thoughts on a Book by Hans Blumenberg" (1968), in Pannenberg, *The Idea of God and Human Freedom*, trans. R. A. Wilson (Philadelphia: Westminster Press, 1973): 178–191, 183.
[423] Pannenberg, "Christianity", 183.
[424] Blumenberg, *The Legitimacy of the Modern Age*, 53.

7.1 Modernity as grounded in, or as a revolt against, the late Middle Ages? — 163

God, the Bishop of Hippo seeks to exonerate God by attributing evil in all its forms (with the Latin term *malum* collapsing the difference between evil events caused by nature and by the human will)[425] to the human creature. Blumenberg notes correctly that this attempt to exonerate God must fail since the blame falls back on the almighty God of creation. The second attempt occurs with late medieval theology, all subsumed under the term "Nominalism", which emphasises God's absolute power to such a degree of detachment that humans feel cast out from their previous position – biblical, patristic and scholastic – of having been created and redeemed for their own sake. Part of the late medieval thinkers' response is to mount inductive enquiries into nature, establishing truth by their own means. It contributed to the liberation from the bind humans had been put into in the fifth century of being robbed of their agency but nonetheless regarded as guilty:

> the function of a theodicy [...] operates with the argument that man is responsible for all that is bad in the world. According to the exemplary conception developed by Augustine, the physical defects of the created world are simply the just penalties of the evil that proceeded from human freedom. The inevitability of this train of thought in Augustine's actual situation lay in the fact that it made it possible for him to avoid the Gnostic dualism of good and evil world principles. To be sure, the converted Gnostic had to provide an equivalent for the cosmic principle of evil in the bosom of mankind itself. He found it in inherited sinfulness (*Sündigkeit*), as a quantity of corruption (*Verderbnis*) that is constant rather than being the result of the summation of individual faulty actions.[426]

One can regard Blumenberg as confirming the connection detected by theologians in Chapter Five between an anthropology of inescapable, inherited sinfulness which humans can only act out, and predestination – unlikely good acts must stem from God's election enabling these chosen agents. He critically pinpoints the "transition from a general proposition about the teleology of the world for man's benefit to the restricted assertion of its functioning for the benefit of those who are predestined for salvation".[427] Taking predestination as a mainstream position – instead of comparing it to earlier patristic and contempo-

---

425 Cf. Blumenberg, *The Legitimacy of the Modern Age*, 136. Part II, entitled, "Theological Absolutism and Human Self-Assertion" (123) begins with Chapter 1, "The Failure of the First Attempt at Warding Off Gnosticism Ensures its Return" (127). It opens with the statement: "The problem left unsolved by the ancient world was the question of the origin of what is bad in the world". In his Translator's Note, R. Wallace specifies regarding "*Übel*", "evil" or "badness" that "Augustine's term, *malum*, does not prejudge the answer as our terminology (no doubt largely owing to his influence) does" (136).
426 Blumenberg, *The Legitimacy of the Modern Age*, 53.
427 Blumenberg, *The Legitimacy of the Modern Age*, 171–172.

rary theologians like Ambrose and counterparts like Pelagius or Julian of Eclanum – the German philosopher's critique targets the new contradictions emerging from this answer to Gnosticism: it merely manages to shift the cause of evil, thereby paralysing the human agent from the depth of her being. It is only the Modern Age that succeeds in overcoming the Gnostic dualism by freeing the human person to cultivate an affirmative relationship to the world and to engage in its transformation through action. As the theologian Peter Behrenberg observes in his study of Blumenberg's critique of theology, "falling back into dualistic formulas of God and world" constitutes "the most excessive realisation of the failure to take on responsibility for the world [...] The reoccupation of inherited questions in the Modern Era makes it possible for humans to enter into a positive world relationship, and to take on a responsibility of their own."[428]

Which elements of the sequence of responses since Late Antiquity constructed in this way does Pannenberg take up in his review of different uses of "secularisation", backed by his prior detailed research into exchanges between philosophy and theology in the early patristic and the late scholastic eras?

7.1.4 Incarnation as the guideline: Wolfhart Pannenberg's theological response

From his theological background as one of the initiators of the "Revelation as History" movement which questioned the reduction of the Christian message to the individualist terms of existential appropriation, Pannenberg shares the interest in reconstructing the major steps of the interaction of philosophy with monotheism in European thinking. Yet he problematises the selection of the guiding theme, the problem of evil, which sidelines motifs that can be regarded as equally definitive: the incarnation of God, and the promise of reconciliation, constituting the framework in which such issues arose: "the question of theodicy never had such a simple significance for the history of Christian theology".[429] The reason for this is that Christian belief in the incarnation spelt out God's willingness to take on the burden of evil and suffering in the world and to provide rescue and restoration.

In his article published two years after the first appearance of *The Legitimacy of the Modern Age*, he proposes re-evaluations from two sides: from the history of

---

[428] Peter Behrenberg, *Endliche Unsterblichkeit. Studien zur Theologiekritik Hans Blumenbergs* (Würzburg: Königshausen & Neumann, 1994), 61.
[429] Pannenberg, "Christianity", 183.

Christian thinking, especially regarding the late medieval authors interpreted by Blumenberg, and from a general historical consideration of key factors promoting the turn to new eras, such as the role of the Reformation against an absolutist church government. Pannenberg disputes summarising statements which attribute to medieval theology as such specific authors' positions that were, moreover, not carried but rejected. An example of this is the idea that humans were only replacements for the fallen angels – which for Blumenberg illustrates the growing distance from conceiving the world as having been created for humans to enjoy and care for. Pannenberg clarifies that this conception of Anselm's was not accepted but refuted by the position which came to be widely shared in the twelfth century – that humans are not subordinate to angels.[430] A further important inaccuracy is identified regarding the reasons for electing or rejecting human agents: Duns Scotus is portrayed as promoting the concept of an arbitrary God who "undeservedly rejects" individuals despite his specification that it depended on divine foreknowledge of their evil acts whether they were rejected.[431]

In spite of the erudition shown by Blumenberg, the positions ascribed sweepingly to the whole era, and especially the lack of distinction between the argumentations of Scotus and Ockham, give cause for doubting the accuracy of his reconstructions. Overarching conclusions are drawn from quotes that are not related to their contexts, failing to note the actual direction taken which can be diametrically opposed to his verdicts. It is not clear, for example, how to reconcile Scotus's actual proposals with a summary like this:

> the theological absolutism of the declining Middle Ages (*ausgehenden Mittelalters*) can be characterized as the extreme of taking from ourselves, as a self-divestiture of all pregiven guarantees of a privileged position, established at Creation, in the "order" of reality. For this loss of order there could no longer be the escape and the solution of late-antique distance from the world. But man's negation of even the last physical and metaphysical "assurances" of his role in the world, in favour of the logic of the 'maximal God' allows the question of the minimum potential of his self-assertion – of the minimum of a potential that had remained unquestioned in the late-antique involvement in the cosmos (*Kosmos-Implikation*) to pose itself now in its full rigor.[432]

Does the divine self-limiting of *potentia Dei absoluta* to the predictability of a *potentia ordinata* not count? Does the establishment of a univocal concept of truth as valid also for theology not indicate an anti-absolutist path? Is the reason for

---

430 Cf. Pannenberg, "Christianity", 186.
431 Cf. Pannenberg, "Christianity", 187.
432 Blumenberg, *The Legitimacy of the Modern Age*, 178.

creation, to have *alios condiligentes*, not the opposite of "divesting" these intended fellow lovers of their "privileged" position? It is true that God renounces to "pregiven guarantees" in the opening up of a history of free encounters and conflicts, but this exactly precludes the interpretation of quotes taken out of context as "prohibiting questions".[433] A serious equivocation is not spotted: the context-dependent use of the concept of "predestination". In his subsequent reference to Scotus when treating Nicholas of Cusa, Blumenberg employs this term not in the Augustinian sense but in line with Scotus's supralapsarian position regarding the divine decree of incarnation as independent of human sin:

> To represent the Incarnation as the inner consequence of the Creation, to lead the eternal predestination of the Son of God to become man, of which Duns Scotus had already spoken, out of the voluntarism of the concept of predestination and to bring it nearer to human comprehension by means of a rational deduction, is the program of the first four chapters of *Docta ignorantia*.[434]

These are clearly two different references of "predestination": the Augustinian meaning of election or damnation in the context of human sin that is deemed

---

433 In *The Legitimacy of the Modern Age*, 171, Blumenberg bases the following judgement on a quote from Scotus, referenced as *Sentenzenkommentar* without specification of the version, I distinctio 8 quaestio 5: "*quare voluntas voluit hoc, nulla est causa, nisi quia voluntas est voluntas*" (n. 49 ET; German edn. 194, Fn. 73): "since the will wills this, there is no reason except that the will is the will". He interprets this characterisation of the underivable status of the will, although it is also stated in relation to the human faculty, as a prohibition of questions: "Finally, the formula that the Creator had done His work for no other purpose than to demonstrate His power omitted man entirely from the determination of the world's meaning (*ließ den Menschen aus der Bestimmung des Weltsinnes ganz herausfallen*) and approached the voluntaristic formulas that closed the sequence of development, formulas whose function was not to answer but to reject the question." He concludes: "The world as the pure performance of reified omnipotence, as a demonstration of the unlimited sovereignty of a will to which no questions can be addressed – this eradication even of the right to perceive a problem meant that, at least for man, the world no longer possessed an accessible order." Other scholars, such as Axel Schmidt, read the quote as establishing the will as a principle which, since it is "first and immediate, cannot be traced back to anything else [...] an underivable reason for action (*Handlungsgrund*) is effective which simply escapes (*schlechthin entzogen*) causal explanation due to its contrast (*Gegensatzes*) to principles of nature." In "Der Denkansatz des Johannes Duns Scotus", in *Duns-Scotus-Lesebuch*, Vol. 26, ed. by Herbert Schneider, Marianne Schlosser and Paul Zahner (Mönchengladbach: B. Kühlen Verlag, 2008): 39–81, 68, Axel Schmidt locates the quote in the final stage of the Lectures on the Sentences of Petrus Lombardus in *Ordinatio*. I d. 8 p. 2 q. un. n. 299 (Vat. IV 324f) and adds that "Scotus argues in the same way for the human will: *Met* IX q. 15 n. 24 (OP IV 681)" (*Quaestiones super libros Metaphysicorum Aristotelis*. ed. G. Etzkorn et al., *Opera Philosophica* III–IV).
434 Blumenberg, *The Legitimacy of the Modern Age*, 543.

both an unavoidable fate and a personal deed – fitting Blumenberg's and Augustine's interest in theodicy – and its use relating to Christ in Scotus's theology of "absolute incarnation". The term "voluntarism" is used without differentiation.[435] He adds a comment that recognises the momentous change effected by the Christian belief in the incarnation: "Christian theology also contains, in the form of the God Who became man, a potential for human assurance, to realize which – if one finds the late attempt of the Cusan instructive – would have been its noblest endeavour."[436] A breakthrough role could have been ascribed not only to Nicholas of Cusa, but already to Duns Scotus. He cannot be counted as a continuation of Augustine, but as offering a point of departure that is the polar opposite to his. It opens the door to an understanding of freedom as the foundation of the human response to the Creator whose absolute freedom is channelled into a *potentia ordinata* on which God's human counterparts can set their trust.

7.1.5 Ongoing theological questions and answers relevant for Modernity

That the Modern Age has an independent, underived legitimacy of its own is a conclusion shared by Habermas. In keeping with the genealogical perspective of the Axial Age thesis, his interest is as much in precursors as in obstacles to the project pursued in Modernity, a theoretically and practically "postmetaphysical" approach. Therefore, the continuities from the Middle Ages onwards are identified with a clear eye for its character as a laboratory of future trajectories worked out in assiduous exchanges with other intellectual streams, reflecting unprecedented political and religious, economic and societal developments. No longer required to defend the validity of the Modern Age, Habermas's approach leads to a different type of assessment that is measured rather than po-

---

435 As Behrenberg observes in *Endliche Unsterblichkeit*, 71, "theodicy" acquires an equally loaded and "stylised" meaning as the "complex of voluntarism" does.
436 Blumenberg, *The Legitimacy of the Modern Age*, 177. He goes on (177–178), however, in a way that seems to underrate the Christian understanding of the incarnation as the revelation of God's being as love by the human person of Jesus: "Here there was a barrier: The assiduous labor on both the image and the unimaginability (*Bildlosigkeit*) of the divinity seemed to be capable of success only at the expense of this human substance. The basic conflict that was never admitted, perhaps was never perceived, but was latent in the Middle Ages was unsparingly articulated by Ludwig Feuerbach as the antinomy between theology and Christology [...] The medieval system ended in such a phase of objectivization that has become autonomous, of hardening that is insulated from what is human. What is here called 'self-assertion' (*Selbstbehauptung*) is the countermove of retrieving the lost motives, of new concentration on man's self-interest."

lemical, and multifactorial rather than focused on analysing the dwindling power of a specific narrative of an illegitimate "secularisation".

At this juncture of two eras in the reception of Christian monotheism, it is important to sum up open questions directed at Blumenberg's project and indicate ongoing issues, some of which Kant will take up in his foundation of the new era on the concept of "autonomy". Questions regarding a historical verification of the claimed reoccupations were put to Blumenberg also by philosophical colleagues. From the history of philosophy, Wolfgang Hübener pointed out the lack of a connection between Ockham's critique of universals and theological voluntarism.[437] This objection is also relevant for Duns Scotus whose theory of truth was realist, not nominalist; yet he reasserted the biblical emphasis on God's will from his Franciscan starting point, with God's "love" as the supreme attribute, subordinating, as mentioned, the divine "wisdom" favoured by the Dominican theologians. Also the downplaying of other factors, including the Reformation, is noted, as did Pannenberg in his response of 1968. From the perspective of Political Theology, Johann Baptist Metz agrees with parts of Blumenberg's critique but objects to encompassing the "saviour (*soter*) of the biblical traditions" under Augustine's individualising concern with sin. The "*soter*" is

> thought as "redeemer" but no longer as "rescuer". The component of universal justice, of rescue (*Rettung*) from unjust suffering, also from unatoned (*ungesühnten*) past suffering is lost in favour of redemption from sin. The biblical vision, the promise of rescue contained in the biblical name for God (*soter*) [...] also relates to being rescued from abysmal human situations of suffering. Augustine replaces the question for God led by the hunger and thirst for justice, that is, the eschatological question about God's justice with the anthropocentric question about human sin. The theodicy question is thereby immobilised (*stillgestellt*) [...] This has had two fatal consequences. a) Theology no longer allowed humans to put questions to God [...] b) The indirect result of the Augustinian paradigm was an extreme exaggeration (*Übersteigerung*) of the idea of guilt, a hamartiological overtaxing of humans that one could call with a formulation close to Blumenberg the absolutism of sin in Christianity [...] the momentous counterreaction was that being capable of guilt counted increasingly

---

437 In *Endliche Unsterblichkeit*, 62, Behrenberg quotes Hübener's critique of the "legend of Nominalism" with the "fiction (*Fabel*) of a '*deus mutabilissimus*' of Nominalism" as an "ingenious invention of Blumenberg's [...] A specific closeness of the core complex of Nominalist theory – namely the doctrine of universals – to early bourgeois social revolutionary efforts and to an excessive theological voluntarism remains unproven (*unerwiesen*), in my view, as long as the assumption is not refuted that they could have equally linked up with a different doctrine of universals." Wolfgang Hübener, "Die Nominalismus-Legende. Über das Missverhältnis zwischen Dichtung und Wahrheit in der Deutung der Wirkungsgeschichte des Ockhamismus", in *Spiegel und Gleichnis. Festschrift für Jacob Taubes*, ed. Norbert W. Bolz and Wolfgang Hübener (Würzburg: Königshausen und Neumann, 1983): 87–111, 105.

less as a distinction (*Auszeichung*), as the dignity of freedom itself, a view that would have been in deep correspondence with biblical anthropology.[438]

Thus, in Metz's analysis, it is necessary to scrutinise and evaluate problematic innovations within the history of Christian thinking and measure them by the standard of the original message they are meant to rearticulate in new eras. Being capable of accepting one's imputability for concrete deeds is distinct from Augustine's attribution of a generic "original sin" to each individual as their own fault. The encompassing question is about a God who rescues in a history marked by human suffering, injustice and violence. Refocusing the theodicy problem in this way leads to the question of criteria for assessing the "reoccupations": in function of which views of human life and history are they judged? A "substantialist", objectifying perspective may have been abandoned for a view that takes the role of human consciousness and practical self-understanding into account. Yet, it remains necessary to evaluate the new candidates that have filled the vacancies.[439] The authors of Modernity must be examined for their sensitivity to such issues. In earlier publications, Habermas had replaced the question about the totality of history with a more limited horizon: the whole of the lifeworld. How will the problem of meaning that becomes more acute for a subjectivity unsupported by teleological conceptions be addressed after the anthropological turn?

7.2 The anthropological turn achieved through Kant's transcendental method

Habermas attributes a decisive role to Duns Scotus for breakthroughs in theoretical and practical reason. As we have seen, he credits him with an "epistemologically transformed point of view" that accesses God no longer through "ontolog-

---

[438] Cf. Johann Baptist Metz, "Plädoyer für mehr Theodizee-Empfindlichkeit in der Theologie", in *Worüber man nicht schweigen kann. Neue Diskussionen zur Theodizeefrage*, ed. Willi Oelmüller (München: Wilhelm Fink Verlag, 1992) 107–160, 133–134.
[439] In *Endliche Unsterblichkeit* , 71–72, with reference to Blumenberg's *St Matthew Passion*, trans. Helmut Müller-Sievers and Paul Fleming (Ithaca, NY: Cornell University Press, 2021, German original 1988), Behrenberg points out how Blumenberg evokes the human vulnerability that arises from finitude and mortality marked by the "concern (*Sorge*) not to experience enough empathy (*Anteilnahme*) as a being that is in need of consolation *(trostbedürftiges Wesen)*. The concentration of the human person on himself and the will not to fall into oblivion through consolation is for Blumenberg the decisive 'reoccupation' of theodicy."

ical statements about God as the 'First Being'" but through "transcendental statements about the 'First Known'."[440] Similarly, the Aristotelian tie of practical reason to a natural teleology is replaced with a different understanding of ethics:

> Only Duns Scotus disconnects natural law from the metaphysical justification within a hierarchy of "naturally wanted (*gewollt*) goods". He anchors the natural law principle to do good [...] without the mediation of basic needs of human nature – in the absolute commandment of love to God and to the neighbour. But it has the character of a law [...] to code all alternatives for action in a binary way as good or evil in light of this divine law translated into the idiom of natural reason. This will is challenged (*zugemutet*) to bind itself to what has been *grasped as normatively binding*. With this idea of self-binding to a general norm Duns Scotus removes natural law from the context of a natural teleology and thus steps onto the path that will lead to Kant's deontological ethics.[441]

By changing theology as a whole into a practical discipline, also this part of Scotus's programmatic innovation is a precursor to Kant's priority of practical reason. What must be examined first, however, is the departure from substance ontological terms, based on theological sources of change in philosophical thinking. In this shift, the meaning and relevance of the transcendental method is contested. Habermas regards it as needing replacement itself, in view of the paradoxes he identifies in the "philosophy of consciousness" (7.2.1). Secondly, he traces the Kantian distinction of a transcendental from an empirical level back to the theological doctrine of the two kingdoms. The question to him will be whether Kant's method cannot stand on its own, on a philosophical foundation that is independent of a religious tradition (7.2.2).

7.2.1 Breaking with substance ontology: Theological factors, and a new method

While recognising the late Middle Ages as providing the decisive shifts that lead towards postmetaphysical thinking, Habermas also reaches back further to changes of focus that begin with Paul and Augustine. In view of Blumenberg's critiques of Augustinian and Nominalist theologies, the driving motifs identified need to be scrutinised. Following this, the transcendental method that carries Kant's analysis of the power and the limits of reason will be examined in relation to Habermas's objections.

---

440 Habermas, Vol. I, 766.
441 Habermas, Vol. II, 85.

7.2 The anthropological turn achieved through Kant's transcendental method — 171

In an overview of new accentuations and priorities that shaped the subsequent course of philosophical thinking, Habermas specifies "four new perspectives and weightings since Augustine": the "disclosing (*Erschließung*) of subjectivity from the viewpoint of the soul struggling for its salvation" as the "most important innovation"; "freedom of the will" spelled out from the "radicalisation of the Pauline doctrine of grace"; "God intervening into history and the history of salvation"; and "the Last Judgement".[442] What is remarkable about their elucidation is that they are not only portrayed as disrupting several givens of antique thought (such a cyclical understanding of nature) but also as ultimately – at least through the controversies they caused – as leading to the modern concept of freedom. In some instances, however, typical features of biblical monotheism that the early patristic authors seized upon in their dispute with Gnosticism are attributed to their counterpart, Augustine, who in effect contravened their theological anthropologies, doctrines of God and eschatologies. Against the straight line drawn by Habermas from Augustine to Scotus and the Reformation, it must be recalled that the eminent history of reception he has had in theology and in Christian religious practices included only an attenuated version of his view of salvation as granted only to the few. It offered a vision of divinely created humanity and its destiny that is, as also Habermas states, marked by "anthropological pessimism".[443] Both for the sake of a genealogy, and from a normative theological perspective assessing the antithetical swings between different eras and authors in spelling out the essence of Christianity, it is important to distinguish between directions: mainstream developments, counter-movements, challenges, rejections, alternatives, and also dead ends.

The "individuating power of personal responsibility in front of God" which Habermas identifies perceptively can indeed be regarded as a key biblical inheritance. From Adam and Eve to Cain, Abraham, Moses, and the prophets, Job, Mary, to the calling of unlikely individuals as disciples – multiple stories focus on how the persons addressed react in different ways to God or Jesus. Regarding this "individuating power", Augustine is interpreted in key terms of communicative rationality, such as the ability to see oneself from the other's perspective:

> Subjectivity becomes the scene of a scrupulous self-investigation of the Ego as a counterpart seeking a response from an invisible power on whose inscrutable (*undurchschaubar*) decree the motivating aim (*Worumwillen*) of one's own life depends [...] taking over the perspective that a counterpart, a second person directs towards me as a first person. Three Christian themes of Augustine's – freedom of the will and predestination, temporal expe-

---

442 Habermas, Vol. II, 194–197.
443 Habermas, Vol. I, 569.

rience and history of salvation as well as the individuating power of personal responsibility in front of God have had a sustained (*nachhaltig*) significance for the development of practical philosophy.[444]

It must be asked, however, if this characterisation of God's "inscrutable decree" that can be accurately applied to Augustine's late doctrine of predestination, should be extended to subsequent theological approaches. We have already seen how Anselm's option for "*satisfactio*" provides a reasoned alternative to damnation. Pannenberg critiqued Blumenberg for wrongly including Duns Scotus under the position of an "intransparent decree" which condemns the individual without regard for their actual life. It must be asked, too, if "personal responsibility" is at all possible when the constraint to sin is expressed as "*non posse non peccare*", abolishing the difference between actual uses of human freedom and its generic capability for good as well as for evil.[445] This doubt also affects the view that freedom of the will can be derived from the Pauline doctrine of grace. As discussed before, the capability for agency which the Gospels emphasise in their narratives of responses to Jesus is subsumed into a mystical experience of being "in Christ" and into Paul's antithesis of grace and "law" for all religious and social practice.

While it is true that the analysis of temporality in an internal enquiry into subjectivity is a decisive breakthrough achieved by Augustine,[446] it would be more accurate to credit his predecessors, such as Irenaeus and Origen, with the concepts of a history of salvation and of freedom. From the perspective of a theory of agency implied in the idea of responsibility, a direct connection to Augustine could only be made at the price of an equivocation. The reason for seeking the solution in divine predestination to heaven or hell is because humans, while still being deemed blameworthy for sin, are not attributed the power to act of their own volition. A theological judgement quoted before on the space left for the course of human history must be recalled: it was diagnosed as being over before it could really begin, with the one single human individual able to act being Adam, and with his Fall destroying this capability for all sub-

---

444 Habermas, Vol. II, 194.
445 In *The Legitimacy of the Modern Age*, 53, Blumenberg does not see a continuity but a reversal of Augustine's innovation, an inherited original sin, by Kant: "While this sinfulness is inherited, it is at the same time a disposition to increase the actual evil and thus continually to reduce the chances of the good being realized – a negative concept of progress that Kant would be the first to reverse." He adds (54): "The idea of progress, as was to become evident much later on, requires a reversal of the causal relation between moral and physical evils; it is founded on the assumption that in a better world it would be easier to be a better person."
446 Habermas, Vol. I, 577–579.

sequent humans created in the image of God.⁴⁴⁷ The problem of the level at which the human will is treated by Paul and Augustine will be returned to in the following subsection on practical reason.

What Kant distinguishes as two standpoints, the intelligible and the empirical, could be derived from the idea of the inner person, already promoted by early patristic theologians. Habermas, however, traces the connection to this distinction devised in the *Critique of Pure Reason* back to an ecclesiological-political theme: to the much-analysed Augustinian "distinction between *civitas divina* and *civitas terrena*" which was received by Luther. "In this version that was converted (*umgestellt*) to the interiority of the believer and that accommodated (*entgegenkommend*) the subject philosophical terminology, it gave the impetus (*Anstoß*) to Kant's momentous transcendental delimitation (*Abgrenzung*) of the realm of the intelligible from the reign (*Reich*) of appearances."⁴⁴⁸ Yet does this critical distinction of Kant's need a religious origin? Or can it be found in Plato and in the univocal use of concepts by Scotus who assumes two levels, one transcendental, the other empirical? This question relevant for the relationship between "knowledge" and "faith" needs to be investigated next.

7.2.2 Reconceiving theoretical reason based on philosophical or theological distinctions?

The critical enquiry into the power and the limits of reason that resulted in the "Copernican turn" employed a method which Kant called "transcendental". It is decisive also for theology's anthropological turn, as the treatment of Schleiermacher's groundbreaking re-conception of a dogmatics under modern conditions in the following chapter will show. Not reducible to psychological experience, the analysis of self-consciousness in the second edition of the *Glaubenslehre* claims the status of a necessary philosophical insight, as ²§4.1 states.⁴⁴⁹ For Habermas, however, it is a contested method, and it is part of

---

447 Pröpper, *Theologische Anthropologie*, 1023, cf. above, Chapter 5.5.3.
448 Habermas, Vol. II, 196–197.
449 Friedrich D. E. Schleiermacher, *Christian Faith – A New Translation and Critical Edition*, trans. Terrence N. Tice, Catherine L. Kelsey and Edwina Lawler; ed. Catherine L. Kelsey and Terrence N. Tice (Louisville, KY: Westminster John Knox Press, 2016, 2 vols.), Vol. I, 20: "Assent to these statements can be expected without qualification. No one would gainsay them, moreover, who is capable of self-observation to any degree and who can deem the distinctive object of our investigations to be of interest." Cf. *The Christian Faith*, trans. H.R. Mackintosh and J.S. Stewart (Edinburgh: T & T Clark, 1928; 1986), 13: "To these propositions assent can be unconditionally

the reason for his rejection of the "philosophy of consciousness". The question of the justifiability of religious faith is a crucial task at the intersection of faith and reason, on which its "opacity" or "transparency", "exterritorial" or rationally arguable character hinges. Thus, how the transcendental method, the terms used and the sources given are portrayed by the theorist of communicative action will be a decisive turning point for philosophy in its exchange on truth claims with theology.

The terms "introspection", "interiority" as distinct from relating to the world, "subjectivity" and "performative" are used to convey an approach which for Kant requires a distinction of two levels: that of phenomena accessible by the senses, and the "condition of their possibility" – the decisive step back to a faculty that is able to constitute the subject's relationship to the world. For the *Critique of Pure Reason*, this problem of the constitution of objects must be clarified in its possibility at a level prior to actual research processes.[450] As the term, "anthropological turn", indicates, there is no way of making philosophical propositions about the world that does not include the reference back to the speaker. It is a general feature of truth claims in Kant's critical philosophy that they relate to the I of the "original synthetic apperception": "It must be possible for the 'I think' to accompany all my representations".[451]

In Habermas's reconstruction, the Kantian distinction between a priori and empirical elements in the act of knowing is turned into a separation. The consciousness in which this takes place is portrayed as a reduplication that creates unsolvable paradoxes in the thinking person. The fact that Kant carries out his analysis of human consciousness at the level of the individual is a further problem in his assessment since it seems to indicate a "monological" stance. The counterargument to Habermas's introduction of the need for intersubjective validation already at this level is that it does not thematise the conditions of the possibility of objective knowledge. To call for discourse between multiple perspectives here leaves the Cartesian problem unsolved that *res cogitans* and *res extensa* cannot be treated as parallel dimensions. A discourse on concrete truth claims presupposes that the human subject is structurally equipped with

---

demanded; and no one will deny them who is capable of a little introspection (*Selbstbeobachtung*) and can find interest in the real (*eigentlichen*) subject of our present inquiries."

450 Cf. Rudolf Langthaler, *Nachmetaphysisches Denken? Kritische Anfragen an Jürgen Habermas* (Berlin: Duncker & Humblot, 1997), 112–114. His in-depth, intricate and thorough comparison of Kant's argumentations with Habermas's will be drawn on in Chapter Eight in the context of the move to language.

451 Kant, *Critique of Pure Reason*, trans. Norman Kemp Smith (New York: St Martin's Press and Toronto: Macmillan, 1929), 152 (B 132–133).

the means of ascertaining a reality that exists outside of itself: categories and forms of intuition operative in the act of knowing which derives not merely from a passive sense impression but from its conjunction with the subject's own constructive spontaneity. The process enacted is not one of "introspection" at the same level as attention directed to the existing world of objects. Kant's analysis discovers two levels: a priori structures enabling the constitution of the world relation as such, and concrete individual acts of cognition. By assimilating Kant's new method to Luther's position through the term "introspection", Habermas claims a parallel with interior religious affections which turns out to be misleading: a faith commitment, a person's self-reflection in front of God, or "religious experience" are concrete, situated occurrences, while Kant enquires into the general a priori structures of any act of cognition. Thus, the discrepancy between Kant's own account of the elements at work in this process and its evaluation by the discourse ethicist seems unbridgeable. Habermas identifies not only a parallel, but even a relationship of derivation between Luther and Kant on two points:

> By restricting the glance (*Blick*) theologically to the focal point of the event of faith (*Glaubensgeschehens*) in the inner space (*im Inneren*) of a subjectivity which knows itself to be radically separate from the exteriority of the world, two consequences arise [...]
>
> On the one hand, the strict distinction between the attitudes that the believing subject takes to being either *coram Deo* or *coram mundi*, leads to the two-kingdoms-doctrine [...] Its floor plan (*Grundriss*) is mirrored – now, however, in an egocentric way and without the relation to God – in the basic terms of subject philosophy in the counter positions of the sphere of consciousness, accessible by introspection [...], and the world of the objects of representation (*vorstellbar*).[452]

The second point consists in tracing the epistemological distinction between the intelligible and the empirical levels, derived from the two kingdoms doctrine, also into the heightened anthropological antitheses of the late Augustine's position in which the believer anxiously awaits God's final judgement:

> In Augustinian tradition [...], Luther directs attention to the subjectivity of a soul struggling with God about its salvation, describing this event of faith (*Glaubensgeschehen*) from the believer's performative attitude towards God. He thereby dramatises the realm of experience which cannot be grasped from the *epistemological attitude of an observer*, but solely from the *performative attitude of a communicatively acting person*. In the role of a first per-

---

[452] Habermas, Vol. I, 163–164.

son, she relates to the anticipative (*zuvorkommende*) offer of a second person, on whose decision her own salvific destiny depends.⁴⁵³

In conclusion, the categories of the philosophy of consciousness are identified as elements that Kant has taken over from this theological tradition:

> In the framework of the basic concepts of subject philosophy, Kant will be the first to appropriate this reconstructive implementation (*Nachvollzug*) of performative knowledge for the examination of the spontaneous achievements of the knowing, experiencing and acting subject. The point (*Witz*) of transcendental philosophy consists in Kant taking possession (*sich bemächtigt*) of the sphere that Luther thought as intelligible, separated from the world, as that of transcendental consciousness. For Luther everything essential takes place in the interiority of the believer – the interactions with the God of salvation that decide on the weal and woe (*Wohl und Wehe*) of each singular individual. With Kant the legislating activity of reason takes the place of the communication between sinner and saviour.⁴⁵⁴

Thus, Kant's distinction between two levels of reason is put on a par with a division between two comparable territories, world/state and religion/church. While reflection is not identified with inwardness in the sense of a self-observation of the internal objects of one's mind,⁴⁵⁵ it is still traced back to the "performative" experience of the believer in front of God, exemplified by Luther's reconnecting with Augustine. This "performative" dimension could have been found also in the history of effects of other theological works that change into the form of prayer, as in Anselm's *Proslogion*, in Duns Scotus and medieval mysticism. It is possible to make a case for linking the transcendental method to the history of reception of "inner freedom" emphasised in Christian theology from the early Patristic age onwards.⁴⁵⁶ It reactualises the biblical emphasis on

---

453 Habermas, Vol. I, 164.
454 Habermas, Vol. I, 164.
455 In Vol. II, 313, in the context of the "primordial-synthetic unity of apperception" in which the "I" is represented as "an agent, an *inherently acting* (*von Haus aus handelndes*) subject", the following differentiations are made: The "self-ascertaining (*Selbstvergewisserung*) of what it does is not accomplished through introspection, that is, through the fixating (*anstarrenden*) glance of an observer directed to his own intuitions (*Vorstellungen*) as objects, nor through an immersion (*Versenkung*) into the stream of self-evident experiences (*Erlebnisse*) but only through reflexion in the sense of an *explicating reenactment (Nachvollzuges)* of a performance attributed to itself, and insofar already familiar (*vertrauten*)". The prior familiarity of the subject with itself that is alluded to here will play an important role in the interpretation of Schleiermacher's concept of religion as a determination of the "immediate self-consciousness" and will be discussed in the following chapter.
456 Cf. Kobusch, *Selbstwerdung und Personalität*, 76–90.

the will when the voluntarism of Duns Scotus breaks with Aristotelian natural teleology. Linking it, however, as Habermas does, to the Augustinian position of discounting the human will as being radically disabled by original sin amplifies a specific interpretation that seems hard to reconcile with Kant's own starting point, the human capability for self-legislation. And how can the soul's struggle with God on whom her destiny depends in an external judgement not be regarded as falling under his term of "heteronomy"? But the parallel drawn by Habermas does not first of all relate to practical reason. What is being compared and derived from the "performative" mode of this encounter is theoretical reason in its foundational operation. It is depicted as a withdrawal from the world into a realm of interiority. The transcendental level of reflection is portrayed as an express decision to turn away from external tasks to the inner life of the subject. This, however, does not capture Kant's argumentation which distinguishes two levels within the act of cognition. Their separation by Habermas risks rejecting the very innovation on which Modernity in the philosophically critical epistemological sense depends, namely the methodological foundation of its anthropological turn. In view of a better alternative, linguistic intersubjectivity, this method is deemed to be superseded and explained away as originating in a theological heritage.[457] It must now be examined how this reconstruction affects his view of Kant's conception of practical reason. Autonomy is defended, but how is it interpreted?

7.3 Practical reason and the question of meaning

In line with the previous argumentation, Habermas also locates Kant's concept of practical reason in the history of reception of Augustine and Luther (7.3.1). After comparing Kant's argumentation with Habermas's interpretation and critique, the new designation which Kant imaginatively projects for philosophy, beyond its remit as a discipline, will be sketched: namely its "public" role which is realised in its "world concept". How "public" is determined will also be instructive for the following chapter on the "linguistic turn" where it denotes the visible, external manifestation of the constitution of subjects through interaction in the grammatical pronouns of the first, second and third persons. Kant's use of the same term for the "world concept" of philosophy includes the question of mean-

---

[457] In Vol. II, 310, Habermas refers to "intuitions which Kant may have acquired in the course of his religious education in a pietistic environment. They are present to the enlightened philosopher even in his old age, although not *as* religious ones but as the slimmed-down (*abgemagert*) postulates of a reasonable faith (*Vernunftglaubens*)".

ing which is established as a matter of public relevance (7.3.2). Kant's argument for the concept of God as a limit idea and "postulate" arises in consequence of a deontological understanding of ethics which nevertheless acknowledges a justified quest for happiness, on the basis of moral "worthiness". For philosophers and theologians,[458] it has provided a key justification of the ongoing relevance of religious faith for the realisation of practical reason (7.3.3). Finally, Kant's designation of an "ethical commonwealth" as founding a philosophical concept of "church" will be reviewed regarding the link proposed by "*This Too a History of Philosophy*" once again to Augustine (7.3.4).

7.3.1 Finding parallels between the Augustinian heritage and Kant

Having already accessed the transcendental level of Kant's account of theoretical reason from the "performative" attitude of religious interiority addressing God as one's counterpart, Habermas now confirms that the analysis of the presuppositions of cognition has always been oriented towards practical reason: "Since the concept of subjectivity is essentially practical, already theoretical reason is the expression of a transcendentally legislating subjectivity which, so-to-speak, only attains itself as morally-practical reason by binding subjective wilfulness (*Willkür*) to self-given general laws".[459] This connection means that the religious heritage he sees at work also extends to the conception of morality. The line thus established, however, is not direct but marked by deflections and modifications to such a degree that the dependence claimed can at times take the shape of an outright opposition. It is important to pay attention to the relationships indicated when "transformations" are traced, when a religious heritage is "appropriated", or its result is found to be "dialectical".

The context of his interpretation is the comparison with David Hume who stands as the protagonist of the empiricist route which bases morality on psychological feeling and taste. The concluding view offered of the contrasting deonto-

---

[458] The key point is that religion allows the connection of agency to hope. Cf. P. Ricoeur, "Freedom in the Light of Hope" (1968), in *The Conflict of Interpretations*, 402–424, 417–418: "Kant explicitly brings religion to the question: 'What can I hope for?' I do not know any other philosopher who has defined religion exclusively with that question." In her enquiry into the "Doctrine of postulates and moral faith", in Saskia Wendel and Martin Breul, *Vernünftig glauben – begründet hoffen. Praktische Metaphysik als Denkform rationaler Theologie* (Freiburg: Herder, 2020), 98–111, Wendel states: "The concept of hope [...] is ultimately the concept for Kant by which religion can be determined, and vice versa" (103).
[459] Habermas, Vol. II, 209.

logical approach is that "with this revolutionary concept of autonomy developed in the sequence of Rousseau, Kant transforms the Christian theme of the freedom of the will of the human person who at any rate (*so oder so*) knows his fate to be anchored (*aufgehoben*) in the providence of an omnipotent God, into the theme of reason-led (*vernünftige*) freedom of a subject that must *rely on itself* (*eines* auf sich gestellten *Subjekts*)". It will have to be examined in the following subsection at what level this need for self-reliance applies, whether in taking on the obligation, or also in fully accomplishing its intention. Habermas observes: "The *liberation towards self-legislation* makes the awareness of the finitude of one's own forces only more acute".[460] While both Hume and Kant are identified as "secular thinkers", there is a major difference in that the latter's "critique of religion has a constructive intention [...] Kant appropriates from the content (*Gehalt*) of religious tradition what is reasonable according to secular standards [...] He has taken over (*abschaut*) the consciousness of sin of Protestant subjectivity into the interiority (*Innerlichkeit*) of an active subject ascertaining itself (*sich selbst vergewissernden*)".[461] On the one hand, this transfer is "sobering" for religion; on the other, the theological content remains present in its traces:

> Due to this change of perspective, the Lutheran conception of an existential battle place of the remorseful sinner who struggles *coram Deo* for his salvation must be rededicated to self-critical reason and changed in a sobering way (*ernüchtert*) into the worldly stage of the subjectivity in its cognitive performance and moral self-legislation [...] The writings on philosophy of religion show that important thought motifs and basic concepts go back to a religion-critical appropriation and philosophical translation of Luther's doctrine of justification which was based on Paul and Augustine.[462]

The question remains regarding these supposed transformations whether some conceptions that are here portrayed as "translations" are not owed to different roots, or represent genuinely opposite views; the term "reduction (*Ermäßigung*)" is not sufficiently precise, since the content is not even similar. Between "justification" which, as Luther insists, is enacted on the human person who remains *mere passive*, and Kant's appraisal of the human capacity for self-determination, there seems to be no parallel, but a clear alternative regarding their anthropological models. The express priority Kant gives to the "disposition towards the good" against which evil is given a secondary status, becomes a "dialectical" and "equally primordial" relationship for Habermas. This reading moves Kant

---

460 Habermas, Vol. II, 209.
461 Habermas, Vol. II, 210.
462 Habermas, Vol. II, 310–311.

closer to Augustine than his emphasis on the constitutive human ability to follow the moral law allows for. After quoting from *Religion within the Boundaries of Mere Reason Alone* that the "original disposition [...] is a disposition for the good" and that "there is no conceivable reason for us from where moral evil could have first come into us", Habermas concludes: "In other words: Freedom and morality are equally original with radical evil. The meaning of this interpretation of original sin as the dialectical connection (*Zusammenhang*) between good and evil becomes clearer when we recall the role that the consciousness of sin plays for Luther regarding the liberating conversion towards faith [...] *stimulating* a remorseful turn (*Umkehr*)". Kant converts this discrepancy into a "dynamising [...] challenge (*Zumutung*) of self-improvement (*Selbstbesserung*)".[463]

If the starting position and the content that is being renewed are not laid out clearly, it becomes impossible to judge the "translation" from theology to general reason on what it gives up in its sobriety, and what it "rescues". Before pursuing this problem in relation to the experience of the "antinomy of practical reason" outlined in the "Dialectic" of the *Critique of Practical Reason*, the extensive horizon Kant gives to philosophy in its "world concept" will be examined. It also includes the question of meaning which accompanies the active pursuit of practical reason that humans are capable of.

7.3.2 The "world concept" of philosophy and the public sphere

Kant's determination of the subject area and task of philosophy reflects the anthropological turn. As the "academic study (*Wissenschaft*) of the conditions, aims, reasons and limits of human knowing (*Erkenntnis*)", it "engages with (*befasst sich*) the questions: '1. What can I know? 2. What ought (*soll*) I do? 3. What may I hope for?', which find their unity in a fourth question: 'What is the human being?'".[464] From the first *Critique* onwards, the Enlightenment philosopher is oriented towards the public, "directing himself to the reason of human beings whose 'interest(s)' he seeks to promote in all his works".[465] It is an understand-

---

[463] Habermas, Vol. II, 330–331, with reference to Kant, *Die Religion innerhalb der Grenzen der reinen Vernunft*, Akademie-Ausgabe Vol. 6, 43 and Vol. 6, 51.
[464] Volker Gerhardt, "Art. Philosophie", in *Kant-Lexikon. Studienausgabe*, ed. Marcus Willaschek, Jürgen Stolzenberg, Georg Mohr, Stefano Bacin (Berlin: De Gruyter, 2017): 433–444, 433, with reference to the *Critique of Pure Reason* A 805/B 833.
[465] Gerhardt, "Art. Philosophie", 436, with reference to the "Publicum" (*Critique of Pure Reason* B XXXIV and A 745/B 733).

ing that Habermas shares and takes to a new level in his analyses of the changing forms of the "public sphere", a concept that has been compared in its significance as enjoying "a status akin to that of a scientific discovery".[466] Yet how far does he follow Kant in his comprehensive definition of the remit of philosophical enquiry, combining knowledge, moral agency, and hope? The creation of a public domain of interaction in which objective knowledge and moral insight are elaborated from multiple perspectives is a hallmark and uniting horizon of Habermas's theory enterprise from the start. Thus, the "world concept" of philosophy which Kant distinguishes from its expert pursuit as a discipline can be regarded as a shared basis:

> There is more chance of an entire public enlightening itself. This is indeed almost inevitable, if only the public concerned is left in freedom [...] For enlightenment of this kind, all that is needed is *freedom*. And the freedom in question is the most innocuous (*unschädlichste*) form of all – freedom to make public use of one's reason in all matters [...] The public use of man's reason must always be free, and it alone can bring about enlightenment among men (*unter Menschen*).[467]

In the context of outlining Kant's refutation of empiricism as "aiming at the restitution of a philosophy that satisfies its 'world concept'", Habermas specifies this goal: "It does not resign itself (*sich abfinden*) to the price of a deflationing of the validity of the ought (*Sollgeltung*) of practical prescriptions (*Gebote*) to prudential rules (*Klugheitsregeln*) respectively to compassion (*Mitgefühl*) that had been paid for the scientisation (*Verwissenschaftlichung*) of philosophical thinking".[468] The deontological approach to morality is distinguished from the teleological quest for a flourishing life which restricts itself to keeping virtues alive that are internal to a community. In Kant's outline, it starts from the basis of a self-imposed moral obligation which is marked by an unconditionality that is independent of actual reciprocity. Kant's "world concept" can be read as including this dimension which is addressed to every human being due to the capacity of their conscience to hear its call. François Marty explains the final orientation that characterises the "world concept" of philosophy: "As a 'freely acting' being, the human person enters the realm of the unconditioned (*Unbedingten*)" in which "a 'canon', that is, a legitimate use of pure reason as *practical* reason

---

[466] Nancy Fraser, "The Theory of the Public Sphere: *The Structural Transformation of the Public Sphere* (1962)", in *Habermas Handbook*, ed. Hauke Brunkhorst, Regina Kreide and Cristina Lafont (New York: Columbia University Press, 2017): 245–255, 245.
[467] Kant, "An Answer to the Question: 'What is Enlightenment?'", in *Kant's Political Writings*, 54–60, 55. Cf. also Sarah Holtman, "Öffentlichkeit", in *Kant-Lexikon*: 408–410.
[468] Habermas, Vol. II, 317.

exists [...] As the final purpose (*Endzweck*) of the whole activity of human reason it characterises all of philosophy in its *world concept*, its '*conceptus cosmicus*'."[469]

The "publicness" that Kant aims at here includes a cosmopolitan scope of morality. Yet in the demanding normative sense proposed by him, doing justice to this horizon requires the anticipation of a meaning that is not at the agent's disposal but remains a hope. It is this gaping discrepancy between the good intention and the actual ability to fulfil it in reality that Kant reflects on in what he terms the "antinomy of practical reason".

7.3.3 Overtaxed by too great a scope for morality? The antinomy of practical reason and the postulate of God

This part of Kant's philosophy has been extensively discussed with Habermas by philosophers and theologians, even before his thinking on religion entered a new phase in 2001 with his call for mutual translations between religious and secular interlocutors. The questions from a philosophically informed theology have been specified since 1976 when Helmut Peukert based his positive analysis and internal critique of Habermas's research programme, constituting the third stage of the Frankfurt School, on the "analytics and dialectics of reason" that had been so sharply analysed by Kant.[470] From the earlier positions of Critical Theory, as marked by the reflections of Max Horkheimer, Theodor W. Adorno and Walter Benjamin, he introduced the horizon of biblical monotheism into a concept of universality which in Habermas's theory had become restricted to the present and the future. This left the suffering endured by the victims of

---

[469] François Marty, "Die Analogie zwischen 'ethischem' und 'bürgerlichem gemeinen Wesen'. Ein Beitrag zur Frage der Erreichbarkeit des höchsten politischen Gutes", in *Recht – Geschichte – Religion. Die Bedeutung Kants für die Gegenwart*, ed. Rudolf Langthaler and Herta Nagl-Docekal (Berlin: Akademie Verlag, 2004): 63–70, 64, with reference to Kant, *Akademie-Ausgabe*, Vol. 3, 518. 542–543.

[470] The argumentation and significance of the pioneering work by Helmut Peukert, *Science, Action and Fundamental Theology: Toward a Theology of Communicative Action*, trans. James Bohman (Cambridge, MA: MIT Press, 1984, German original 1976) have been analysed by Magnus Striet, "*Wissenschaftstheorie – Handlungstheorie – Fundamentale Theologie*", in *Lexikon der theologischen Werke*, ed. Michael Eckert et al. (Stuttgart: Kröner, 2003): 812–813. Regarding the second phase of Habermas's discussion of religion as "co-existing" with philosophy, cf. Peukert, "Enlightenment and Theology as Unfinished Projects", trans. Eric Crump and Peter Kenny, in *Habermas, Modernity, and Public Theology*, ed. Don Browning and Francis Schüssler Fiorenza (New York: Crossroad, 1992): 43–65.

human cruelty in the past unanswered. Renewing the motivation to continue such struggles for justice can make a difference for the future but remains helpless regarding the price others have already been forced to pay. The philosophical critics of Habermas's programme and his own responses do not draw on the biblical promise of the power of a God who rescues from death with its critical edge in relation to only forward-looking theories. They do insist, however, on the far more encompassing scale of Kant's problem analysis. In his "Postscript" to the new publication which maps out the motivation behind the course of enquiry carried out over more than a decade, Habermas points to "learning processes" that, it is hoped, cannot be undone. By naming some recent steps of incremental historical progress, he intends to counteract the "defeatism of reason" that is part of modern cultural pathologies: "These empirical reasons can support the fragile trust in one's own powers (*Kräfte*)".[471] At the same time, he discovers a public location where the motivation for solidarity is renewed in the rituals still performed in religious communities. The question remains whether such believers in God are designated as living in parallel symbolic worlds, or whether any connections to autonomous reason can be identified. This is where other philosophers in the tradition of Kant differ from Habermas. For him, the gaping disconnection Kant diagnoses between "worthiness of happiness" due to a person's sustained moral effort, and its actual fulfilment is due to an "overtaxing" (*überfordernd*) idea of moral action. The terms he uses in this context bear a clear resemblance to Hegel's objection to an 'empty ought' (*einem 'leeren Sollen'*)".[472] The radicality of Kant's analysis – which goes as far as expressly suspending his whole approach if no answer can be found since it would then reveal itself as "empty", "fantastic", "unfounded" – is not nearly captured.[473]

---

471 Habermas, Vol II, 806 (Postscript).
472 Nagl-Docekal, *Innere Freiheit. Grenzen der nachmetaphysischen Moralkonzeptionen* (Berlin/Boston: De Gruyter, 2014), 167: "Evidently, Habermas allows himself to be guided by the Hegelian critique according to which Kant's moral philosophy is said to have only reached an 'empty ought'." In his "Postscript", Vol. II, 803, Habermas can be seen to confirm her interpretation when he notes in the context of the moral justification of the validity of human rights in international law: "one can hardly rely on the global expansion of a corresponding feeling of duty that has been deprived (*beraubt*) of its transcendental status. With this, the embarrassment (*Verlegenheit*) of the missing motivational embedding of abstract ought that Hegel already criticised (*moniert*) Kant himself for, is only intensified."
473 Cf. Kant, *Critique of Practical Reason*, trans. Lewis W. Beck (New York: Liberal Arts Press, 1956), 114. In "Der praktische Vernunftglaube und das Paradox der kulturellen Weltbilder", in *Glauben und Wissen*, ed. Langthaler and Nagl-Docekal, 120 – 155, esp. 120 – 139, Wilhelm Lütter-

The question that imposes itself therefore is if the "dialectic of practical reason" can be offset by referring to the "signs of history" which Habermas's new work falls back on, endorsing Kant's inclusion of the French Revolution as a momentous political event that has resonated with the hopes of the ordinary members of the public. If this seems to be the path to be chosen, should Kant himself have taken back the "antinomy" reflections written a few years earlier? It is clear that Habermas regards them as a dubious legacy with an uncertain status in Kant's overall conception.[474] If the "postulate of the existence of God" is deemed superseded, however, the gradual enlargement of circles of inclusion that Habermas points to as "experiences of learning" may not be enough to counterbalance the lacunae of meaning that open up for individual agents when their good actions falter.[475] Hoping in the progress of learning in the course of history should also come with Kant's warning that two aspects need to be distinguished: historical events that may provide more equitable conditions for the future, and their moral evaluation which in the case of July 14, 1789 is its judgement as a "bloodbath". Unlike Hegel, he was not willing to submerge the second perspective into an exercise of stocktaking at some higher, historical level.[476]

---

felds outlines the discrepancy described in stark words by Kant and explains the urgency of the "need of reason" (*Vernunft-Bedürfnis*) arising from it.

[474] Habermas's judgements, for example, include that "the credit which Kant bestows on the doctrine of postulates is not vouched for (*nicht gedeckt*) (Vol II, 333); that its "mode of taking-to-be-true oscillates (*schillernde*) (348) and that the "enlargement of the moral law by the doctrine of postulates fails under Kant's own premises" (360).

[475] In her article, "Nach einer erneuten Lektüre: Max Horkheimer, *Die Sehnsucht nach dem ganz Anderen*", *Deutsche Zeitschrift für Philosophie* 68 (2020): 659–688, 683–684, Nagl-Docekal notes that the challenge posed for the individual that is key for Kant is no longer the focus for Habermas: "A change in the initial question becomes noticeable: While Kant indicates with the question, 'What may I hope?' that he sets out from the perspective of the first person singular, the use of "we" by Habermas instead already reveals a social theoretical approach. It is also significant that Habermas's presentation sounds as if Kant's conception of the postulates was meant as a theory that could be offered to human beings in their despair due to their experiences of finitude as a philosophical word of consolation. What is lost out of sight in this way, however, is that for Kant the genuine location of the postulates is the practical reason of each individual even if they do not reflect on it explicitly; only because they are anchored in the need of reason (*Vernunft-Bedürfnis*) of each single person can the ideas of God and of a future life attain the power of conviction."

[476] Ricoeur comments on this difference between the perspectives of Kant and Hegel also in reference to Hannah Arendt's analysis in *The Just*, trans. David Pellauer (Chicago: Chicago University Press, 2000), 102–108. Cf. also Heiner Bielefeldt, "Verrechtlichung als Reformprozess. Kants Konstruktion der Rechtsentwicklung", in *Recht – Geschichte – Religion*, ed. Langthaler and Nagl-Docekal, 73–84, 80–81.

Kant's insistence on staying with the perspective of the human subject and not to replace it by an overarching viewpoint is also evident in his proposal of an "ethical", self-organised gathering independent of the state. It is an idea that connects the anticipatory features which law is endowed with in his conception with a mutual provider of voluntary support for individuals in their onerous moral awareness: a "philosophical" concept of "church".

7.3.4 The "ethical commonwealth": Borrowing from Augustine, or supporting the will's capability for self-legislation?

In the work's reconstruction of the two major contributory streams of European thinking – as part of the programme of elucidating the stages of turning away from metaphysics – this communal element in Kant's moral philosophy appears as a further building block in the thesis of the extended history of effects of Augustine. It is presented as one of the two "Augustinian themes" appearing in Kant's 1793 treatment of religion, and it is subsumed to a defining feature of the Critiques that Habermas sees as part of the paradigm he wants to supersede: the distinction between a transcendental and an empirical level. It seems that with this trait removed there would be no need for Kant's proposal of a parallel organisation to a state of law:

> In *Religion within the Boundaries of Mere Reason*, Kant treats two Augustinian themes: evil, that is, the struggle of the good with the principle of evil, and the *civitas Dei* as the "unification point (*Vereinigungspunkt*)" for all who want to bring about (*herbeiführen wollen*) the kingdom of God as an ethical community on earth. With this, not only a sore point of Kantian moral theory, the orientation towards the "highest good", is articulated (*kommt zur Sprache*); rather, the construction of reason in general is shaken (*kommt ins Wanken*). Attention is thus directed to the systematic reason why Kant could not be satisfied with the secular (*profanen*) answer of philosophy of history [...], a process of civilisation. As long as the transcendental lay-out (*Anlage*) of the theory of knowledge forces him to attribute the sphere of society, culture and history to the side of nature as appearance (*der erscheinenden Natur*), the intelligible subject cannot draw any encouragement from the processes of learning of the human species.[477]

Apart from the ongoing question of the need for a transcendental level, to be followed up in the next chapter, one issue to be examined is the adequacy of aligning Kant's conception of an "ethical commonwealth" with Augustine's idea of *civitas Dei*. Contemporary theological interpretations diverge widely – from its

---

477 Habermas, Vol. II, 310.

Radical Orthodox inclusion into an integralist conception of church, to a critique of this interpretation by the historian Robert Markus,[478] and to various theological assessments of his ecclesiology. The different evaluations turn out to be dependent on prior assumptions on the legitimacy of the state – church separation, on the theological anthropology expressed in it as well as on views about the legal and institutional orientation of Latin thinking referred to before.[479] Judging merely from Habermas's own comments on this towering figure from the patristic to the modern era, some discrepancies should be noted. Do the following basic points of Kantian philosophy not constitute major differences to Augustine: his appreciation of the human will as capable of self-legislation, his subordination of evil as only a propensity (*Hang*) to the elementary human predisposition (*Anlage*) to the good,[480] his inclusion of law into a framework of mutual recognition, and the cosmopolitan scale of the obligation for inclusion over against an eschatological separation of the elected from the damned? In Volume I, Augustine's position was rightly analysed as "Hobbesian" in its view and use of the state as a coercive power against "sin".[481] How does this stance agree with the opposite argumentation to Hobbes which Kant provides: an anticipation of a future legal self-organisation already in the state of nature? Is the line of continuity from Thomas and Duns Scotus, laid out so impressively in its groundbreaking elements in the first volume, not much more pronounced in these key issues, the very turning points to Modernity? To recall the alternative position to Hobbes which Kant elaborates from the starting point of his critical philosophy, the human capability for morality: As the philosopher Heiner Bielefeldt has shown, he distinguishes three stages in the development of law, first, to overcome the state of nature, second, to work towards a republic, and third, to institute a framework of international law. Thus, the legitimation for the state is pro-

---

478 In *Christianity and the Secular* , Robert A. Markus contextualises and compares Augustine with the receptions he has been given by Radical Orthodoxy, by Oliver O'Donovan and John Yoder. He counters a reading of *Civitas Dei* as a rejection of the legitimacy of political agency with the thesis that on the contrary, a neutral space of the "*saeculum*" has been opened up. The distinction from the political community must be located in the context of the Roman Empire's elevation of Christianity into the new state religion and is interpreted as a countermove to a triumphalism that forgets about the earlier stages marked by persecution.
479 Ansorge, *Kleine Geschichte*, 107.
480 Cf. Kant, *Religion Within the Boundaries of Mere Reason And Other Writings*, ed. Allen Wood and George di Giovanni. Introduction by Robert M. Adams (Cambridge: Cambridge University Press, 1998): 50.52 (A 13/B 15. A 18/B 19–20).
481 In the context of treating the "instrumental conception of the relationship between church and state" shown by Augustine, Habermas judges that he "paves the way to a Hobbesian understanding of state" (Vol. I, 614).

vided from a moral perspective which assigns an "anticipatory" dimension to the establishment of legal structures.[482] It is a refutation of the Hobbesian argument for the state's monopoly of violence which is defended instead by regarding already the "state of nature" as marked by an anticipation of public law. The reason for this is the cosmopolitan stance of attributing to each living individual an equal claim to the surface of the earth and its plentiful resources. From the common ownership of the earth recognised as valid prior to the foundation of states, this right must then be institutionalised in law; it is not, by contrast, first inaugurated by the state. Important for Kant's conception of "public" is the following level of extension, once a state has been achieved, while it operates by authoritarian governance (*Obrigkeitsstaat*): the anticipation of a constitutional republic. The medium of this process of reform is the citizens' public use of reason. It would be hard to find parallels in Augustine for so much investment into the agents' own capacity for moral judgement and political commitment to greater justice and attentiveness to their fellow humans' hope for happiness.

In Volume II, Habermas takes account of this "aim" in a subsection dedicated to Kant's view of society, culture and history. It is worked out

> in the juridical concepts of a "cosmopolitan state (*weltbürgerlichen Zustandes*)" in his philosophy of history, not in the religiously inspired concepts of an "ethical commonwealth", as in his philosophy of religion […] It is not informal, but binding (*zwingendes*) law. The *Critique of Judgement* projects the whole of history from the perspective of progressing to a "cosmopolitan state" as the "best in the world" […] as a globally implemented (*in Kraft gesetzte*) order of human rights […] Law is a dual entity (*Zwitter*) that can be considered from the outside under the aspect of legality, but also from the inside under the aspect of morality".[483]

This position, including its decision not to delay the question of validation to a condition to be achieved in the future, but to insist on the current validity and urgency to implement this framework,[484] however, is built on an expectation to each individual. This is where it becomes evident not only that Kant's "philosophy of law necessarily leads to a philosophy of history"[485] but also that it is not possible to separate Kant's philosophy of history from his philosophy of religion. His ethics which feeds into his conception of history is marked by an inherent quest for the unconditioned that will require the religious assumption of divine

---

482 Bielefeldt, "Verrechtlichung", 75–83.
483 Habermas, Vol. II, 363–364.
484 Bielefeldt, "Verrechtlichung", 81.
485 Bielefeldt, "Verrechtlichung", 79.

support. God as the creator of a "morally sensitive" universe[486] is trusted with having provided a framework in which moral intentions will ultimately be fulfilled, and the happiness deserved, but contravened so often in the interaction of free human beings, will be achieved.[487]

How does the "philosophical concept of church" fit into this outline? It has become clear that it bears no resemblance to the competitive mode of sinners hoping for their own salvation by a God of retributory justice. This Augustinian vision will be rejected by Schleiermacher for the reason that beatitude could not be envisaged by the individual Christian if it excluded others. Yet it is equally misleading to speak of a rejection of religion by Kant, as the title of a "religion-critical appropriation (*Aneignung*) and translation of Luther's doctrine of justification based on Paul and Augustine" suggests.[488] The "religiously inspired" concept of an "ethical commonwealth" is located at the border between two disciplines and two types of agency, one legal, the other "ethical" in the sense of striving for a flourishing life. Precisely in view of the universal direction of the moral and the legal enterprises, religions are given a non-substitutable function as communities serving the renewal of virtue, especially after humans have failed. As public communities within society they are dedicated to mutual encouragement, to a heuristics of perceiving nascent conflicts and to the task of addressing the participants as autonomous agents. Thus, an "ethical commonwealth" is needed alongside the realm of the state:

> As Kant explains, such an "ethico-civil state" is clearly distinguished from a "juridico-civil (political) state," since it unites people "under laws of virtue alone" (*RR*, 106). This implies that the task of establishing an "ethical community" cannot be performed by means of politics [...] In Kant's view, our duty to engage in developing an "ethico-civil state" is tanta-

---

[486] This is the expression Habermas uses in "Faith and Knowledge", in *The Future of Human Nature*, trans. William Rehg, Max Pensky and Hella Beisker (Cambridge: Polity Press, 2003), 101–115, 115: "From the very beginning, the voice of God calling into life communicates with a morally sensitive universe."

[487] Cf. Nagl-Docekal, "Immanuel Kant's Concept of Reasonable Hope", in *Hope: Where does our Hope lie? International Congress of the European Society for Catholic Theology* (August 2019 – Bratislava, Slovakia), edited by Miloš Lichner (Wien: LIT Verlag, 2020), 177–192. On the relevance of this endpoint of Kant's argument for how the scope of ethics is conceived, cf. my comparison of its reception by Rawls and Habermas in "What Scope for Ethics in the Public Sphere? Principled Autonomy and the Antinomy of Practical Reason", in *Theology and Reason in the Public Sphere*, Special Issue, ed. Christoph Hübenthal, *Studies in Christian Ethics* 32 (2019): 485–498.

[488] Habermas, Vol. II, 311. 320.

mount to the obligation of "founding a kingdom of God on earth," which needs to be expounded in terms of a philosophy of religion.[489]

Its key term is "hope" that provides an answer to the questions arising unavoidably in moral agency which is therefore marked not only by "obligation" as its single definitive hallmark: "With an internal necessity, the essence of morality raises the question of meaning [...] the problem what the ultimate purpose of all moral action is [...] The practical interest of reason not only announces itself in the question of obligation (*Sollen*) but at least as urgently in the question of hope".[490]

Habermas has highlighted convincingly that "in reason itself an *interest* belonging to its practical use is hidden *regarding its own chances of having an effect* (*Wirkungschancen*) in the world.[491] But in his view this question is caused by the "exaggerated (*überschießenden*) demands of the moral law" facing the real-world individual with its tall orders: "In the Incognito of the reason-led (*vernünftige*) self-legislation of the I of transcendental apperception the assailable (*anfechtbare*), *acting* subject in the literal sense is already hidden from the start, its autonomy challenged by the fight between good and evil".[492] Habermas's view seems to be that by rescinding the distinction of the empirical from the noumenal, such tension and desperate conflicts may no longer arise. In the following chapter it will be instructive to examine the "paradigm change" at work, the beginnings of which Habermas finds in the work of Wilhelm von Humboldt and his contemporaries.

---

489 Nagl-Docekal, "Why Ethics Needs Politics: A Cosmopolitan Perspective (With a Little Help from Kant)", in *Chiasmatic Encounters: Art, Ethics, Politics*, ed. Kuisma Korhonen, Arto Haapala, Sara Heinämaa, Kristian Klockars, and Pajari Räsänen (Lanham, MD: Lexington Books, 2018): 151–169, 168, with reference to Kant, *Religion Within the Boundaries of Mere Reason And Other Writings*, 106. Kant's critique of religious ritual and paternalism goes along with a clear recognition of the philosophical place of a concept of church. Cf. Nagl-Docekal, "Eine rettende Übersetzung? Jürgen Habermas interpretiert Kants Religionsphilosophie", in *Glauben und Wissen. Ein Symposium mit Jürgen Habermas*, ed. Rudolf Langthaler and Herta Nagl-Docekal (Wien: Oldenbourg Verlag/Akademie Verlag, 2007): 93–113.
490 Christoph Hübenthal, "Autonomie als Prinzip. Zur Neubegründung der Moralität bei Kant", in *Kant und die Theologie*, ed. Georg Essen and Magnus Striet (Darmstadt: Wissenschaftliche Buchgesellschaft, 2005): 95–128, 115.
491 Habermas, Vol. II, 319.
492 Habermas, Vol. II, 319.

8 Post-Kantian Theories of Language – Pacemakers for the Paradigm Change from Subject Philosophy to Linguistic Interaction

In the second volume entitled, "Rational" (*vernünftige*, i.e., reason-based) Freedom: Traces of the Discourse on Faith and Knowledge", Chapter Nine is dedicated to the "linguistic embodiment (*Verkörperung*) of reason", regarded as the move "from subjective to 'objective' spirit".[493] The chapter treats Schleiermacher together with Herder and Wilhelm von Humboldt as representing the decisive step beyond Kant towards situating reason in language, interaction and a reservoir of shared meanings. I will first examine aspects of the "linguistic turn" that is seen to begin with these late eighteenth- and early nineteenth-century language theorists (8.1). Secondly, I will compare Habermas's with other reconstructions of Schleiermacher's hermeneutics (8.2) and include his earlier analysis of his work as a post-Kantian theologian (8.3). The final point of discussion will be how the inclusion of the new approaches after Kant into "postmetaphysical thinking" affects the relationship between faith and knowledge (8.4). This will prepare the theme of the final chapter which investigates the location proposed as the core of lived religion: ritual. It is presented as the determining feature of a still active "form of the spirit" that is the enduring counterpart to a faculty of reason which has become defined by an inherent secularity.

8.1 Discovering language as the medium of reason: Herder, Schleiermacher and Humboldt

One of the key problems of "subject philosophy" that the "paradigm change" to linguistic interaction is charged with resolving is its seeming unsuitability for capturing individuality. The position which Habermas has elaborated over five decades, that major themes only became possible after departing from the initial approach of Modernity, a philosophy of consciousness, is confirmed also in 2019: the issue that persons

> need to be identified also by others through the *life histories* (*Lebensgeschichten*) that are localised in *social* space and *historical* time [...] receives more of a detour than a solution by the turn to subject philosophy. By distinguishing the individual empirical subject

---

[493] Habermas, Vol. II, 375–589.

from a general "subject as such (*Subjekt überhaupt*)", the question of identifying persons as individuals seems to be settled (*sich erledigen*); for it can be comprehended from the perspective of self-observation how the subject himself distinguishes himself from all other persons. Yet the internal connection between identifying oneself and identifying an other (*Fremdidentifizierung*) [...] will only be able to be conceptualised after the linguistic turn [...] New themes such as freedom of the will that is tied to obligating laws, the historicity of human existence, and the individuality of a person only ascertaining (*vergewissernden*) her identity have imposed themselves (*aufgedrängt*) on philosophical reflection.[494]

In Volume II, changes in cultural, political and social structures that underlie the rise of these new conceptions are outlined before each of the three language thinkers is treated. The overarching themes that unite their distinct contributions are, first, their realisation of the need to "situate reason" (8.1.1). On this basis, the priority of coming to an agreed view of the world results in a new concept of individuality as emerging from intersubjectivity (8.1.2). At the same time, a productive tension between individual speech acts and the language system is elaborated (8.1.3). These positions, reaffirmed in the 2019 work, will be discussed in view of the objections raised against them by defenders of the paradigm Habermas deems to be superseded, a "philosophy of consciousness" traced back to the human subject.

8.1.1 "Situating reason" in language – an overdue revision of foundations, or a question of levels?

In order to overcome what are considered to be fruitless dichotomies of the philosophy of consciousness, a variety of starting points is taken up and their potential to lead out of the existing cul-de-sacs highlighted: the moves to situate reason in language, in thoroughly transformed economic structures, and in intersubjectivity. They are found in Herder's anthropology and cultural history, in Schleiermacher's hermeneutics and Humboldt's comparative study of languages, in the Young Hegelians, and in social sciences that link empirical and philosophical analyses, such as George Herbert Mead's Symbolic Interactionism. From different foundations, they attempt to anchor the concept of the transcendental subject – which Kant had introduced as a necessary distinction from concrete empirical individuality – at a prior material level; it is acknowledged as the enabling ground for the pursuits of human life in its shared language-based rationality. This programmatic departure from the methodological foundations of

---

[494] Habermas, Vol. II, 197–198.

8 Post-Kantian Theories of Language

Kant's *Critiques* has been the subject of long-standing discussions involving a range of philosophical positions. Contested questions have been the connection between thinking and language, and the subject's relation to the objective world and to fellow humans. These can all be read as aspects of "individuality" which in the view of Habermas's interdisciplinary research project requires a substantially transformed framework. On the road to the new paradigm of intersubjective communicative action that overcomes the features typical of metaphysics – identity thinking, idealism with its preponderance of the general, a "strong" concept of theory[495] –, they are credited with offering a critical alternative to Kant. Constitutional norms, accelerated social change, capitalist economic circuits, new classes and class conflicts represent developments that bring to awareness

> the weakness of a subject philosophy which is insensitive to the *social-ontological obduracy* (*Eigensinn*) of the historically experienced reality of the symbolically structured contexts of the lifeworld, having assimilated the reality of history and culture to a nature objectivised by the natural sciences; [...] Even if Herder, Schleiermacher, and Humboldt were deeply marked by Kant and idealistic philosophy, [...] they owed their scholarly education and their ways of thinking to other disciplines [...] They unfold (*entfalten*) the [...] basic conception of the world-constitutive power (*Kraft*) of language that is equally original (*gleichursprünglich*) to reason. They pursue the idea that speaking is as original as thinking in a systematic perspective (*Hinsicht*) and already elaborate the basic terms that will be effective (*zum Zuge kommen*) in the paradigm change.[496]

Herder uncovers the "organic empowerment of the linguistically socialised humans as authors of their multiple ways of life who *learn collectively*", for whom "language as the medium of socialisation and of rational 'formation' (*vernünftige 'Bildung'*) [...] stands in an internal connection with reason".[497] In his "analysis of the linguistic embodiment of reason", Schleiermacher succeeds in developing a hermeneutics which "reconciles (*vereinbaren*) reason's claim to universality with a hermeneutical respect for the peculiarity (*Eigenart*) of the respective language and the individuation of linguistic meanings (*Bedeutungen*) in individual texts or speech acts".[498] Yet only Humboldt is seen as achieving the

---

[495] Habermas, *Postmetaphysical Thinking*, 29–34.
[496] Habermas, Vol. II, 380–381.
[497] Habermas, Vol. II, 429. In 426, he points out how Herder's "ethos of a comparison-based differentiation is resonant with the moral demand to respect the intrinsic dignity of the individual in his singularity (*Einzigartigkeit*). Herder cannot comprehend how one can judge the happiness of a people by standards other than its own."
[498] Habermas, Vol. II, 429.

breakthrough of ending the Platonic subordination of language to thought, of deriving individuality from intersubjectivity, and of establishing the humanistic goal of cosmopolitanism in a new discipline of comparative language research. For Schleiermacher, "language is only the medium of articulation for *unfolding the thought*" but it does not belong to the "genesis of consciousness" itself since "the grammar of language does not at all (*keineswegs*) structure and pervade *consciousness as a whole*".[499] Humboldt, however, is portrayed as connecting the two internally:

> Since he does not posit the subject as an intelligible being in contrast to the world of appearances, Humboldt is able to attach the formation of rules according to which the performing subject unites the multiplicity of his impressions into reproducible units, to the power of segmentation of the sensory signs. By thus fixing an inner process to something visible, the representing subject (*vorstellende Subjekt*) achieves a distance from the content captured (*festgehaltenen*) in this way. Humboldt explains the linguistic sign that is generated spontaneously and establishes order as the "forming (*bildende*) organ of the thought" [...] The legislating spontaneity of Kant's world-removed (*weltenthobenen*) transcendental subject thus shifts to (*geht über*) the rule-constituting medium of language.[500]

The activity of understanding (*Verstandestätigkeit*) is now "mediated by signs".[501] Yet already earlier, in the 1990s, Habermas's interpretation of Humboldt has been contested regarding the degree and the details by which both he and Schleiermacher can be seen to go beyond the transcendental method as devised by Kant. Is it their aim to supersede it, or instead, to illuminate and concretise it by analysing how the transcendental subject – who still needs to be presupposed as a speaker and as an active recipient – engages in the process of making herself understood? The theory decisions that are at stake here are relevant for what "postmetaphysical thinking" will consider to be themes that are still reasonable, including the type of connection assumed between "faith" and "knowledge". Before examining the relationship between the subject's reflexivity and human intersubjectivity, as well as between speaker and language system, the objections to the way in which Humboldt is claimed for a linguistic turn that departs from subject philosophy need to be treated. Rudolf Langthaler has disputed the alternatives into which the transcendental method is cast: an "intelligible" subject, removed from the world, who conceives of herself as "world-constituting", over against an empirical, contextual subject who is already part of a "lifeworld". The Habermasian charge that Kant ends up with a

---

499 Habermas, Vol. II, 449.
500 Habermas, Vol. II, 452.
501 Habermas, Vol. II, 453.

"transcendental-empirical reduplication" of the subject[502] is identified as a failure to distinguish two levels which in the actual exercise of one's relation to the world are always intertwined but remain formally distinct: without the Kantian concept of "transcendental apperception", namely that it "must be possible for the 'I think' to accompany all my representations (*Vorstellungen*)"[503] – denoting the subject's consciousness that these impressions are hers – there would not be any reference point for making and validating truth claims. Langthaler sees Habermas's rejection of Kant's enquiry into the conditions of the possibility of human performances, his step behind the actual pursuits to the conditions that enable them, as subordinating claims to knowledge of objects to a different question, that of intersubjective relations.[504] This leaves unclarified the issue of how the human subject is able to relate to the world at all. The "third categories" of "interaction" and "lifeworld" through which Habermas wishes to replace the "subject-object dichotomy" and turn the "introspection" of such reflection into visible entities, such as grammatical pronouns, risk obfuscating the role of the "I": it is not on a par with the entities or objects it is able to experience due to its own a priori structures of knowing that make perception possible. For Langthaler, there is no way around the "transcendental anchoring role" of subjectivity.[505] It is true that it only ever functions in the *actual* pursuits of a concrete historical agent but as a condition, it is the same in all these distinct individuals. By collapsing the two levels, Langthaler sees Habermas as promoting a "naturalisation"[506] of the act of consciousness that needs to be explicated. His "recon-

---

502 Langthaler, *Nachmetaphysisches Denken?*, 152, quoting Habermas, *Nachmetaphysisches Denken. Philosophische Aufsätze* (Frankfurt: Suhrkamp, 1988), 275.
503 Langthaler, *Nachmetaphysisches Denken?*, 161, cf. Kant, *Critique of Pure Reason*, 152 (B 132–133).
504 Langthaler, *Nachmetaphysisches Denken?*, 324. In Vol. II, 453, Habermas notes also regarding Humboldt that a "certain privileging of the function of representation over that of communication (*Darstellungs- vor der Mitteilungsfunktion*) of language" takes place.
505 Langthaler, *Nachmetaphysisches Denken?*, 337. He regards the oppositional framework employed by Habermas as the result of an abstraction, derived from an "unquestioned [...] nominalistic contrast" that pits "individual" against "universal". This "undialectical opposition (*Gegenüberstellung*) insinuates a slanted (*schiefes*) understanding (respectively a one-sided dissolution) of the metaphysical problem of 'individuality'" which needs to be conceptualised as "'qualitatively determined'" (100–101), placing it in a more encompassing totality. He questions Habermas's critique of metaphysics and subject philosophy as not being able to grasp individuality by reminding interlocutors that "the principle, '*individuum est ineffabile*' originated in the ontological tradition". Thus the "claim to have shown that 'the philosophical tradition [...] has always held only privative concepts or negatively encircling formulas ready for what is individual' is misleading" (101), with reference to Habermas, *Postmetaphysical Thinking*, 143.
506 Langthaler, *Nachmetaphysisches Denken?*, 126–133.

structive" method ends up attributing to anonymous carriers – such as "language" and "lifeworld" – what can only be understood by means of a more intricate structure: by presupposing a non-empirical level that makes the subject's world relation possible. It is the individual participant in a given language whose act of speaking determines this language as a living, changeable totality.

This is what Schleiermacher and Humboldt elaborate in strikingly compatible approaches.[507] Habermas's view is that their theories prepare or even perform the "linguistic turn" and that they lend themselves to being incorporated into a paradigm which supersedes that of consciousness. In contrast, an analysis of their premises and argumentations will show that the capacities and results he draws on point to the need for a transcendental approach which both nineteenth-century thinkers maintain and concretise.

8.1.2 Individuality as a result of intersubjectivity?

The scholars opposed to the "detranscendentalisation" pursued programmatically in the concepts and research design proposed in the project of postmetaphysical thinking also elaborate a different view of the connection between the "I" and fellow human subjects. The subject's perspective is not replaceable in its relation to the objective world nor to others. In this debate Dieter Henrich had identified crucial points of disagreement already in the 1980s. The question is which positions Schleiermacher and Humboldt develop on this matter.

Schleiermacher's lectures on Hermeneutics (beginning in 1805) and several of his Academy Addresses (for example on methods of translation in 1813) predate Humboldt's writings. Similarities in the constellation into which they cast the players and key factors have been explained by shared thought models of the era, such as conceiving of the speaker and the language system as a polarity.[508] That each of them refers to the determining power of language as "force"

---

[507] Having compared their frameworks and their application in "Passer entre les langues. Réflexions en marge du discours de Schleiermacher sur la traduction", in *Friedrich Schleiermacher and the Question of Translation*, ed. Larisa Cercel and Adriana Serban (Berlin/Boston: Walter De Gruyter, 2015): 59–73, 60, Denis Thouard speaks also in relation to their theories of translation of "d'étonnantes harmonies" between the outlines of the two authors who "semblent être tellement sur la même ligne".
[508] Gunter Scholtz, "Schleiermacher im Kontext der neuzeitlichen Hermeneutikentwicklung", in *Friedrich Schleiermachers Hermeneutik. Interpretationen und Perspektiven*, ed. Andreas Arndt and Jörg Dierken (Berlin/Boston: De Gruyter, 2016): 1–26, 11.

or "violence" (*Gewalt*)⁵⁰⁹ from the perspective of the individual speaker, manifests the concern of both theorists with the space it leaves for the human subject. By the time that an influence of examples and insights from Humboldt's Academy Addresses in the 1820s has been noted in Schleiermacher's lectures, his philosophical framework in which Hermeneutics appeared as a "technical discipline" had been mainly completed.⁵¹⁰ "New accentuations" were incorporated into them – for example, a greater emphasis on knowledge as resulting from a process of conversation and contestation in the 1822 lectures on *Dialectic*,⁵¹¹ as well as the relevance of the "world intuition (*Weltansicht*)" of each particular language.⁵¹²

While Schleiermacher's Lectures were known to his students, the Academy Addresses were publicly available to its members. One of the issues on which he predates Humboldt's writings is his use of the case of language acquisition by infants.⁵¹³ For the problem under debate, the priority of either individuality or intersubjectivity, which Habermas decides in favour of the latter, this achievement of human thinkers in their infancy has provided an instructive example. For Dieter Henrich, it constitutes as much of a proof as is possible of the priority of the self-relationship of the individual. Habermas refers to Humboldt on this

---

509 Schleiermacher, *Akademievorträge*, ed. Martin Rössler with cooperation by Lars Emersleben in Schleiermacher, *Kritische Gesamtausgabe* (= KGA) I/11 (Berlin/New York: De Gruyter, 2002), 71. Cf. Scholtz, "Schleiermacher im Kontext der neuzeitlichen Hermeneutikentwicklung, 11, Fn. 34, and Christian Berner,"Das Übersetzen verstehen", in *Schleiermacher and the Question of Translation*, 43–58, 47. 51.
510 In "Das Übersetzen verstehen", 43, Berner sees the 1813 Academy Address on translation as belonging to a "philosophical system" that "was already achieved". One major change, however, had not yet occurred: the move from a phenomenological to a transcendental analysis which will take place in paragraphs 3 and 4 of the Introduction to *The Christian Faith*, second edition, which will be relevant for a precise evaluation of his pioneering role as a post-Kantian theologian, to be treated in 8.3.
511 Thouard, "Die Sprachphilosophie der Hermeneutik", 85. Cf. Thouard, "Passer entre les langues", 94. "They certainly made a strong impression on Schleiermacher, without, however, moving him to fundamental changes" (95).
512 Thouard underlines the balance between the general structures of knowledge, and the variety introduced by the particular languages, in "Passer entre les langues", 63: "Ces concepts correspondent aux conditions générales du savoir, qui sont monnayées différemment selon différentes langues, mais restent cependant les garanties de la possibilité même de la connaissance".
513 Cf. Schleiermacher, *Hermeneutics and Criticism*, ed. Andrew Bowie (Cambridge: Cambridge University Press, 1998), 233–235 [= ET, 1998].

matter,⁵¹⁴ and correctly regards Schleiermacher as not fully subscribing to the equal primordiality of thinking and language. But irrespective of whose work is being used, the point is the spontaneous ability of children when they empower themselves of language to identify two things at once: the "general", and the "specific" value of a word.⁵¹⁵ This can only be done by an inventive leap between the general schema and the "local worth (*Lokalwerth*)" of a word. In every act of understanding, the comparative and the divinating operations complement each other. Learning to speak for the first time, children succeed in guessing and establishing both the general meaning and the specific, context-determined sense of a word. Their "learning" is not based on imitation and routine but consists of a spontaneous double achievement of their own. This fact undermines any attempts to posit the language system as the dominant factor and calls for a proper recognition of the divinating power of even its smallest, barely articulate participants. For Henrich, it is an observation that is sufficient to refute the reversal Habermas proposes, according to which individuality is produced by intersubjectivity:

> the capacity for language can only develop *along with* (*in einem* mit) the spontaneous emergence of a self-relation (*Selbstverhältnis*). This emergence [...] would require us to speak of an implicit self-relation, which already appears or functions at the most elementary level of language acquisition. For it is clear that the capacity to use the grammatical first-person singular (the pronoun "I") is acquired only at a late stage in the process [...] But if it can be shown that the mastery of demonstratives, the correct use of one's name, the developed use of negation, and thus one of the elementary conditions for the understanding of truth, can only be understood when a self-relation is presupposed, then the situation is quite different.⁵¹⁶

---

514 In Vol. II, 455, Habermas refers to Humboldt's finding that "children learn language not at all in a mechanical way, thus not piece by piece through imitation", discovering "generative rules [...] long before Chomsky".
515 Cf. Schleiermacher, *Hermeneutik 1809/10*, in Schleiermacher, *Vorlesungen zur Hermeneutik und Kritik*, ed. Wolfgang Virmond, with cooperation by Hermann Patsch, KGA II/4 (Berlin/New York: De Gruyter, 2012), 80.
516 Dieter Henrich, "What is Metaphysics – What is Modernity?", trans. Peter Dews, in *Habermas: A Critical Reader*, ed. P. Dews (Oxford: Blackwell, 1999), 291–319, 311–312, quoted also in Langthaler, 377, from Henrich, *Konzepte. Essays zur Philosophie in der Zeit* (Frankfurt: Suhrkamp, 1987): 11–43, 35. I have discussed the exchanges between Henrich and Habermas on the primacy or the equal originality of intersubjectivity with a self-relation in greater detail in *Argumentationsethik und christliches Handeln* (Stuttgart: Kohlhammer, 1998), 75–82, in *Habermas and Theology* (London: T & T Clark, 2011), 46–50 and *in Religion and Public Reason* (Berlin/Boston: De Gruyter 2014), 118–121.

Appearing in the capability to speak a language, the observation of how "understanding along with the capability (*das Verstehen in einem mit dem Können*) emerge spontaneously" makes the priority of intersubjectivity to reflexivity questionable. The explanation provided by Mead's Symbolic Interactionism falters for the same reason, its lack of accounting for the prior self-relation as the decisive factor. How can the change of perspective between the self and the other take place if there is no prior ability of the "I" to recognise itself? This is where Henrich introduces the idea of an "immediate familiarity with oneself" that can only be elucidated in a transcendental reflection, as distinct from a psychological interpretation. This point will become relevant also when following up in section 8.3 the steps of Schleiermacher's determination of religion as the "feeling of absolute dependence" in a structural analysis that uncovers an "immediate self-consciousness".

8.1.3 Models of relating speech acts and the language system

In 2019 as much as at the beginnings of *Postmetaphysical Thinking*,[517] the goals of delivering on the intentions of the Enlightenment worked out by Kant and succeeding philosophers are maintained, while the means developed to reach these targets are questioned and rejected. Thus, the aim "not to renounce to the spontaneous performances (*Leistungen*) of a world constituting and legislating subjectivity" is accepted, but the conceptions themselves are deemed unsalvageable: an "inflated subjectivity" whose "transcendental husk" has been "punctured" (*durchlöchert*), cast in a framework that is marked by the "separation between the intelligible and the world of appearances" and thus caught in "spheres that persist contactless beside each other".[518]

In view of this discrepancy between the – seemingly untenable – theoretical premises and the shared destinations, Habermas identifies two strategies: Either "one sticks to the basic concepts of subject philosophy and subordinates the finite subject of transcendental philosophy to an inflated subjectivity [...] Or one changes the prior subject theoretical decisions (*Vorentscheidungen*)" in favour of "detranscendentalised, [...] embodied and communicatively socialised subjects who find themselves in a nexus of life that is intersubjectively shared and symbolically structured."[519]

---

517 *Nachmetaphysisches Denken* was first published in 1988.
518 Habermas, Vol. II, 371–372.
519 Habermas, Vol. II, 372.

In his view, only the second option offers "subjective reason" the chance to "step beyond the transcendental armour (*Panzer*)" and to be grasped correctly as an "intellectual activity (*geistige Tätigkeit*) that is situated in a social realm". By descending from the intelligible world into the realm of intersubjectivity, "essential elements of the heritage of the transcendental I are kept: the learning ability of world-disclosing intelligences who project hypotheses and the spontaneity of reason-led and freely acting subjects".[520]

Schleiermacher and Humboldt are read as "anticipating the paradigm of linguistic socialisation" by providing a "pragmatic language theory" in which "reason embodies itself symbolically in the meanings of intersubjectively understandable sign substrates and in cognitive operations [...] reason objectivises itself in dispositions, orientations for action and life stories of persons, artefacts and practices of lifeworlds".[521] The shift to "techniques, procedures and institutions, social structures and stored cultural knowledge" provides the sought-after visibility of a faculty of reason that has given up its distance from everyday life and resides in cultures of knowledge.[522] The intention clearly is to offer a more adequate conceptual framework for the indispensable role of individuality by turning to the new paradigm of communicative action with its social science-led research projects in which philosophy can still provide direction and critical impulses. The question is whether the two post-Kantian thinkers he regards as precursors share this project. The polarity between system and speaker is also crucial for Habermas. It is attributed to the "indissoluble *(unauflösbaren)* relationship of tension between language and consciousness" that the "language system enables speech acts which in their turn reproduce the language and thereby change it, however imperceptibly, in an innovative way".[523] At what levels do Schleiermacher and Humboldt establish their analyses of reason in relation to language, and in which terms do they configure their polarity?

For Humboldt, "*ergon*" and "*energeia*" are the two terms in which the language system and the speaker's action are captured. The first pole, language as an "'effective", indeed, "coercive" power *("wirkende", ja "nötigende" Macht)* is depicted as potentially overwhelming in relation to its counterpart.[524] Humboldt points out "how small the strength (*Kraft*) of the individual against the

---

[520] Habermas, Vol. II, 373.
[521] Habermas, Vol. II, 374.
[522] Habermas, Vol. II, 373–374. Yet, as he clarifies in Vol. I, 265 in the context of the problem of solidarity, the "weak grammatical normativity of language does not have the power to steer affects and create motives."
[523] Habermas Vol. II, 386–387.
[524] Habermas Vol. II, 455.

power of language actually is (*wie gering eigentlich die Kraft des Einzelnen gegen die Macht der Sprache ist*)".[525] Habermas notes Humboldt's awareness that the system could swallow up the individual's intention. Yet, the power of the "*ergon*" is counterbalanced by Humboldt's concept of "*energeia*", a term that Langthaler identifies as implying a transcendental subject.[526] Schleiermacher offers a similar, yet even more radical analysis than his by beginning with a generalised "misunderstanding". He equally distinguishes the concrete individual speaker from the level of the constitution of experience as such, and examines the first in his Hermeneutics, the second in the discipline of Dialectics.

While Habermas seeks a solution in "directing the gaze towards a middle point (*Mitte*) between natural necessity and intelligible freedom",[527] which is where the "third categories" are located, his nineteenth-century predecessors in language theory capture the constitutive factors in the model of an ellipse with two focal points.[528] They develop structural theories in which the polarity of the formal factors can be seen from above, yet take their entry point nonetheless in the concrete perspective of the individual participants. These experience a tension between the new thought each of them aims to express, and the pre-given, historically accrued totality of a specific language with its syntax and semantics composed of the current units of meaning. The creativity and innovation within the historical, finite system of a language lies at the individual's end of the polarity, with the speaking subject who is

---

[525] In "Schleiermacher im Kontext der neuzeitlichen Hermeneutikentwicklung", 11, Fn. 34, Scholtz compares the similar positions of Schleiermacher in his 1813 Academy Address, "On the different methods of translation", KGA I/11, 64–93, 72, and of Humboldt on the "violence" (*Gewalt*) of language that is counteracted by the individual speaker's influence. Humboldt states in *Ueber die Verschiedenheit des menschlichen Sprachbaues* (1830–35) that "language has an 'independent, external existence (*Daseyn*) that exercises violence against the human person himself ." "Yet since everyone individually and incessantly (*unaufhörlich*) retroacts on it (*auf sie zurückwirkt*), each generation nevertheless produces a change in it" (*Werke in fünf Bänden*, ed. Andreas Flitner and Klaus Giel (Darmstadt: Wissenschaftliche Buchgesellschaft, 1964, 4th edn), Vol. 3, 392. 439). Scholtz sees the reason for the similarity of Schleiermacher's and Humboldt's analyses in that taking "recourse to the speaker and language was suggested by the matter itself and the polar relationship by the era's style of thought" (11).
[526] Langthaler, *Nachmetaphysisches Denken?*, 385–395.
[527] Habermas, Vol. II, 370.
[528] Schleiermacher does so expressly and perceptibly for his readers by prefacing his text with the design of two ellipses crossing each other. Cf. the title page, *New Athenaeum/Neues Athenaeum* 3 (1992): 4. In "Schleiermacher im Kontext der neuzeitlichen Hermeneutikentwicklung", 10–11, Scholtz refers to this figure in the "Kritik der bisherigen Sittenlehre" of 1803.

on the one hand, "organ" of the language and "is only able to say what language wants" (*will*), but on the other hand, language is "his" [...] This means, all real thinking is language forming (*sprachbildend*) [...] Speaking is "the mediation for the communality (*Gemeinschaftlichkeit*) of thinking" [...] the realisation of reason is always determined by the internal condition of the individual factor (*Beschaffenheit des Individuellen*). Each language is constituted in an individual way (*individuell beschaffen*) and therefore non-transferable (*unübertragbar*) in its incomparability (Schleiermacher states, "irrationality").[529]

The transfer that happens when Habermas relocates the achievement of "innovation" to the linguistic system is not endorsed by their writings. Commenting on Schleiermacher's analysis of translation, Thouard identifies the contrast between the "constraint" and the "unforeseeable" actualisation of a "new speech" which the translator tries to render: "Le jeu de contrainte et de l'effectuation imprévisible de nouveaux discours constitue l'historicité des langues. Le traducteur s'efforce de traduire non une langue, mais le discours singulier qui la modifie."[530]

Thouard highlights how the language system is the "historical" aspect and the modification it undergoes through the speaker a manifestation of the subject's spontaneity. Also Berner points out that language is "virtual" for Schleiermacher and only exists when it is concretised by speakers: "Language must individualise itself. Otherwise it can only be thought of as a potentiality (*Vermögen*), but it cannot really exist".[531] Although the link between a language and the world conception (*Weltansicht*) it portrays is highlighted, this does not happen at the expense of the universally shared a priori structures of reason, as Thouard explains:

> Il y a un système de concepts propre à chaque langue au sens d'une sémantique spécifique (au niveau de l'herméneutique), mais aussi un système de concepts qui transcende la différence des langues et qui rend possible ultimement la connaissance (au niveau de la dialectique) [...] cette construction produit bien une identité de la raison humaine. Cette di-

---

529 Berner, "Das Übersetzen verstehen", 51–52.
530 Thouard, "Passer entre les langues", 62. He sees a contrast to Humboldt in Schleiermacher's systematic interest, despite his own experience of scholarly translation, especially of Plato's works, but also of sermons from English: "Schleiermacher, au contraire de Humboldt, s'appuie sur une réflexion préalable concernant les implications cognitives de la compréhension. S'il partage l'idée que les langues naturelles donnent des perspectives sur le monde, il comprend autrement cette multiplicité, car son ambition reste systématique [...] Il ne s'agit pas tant pour lui du projet d'une 'science de la traduction' comme on a pu parfois être tenté de l'identifier [...] que d'une réflexion philosophique sur les conditions de l'acte de traduire, réflexion qui s'appuie sur la cohérence systématique de sa pensée." (60–61).
531 Schleiermacher, *Brouillon zur Ethik* (1805/06), ed. Hans-Joachim Birkner (Hamburg: Meiner, 1981), 24, quoted by Berner, "Das Übersetzen verstehen", 50–51.

mension métaphysique, rarement perçue des lecteurs de Schleiermacher, constitue néanmoins le cadre dans lequel se meut le discours sur la traduction.[532]

Schleiermacher's position is, as Berner as well underlines, that "knowledge (*das Wissen*) presupposes [...] in all individuals an identical production or construction [...] a foundational identity of individuals must be presupposed: 'In short, with the idea of knowledge a communality (*Gemeinsamkeit*) of experience and communality of the principles among all is posited (*gesetzt*), by means (*mittelst*) of the identity of reason and of the organisation in all'".[533]

The model which the two post-Kantian language theorists outline in their separate approaches with different applications thus focuses on the innovation that using a language brings to it. What Langthaler calls the "unrelinquishable (*unaufgebbare*) anchoring role of subjectivity" is exemplified or "concretised",[534] not superseded, in each of these speech acts. Regarding Habermas's sustained appreciation of "third categories" as the solution to the subject-object dichotomy of the philosophy of consciousness, one must conclude: while these terms capture the embedded position of speakers at the historical, material or concrete level, they are in danger of being turned into an objectivising, alienating framework if they eclipse the crucial, system-modifying role of the individual speaker and listener. They silence the voice of the only source of change, each agent in their particularity, by abolishing the tension for the benefit of the encompassing system of conventional language.

Within the model shared with Humboldt, of relating the two focal points of the ellipse that begins with the agent, what is specific for Schleiermacher's language theory as it is developed in his Hermeneutics (8.2)? And which points of structure and method are equally relevant within his theory of religion (8.3)?

8.2 Schleiermacher as language theorist

The unprecedented starting point proposed for hermeneutics, casting it as a discipline that actively engages in undoing "non-understanding" (8.2.1), leads to two distinct enquiries into both focal points of the ellipse: into the language system, entitled "grammatical", and into the speaker and recipient, called "techni-

---

[532] Thouard, "Passer entre les langues", 64.
[533] Berner, "Das Übersetzen verstehen", 56, with reference to Schleiermacher, *Vorlesungen über die Dialektik*, ed. Andreas Arndt, KGA II/10/1–2 (Berlin/New York: De Gruyter, 2002), 58.
[534] Langthaler, *Nachmetaphysisches Denken?*, 205.

cal" and "psychological" (8.2.2). The final section examines the role of individuality as involving both general and unique elements (8.2.3).

8.2.1 Radicalising the starting point of hermeneutics: Non-understanding

A different perspective from the external descriptions of linguistics and the social sciences opens up when the matter of enquiry is framed from the outset as a precarious performance that cannot be taken for granted. In this perspective, one cannot assume the outcome of speaking as being automatically successful. With the entry point of the discipline identified as the fact of "non-understanding", it seems that terms like "perlocutionary effect", as the third component posited in speech act theory, appear as in need of scrutiny.[535] The philosopher Sarah Schmidt identifies Schleiermacher's approach as based on a "universalisation of suspicion", instead of continuing the previous, now naïve-seeming expectation that most of the time, a one-to-one comprehensibility can be assumed. This leads to a far more ambitious goal regarding the extent to which an utterance must be reconstructed. It also includes a keen awareness that the listener's contribution must be taken into account. "Understanding" is restricted by the knowledge that their concepts overlap to some degree, but never coincide completely.[536] The investigation of the internal components of the acts of speaking and understanding, however, results in an insight which seems to become less prominent in some of the linguistic theories of subsequent eras: that with the "perspective directed towards the origin of what is new",[537] the impact of the individual's unique selection and combination of words is given a co-constitutive role for language as a system. As noted before, Habermas acknowledges the double point of reconstruction but seems to attribute the "innovation" not to the pole of the individual speaker but to language. Under the heading, "On the indissoluble relationship of tension (*unauflösbaren Spannungs-*

---

[535] In Vol. II, 459, Habermas draws on this theory and distinguishes between the view "of the 'logician' that is fixed on the representative function of language, and the performative sense which the pronouns of the first and second person acquire from the *perspective of the participants* that is missed by it".
[536] Cf. KGA II/10/2, 406, quoted by Sarah Schmidt, "Die Kunst der Kritik: Schleiermachers Vorlesungen zur Kritik und ihre Einordnung in das philosophische System", in *Friedrich Schleiermachers Hermeneutik*: 101–117, 108.
[537] Thouard, "Die Sprachphilosophie der Hermeneutik", 90: "Hermeneutics has the task of taking up this new element (*dieses Neue*) [...], which cannot be achieved from what is already known."

verhältnis) between 'language' and 'consciousness'", he concludes that the "language system enables acts of speaking (*Sprechhandlungen*) which themselves reproduce the language and thereby, however imperceptibly, change it in an innovative way".[538] Will the "acts of speaking" be traced back to the subject in her world relation and in her wish to communicate with others, or are they regarded as self-sufficient components with their own "agency" or power to cause effects? This will be a key indicator on whether Schleiermacher's and Humboldt's founding efforts can be regarded as belonging to the "linguistic turn", seen as opening up the path away from consciousness to language, or whether their models should be assessed as an alternative.

Beginning from the context of the early nineteenth century, the tasks ascribed to hermeneutics already by the 1805 Lectures, given by Schleiermacher at his first university appointment in Halle, differ not only from the then existing handbooks which are overturned in their starting points. They also reject a key premise of fellow Romantic philosopher and intended partner in the project of translating the works of Plato, Friedrich Schlegel. A corollary of the principled assumption of misunderstanding – which is the "reason for the universality of hermeneutics" – is that all human beings, not only the geniuses, are regarded as artists:

> Schleiermacher's interest is not directed towards art criticism (*Kunsturteil*) (and its programmatic entanglement in the artistic process), but – similar to Schiller's *Letters on Aesthetic Education* – towards the artistic activity proper to *every* human being as a free play of thoughts and to its meaning and function in the process of reason unfolding itself [...] the concept of criticism has a central function as the critical procedure (*Verfahren*) in the process of knowledge being generated (*des werdenden Wissens*) and as philological criticism".[539]

By relating the task of hermeneutics to "everyday life", artistic production is included, but no longer treated as an exceptional case on a different plane to the inventiveness with which every human being operates. Scholtz explains the new standard which the discipline is held to attain:

> What is new with Schleiermacher and his era is [...] that the individuality – and that means the alterity (*Andersartigkeit*) – of the Other is conceived of much more radically – yet that at the same time far more than before is demanded from an understanding of his utterances. The Other becomes, so-to-speak, even more inaccessible (*unzugänglicher*) and the consciousness of distance is thereby sharpened: Schleiermacher declares the most inner

---

[538] Habermas, Vol. II, 386–387.
[539] Schmidt, "Die Kunst der Kritik", 102.

realm of the human being as closed (*verschlossen*), as a mystery, and – unlike, for example, Chladenius – he does not expect any aids for understanding texts from a general psychology. At the same time, a much higher accuracy (*Genauigkeit*) is demanded from understanding.[540]

On the backdrop of a "permanent latent misunderstanding",[541] the benchmark is set high: "Misunderstanding ensues by itself, and understanding must be willed and sought at every point".[542] For the analysis of actual acts of composing and understanding utterances, this means that the two focal points of the ellipse must be investigated: the surrounding language system which is an enabling but also a limiting condition, and the speaker whose finished proposition or text is to be traced backwards to the origin of its production. This task of a "double reconstruction" (*Nachconstruiren*) in the language and in the individual has as its premise that either side constitutes a "totality": "A presupposition of this universalisation of misunderstanding and suspicion is [...] the assumption of a totality and wholeness of the text [...] which is to be understood, respectively to be reconstructed, as totality and wholeness."[543]

It has become clear that for hermeneutics as a discipline reconfigured after the anthropological turn, the factors operative in "understanding" must be problematised and turned into objects of enquiry. It cannot be assumed as ordinarily given but only as an infinite aim relating to an evolving matter towards which the outreach always remains approximate.

8.2.2 Interpretation as a dual task, grammatical and technical/psychological

In view of the history of reception that has focused inordinately on the second aspect, it is important to examine both directions of the twofold task of hermeneutics, maintained from the first (1805) to the final Lectures manuscripts (1832/33) and the Academy Addresses (1829).[544] Which factors are constitutive for the

---

540 Scholtz, "Schleiermacher im Kontext der neuzeitlichen Hermeneutikentwicklung", 16.
541 Schmidt, "Die Kunst der Kritik", 107.
542 KGA II/4, 127 (1819), and similarly in KGA II/4, 6 (1805 and 1809/10) that "one does not understand anything as long as one does not grasp it as necessary and can 'construe' it", quoted by Schmidt, "Die Kunst der Kritik", 107, and Scholtz, "Schleiermacher im Kontext der neuzeitlichen Hermeneutikentwicklung", 16. Thus, one needs to "reconstruct the act of production" (KGA II/4, 65).
543 Schmidt, "Die Kunst der Kritik", 107, Fn. 27, with reference to KGA II/4, 628.
544 With the publication of Wolfgang Virmond's "Neue Textgrundlagen zu Schleiermachers früher Hermeneutik", in *Internationaler Schleiermacher-Kongress Berlin 1984*, ed. Kurt-Viktor

grammatical side, and where is the point of transition to the complementary enquiry into the author? If this post-Kantian hermeneutics is marked by allowing for the role of subjectivity, how does the "individual" appear in it, and what makes his or her unique expression comprehensible?

The "grammatical" part of the operation of understanding deals with the "material" elements,[545] that is, with the "visible" structures which for Habermas provide the advantage of providing researchable elements beyond the speakers' interiority. It focuses on an utterance or text from "language as the embodiment (*Inbegriff*) of everything that can be thought in it, because it is a closed whole and relates to a particular manner of thinking".[546] The reason for the need for enquiry is that the words or lexical items are marked by an "indeterminacy" (*Unbestimmtheit*), and "ambiguity of the content" (*Zweydeutigkeit*), a property of language itself, "without any fault (*Schuld*) on the part of the utterer".[547] How can these characteristics be explained and dealt with?

Schleiermacher distinguishes between a "unity of the meaning" which "appears nowhere in an individual case", and a "multiplicity of use", of which "(e)very individual occurrence (*Vorkommen*) of an element" is a different one.[548] He explains this distinction of levels with the contrast of "idea" and "appearance": "The unity is really the idea of the word, the occurrences are its appearances. The latter are always affected (*afficirt*) by the context".[549] The task involves two operations: "1.) to determine the meaning from the given usage 2.) to find the yet unknown specific usage from the meaning".[550] The first happens through an act of the imagination (*Einbildungskraft*) that moves from the specific

---

Selge (Berlin/New York: De Gruyter, 1985), Vol. I, 576–590, based on his publication of the 1809/10 lecture copy of A.D. Twesten, *Internationaler Schleiermacher-Kongress Berlin 1984*, Vol. II, 1271–1310, the sequence of the manuscripts has been revised comprehensively. Cf. Peter Kenny, "Correcting the History: The Significance of Schleiermacher's Early Hermeneutics Manuscripts", in *New Athenaeum/Neues Athenaeum* 3 (1992): 43–66, 43–49. In the collection edited by Arndt and Dierken in 2015, Heinz Kimmerle comments on the context of the earlier datings in "Interpretationen der Hermeneutik Schleiermachers in den 1950er Jahren in Heidelberg", 183–196.

545 KGA II/4, 83/ET 1998, 237.
546 KGA II/4, 75/ET 1998, 229.
547 KGA II/4, 73/ET 1998, 227.
548 KGA II/4, 80/ET 1998, 233.
549 KGA II/4, 80/ET 1998, 234.
550 HK 61 / cf. ET 1977, 76. The ET of 1977, *Hermeneutics: The Handwritten Manuscripts*, trans. by James Duke and Jack Forstman (Missoula: Montana: Scholars Press, 1977), is of the Kimmerle edition (= HK) of Schleiermacher, *Hermeneutik*, 2nd edn, ed. Heinz Kimmerle (Heidelberg: Carl Winter Universitätsverlag, 1974).

usage up to the general meaning;[551] the second is carried out by testing this hypothetical unity with comparisons of other examples of usage.[552] By giving it the title, "Schema", he is applying a term that Kant used for the mediation between sensibility (*Sinnlichkeit*) and understanding (*Verstand*) to language.

While the "power" of language prior to its actual utilisation for statements is certainly recognised, the opportunity of the speaker to imprint their individuality on language is given by the "indeterminacy" (*Unbestimmtheit*) and "equivocalness" or "ambiguity" (*Zweydeutigkeit*), that require and allow for specification. This explains as well why hermeneutics does not only begin with literary writings but already with "misunderstanding in the mother tongue and in everyday life".[553] On its own, however, the grammatical operation only delivers an "aggregate"[554] that lacks a unifying factor. It provides the means for achieving the positive task of finding the "specific sense" of an utterance. This part of the task has been defined to an ambitious scale, "understanding in the highest sense" which follows the "higher maxim" that one has only understood "what one has reconstructed in all its relationships and in its context" (*Zusammenhang*).[555] Yet now the second perspective must be called on, that of the subject: language "as a fact (*Thatsache*) in the thinking person"[556] or towards the author's "creativity".[557]

Here the description of the matter to be investigated changes in its title and task between "technical" and "psychological". While these are connected aspects, commentators have identified them as "dissimilar" and as constituting two distinct operations.[558] It seeks to nail down the "guiding idea of the whole" which can only come from the speaker. It is helpful to understand the reason for calling the aspect relating to the role of the individual "technical", thus specifying the meaning of "psychological". As Berner explains, technical interpretation "shows the way in which an author uses language individually

---

551 Arndt refers to this function of the imagination as "totalising", while it could also be attributed to the role of the imagination in reflective judgement. In "Die Sprachphilosophie der Hermeneutik", 91–92, Thouard marks Schleiermacher's use of the Kantian concept of "Schema" for the unity of meaning in language as a most original application.
552 HK 61–62/ET 1977, 76–77.
553 KGA II/4, 73/ET 1998, 227.
554 KGA II/4, 101.
555 KGA II/4, 74–75/ET 1998, 228.
556 HK 76/ET 1977, 98.
557 HK 139/ET 192–193.
558 One of them is Paul Ricoeur, in "Schleiermacher's Hermeneutics", in *The Monist* 60 (1977): 181–197. Sarah Schmidt distinguishes them as follows: "Technically or psychologically it is about an ideal-typical genesis of thoughts and their deviation by the individual circumstances of life of the speaker" ("Die Kunst der Kritik", 109).

for his thoughts (thus the word 'technical', since the general language is the means for the purpose of an individual proposition (*Aussage*)".[559] In 1805, "psychological" was reserved for "secondary thoughts (*Nebenvorstellungen*)", pointing to the difficult task of distinguishing them from the guiding idea. Already in the rediscovered manuscript of the "*Allgemeine Hermeneutik*" of 1809/10, lectures held even before the opening of the new University of Berlin, the term expresses the growing interest in the individuality of the speaker. In the second Academy Address, the "psychological" task is described in terms that seem to pave the way to Dilthey's and Gadamer's isolation of this aspect, despite the ongoing grammatical task, since it invites to capture the thought as "breaking forth from life" (*hervorbrechenden Lebensmoment*).[560] It requires the backdrop of the whole personality of the individual author, which can, however, also only be reached to a degree.

Is the career of the non-grammatical course of enquiry an indication of unresolved tensions in identifying the specific goal? While based on the earlier stage of the edition with a sequence that has now been revised and does not justify a trajectory that leaves the grammatical behind, Paul Ricoeur judges it as hovering between two directions: towards the guiding idea, and towards the author. He sees both connected, however, in the emphasis on "style":

> Schleiermacher never managed to distinguish clearly between these two possible orientations of technical interpretation: towards the idea that governs the work or towards the author considered as a psychological being. Between these two directions – pointing to the text and pointing to the author – hermeneutics hesitates [...] yet, Schleiermacher did, in the idea of "style" glimpse their profound unity [...] Style marks the union of thought and language, the union of the common and the singular in an author's project [...] Schleiermacher saw a level of articulation that provided for the continuity of the two hermeneutics.[561]

Thus, both for earlier and for more recent research, reconstructing the input of the individual is a decisive part of the activity of understanding. As Andreas Arndt points out, restricting hermeneutics to the "grammatical" task would result in a mere "register of words".[562] His judgement matches Schleiermacher's

---

[559] Berner, "Das Übersetzen verstehen", 46.
[560] Schleiermacher, *Hermeneutik und Kritik*, ed. Manfred Frank (Frankfurt: Suhrkamp, 1977), 316. While Andrew Bowie's 1998 translation generally follows Manfred Frank's edition, he does not include the Academy Addresses into the translation.
[561] Ricoeur, "Schleiermacher's Hermeneutics", in *The Monist* 60 (1977): 188.
[562] Arndt, "Hermeneutik und Einbildungskraft", in *Friedrich Schleiermachers Hermeneutik*, 128: "Without the play of imagination, also of divinating imagination, interpretation would hardly get beyond a register of words."

own, quoted above, that working from the examination of a language in its totality will only result in an "aggregate"[563] – as important as such thorough knowledge is, especially for ancient languages with the additional threshold they pose to non-contemporary interpreters, separated by at least two epochs.

Yet, despite the growing interest in trying to understand an author's output from the interior source discernible in the organisation of thoughts, the operative element of generality is not dropped, as is also evident from the placement of hermeneutics alongside the *Dialectics* and *Criticism*. However, already regarding the Hermeneutics itself, interpretations which extoll the "individual" at the expense of the "general" are critiqued as leading to underrepresenting the other side of the dual task, namely the objective grammatical system.[564] Thus, while the subject-related factor is irreplaceable, its exact position and capability need to be determined.

8.2.3 The irreplaceable position of individuality

The need for adding a separate operation to the project of understanding arose from the inability of the grammatical focus to answer the question of why a proposition or text is composed the way it is. The aim of the new enquiry is "to reproduce the subjective reason for the combination of the particular elements"[565] as "belonging in the specific sequence of thoughts of the author".[566] What needs to be reconstructed, as the Hermeneutics of 1826/27 states, is how the "real" has been created from the "possible",[567] casting the process in two contrasting terms that depict language as a virtual totality. In relation to this reservoir, it can only be the "individuality (*Eigenthümlichkeit*)" of the author that makes these elements "real" by selecting and combining them. It needs to be in-

---

563 KGA II/4, 101.
564 Thouard, "Die Sprachphilosophie der Hermeneutik", 87, and Reinhold Rieger, among others, criticise Manfred Frank's innovative interpretation in *Das individuelle Allgemeine* (Frankfurt: Suhrkamp, 1977) as overplaying the pole of individuality. Regarding the "non-negotiability" (*Unübertragbarkeit*) of the sense, Reinhold Rieger observes in *Interpretation und Wissen. Zur philosophischen Begründung der Hermeneutik bei Friedrich Schleiermacher und ihrem geschichtlichen Hintergrund* (Berlin/New York: De Gruyter, 1988), 301, Fn. 186: "Frank [...] overlooks the fact that it is precisely the sense that makes communication possible because it contains something general that enables us to reach an understanding."
565 HK 106/ET 1977, 153.
566 KGA II/4, 101/ET 1998, 254 (II,1).
567 KGA II/4, 609.

vestigated as the force that creates the "inner unity" of the sentences.⁵⁶⁸ It is up to technical interpretation to propose a first idea of "the whole (*das Ganze*)" which is present solely as a line of thought and can only be understood as such.⁵⁶⁹ The interpreter's task on the technical side is defined as "relating the single element [...] to the idea of the whole". The paragraph treating Hermeneutics as one of the disciplines relevant for theology in the 1811 *Brief Outline* states: "The goal of all interpretation consists in correctly apprehending each individual thought in its relationship to the idea of the whole and, in doing this, likewise in re-constructing the act of writing".⁵⁷⁰ The 1819 Compendium intensifies the interest in the person: "By leading the interpreter to transform himself, so to speak, into the author, the divinatory method seeks to gain an immediate comprehension of the author as an individual", now identifying the "idea of the work" as "the will that leads to the actual composition".⁵⁷¹ The individuality or "idiosyncrasy" in apprehending and treating the theme becomes manifest in the "style" that is expressed both in the "composition" and the "use of language (*Sprachgebrauch*)".⁵⁷² At the same time, Schleiermacher notes the open-ended and provisional character of this attempt of reconstructing the relations between the parts and the whole and restricts its pursuit to capturing the guiding thought from the spoken or written product. A distinction he makes in this context confirms Habermas's view that "thinking" and "linguistic expression" remain separate performances for him, which places him outside the full "linguistic turn".⁵⁷³ The aim of discovering "the subjective principle by which some elements are chosen to represent the whole (of the object)"⁵⁷⁴ only deals with thinking as it relates to outward expression, not to the internal thought process: "For thought without reference to representation does not belong here, because one can only infer very indirectly from the composition [i.e. the particular product being interpreted] to the meditation [i.e. the thoughts that gave rise to it]."⁵⁷⁵ Since the method of inference (*Rückschlussverfahren*) is directed towards the outward-fac-

---

568 Cf. KGA II/4, 101/ET 1998, 254 (II,5).
569 KGA II/4, 101/ET 1998, 254 (II,3).
570 Schleiermacher, *Brief Outline of Theology as a Field of Study* [1811 and 1830], trans. with an introduction by Terrence N. Tice (Lewiston, NY: The Edwin Mellen Press, 1988), 72–73, I § 31.
571 HK 105/ET 1977, 150–151. Cf. Kenny, "Correcting the History", 56.
572 HK 116/ET 166; KGA II/4, 102/ET 1998, 256 (II 11).
573 Habermas, Vol. II, 449.
574 KGA II/4, 108/ET 1998, 261 (II 27).
575 KGA II/4, 102/ET 1998, 255 (II 6).

ing thought production, it aims to grasp the specific way of thinking that produced the text, not the total personality of the author.[576]

The operation that hovers between the "technical" and the "psychological" seems to aim at an intermediate level: between the spontaneity of thinking, located at the level of the transcendental subject as the condition of the possibility of individual expression, and the concrete historical individual. Distinct speakers can make themselves comprehensible to each other on account of this general level. In its world relation as such, subjectivity displays shared, general capacities. It is at the level of linguistic expression that concrete individuality comes into play. It is not possible to deduce the "sense (*Sinn*)" of a sentence from the unities of meaning (the object of the grammatical interpretation); it can only be recreated by the listener whose own imagination (*Einbildungskraft*) is required for a creative unlocking of the individual "sense" in his or her interpretation.[577]

Reinhold Rieger underlines these two linked aspects: Schleiermacher's philosophical foundation for Hermeneutics is post-Kantian, that is, it no longer relates to an objectivised "meaning", as Rationalist treatments did, but to individual "sense" (*Sinn*).[578] But the capacity to do so is based on something shared by all individuals, a formal level from which the material, concrete exercise must be distinguished:

> The sense cannot be solely deduced from the meaning but must be created anew each time in the interpretation. The task of understanding is exactly this determination of sense. The sense of a text does not arise automatically (*ergibt sich nicht von selbst*) because it is co-de-

---

[576] HK 114/ET 1977, 163–164: "The individuality manifest in a person's way of combining and presenting thoughts is connected with every other expression of his individuality [...] Again, we do not deal with this connection and its mid-point, but only with the peculiarity of the presentation = style".

[577] In "Schleiermacher im Kontext der neuzeitlichen Hermeneutikentwicklung", 21, Scholtz emphasises the creative aspects of his theory for both using and understanding language: "If style is the whole person, then the text is not only a manifestation of his faculty of understanding (*Verstandes*), but also of his imagination (*Einbildungskraft*). In order to do justice already to this fact, the interpreter needs also his own imagination."

[578] Rieger, *Wissen*, 333: "The turn away from an objective hermeneutics and the elaboration of a decisively subject-oriented hermeneutics of sense is a consequence of the transcendental turn to the subject by Kant's *Critique of Pure Reason*. It put an end to the illusion of an immediate access to what is objective and provided space for the spontaneity and creativity of the subject for the constitution of objectivity. What is objective is no longer something that is independent of the subject but is something which has been created in its determinedness (*in seiner Bestimmtheit Geschaffenes*) by the subject. Its ground of being however eludes (*ist entzogen*) the spontaneity of the subject."

termined by individuality [...] the use of method and rules is necessary to allow for a transformation of what is individual into what is general. But since the rules are general themselves, they cannot completely do justice to the individual [...] and a creative act of generating the sense must be added.[579]

These analyses help in specifying where the innovation – which Habermas, too, wants to maintain as part of the interaction of speaker and language – is to be located, and they also explain the contribution of the listener. They insist on the inventiveness of both, having traced the radicality of Schleiermacher's theory design, and thus protect his conception against critiques that regard it as lacking acceptance of the truly enabling power of language.[580] Between an overemphasis either on individuality or on the totality of language, Schleiermacher maintains a balance which begins, however, with the individual's power to use and understand it.

8.3 Schleiermacher as a post-Kantian theologian

The "general" element required to prevent "irrationality"[581] or lack of comprehensibility, and defended by scholars of the Hermeneutics against an interpretation that links it to a Romantic theory of feeling,[582] is equally relevant for the analysis of self-consciousness in the second edition of the *Glaubenslehre*. Thouard identifies the need, but also the possibility to argue for the compatibil-

---

579 Rieger, *Wissen*, 302. Cf. Kenny, "Correcting the History", 52–53, Fn. 17, and Thouard, "Passer entre les langues", 64, quoted above, 8.1.3.
580 Cf., for example, Joachim Ringleben, "Die Sprache bei Schleiermacher und Humboldt. Ein Versuch zum Verhältnis von Sprachdenken und Hermeneutik", in *Schleiermacher und die wissenschaftliche Kultur des Christentums*, edited by Günter Meckenstock, with Joachim Ringleben (Berlin/New York: De Gruyter, 1991, reprint 2019): 473–492, in which he subordinates the role of individuality to the language system.
581 This is Schleiermacher's term in the *Dialectic* of 1814, as Berner points out with the following quote: "The irrationality of the individual can only be balanced (*ausgeglichen*) by the unity of language and the irrationality of language only by the unity of reason. The irrationality of the individual can only be balanced by the identity of language since everyone with their thinking is integrated (*aufgeht in*) into language. This is the dam against the sceptical tendency which wishes to present it as unlimited". Berner, "Das Übersetzen verstehen", 52–53, with reference to *Vorlesungen über die Dialektik*, KGA II/10/1, 190.
582 Scholtz, "Schleiermacher im Kontext der neuzeitlichen Hermeneutik-Entwicklung", 4, comments: "Only that divination and presentiment (*Ahnung*) make a better fit for the prejudice about the Romantic philosopher of feeling (*Nur passen Divination und Ahnung besser in das Vorurteil vom romantischen Gefühlsphilosophen*)."

ity of the language theory with the enquiry into the structures of self-consciousness elaborated in the philosophical "Introduction" prior to the material dogmatics: "The fact that language is already a prior given for us (*dass uns die Sprache schon vorher gegeben ist*) [...] does not in any way contradict the results (*Erträge*) of the *Glaubenslehre* on the 'immediate self-consciousness', but is indeed compatible with it (*verträgt sich sehr wohl damit*)".[583] The two propositions at the centre of all the subsequent attempts of interpretation are:

"§ 3. The piety which forms the basis of all ecclesiastical communions is, considered purely in itself, neither a Knowing nor a Doing, but a modification of Feeling, or of immediate self-consciousness."[584]

"§ 4. The common element in all howsoever diverse expressions of piety, by which these are conjointly distinguished from all other feelings, or, in other words, the self-identical essence of piety, is this: the consciousness of being absolutely dependent, or, which is the same thing, of being in relation with God."[585]

Before examining in greater detail the much-discussed argumentation of these two propositions in comparison with their summary by Habermas (8.3.2), I will outline three typical misinterpretations that §§ 3 and 4 have attracted (8.3.1). Recognising the analysis of the "immediate self-consciousness" as transcendental still leaves it open how this pre-reflective level is determined (8.3.3). In conclusion, Habermas's inclusion of Schleiermacher's argumentation into postmetaphysical thinking will be discussed in its relevance for the relationship between faith and knowledge (8.3.4).

8.3.1 Three misinterpretations

One familiar line of interpretation is to read "feeling" as the singular of "feelings", thus as equivalent to emotions in the plural, at the level of everyday human experience. Schleiermacher's own formulation in § 4 allows for this read-

---

[583] Thouard, "Die Sprachphilosophie der Hermeneutik", 97.
[584] Schleiermacher, *The Christian Faith*, ET 1928, 5. ET 2016, vol. I, 9 translates: "The piety that constitutes the basis of all ecclesial communities, regarded purely in and of itself, is neither a knowing nor a doing but a distinct formation of feeling, or of immediate self-consciousness." However, "modification" is more precise for "*Bestimmtheit des Gefühls*" than "formation" since it presents piety as a specific determination of feeling and avoids the empirical connotation of "formation" in a community.
[585] ET 1928, 12. ET 2016, vol. I, 18 translates: "However diverse they might be, what all the expressions of piety have in common, whereby they are at the same time distinguished from all other feelings – thus the selfsame nature of piety – is this: that we are conscious of ourselves as absolutely dependent or, which intends the same meaning, as being in relation with God."

ing, even if § 3 has already identified a location in the singular presented as synonymous, namely "immediate self-consciousness" of which there can be no plural. In theology, subsuming the latter under "feelings" in the plural is a reading which is connected with the judgement that the anthropological turn conceived in these terms opens up the road towards Feuerbach's projection theory. The only remedy available is seen in securing a starting point for theology that is held to be unimpeachable by the critique of religion, namely the Word of God, spoken authoritatively in the Bible, which cannot be subjected to a human origin. Alister McGrath sees a direct connection between the work's "theological programme" based on "introspection" and Feuerbach's unveiling of religion as a projection: "Feuerbach's critique of religion called into question the propriety of inferring the existence or nature of 'God' from religious feeling, in that this feeling could only be interpreted anthropologically, and not theologically."[586] Since then, the *Glaubenslehre's* "unsatisfactory foundation" has been "exposed, its inadequacy" has become "obvious to all."[587]

Faced with this reading, the question arises how unavoidable a descent into the unveiling of the idea of God as a human projection is. For those who reject its alleged inevitability, the task is to show that the epistemological turn to the subject does not equate with giving up the difference between God and humans. This is why Thouard's comment is so insightful: it neither accepts the alignment of "feeling" with the subjective phenomena that are studied in psychology, nor does it establish language as interfering with the thesis of an "immediate" self-consciousness. On the contrary, he takes the elliptical structure of language system and speaker as an indication of the "historicity" and "finitude" of the human subject.[588] As will be shown in the following subsection, this awareness is key for the theory of self sketched in these two foundational paragraphs of the Introduction.

A second misrepresentation is to try to read the theory of "feeling" as a continuation of the *Speeches* which, after all, also use "feeling", as well as "intuition" and "sense", in their aim to connect the individual with the "universe" in their plea for religion as a genuine and irreducible human pursuit alongside "thinking" or metaphysics, and "morality". Key terms of this interpretation are "totalising", "encompassing" or "comprehensive" – in the sense of including the individual into a cosmic process. The well-thought-out change of framework

---

586 Alister McGrath, *The Making of Modern German Christology: From the Enlightenment to Pannenberg* (Oxford: Oxford University Press, 1986), 19.
587 McGrath, *The Making of Modern German Christology*, 47.
588 Thouard, "Passer entre les langues", 69: "La condition linguistique de la pensée est une des marques de sa finitude et de son historicité."

three decades after early Romanticism, also in response to the rapid succession of philosophical approaches which his theology seeks to relate to, is not explored. Organic metaphors such as "pulse" and "vascular system", "circulation", "temperature" and "assimilative power"[589] are replaced in the *Glaubenslehre* by a different analysis of the constitutive modes of "life": "a subject's remaining-within-oneself" (*Insichbleiben*) and "stepping-out-of-oneself" or "passing-beyond-self" (*Aussichheraustreten*).[590] They are traced back to the structure of self-consciousness which is marked by a "double constitution" consisting of two co-equal factors, "self-activity" and "receptivity". The move to the level of a transcendental analysis of the subject becomes evident in the terms used, "self-positing" and "not-having-posited-oneself-in-this-particular-way".[591] These concepts do not lend themselves to a simple contrast of "finite" and "infinite" but demand the use of a more intricate enquiry to explore the distinctions between self, world, and God. A reconstruction in Spinozist or Hegelian terms does not do justice to the stage reached in the *Glaubenslehre*, neither to the steps of the phenomenological enquiry presented in the first edition, nor to the transcendental enquiry achieved in the second version of 1830/31.

Thus, neither the psychological nor the Spinozist route can capture the theoretical assumptions discernible in the uncovering of temporal self-consciousness as a "feeling of absolute dependence" and as connected to a "Whence" of each individual's existence. Is its classification as "introspection" a better

---

589 Schleiermacher, *On Religion: Speeches to its Cultured Despisers*. Introduction, Translation and Notes by Richard Crouter (Cambridge: Cambridge University Press, 1988), 205. What already the *Speeches* had put forward, the equal standing of religion beside metaphysics and morality, is now proven in it is validity with the help of the new distinction of *Insichbleiben* and *Aussichheraustreten:* that knowing, doing, and feeling do indeed represent an exhaustive analysis of the basic functions of the human spirit.
590 Cf. ET 2016, I, 12. ET 1928, 8 uses "passing-beyond-self" for *Aussichheraustreten*.
591 Instead of the 1928 ET which calls the first "a self-caused" and the second "a non-self-caused element" (13), I am adapting Richard R. Niebuhr's translation in *Schleiermacher on Christ and Religion* (New York: Ch. Scribner's Sons, 1964) 122, which is faithful to the verbal (and therefore "process" rather than "object" oriented) character of Schleiermacher's choice of terms. The contrast is between "self-positing" (*Sichselbstsetzen*) and "not-having-posited-oneself-in-a-particular-way" (*Sichselbstnichtsogesetzthaben*), in other words, finding oneself determined prior to and without one's own doing. The second concept could also be translated as "not-having-posited-oneself-in-this-particular-way". The 2016 ET changes the meaning by rendering the first, active self-positing of the subject as a passive experience, as "a being positioned-as-a-self" over against "a not-having-been-positioned-as-such" (§ 4,1. I, 19). I have discussed the relevance of these translations for the interpretation of the analysis in *Self, Christ and God in Schleiermacher's Dogmatics. A Theology Reconceived for Modernity* (Berlin/Boston: De Gruyter, 2020), 42–44.

way forward? Can this be regarded as a general and neutral term for a process that is not concerned with self, others, and society as publicly visible units but with an interior reflection? Even before turning to Schleiermacher's Dogmatics, the warnings of commentators on the Hermeneutics should be heard. From their interest in distinguishing levels, their question is, whether the agent carrying out the introspection denotes a particular, concrete "person", or a "subject" whose formal capacities are being investigated.[592] From the context of the term in Habermas's outline of key positions in post-Kantian thinking, it becomes clear that he means the alleged "turn away from the world"[593] as an actual decision of a pious person who retreats from the public into the private life of her religiosity. This reading is linked to locating the author biographically in his Moravian upbringing, in the easily imaginable seclusion of Niesky and Barby, the institutional settings of his pietist education. Consistent with this explanation of his argument from the context of its author's youth is that Habermas establishes the "feeling of piety"[594] as its foundation. However, in §§ 3 and 4 the argument proceeds more precisely from "piety" expressly defined as a "modification (*Bestimmtheit*)" of feeling or immediate self-consciousness, thus, of a general basis given in every human being. The disputed interpretation of these propositions will now be investigated.

8.3.2 "Feeling or immediate self-consciousness" as the object of a transcendental enquiry

The argumentation offered within a philosophical anthropology, entitled "Ethics", forms part of the connection to the general consciousness of truth elaborated in the "Introduction". Engaging with philosophy and individual disciplines like history, hermeneutics and comparative religions takes the place of the usual explanation of the basis of dogmatics as reflecting on revelation as it is authoritatively laid down in the Bible. The innovation of outlining an entry route to a dogmatic system therefore documents to Christians as well as

---

[592] This crucial distinction used by Dieter Henrich, Konrad Cramer, Rudolf Langthaler and the theological commentators to be discussed next keeps the level of analysis of the transcendental subject separate from that of the "person" who is potentially identifiable in their lifeworld, a connection to which Habermas's theory shifts in a programmatic move. Cf. Langthaler, *Nachmetaphysisches Denken?*, 124–126.
[593] Habermas, "The Boundary between Faith and Knowledge", in *Between Naturalism and Religion*, trans. Ciaran Cronin (Cambridge: Polity, 2008): 209–247, 233.
[594] Habermas, "Boundary", 233.

to non-believers how the systematic reflection on a faith tradition is connected to a theory of human agency as such. "Piety" is not a "private" theme, it is claimed on the contrary as an irreducible element of every human existence.

Habermas's appraisal of Schleiermacher's position, identified as "simultaneously Christian and postmetaphysical",[595] combines two perspectives. On the one hand, he takes the term "feeling" to indicate a Romantic and "pietistic valorization (*Auszeichnung*) of religious inwardness (*Innerlichkeit*)":[596] Schleiermacher "shifts the boundary-line between faith and knowledge to the advantage of an authentic faith beyond mere reason".[597] On the other hand, when proposing religion as enjoying equal standing with the other two operative modes of reason, he is explained as "working out the intrinsic logic and the autonomy of religion (*Eigensinn und Eigenrecht des Religiösen*) using the basic concepts of the philosophy of consciousness".[598] Habermas agrees that it is through a transcendental argumentation that the author of the *Glaubenslehre* justifies this claim. How do the two interpretations go together? This becomes clear in the 2019 book which across its two volumes refers in various contexts to Kant's distinction between intelligible and empirical as part of the reception history of the Lutheran two kingdoms doctrine. Classifying the argumentation of §§ 3 and 4 as "transcendental" does not imply for Habermas that it is philosophical, since this method itself derives from religious origins. The rubric quoted above, of a "pietistic valorisation of religious inwardness" under which it is put does not contradict labelling it also as transcendental. For Schleiermacher however, the structural analysis of finite freedom elaborated in these two propositions stands as an undeniable insight of human reason into its constitution. A comparison will show that decisive steps and statements (8.3.2.1) as well as the method (8.3.2.2) of the reasoning by which a "God-consciousness" is to be established are reduced in their scope or misrepresented in Habermas's reconstruction.

8.3.2.1 Determining piety in a general theory of self-consciousness, or as a chosen "performance" and "conduct" of religious persons?

A problematic direction of moving the analysis away from a theory of consciousness becomes visible in the way in which the alternative interest to a "*fides quae creditur*" is defined:

---

595 Habermas, "Boundary", 232.
596 Habermas, "Boundary", 234.
597 Habermas, "Boundary", 232.
598 Habermas, "Boundary", 232.

As a philosopher, Schleiermacher is not interested in the contents of religious faith (*fides quae creditur*), but in the question of what it means in a performative sense to have faith (*fides qua creditur*). He distinguishes between a scientific theology that treats the content of faith in a dogmatic manner and the piety that inspires and sustains the personal conduct of the believer.[599]

Yet the analysis is neither about "conduct" nor merely about the believer but is intended as an enquiry into general human self-consciousness. Habermas's shift from piety "as a determination (*Bestimmtheit*) of feeling" (§ 3, Thesis) which requires a philosophical analysis of its own, to a "feeling of piety" also causes a change of level from investigating the depth structure of human subjectivity to identifying the content of an empirical feeling:

> Schleiermacher extends the Kantian architectonics of the faculties of reason without going beyond it when he assigns religious belief (*Glauben*) a transcendental place of its own alongside knowledge, moral insight and aesthetic experience. The religiosity of the person of faith now takes its place alongside the familiar faculties of reason. In the feeling of piety the person of faith is immediately aware of his own spontaneity and his absolute dependence on an other.[600]

Habermas's presentation is correct in pointing out the ongoing role of self-activity without which the "feeling of absolute dependence" could not be grasped. But the dual structure consisting of self-activity (*Selbstthätigkeit*) and receptivity (*Empfänglichkeit*) in which the subject already finds itself, that is the basis of the subsequent steps, is not followed up.[601] Habermas depicts as a choice, as turning away from the world to one's own inner life, what is an analysis of the ineluctable structural constitution of finite freedom:

> once it turns away from the world, the subject is overcome (*erfasst*) by a feeling of utter dependence as it becomes aware of the spontaneity of its own conscious life. In the process of intuitive self-assurance, it becomes conscious of its dependence on another being who first makes conscious life possible prior to our intentional distance from what we receive from the world and what we bring about in it.[602]

---

599 Habermas, "Boundary", 232–233.
600 Habermas, "Boundary", 233.
601 The English translation of Habermas's article chooses "responsiveness" for "*Empfänglichkeit*" and "autonomy" for "*Selbstthätigkeit*", instead of "self-activity". Both the 1928 and the 2016 translations of the *Glaubenslehre*, however, render the original more literally. The term "*Autonomie*" would have been available to Schleiermacher in German if he had wished to refer to human freedom with this concept.
602 Habermas, "Boundary", 233.

8.3.2.2 The method used in arguing for "absolute dependence"

It downplays the method and misses a key point of the argument when the reason for only assuming a "relative freedom" is attributed merely to external conditions: "Neither absolute freedom nor absolute dependence is conceivable for a finite subject turned toward the world. Just as absolute freedom is incompatible with the restrictions that the world places on situated agency, so, too conversely, absolute dependence is incompatible with the intentional distance from the world without which states of affairs cannot be grasped objectively".[603]

While Schleiermacher's analysis takes as its starting point the level of concrete, historically situated freedom, the enquiry is then carried out in the terms of transcendental logic. Thus, explaining his rejection of an absolute feeling of freedom only through limiting external circumstances fails to recognise that in the second edition, Schleiermacher breaks through to a structural analysis of human subjectivity. Its decisive insight is to identify the configuration of finite freedom in its own inescapable double constitution. Already the first edition of 1821/22 had insisted on freedom over against the world but had in its phenomenological description only distinguished between two types of a "co-determining cause" (*des Mitbestimmenden*) in temporal self-consciousness: one, the "interdivided (*in sich geteilte*) and finitely composed infinity" of the world towards which there is a "consciousness of freedom"; second, the experience of a "perfect, steady dependence that in no way is limited or pervaded (*durchschnitten*) by reciprocity (*Wechselwirkung*)". The second type is correlated with a "simple and absolute infinity" of the co-determining cause which is identified with dependence from God. The "Postscript" to this subsection ("*Zusaz*") explains that a decision on which comes first, the feeling or the concept of God, "does not belong here".[604] But the concept of God is presupposed as known, and has been analysed in the *Dialectic*. Due to the critiques from theological colleagues like Karl Gottlieb Bretschneider as well as from Hegel, Schleiermacher revised the argumentation in order to show the compatibility of an absolute dependence with the feeling of freedom. In the second edition it is the "double constitution" that has been found as the invariant structure of self-consciousness itself which indicates its "absolute dependence" to it. Thus, what is at stake at the level of transcendental logic is more than the "spontaneity of one's own conscious life", namely what has been called the elementary "essential constitution of finite freedom: Precisely *as free* human beings are we conscious of being *un*-

---

[603] Habermas, "Boundary", 233.
[604] F.D.E. Schleiermacher, *Der christliche Glaube 1821/22*, 2 Vols., ed. Hermann Peiter (Berlin/New York: De Gruyter, 1984) (= KGA 1/7.1.2), § 9,3, Vol. 1, 32.

free, as being tied to the structure of self-activity and receptivity"[605] which we can only enact and are unable to shake off.

Habermas is correct in pointing out that the thesis of a "Whence" (§ 4,4) claims a constitutive relationship to God. Yet his wording seems to align it with the different position that was developed in the *Speeches*: the "reassuring feeling of dependence on an all-encompassing cosmic being (*Gefühl der geborgenen Abhängigkeit von einem kosmisch Umgreifenden*)".[606] However, the cosmos or the totality of the world belongs to the realm towards which a "counter-action (*Gegenwirkung*)" of human freedom is possible in principle; thus, it is something towards which no absolute dependence obtains. Either both the human person and the cosmos (as a totality that is interdivided and finitely composed) are utterly dependent, or neither of them is.

It is true that in § 4,4, Schleiermacher overdraws the result of the philosophical analysis by claiming a "Whence", which in the material dogmatics will be explained as the absolute causality of God. Even the term "dependence" in § 3 already insinuates an anchor point rather than a void, a question which the philosophical insight into the facticity of human existence would have had to leave open. Yet the fact of this final conclusion does not turn each step of the argumentation into a theological one. The only way to do justice to §§ 3 and 4 is to reconstruct them as a reflection on the presuppositions of the pursuits of subjectivity, a level which Habermas considers as having been superseded by the linguistic turn. Thus, the following issue to be examined reconnects with the debate on language theory, treated in the first two subsections of this chapter: Schleiermacher claims that the location in which the thought of God arises is the "immediate self-consciousness". Interpreted as the subject's "pre-reflective familiarity" with itself, which one of two possible directions is it seen to take?

8.3.3 Two directions of interpreting the "immediate" or "pre-reflective" consciousness – egological or monist?

To summarise the progress of the second edition, the concept of God is no longer assumed as known from the *Dialectic*, that is, borrowed from the realm of theoretical reason, but is now originally derived from the consciousness of absolute dependence. Only through this correction is the independence of religion from

---

[605] Pröpper, *Theologische Anthropologie*, Vol. I, 471. He concludes: "It is this essential constitution of finite freedom itself which excludes an absolute feeling of freedom."
[606] Habermas, "Boundary", 237.

metaphysics and morality in effect established. The feeling of absolute dependence serves as the hermeneutical key to the word "God", as pointing to the absolute ground presupposed by the world and not simply opposed to it (as in the original Introduction). That is, only in the second edition is the meaning of the concept of God determined in an independent, underived way.

But what is the status of the "immediate self-consciousness" that Schleiermacher claims as the location of this "original revelation" (§ 4,4)? The options arising here connect with the question discussed before whether subjectivity is the result or the counterpart of intersubjectivity. Identified by Henrich as a "prior familiarity with oneself", "immediate self-consciousness" marks a difference in principle between the "I" and everyone else as second or third grammatical persons. It explains what the "special transcendental position" (*transzendentale Sonderstellung*), insisted on by Langthaler, is based on and why it is the condition for being able to recognise what is other than oneself. The "I" cannot be assimilated to the second or third person pronoun, and Habermas's theory is considered to be in danger of doing so.[607] In order to complete the discussion referred to earlier when Humboldt's and Schleiermacher's language theories were set off from the linguistic turn for which Habermas claimed them at least partly, this issue will now be treated in relation to its appearance in the Introduction of the *Glaubenslehre*. The further discussion that arises here is alluded to when Habermas mentions the "anonymous" ground proposed by Henrich and rejects it in favour of an explanation based on the linguistic turn.[608] The follow-

---

[607] In *Nachmetaphysisches Denken?*, 215, Langthaler discusses Habermas's use of G. H. Mead's theory to replace the original status of self-consciousness by "deriving it as a 'communicatively constituted phenomenon'", resulting in an "intersubjective core" of the I. He quotes Habermas's acknowledgement of the "surprising result" of the "intersubjectivistic" turn that "the consciousness that is centered, as it seems, in the ego is not something immediate or purely inward. Rather, self-consciousness forms itself on the path from without to within, through the symbolically mediated relationship to a partner in interaction" (*Postmetaphysical Thinking I*, 178. 177). In this context, Langthaler refers to the alternative "way out of the aporia" offered by Henrich: an "ego-less consciousness [...] which is no longer supposed to be distinguished by a self-relationship but still by a kind of originary familiarity [...] with oneself, however, as an impersonal factor" (217). Habermas discusses it critically as the "prereflexively familiar anonym of conscious life, which is open to Buddhistic as well as Platonistic interpretations" (*Postmetaphysical Thinking I*, 25) (cf. Langthaler, 219).

[608] In his response to the "Symposium on Faith and Knowledge" held in Vienna in 2005, Habermas refers to Henrich's approach in similar terms: "If the absolute, as in Henrich, is supposed to be revealed through the meditative dissolution of the problem of self-consciousness in an original awareness-of-oneself (*Mit-sich-vertraut-Sein*), this message betrays the original affinity between Platonism and the Far Eastern world religions" (*Postmetaphysical Thinking II*: 122–160, 146).

ing outline of two possibilities of thinking competing in their analyses of §§ 3 and 4 of *The Christian Faith*[609] is meant to show that also in a transcendental analysis, an alternative to the direction taken by Henrich exists; thus, abandoning the transcendental level as such in favour of the quasi-empirical reconstruction of linguistic interaction, as chosen by the *Theory of Communicative Action*, is not the only option. There are two readings of this level to choose between.

Does the concept of an "immediate self-consciousness" follow an "egological" approach, or a "monist" interpretation for which the world and humans are comprised in God? "Immediate" denotes a self-consciousness that is prior to the division between acting and thinking, thus at a pre-reflective level. The joint starting point of both positions is a philosophy of the subject. Disputed is whether a prior, ontological foundation between God and the human subject is being assumed, or whether God remains distinct from humans and the world as the absolute initiator of all out of nothing, *ex nihilo*. One approach prioritises unity, the other distinction and multiplicity. Henrich judges that the "two self-interpretations of self-consciousness can be deduced with equal justification (*mit gleichem Recht*) from the basic relationship".[610] Regarding §§ 3 and 4, by using the Fichtean term, "self-positing" and by identifying the subject as the centre of unity by making the changing impressions from the world its own, Schleiermacher's analysis remains centred on the subject as the principle of the reconstruction. The consciousness of God that arises at this level is identified as an "existential relationship".[611] Yet the "pre-reflective familiarity of the Ego with itself" can be interpreted, as Henrich and Manfred Frank do, as arising from an encompassing ground. Tracing this "non-egological theory of consciousness" back to Hölderlin, Novalis, and Schleiermacher, Frank opts for "an 'ego-less' (*ich-los*) theory of an anonymous familiarity with oneself (*Mit-sich-Bekanntsein*)

---

609 The following summary of the alternative between a "monist" and an "egological" interpretation is drawn from the discussion I portray in *Self, Christ and God in Schleiermacher's Dogmatics*, 61–65.
610 Henrich, "Das Selbstbewusstsein und seine Selbstdeutungen", in Henrich, *Fluchtlinien. Philosophische Essays* (Frankfurt: Suhrkamp, 1982): 99–124, 117, quoted by Michael Bongardt in "Einheit ja – aber welche?", in *Dogma und Denkform. Strittiges in der Grundlegung von Offenbarungsbegriff und Gottesgedanke*, ed. Klaus Müller and Magnus Striet (Regensburg: Pustet, 2005): 85–100, 90. Bongardt argues that either type of religion can ground ethical responsibility. Monistic religious traditions based on "life in God" call for equal care by each part of the unity for the others, while monotheistic religions based on "life in front of God" include the obligation to respect and foster the freedom of the other (91).
611 Schleiermacher, *On the Glaubenslehre. Two Letters to Dr. Lücke*, trans. James O. Duke and Francis Fiorenza (Ann Arbor: Scholars Press, 1981), 40.

or feeling".⁶¹² In contrast, Saskia Wendel defends its interpretation as "the first principle of a theory of subjectivity" which seeks to solve the "reflection trap". This term sums up the finding in earlier analyses of Johann Gottlieb Fichte that the subject in its self-reflection gets caught in the dilemma of always being late in trying to achieve its goal of capturing the Ego in its spontaneity.⁶¹³ One way out of this circularity is to assume "an ego-less being [...] as the immanent ground of self-consciousness",⁶¹⁴ an anonymous ground that is at the same time differentiated, comprising others as moments within it. As we have seen, such monist thinking is not convincing for Habermas. Also for Wendel it lacks the decisive factor: it would lead to a "heteronomous understanding of self-consciousness because [...] it is not I who thinks, feels, experiences, but an ego-less ground of which I am a moment, thus, ultimately an anonymous *Id* to which my feeling is owed: but then it is not at all my feeling (*je meines*)."⁶¹⁵

Yet also the avenue proposed by the move to language-based intersubjectivity fails to give a sufficient account of the non-substitutable status of subjectivity. The attempt to replace the constitutive role of the "I" as principle of the world relationship with its alleged constitution by the "other" of language and interaction was critiqued by Langthaler. Substituting the "I" by the "We" risked collapsing the distinction between intersubjectivity and world relation, since reflection on the subjective component is required for access to "objectivity". This does not mean that the material world is caused by the transcendental subject but that it is nevertheless involved in establishing the link between itself and a world which is not just naively accessible. Habermas acknowledges this to some extent when explaining that "absolute dependence is incompatible with the intentional dis-

---

612 Manfred Frank, "Fragmente einer Geschichte der Selbstbewusstseins-Theorie von Kant bis Sartre", in Frank, *Selbstbewusstseinstheorien von Fichte bis Sartre* (Frankfurt: Suhrkamp, 2nd edn 1993): 413–599, 508, quoted by Magnus Lerch, *All-Einheit und Freiheit. Subjektphilosophische Klärungsversuche in der Monismus-Debatte zwischen Klaus Müller und Magnus Striet* (Würzburg: Echter, 2009), 15, Fn. 25, in his analysis of the background positions to this debate.
613 Saskia Wendel, *Affektiv und inkarniert. Ansätze Deutscher Mystik als subjekttheoretische Herausforderung* (ratio fidei 15) (Regensburg: Pustet, 2002), 274, Fn. 117, quoted by Lerch, *All-Einheit*, 178, Fn. 875. Lerch here takes up Wendel's thesis that "the egological theory does not *per se* and automatically lead into the reflection trap; it is only the circular assumption that the free Ego respectively its consciousness of itself is the *result* of reflection that does so." The reconstruction of the core of Schleiermacher's argument as an egological theory is thus based on the view that the much-quoted "reflection trap" is not the necessary fate of this approach. Other theological contributors to this debate between Thomas Pröpper and Klaus Müller have been Georg Essen, Magnus Striet, Susanne Schaefer and Bernhard Nitsche.
614 Lerch, *All-Einheit*, 175.
615 Wendel, *Affektiv und inkarniert*, 275, quoted by Lerch, *All-Einheit*, 75.

tance from the world without which states of affairs cannot be grasped objectively".[616] But the "intentional distance" is not traced back to the "I".

For the advocates of interpreting the "pre-reflective familiarity with oneself" as an egological theory, it is convincing because it avoids a gap between what is to be explained – the Ego in its free capacity for self-reflection – and an anonymous ground which is assumed to be differentiated in itself. The latter view reduces the Ego to one among all the instances of otherness, which are moments but not agents themselves. In contrast, it is important to retain the active part exercised by self-consciousness in this most radical insight into its constitution. If it was not itself the faculty of uniting the impressions it receives from the world as elements affecting it, the insight could not be made.

What Schleiermacher's analysis achieves with his concept of "immediate self-consciousness" that anchors the Ego in a pre-reflective awareness of itself at a level prior to thinking, is to make a new understanding of the unity of self-consciousness possible. It is a position that is compatible with a religious solution to the abyss of its facticity, namely the personal decision to believe in God as the Creator who founded the world and gave life and independence to all its creatures. What the author of the *Glaubenslehre* does not disclose, and what remains hidden by locating God as "given" in this self-consciousness, is the tacit option for ultimate meaning contained in it. Rather than face the ambivalent, if not shattering effect of becoming aware of one's own contingency, a ground is assumed.[617] At this final stage Habermas is right, and in agreement with a number of theologians, that Schleiermacher's transcendental analysis of subjectivity ultimately becomes theological. It claims as an "immediate" consciousness what is really only a hope, an ultimate ground to a self and to a world that are contingent. But as a theory of subjectivity, its starting point and initial conclusions avoid the problems which the alternative to subject philosophy, the linguistic turn, encounters: namely the absorption of the subject into language and intersubjectivity. The subject-object dichotomy and the position of self-consciousness found in Descartes which the "third categories" proposed by Habermas seek to overcome has already been displaced by the nuanced account pio-

---

616 Habermas, "Boundary", 233.
617 Pröpper, *Theologische Anthropologie*, Vol. I, 478: "The contribution of freedom in opting for the positing of God is, however, obscured by Schleiermacher's reference to it as immediate consciousness, thus insinuating its inevitability. Yet what is merely veiled in this way is that it is indeed (also in his own argumentation) a mediated one: namely mediated through the negation of absolute freedom, thus, through the insight of freedom or free reason itself into the abysmal contingency of its existence. This, however, remains a highly ambivalent finding which still very much permits opposite interpretations."

neered by Kant.⁶¹⁸ Habermas entitles as "introspection" what is an enquiry into the conditions of possibility of the subject's relation to the world and to others. He thus abolishes the difference between the actions of an individual in her lifeworld, and a meta-level of identifying the presupposed internal structure of consciousness that enables her to initiate reflections and actions of her own. On the one hand, faced with a hard naturalism that reduces consciousness to neural processes,⁶¹⁹ Habermas has been highlighting "self-reflection" as key for the method of philosophy; on the other, the "postmetaphysical" strictures reduce his ability to reconstruct Schleiermacher's (and Kierkegaard's) analyses of facticity since they require the conceptual means of a philosophy of subjectivity. Pitting this thought-through outline of the factors operative in self-consciousness as a Romantic and Pietist withdrawal into "inwardness" against engagement in the world is especially misleading for Schleiermacher. Concluding this section, Habermas's view of the problems and achievements of Schleiermacher's argumentation will be discussed in its relevance for the relationship between faith and knowledge.

8.4 Consequences of the framework for analysing Schleiermacher and its effect on relating "faith" and "knowledge"

The new work of 2019 discusses Schleiermacher mainly as a language theorist. It reaffirms the necessity of the linguistic turn and accesses "religion" from its foundations. The broader perspective is an analysis of the "pathologies of rationalisation" and the ability of religious traditions to keep "mentalities of solidarity" alive, as well as the question of whether they are capable of endorsing from their own self-conceptions the will to coexist with each other. Thus their contributions to the public sphere are wanted in the interest of jointly working out well-reflected solutions to impasses posed by alternative directions in scientific-technological cultures competing for selection. In order to support this goal, the link between religion and reason appears as less important than the motiva-

---

618 In *Nachmetaphysisches Denken?*, 169, Langthaler refers to Kant's distance from a "self-sufficient and solitary" understanding of self-consciousness, as evident in his critique of Descartes.
619 Cf., for example, Habermas's detailed engagement with naturalism in *Between Naturalism and Religion*, 151–208.

tion these traditions can provide for a communicative understanding of reason that is, however, threatened by "defeatism".[620]

The continuity of this diagnosis of contemporary culture and the role assigned to religion will first be documented (8.4.1) before asking what the assessment of Schleiermacher, the key inaugurator in Modernity of a new approach to theology, means for the relationship between religion and postmetaphysical reason (8.4.2).

8.4.1 Continuities in postmetaphysical thinking on religion

Contributions from religious worldviews to opinion and will formation in civil society continue to be valued for their heuristic and problem-spotting qualities and defended as not requiring prior translation. The status of these positions has been clarified much earlier: Religions "differ from non-religious ethical value orientations in their internal connection with 'truth' claims (of a distinctive kind): religions are worldviews, not values systems. As a result, they possess a cognitive content and a motivational force that secular outlooks on life lack."[621]

This cognitive character gives significance especially to approaches that engage with the modern condition which is increasingly marked by polarities: "naturalism raises epistemological questions, the self-enlightenment of religious consciousness under conditions of modern life brings theological questions into play. This explains my interest in Schleiermacher, Kierkegaard, and twentieth century theology".[622] Already from Karl Jaspers's Axial Age thesis, the insight is taken that "it would be irrational to reject those 'strong' traditions as 'archaic' residua instead of elucidating their internal connection with modern forms of

---

620 Also in his "Postscript" (Vol. II, 767–807), Habermas refers to Kant's "attempt to build bridges in the philosophy of history so that reason does not despair from the defeatism brooding (*brütenden*) in it" (Vol. II, 805). Explaining his motivation to engage in the immense project of reconstructing the dual roots of the Western tradition within the Axial Age formations, he points to the "question of the motivational roots of processes of moral learning. The insight that under conditions of secular thinking we do not avail of an equivalent for the promise of a 'rescuing justice' which had once been articulated in the metaphysical and religious worldviews (*Weltbilder*) illuminates the precarious status of reason-led (*vernünftige*) freedom" (Vol. II, 778).
621 Habermas, *Postmetaphysical Thinking II*, 126. I am drawing on some of the points I have examined in the chapter, "Jürgen Habermas", in *Religion and European Philosophy*, ed. Philip Goodchild and Hollis Phelps (London: Routledge, 2017): 141–155.
622 Habermas, "A Symposium on Faith and Knowledge", in *Postmetaphysical Thinking II*, 122–160, 155.

thought".⁶²³ Yet what this connection consists in, is still in need of determination. Is the reticence against identifying these internal points of connection due to a cautious decision to forego judgement on religion? Habermas defends it as "agnosticism" against "secularistic" proposals which declare it as definitive that secular reason has nothing to learn from religions.⁶²⁴ Or is the silence on the points of connection with "modern forms of thought" the result of a postmetaphysical definition of reason which no longer sustains the questions that were previously posed in philosophy of religion?

On the one hand, postmetaphysical reason is critical of approaches that know too much in this respect, namely the meaninglessness of religion. It will leave open and not refute the truth claim of a religious faith stance that opts for belief in the existence of God. Both philosophy and religious positions share in the reflective ability to critically relate new pieces of empirical knowledge to their own perspectives:

> philosophy shares with religious and metaphysical doctrines that remarkable (*markant*) relation to ourselves which gets lost when philosophy understands itself only as a provider (*Zuliefererbetrieb*) for the cognitive sciences. While the sciences turn their attention exclusively to an object area, philosophy is interested not only in knowledge but in enlightenment – that is, what a newly found piece of world knowledge *means for us*. It allows itself to partake in an interaction between world and self-understanding.⁶²⁵

---

623 Habermas, *Between Naturalism and Religion*, 6.
624 In "Reply to My Critics" in *Habermas and Religion*, ed. Craig Calhoun, Eduardo Mendieta and Jonathan VanAntwerpen, trans. Ciaran Cronin (Cambridge: Polity, 2013): 347–390, 366–367 (reprinted as "Religion and Postmetaphysical Thinking: A Reply", in *Postmetaphysical Thinking II*, 77–121), he rejects as "secularistic" the proposal by J. M. Bernstein who stated: "This is not to deny that there is an existential excess to religious beliefs that defies the translation procedure; *but for us that excess is not simply unavailable to philosophical reflection, it is what is permanently lost in the transition to modernity.*" Habermas responds: "What does 'permanently lost' mean here? The agnostic only asserts that these semantic contents are *inaccessible* and refrains from making judgments concerning the truth claim that believers associate with them. In leaving a truth claim *undecided*, the agnostic expresses his failure to understand a form of discourse [...] I share J. M. Bernstein's adherence to methodological atheism and argue (against John Rawls, for example) that the practical reason of political philosophy, rather than the truths proclaimed by religious communities, must have the final say when it comes to the rational accessibility of secular constitutional essentials. But that does not prevent me from adopting an agnostic stance on the dogmatic foundations of the validity claims of a religious interlocutor."
625 Habermas, "Politik und Religion", in *Politik und Religion. Zur Diagnose der Gegenwart*, ed. Friedrich Wilhelm Graf and Heinrich Meier (München: C. H. Beck, 2013): 287–300, 297.

On the other hand, it is not clear if the "self-understandings" to which also the 2019 work attaches great importance[626] are admitted to the forum of reason. The question remains whether theology as the reflection on the history of thinking and practice of a religious community under the norm of its essence definition is allowed to enter the "space of reasons", or whether these can only be secular. While deemed "cognitive", is its truth claim set apart to a degree that "truth" becomes an equivocal concept?

8.4.2 Problems of fitting Schleiermacher into a postmetaphysical approach

As outlined in subsection 2 of this chapter, the reason for including Schleiermacher into the postmetaphysical stage of reasoning is his endorsement of Kant's anthropological turn. It is specified in theology by endorsing the Dialectic of the *Critique of Pure Reason* that puts an end to arguments for God's existence from the outside world. Having contrasted Kant and Hume also regarding the role given to empirical feeling as a basis for morality, he concludes: "in a quite different way Friedrich Schleiermacher introduced feeling as the systematic connecting link between faith and knowledge in the architectonic of Kant's transcendental philosophy."[627]

What is shared by Schleiermacher's and Habermas's approaches is the rejection of an objectifying metaphysics, and the need to detach the possible truth of religious convictions from the previously held framework of an encompassing philosophical conception of the totality of the world. In order to justify the compatibility of Christian dogmatics with reason in a different way, Schleiermacher's intention is to locate faith in God anthropologically in a dimension that can neither be reduced to the imperative and hope of practical reason, nor to idealist metaphysics. But can his alternative attempt to argue for the reasonableness of faith in God through an analysis of subjectivity be accepted as a competing claim *within* philosophy if the transcendental approach itself has already been

---

626 Habermas, 2019, Vol. II, 99: "From then onwards philosophy and theology share the functions of reaching understandings on world and self (*Welt- und Selbstverständigungsfunktionen*). Philosophy will take the initiative in this competition and determine the level of reflection – so that at the end of the eighteenth century Schleiermacher will react to Kant's *Critique of Pure Reason*." Cf. also Vol. II, 193.
627 Habermas, "A Symposium on Faith and Knowledge", in *Postmetaphysical Thinking II*, 118.

dismissed as "introspective", even "narcissistic", and as "removed from the world"?[628]

As we have seen, Habermas contextualises the analyses of the Introduction of 1830/31 not only in its era, but also in the biography of its author. He supports the diagnosis of "inwardness" by arguing also from the history of reception. Yet what validity claim can be retained if an argumentation is explained from its context and from a part of its history of effects that is, moreover, multi-faceted? After all, Schleiermacher's claim reaches farther than merely to an internal theological audience. In the second edition of the *Glaubenslehre*, as shown before, he adds a statement that expresses the stringency of the argumentation proposed in its difference from the phenomenological mode of reasoning in the original version: "Assent to these statements can be expected without qualification. No one would gainsay them, moreover, who is capable of self-observation to any degree and who can deem the distinctive object of our investigations to be of interest".[629] Also in his language theory, Schleiermacher had maintained that "one does not understand anything as long as one has not grasped it as necessary and has been able to 'construct' it".[630]

Habermas, however, infers backwards from positions that were developed subsequently in "Culture Protestantism" and points out "the price that Schleiermacher has to pay for his elegant reconciliation of religion and modernity, faith, and knowledge. The integration of the Church into society and the privatization of faith rob the religious relation to transcendence of its disruptive power within the world."[631] Habermas derives from the intended reconciliation of religion and modernity that long before the end of the nineteenth century, already Schleiermacher's work champions the privacy of the soul and that its concept of salvation is equally individualistic. It is seen as paving the way to Adolf von Harnack's reduction of the Christian message of the kingdom of God to pious interiority when "the presence of God withdraws into the depths of the individual soul".[632] In a psychologising description, the analysis of self-consciousness as arriving at the insight of its absolute dependence is presented as the pursuit of "self-assurance": "In the process of intuitive self-assurance, it becomes conscious of its dependence on another being who first makes conscious life possi-

---

628 Cf., for example, Habermas, Vol. II, 490, with reference to Hegel's critique of the "narcissism of a knowing subject that imposes its categories on a world that remains exterior", and Vol. II, 369, 371, 452 on the "transcendental subject" as "world-removed *(weltenthobenen)*".
629 Schleiermacher, *Christian Faith*, ET 2016, I, 20. See above, 7.2.2.
630 Schleiermacher, KGA II/4, 6 (1805, 1809/10).
631 Habermas, "Boundary", 234.
632 Habermas, "Boundary", 234.

ble prior to our intentional distance from what we receive from the world and what we bring about in it".[633] This interest is attributed to a perspective that is deemed to be foreign to philosophy: "For Schleiermacher and Kierkegaard [...] *individual* salvation, which poses the greater difficulties for a philosophy oriented to the universal, constitutes the core of faith".[634] This alleged privatisation is contrasted to "the idea of the 'people of God' inherited from Kant" by Hegel and Marx and their combination in a "philosophy that attempts to assimilate the *collective* emancipatory moment of the Judeo-Christian promise of salvation".[635] Not only does this judgement fail to note the political, civic, and academic struggles Schleiermacher engaged in; it also does not account for the theological stance he took in arguing against Augustine's and Calvin's distinction of the elected from the damned, for an eschatology that declared an isolated, less than universal salvation to be deficient from a Christian point of view.[636]

Habermas's concluding judgement that the *Glaubenslehre* provides a "comforting (*besänftigenden*) analysis of the pious existence reconciled with modernity"[637] is built on mistaking a transcendental analysis for an interiorisation and privatisation. The misinterpretation of his argument which, bar the final step, is a philosophical one, seems to reflect Habermas's view that the "reasons and abysses of reason (*Gründe und Abgründe der Vernunft*)"[638] followed up in the philosophy of consciousness are an unnecessary dramatisation; it is possible to remedy them by going to the level of a publicly visible prior connectedness within the lifeworld. This means that the connection between religion and a concept of reason marked by its ongoing questioning towards what is unconditioned is disrupted. His assessment that philosophy of religion belongs to the apologetics of a faith tradition[639] confirms, rather than contradicts this view. Reason itself has no link to such reflection, and it does not constitute an internal philosophical discipline. In line with this position, the 2019 work does not claim to be a

---

633 Habermas, "Boundary", 233.
634 Habermas, "Boundary", 232.
635 Habermas, "Boundary", 232.
636 Cf. Matthias Gockel's discussion of Schleiermacher's defence of the *apokatastasis panton*, the reconciliation of all, in *Barth and Schleiermacher on the Doctrine of Election* (Oxford: Oxford University Press, 2006), 30–36.
637 Habermas, "Boundary", 235.
638 Habermas, *Moralbewusstsein und kommunikatives Handeln* (Frankfurt: Suhrkamp, 1983), 26. The ET, *Moral Consciousness and Communicative Action*, trans. Christian Lenhardt and Shierry Weber Nicholsen (Cambridge, MA: MIT Press, 1991), 18, sums up this formulation as "yesteryear's classical philosophy of reason".
639 Habermas, *Kritik der Vernunft*, Vol. 5 (Frankfurt: Suhrkamp, 2009), 31.

philosophy of religion,⁶⁴⁰ and it has become clearer why this is so. Reason is not identified as "autonomous" in a sense that leaves the connection from the limit questions of practical reason to philosophy of religion open, but as "secular". This limitation, however, also undermines the possibility of accounting for the basis on which secular outlooks may benefit from taking an interest in insights from religions: "The imposition consists in the demand that state citizens should not rule out the possibility of recognizing in the articulated language of religious positions and expressions resonances of suppressed intuitions of their own".⁶⁴¹

A question that becomes inescapable, but that is not asked, in view of "intuitions of their own" coming at secular fellow citizens from a religious tradition, is, what makes this point of coincidence between two traditions of reflection possible?⁶⁴² What Herta Nagl-Docekal points out in relation to Rawls is also true in Habermas's case: without Kant's thesis that "all religions have their origin in the same need of reason (*Bedürfnis der Vernunft*)", it is not possible to maintain the implicit assumption that they can indeed overlap in supporting freedom and equality.⁶⁴³ Without this link to reason, religions can only appear in their difference. Their specificity must then be sought in an alternative factor of their presence as traditions in the public sphere: their "ritual" basis.

---

640 Cf. Georg Essen, "Rezension Jürgen Habermas, *Auch eine Geschichte der Philosophie, 1–2*, Berlin: Suhrkamp Verlag 2019, in *Zeitschrift für Neuere Theologiegeschichte* 28 (2021) (forthcoming).
641 Habermas, "Politik und Religion", 293.
642 In *Studienausgabe* (Frankfurt: Suhrkamp, 2009), Vol. III, 287, Habermas treats a related matter, namely the need to assume an "area of rational overlapping" between traditions, a "*tertium comparationis* which allows us to relate the two linguistic worlds to each other", quoted by Martin Breul, *Diskurstheoretische Glaubensverantwortung. Konturen einer religiösen Epistemologie in Auseinandersetzung mit Jürgen Habermas*, (Regensburg: Pustet, 2019), 97.
643 Nagl-Docekal, "Moral und Religion aus der Optik der heutigen rechtsphilosophischen Debatte", in *Deutsche Zeitschrift für Philosophie* 56 (2008): 843–855, 854.

9 Reappraising the Counterparts: Secular Reason as the Default Position, Religion as "Other"?

In conclusion, the steps of the enquiry of the foregoing chapters (9.1.1) and crucial findings (9.1.2) will be summarised. Then two questions that have turned out to be key theory decisions will be discussed. One, with "ritual" emerging as the anchor point of religion for postmetaphysical thinking, its role in the origins of Christianity and in the turns of its history of thinking will be recalled. The necessity of theological interpretation will be exemplified in relation to three rituals at crossroads of future developments: sacrifice as a means of attaining forgiveness, baptism, and the Lord's Supper (9.2). Thirdly, the choice of the guiding categories for the analysis of the two strands of European thinking will be examined. Does it affect the enquiry to distinguish them as "faith" and "knowledge", instead of "faith" and "reason", and which determination of "reason" is to be endorsed, if this is judged to be the more encompassing category (9.3)?

9.1 A summary of the course of enquiry

9.1.1 Its guiding thesis and steps

In his new work, the theorist of communicative action carries out an in-depth and wide-ranging account of the origins of modern self-understandings in the two formations emerging together in the Axial Age: philosophy and the world religions. Focusing from his fourth chapter onwards on the contingent roots of European thinking, their encounters, transformations and separations from Antiquity onwards, he explains the strands that have resulted in the appearance of a postmetaphysical stage of thinking. Its emergence was helped by core intuitions of the Jewish and Christian monotheisms that broke through the substance ontological categories and a latent monism of the Greek approaches. Spurred by changes in knowledge and the need to account for them, as well as by the internal transformation of concepts affected by the encounter of conflicting worldviews, new understandings of self and world were reflected in theology, religious practice, and philosophy.

The chapters of this study have followed Habermas's outline of the moves from earlier to later guiding assumptions and frameworks. Chapter One examined current discourses on history and their relevance for studies on Christian origins. This entry point was chosen in order to clarify disputes about understandings of objectivity, premises and methods of research. Chapters Two, Three and Four examined debates on the foundations of the Christian tradition in Second Temple Judaism and its expansion into Gentile cultures, Chapter Five on the authors and Councils of the patristic era. From the directions taken by the first patristic theologians against Gnosticism, it offered a contrasting evaluation to Habermas's view of Augustine's complex work as a culmination, not as a counterposition to earlier patristic thinking. The need for such distinctions arose from the singular importance given to his work as the epitome of Christian theology in comparison with which, as it turned out, modern approaches were judged as too accommodating. The question guiding this enquiry was whether an implicit option for a normative self-understanding of Christianity on Augustinian lines was prefiguring the subsequent framework for assessing the properties and potential of religion in the contemporary world. Is its placement as the opposite to reason – which as a consequence of Nominalism itself diverged into two different tracks in the eighteenth century – not based on quite specific and controversial understandings of sin and salvation, Christ and the doctrine of God? By privileging the link from Paul to Augustine and by portraying Kant as a response to Luther, other lines of continuity appear as underrepresented. For an assessment of "faith" in relation to "knowledge", however, the connection from early patristic theology to Duns Scotus, whose work Habermas highlights perceptively, would have been crucial. As explained in Chapter Six, it accepts a general consciousness of truth as the independent dialogue partner of theology, using univocal philosophical terms. This position is continued by Schleiermacher in his positive theological response to the anthropological turn inaugurated by Kant. By taking Paul and Augustine as the measure of Christian identity, instead of as influential but not unquestioned positions at the origin and later turning points of Christianity, the path to casting "faith" as the "other" of reason is facilitated. The interpretation of Kant's new starting point in Volume Two is discussed in Chapters Seven and Eight: first, regarding the thesis of Hans Blumenberg that Modernity is a counterposition to the arbitrary power of the God of Nominalism, and regarding the relationship of theoretical and practical reason; secondly, in relation to the linguistic turn which the Frankfurt discourse ethicist sees as beginning with Wilhelm von Humboldt and interprets as a departure from Kant's philosophy of consciousness. Having subjected the understanding of "reason" in the relationship between language and thinking to scrutiny in the first parts of Chapter Eight, the third section turns to examining the "faith" side. It shows Schleiermacher's foundation of theology in Modernity to be based on a transcendental-philosophical analysis of human self-consciousness which contrasts with its reconstruction by Habermas as a religious turn to Pietist interiority. With Kant and Schleiermacher, two distinct approaches to the interaction between "reason" and "faith" could have been found which – instead of turning religion into the "other" of a reason understood as "secular" – elucidate it as a *further determination* (*Weiterbestimmung*) of reason in its undiminished orientation towards meaning.

9.1.2 Assessments of the course of European thought depending on their starting points

As is evident from the reviews of the work, the systematic strength, perceptiveness and clarity in structuring three millennia of intellectual streams, their backdrops and outcomes as well as the ongoing disputes between different disciplines on the issues they raise have been greeted with great respect and admiration. It takes nothing from the eminence and unparalleled stature of the studies themselves to state that corrections of starting points and subsequent intersections will affect their overall direction and conclusions. The significance of the point of departure chosen for the further unfolding of the overall thesis becomes clear with the dominant position accorded to Paul's interpretation of the salvific role of Jesus Christ. It exemplifies one reading of the impact of Christianity on the course of European thinking that results in pitting "faith" as the opposite to "reason" and agency. The recurrent shorthand term for the Christian concept of the human person signifies this unmistakeably: the "remorseful sinner". The assumption that Augustine's idea of an inherited original sin is already rooted in Paul drives the contraction of theological anthropology to this aspect assumed to be dominant through all the stages of Christian thinking.[644] An alternative starting point would have been the designation of *imago Dei*. It gives value to human agency, to the capability to be a faithful witness to Jesus Christ and to the visible effects of encouraging human inventiveness in new institutions and forms of living. Recognising the role of law for equality, knowledge as requiring the interaction of disciplines at universities, or compassion demanding struc-

---

[644] Cf. Habermas, Vol. I, 565–566: "Already with Paul this entanglement (*Verstrickung*) – especially in the light of the narrative of Adam's Fall and expulsion with which evil (*das Böse*), *also death and sin first arrive in the world* (*in die Welt gelangen*) – acquires the character of an 'inherited' sin. The legend of Adam was properly (*eigentlich*) destined to solve the theodicy problem: it exonerated God who equips the human being with reason and with the freedom towards good and evil from an authorship of all evil. It takes over the additional function only with the Pauline reading to explain this hereditary sin without which the death on the cross of the incarnated God as vicarious atonement would remain incomprehensible."

tures of caring for the sick and enabling the poor, new foundations established by humans in their vulnerability and capacity for learning can be traced to a biblical heritage. Yet the lines from Irenaeus to the Cappadocians and Maximus Confessor, to Thomas and Duns Scotus that can be seen as developing the human self-understanding as *imago Dei* are missing in this reconstruction: that the "glory of God" is visible in "the human person fully alive",[645] including her capacity for language and her freedom; that "natural law" is the law of reason given by human self-legislation; and that humans were created to be partners and friends of God. Kant is presented as partly responding to and partly rejecting the Augustinian tradition of the sinner struggling with a God of judgement. The "ethical commonwealth" is linked to the *civitas Dei*, although Kant's emphasis and trust here is on human intersubjective agency. His epoch-defining distinction of a formal, transcendental, from a material, empirical level is not placed in the history of effects of Plato but of Luther's two regiments doctrine. Disagreement with any of these points of derivation will affect how the relationship between faith and knowledge is adjudicated. At the end of these exchanges, Habermas interprets reason as secular and religion by definition as "other" – as an unspent reservoir that is still capable of renewal and of surprising the "knowledge" side with fresh intuitions and resonances. It is an outcome that could be expected from the specific determinations following from the directions chosen at the start. I have taken an alternative starting point in the observation that the significance of Paul and Augustine alone cannot explain the history of effects of Christianity (9.1.2.1). Chapters Two to Seven showed the need for more comprehensive and nuanced attempts to determine its core content in the contingent, dialectical history of its syntheses, ruptures and transformations (9.1.2.2).

9.1.2.1 The origins of Christianity in the context of Hellenisation, as assumed in Paul's theology and the Gospels

Chapter Four in Volume I begins the arc of reconstructing the content of the Christian heritage with "atonement" as the cultic concept chosen by Paul to interpret Jesus' death. This is shown in Chapter Two of this study to constitute a narrowing of Christology to a specific tradition.[646] I have argued for a greater sig-

---

645 Irenaeus, Haer. IV 20,7: "*Gloria Dei vivens homo, vita autem hominis visio Dei*", cf. Ansorge, *Kleine Geschichte*, 49–51, and *Gerechtigkeit und Barmherzigkeit Gottes*, 209–220.
646 This is true not only for the subsequent doctrinal development but already for the beginnings, as was clarified by Freyne, *Expansion*, 259: "Certainly there is no mention of an 'atoning death' as elaborated by Paul in either Q or the Gospel of Thomas. Even the Didache's account of

nificance of the Gospels that allowed subsequent generations of Christian communities to relate to the person of Jesus; the essential temporal outline of his life is filled in further, but not replaced by, the theological points developed in Paul's Letters.[647] Crucially, the Gospels put forward a different understanding of Jesus' life, death and resurrection to the "atonement" reading. In his proclamation and praxis, he reveals God's being as love which they see as confirmed when God rescues him from the death he suffered as a result of the conflicts his actions and preaching gave rise to. I will briefly repeat some key findings and the sources on which they are based, including English-speaking exegetical debates.

Against the clear division made by Habermas from a philosophical perspective between Greek metaphysics and monotheistic religion in the first century, a different picture emerges when biblical and cultural studies, archaeology and philology, history of religions and the theological knowledge of the history of reception are included: "Hellenisation" had been under way for centuries, as evident already in the Septuagint, the translation of the Hebrew Bible into Greek. While Habermas does account for the roles of Diaspora Judaism, of Alexandria, of Philo and of concepts like "wisdom", the impression conveyed is that the expansion of post-Easter Christianity beyond Jerusalem is a change singularly owed to Paul: "Post-Easter Christianity was inherently (*von Haus aus*) a formation of spirit that was marked by Hellenism" (*hellenistisch geprägte Gestalt des Geistes*)".[648] This seems to locate Paul on the Hellenistic side. Yet, not only are Paul and the Gospels separate strands but it must also be remembered that the religious background shared by Jesus, Paul and the Gospel writers is Second Temple Judaism. Before Paul, Jesus himself had selected the universalist strands of the Hebrew Bible in which the Gentiles are included. Habermas mentions this motif, but still attributes the move to the nations to Paul's vision.[649] It is also rel-

---

the eucharistic celebrations has no mention of the sacrificial dimension of the meal as reflected in Paul (1 Cor 11:23–26; Didache 9–10)".

647 In *"Gottes Reich – Jesu Geschick"*, 248–249, Schürmann insisted that Pauline soteriology must be "filled in critically with the gospels' material of speeches and narratives. Without it, the proclamation [...] lacks its anchorage in history".

648 Habermas, Vol. I, 515.

649 Habermas's quotes about Jesus restricting his mission to Israel are typically taken from Matthew but would also have to be related to Mt 28:18–20, the mission command, and interpreted in the context of Matthew's overall theological stance. Equally significant for this issue are the representatives of the "nations" figuring in the Gospel narratives. The fact that Jesus chose to place himself in the tradition of Isaiah's view of the Temple and Zion, invoked the banquet with the Patriarchs, the references to the Queen of Sheba in her openness to wisdom, and to Abraham, the "Father of faith" both by Jesus and Paul, are further indicators at the decisive level of symbols rather than concepts.

evant that exegetes have replaced the simple Gentile/Jewish-Christian division by a differentiation into four groups, from those who considered circumcision to be still mandatory, to those who carried the Jewish tradition of Temple critique into the emerging Christian centres. Between these two were the groups led by Paul and James whose positions differed regarding the observance of the food laws, the Sabbath and the Jewish feast days.[650]

Apart from indicating a more differentiated account of "Hellenisation", two further interpretations of key elements of the nascent tradition were questioned. While assuming a dependence of the Gospels on Paul, Habermas contrasts his portrayal of Christ as the "Son of God" with Jesus' own position: "Certainly the evangelists, above all John and Luke, draw on (*zehren von*) Pauline theology and recognise in the historical Jesus the 'Son of God'".[651] The first point raised against this description was that Paul and the Gospels put forward distinct and not overlapping theologies.[652] What required explanation instead was the very appearance of a "Gospel" in the sense of a narrative portrait, in contrast to the existing short credal formulas and Paul's different use of the term "Gospel" only for the salvific death and resurrection of Jesus Christ.[653] Secondly, the absence of an exegetical consensus was pointed out on the thesis that "Jesus himself did not proclaim a Christology".[654] Yet many scholars of Early Christianity and Second Temple Judaism have highlighted that Jesus' symbolic and explicit claims of authority included a clear link to his own role in the coming of the kingdom of God; healings were not just social acts but part of the Messianic expectations.

Overall, the conclusion drawn by Habermas demands so many qualifications that its thesis cannot be upheld: "Jesus proclaimed his teaching with the inten-

---

650 Cf. R. Brown, in *Antioch and Rome*, 2–8.
651 Habermas, Vol. I, 496.
652 The exegetical question is how Paul relates to the oral tradition's portrayal of Jesus in his sayings from which the Gospels arose. In *Jesusüberlieferung bei Paulus?*, 392, Christine Jacobi judges such a link to be absent and concludes that "as founder of the tradition and as teacher, Jesus is not relevant for Paul". What needs to be researched then is the fact that despite his disinterest in the life of Jesus, Paul takes up core points: leading an itinerant life himself, concern for the poor, love of enemy and engagement in reconciliation.
653 In Habermas's examination of Christian origins in Vol. I, Chapter Four, Paul is treated in greater detail than Jesus. Some conclusions are based on citations from Rudolf Bultmann which may indicate a position that has given up on any further quests for the Historical Jesus. Bultmann's view was that only the "that", not the life of the person of Jesus was historically accessible and that the early Christian communities' view was the only "what" that could be researched.
654 Habermas, Vol. I, 495. Cf. 497, with reference to Merz, "Der historische Jesus", 43.

tion of renewing Judaism. In contrast, the Letters of Paul and Acts written by a student of Paul's [...] construct a theology of death on the cross that has determined the history of reception of Christianity at least as much as Jesus' actualisation of the Jewish message of salvation and his radical ethics, condensed in the Sermon on the Mount".[655]

The way towards understanding its history of effects is to examine the four Gospels – thanks to which we know of the Sermon on the Mount, of Jesus' parables of the Kingdom and his symbolic actions – in their historical and religious settings. Jesus' announcement of the "Kingdom of God" arriving through his person reflects the apocalyptic hope in God's liberation from the oppressive forces of the present. Paul's emphasis on the internal realm of the "Spirit"[656] may be one of the reasons for Habermas's correct observation that the political elements of Jesus' message became less pronounced in the subsequent mission to the Roman Empire.[657]

9.1.2.2 Turning points in the history of reception of the New Testament

The impressive and far-reaching judgements made on the cultural significance of the Christian religion bear repetition: It "set in motion the discourse on faith and knowledge [...] In hindsight, in late Antiquity, the cultural programme that was decisive (*maßgebende*) for Europe is formed". It had a "catalysing function" which defined the "basic concepts of practical philosophy that are decisive until today". It "uprooted Greek cosmology" and ultimately "transferred the semantic contents of biblical origin into the basic concepts of postmetaphysical thinking".[658] In view of these long-term effects, it was important to compare the patristic authors in their proposals and their contexts. Against Gnosticism, a theology of history was elaborated by Irenaeus, Origen, Gregory of Nyssa, Ambrose and others in which salvation takes place by God interacting with humans in their freedom. From the second century onwards, Christian theologians made the decision that the content of the message of salvation was to be explained and justified to the general consciousness of truth as unfolded in philosophy, be it Platonic, Stoic, or Aristotelian. In view both of the continuous link they maintained to philosophical understandings of the world, of human beings and the

---

655 Habermas, Vol. I, 495.
656 In *Theology of Paul the Apostle*, 433, James Dunn, however, emphasises the importance of Paul's tying the "Spirit" to Christ: "the redefinition, or tighter definition, of *the Spirit as the Spirit of Christ* [...] in fact constitutes one of Paul's most important contributions to biblical theology".
657 Habermas, Vol. I, 489.
658 Habermas, Vol. I, 537–538.

divine, and their theological emphases on creation, on the "inner person", and on God acting in history, the key question to be decided was: Are they seen as precursors to the position constructed on new foundational concepts by Augustine, or should they count as alternatives? How does it affect the view of the reception of the nascent body of the New Testament writings which position is taken on this stage: is it a "Hellenising" translation, or a resurgence of Gnosis, does it fulfil or disrupt the paths opened up by his theological predecessors?

While Habermas points out the relevance of Augustine's life long quest for the origin of evil and theodicy that motivated his construction of an inherited original sin, he still regards his work as the sum and high point of the patristic era. Yet the differences are so programmatic that it is hard not to see Augustine's anthropology, doctrine of God and eschatology as a *countermovement* to their achievements. The construct of an inevitable, naturally engendered personal sin replaces the far less definitive biblical position as well as the existing patristic anthropologies which had been elaborated against the Gnostic dualism to which his later work returns. It is also a manifestation of the juridical inheritance of Latin theology, conceived in the context of Roman law, focused on institutional membership and the obligations of the human creature to God.[659] While his influence also on subsequent church practice cannot be underrated, the disputed nature of his innovations deserves to be noted with greater clarity than the account of his legacy in the two volumes provides. Augustine's theological heritage was restricted to the Western church, and even there it did not become the essence of orthodoxy. Specifically, the later Augustine's doctrine of damnation was not received, and subsequent Councils stayed silent on it. His influence was less pervasive than Habermas's connection of key motifs of medieval theology to "Augustinian" teachings suggests, for example, regarding the concepts developed by Duns Scotus.[660]

---

[659] Cf. Ansorge, *Kleine Geschichte*, 106–107.
[660] In Vol. I, 769–771, Habermas interprets the question posed by Duns Scotus "to God, 'that you are infinite and incomprehensible by someone finite?'" as referring to sin: "The Franciscan taught by Augustine evidently seems to know how much Adam's Fall has corrupted the world and the nature of the human being. His broken will and his fallen rationality (*Verstand*) have been profoundly weakened [...] Since, however, in the framework of Christian philosophy the question of the precise epistemological determination of the limits of natural reason is posed within the field of tension of the opposition between nature and grace, the answers never only depended from philosophical premises; they always depended as well from the theological interpretation of sin and from the extent of the corruption of human nature caused by the Fall." Thus, the difference between God as infinite and humans as finite seems to be traced back to sin, collapsing two distinct enquiries.

Thus, the next great turning points to be scrutinised in the history of reception of the New Testament were the High and the Late Middle Ages. Evaluating them as a "watershed",[661] Habermas examines the key changes with a focus on the developments of knowledge and of law that reflected and enabled transformations in social, economic and political structures. He reconstructs medieval arguments for a civic legal realm, for subjective rights and a sphere of the world beside the church which is not conceived in Augustine's "Hobbesian" terms.[662] In identifying the sources that will become the two main streams of European philosophy, Habermas highlights the difference in the understanding of "philosophy" between Scotus and Ockham. The bifurcation of philosophy into its major contemporary strands begins with Ockham's fourteenth-century Nominalism: language analysis as distinct from a philosophy oriented towards extramental reality, a difference that also affects the role of theology.

Leaving it undecided whether Scotus's work can be counted as part of Nominalism, Habermas correctly and critically identifies the route to fideism that results from Ockham's separation of philosophy as the logic of natural reason, and theology as a purely internal account. It was worthwhile therefore to pay attention to the theological premises of the turning point in two directions which Duns Scotus represents in his break with Aristotelian monism, substance ontology and natural teleology, but equally with an empirical route which was to be embarked on by Ockham. Scotus insists on the univocal use of language, against the analogical use proposed by Thomas for propositions about God from finite human thinkers, and establishes with insights only possible through revelation – such as God's goodness – that they constitute a *further determination* of the universal philosophical concepts. Instead of teleology, there is a relationship of freedom towards the Creator God. Ockham, in contrast, proposes a view of theology that is completely segregated from philosophy and that is marked solely by its receptivity to the Bible as a whole.

Where does this second classification of the roles of the two disciplines leave the theological task of engagement with new intellectual horizons? Above all, how does a theology oriented towards the insiders, the believers' internal interpretations, determine the essence of the Christian message in view of the heterogeneous accounts one can draw from the Bible? Habermas points out the new

---

661 Habermas, Vol. I, 761, with reference to Kurt Flasch.
662 Habermas, Vol. I, 614: "Augustine nonetheless (*zwar*) has understood what the law achieves as a means of organisation for the exercise (*Ausübung*) of state governance (*Herrschaft*) (as well as for the order and influence of the church); but what remained alien to him was the potential for freedom that is also contained (*beschlossen*) in the form of law with the egalitarian sense of its own (*Eigensinn*) of this medium."

contrast between a philosophy that redefines truth as internal to "a system of propositions without contradictions" and a "fideist understanding of faith" to the previous theological engagement with philosophy. Now, the "scientific character (*Wissenschaftlichkeit*) of theology only consists in the scientific character of the elaboration (*Bearbeitung*) of the presentation (*Darstellung*) of theological truths".[663] This description anticipates with great acuity movements in the twentieth century that make a virtue out of relating entirely to the internal horizon shared by a religious community.[664] The theological question to be put to such attempts of confining the explication of a faith tradition to an in-house exercise is how their choice of an undeclared, tacit selection of a "Canon within the Canon" can be justified. The alternative is to reopen the biblical and theological debate on the core components of the "identity" or "essence of Christianity" in relation to its self-understandings at different points in history.

The final threshold was the turn to Modernity, prepared by the two directions taken in the late Middle Ages. Here, the first of the three pillars holding up the "bold arcs of the history of salvation",[665] namely Adam's Fall, having been submitted to the knocks of historical-critical exegesis, changes its status from an assumed historical event at the dawn of humanity to a literary-symbolic account of the human condition. If the "Fall" is uncovered as an aetiological narrative, the second and third pillars – namely the "atoning death" (*Sühnetod*) of Christ and the Last Judgement – are to be scrutinised as well for the reliability of their construction. Especially for the Augustinian lens through which theology has been surveyed since its patristic beginnings, the loss of anchorage of the first pillar should be serious. It is Schleiermacher who shoulders the task of laying down new foundations to support the two arcs from the beginning of time to its end with God's gracious judgement, centred on the middle pillar, Christ. Schleiermacher's achievement – not treated in the second volume which focuses instead on his contribution to hermeneutics and thus indirectly to the linguistic turn – consists in disconnecting theology from a reading of Genesis as a historical account, and replacing Augustine's conception of a personally inherited original sin as a consequence of Adam's Fall with human "sinfulness". Regarding the third pillar, eschatology, the *massa damnata* gives way to renewing Origen's *apokatastasis panton*, the early patristic promise of the election of all. It is based on the overriding idea of Schleiermacher's Dogmatics, the one unified di-

---

663 Habermas, Vol. I, 808–809.
664 A programmatic proposal of this understanding of theology was put forward by George Lindbeck in *The Nature of Doctrine: Religion and Theology in a Postliberal Age* (Louisville, KY: Westminster John Knox, 1984).
665 Habermas, Vol. I, 513.

vine decree of creation and redemption, affecting theological anthropology, Christology, doctrine of God, and eschatology. From the marginal role Christ had in Augustine's Neoplatonic striving towards God he advances to become the solid middle pillar, which designates, however, not the crucifixion but the whole of his life: it is on the "total impression" of the life of the historical person of Jesus, conveyed by the Gospels, especially John, that the dual perspective towards God's original decree and towards the fulfilment of history is founded. This architecture, however, appears to be missing a crucial element if it is surveyed on the backdrop of the Pauline and Augustinian strands from which Habermas analyses the history of Christian philosophy and theology. He seeks the distinctiveness of the Christian message of salvation in the "awkward (*sperrig*)" elements which are at odds with human reason.[666] Though Augustine's thought is seen as deeply "pessimistic", he is credited with not sacrificing the "darkest theologoumena" (vol. I, 558).[667] Instead of recognising the "elegant reconciliation of faith and reason"[668] achieved through Schleiermacher's transcendental philosophical analysis of consciousness as a valid justification of religion in Modernity's categories of freedom and subjectivity, Habermas seeks a practical justification on the basis of its link to ritual. The final two subsections will indicate the questions arising from this move (9.2) before recalling the full concept of reason used by both Kant and Schleiermacher which is marked by the quest for absolute meaning (9.3).

9.2 Rituals as anchor points of religion, or as sites of discursive contestation?

In tracing the roots of contemporary self-conceptions back to the transformations of the Axial Age, both volumes present ritual as a key component of dealing with the sacred. Already in *Theory of Communicative Action*, at a stage of his theory in which religion was to be superseded by communicative reason, Durkheim's position was discussed regarding the same question that has only increased in relevance since the 1980s: the renewal of solidarity between the members of a society. Apart from sociology, other social sciences have made this theme a research focus, supported by the renewed attention given to Jaspers's Axial Age theory. The sociological assumption that rituals produce or confirm

---

[666] Habermas, Vol. I, 783.
[667] Habermas, Vol. I, 569. 558.
[668] Habermas, "Boundary", 234.

9.2 Rituals as anchor points of religion, or as sites of discursive contestation? — 243

solidarity reflects a perspective from above, the analysis of an observer. Yet also for Jaspers, the appearance of the perspective of the individual thinker was one of the key accomplishments of the intellectual formations emerging in different cultures three thousand years ago.[669] In the three brief reviews that follow I will draw on the exegetical, historical and theological enquiries I have treated to problematise a view that isolates ritual from the ongoing processes of self-understanding of a religious community. Also Habermas acknowledges a major shift in the process of handing on a faith tradition when Sacred Scriptures join rituals as carriers of continuity: "A change in the form (*Gestaltwandel*) of the Holy (*Heiligen*) correlates with the enlargement of media of communication in their momentous effect on social evolution (*sozialevolutionär folgenreichen*). Scriptural cultures (*Schriftkulturen*) and 'religions of the book' relocate (*umstellen*) the ritual dealing (*Umgang*) with the Holy to doctrines handed on in writing and dogmatised".[670]

As the biblical enquiries discussed in the first chapters have shown, rituals are not self-explanatory and have been hotly contested, beginning with the Temple ritual at the time of Jesus, which he attacked, proclaiming forgiveness as available to all, without burnt offerings (9.2.1). Baptism, the rite practised by John the Baptist recalling God's rescue of Israel from the Red Sea on their flight from Egypt, was later inaugurated by Christian communities in and beyond Jerusalem as their new ritual of entry (9.2.2). Based on the Gospels' accounts of the Lord's Supper, the Eucharist became the central Christian ritual. Yet even staying within the categories of substance ontology, already the Middle Ages had more than one term to interpret its meaning: "transubstantiation", the term stemming from the Fourth Lateran Council of 1215, and "consubstantiation", proposed by Scotus, Ockham and other theologians around the turn to the fourteenth century. In the history of theology, a view from above can be detected in the "*ex opere operato*" designation of sacraments in Catholicism, expressing the independence of their validity from the celebrant. Since the Second Vatican Council, the "*participatio actuosa*" of the faithful has officially become a constitutive element, supported by the turn from Latin to the vernacular also for the readings and the prayers. The sacrament is inherently connected to the "Word", and the ritual only exists in this interpretive setting (9.2.3).

The disputes on forgiveness, on baptism and on the Eucharist show the need for conceptual, second order theology to interpret communal rituals and to correct literalist misunderstandings. Religious rituals do represent a decisive differ-

---

[669] Habermas, Vol. I, 463–480, 466.
[670] Habermas, Vol. I, 272.

ence to philosophy, as Habermas impressively reminds his readers also in his Postscript at the end of the two volumes. As a public performance, they constitute a generation-transcending manifestation of a faith tradition. It is necessary, however, to include a philosophical perspective that insists on the subjective dimension in accessing ritual as part of a search for meaning, and to deepen the analysis through the dimension of self-reflection which breaks its immediacy (9.2.4).

9.2.1 The promise of forgiveness: Contesting the Temple's rituals of sacrifice

A social science conception of ritual as renewing solidarity would have to be complemented by historical studies, here by the debates among biblical scholars on the internal critiques of the role of the Temple and of its rituals. The longstanding prophetic questioning of rituals as external practices distracting from the need for internal conversion, for a change of heart, and for action for the poor, is a prominent tradition in the Hebrew Bible. Also the Temple as their location was a matter of dispute, with prophets differing in their critiques. In view of its destruction by the Babylonians, Ezekiel demands its purification from the pagan foreigners. In contrast, the book of Isaiah, parts of which were written in the same sixth century BCE contexts in and after the Exile, welcomes the nations as pilgrims to Zion.[671] A Temple- and cult-critical position can be found in the line that for the Lord, "The heaven is my throne, and the earth is my footstool" (Isa 66:1). John the Baptist's renewal movement and the Essenes created public alternatives to the Jerusalem Temple by relocating to the desert. Thus, if rekindling "solidarity" between the community and the individual is assumed to be the major effect of ritual, the accompanying struggles about the core inspiration of a religious tradition and about the legitimacy of the authority representing it must be included. As Freyne summarises the backdrop to John the Baptist's and Jesus' positions towards the Temple, Judean society "was divided between allegiance to the central symbol system and its guardians and concern about the social deprivation and distance from the power structures that the populace at large was experiencing".[672] Jesus offered "a different interpretation […] in terms of God's original design for all Israel" of the two core symbols of the Temple and the land which stood for a promise:

---

[671] In Habermas, Vol. I, 509, under the heading "universalisation", the "biblical vision of the migration of the nations (*Völkerwanderung*) to Jerusalem" is mentioned, but its relevance for Jesus is not indicated.
[672] Freyne, *Expansion*, 136.

the shape and intention of Jesus' ministry was based on an older, prophetic view of Israel's destiny, one that retained the *symbolism* of temple and land as pledges of Yahweh's presence and protection, while being highly critical of the existing situation that obtained among the dominant elite of the Jerusalem temple state [...] Both the Essenes and the Pharisees, as well as other apocalyptically minded groups, had different visions of how the new Israel should be construed and how the temple symbolism should be represented.[673]

Two insights can be drawn from the study of such particular instances of dealing with the sacred: First, it appears not to be the practice of ritual as such that creates solidarity but its standing as a symbol for something more encompassing from which solidarity might flow, though not directly. Secondly, rituals are a source of ongoing discursive interpretations and struggles for the valid definition of the central content they seek to express symbolically. In Jesus' parables, the power of forgiveness is reallocated to each individual as their implementation of God's greater forgiveness for them. It is not confined to the Temple but available in every local setting. On this background, his cleansing of the Temple of the money changers for buying animals for sacrifice is a critique of ritual and a reminder of its standing for a symbolic reality that can be enacted in a different way. It can be untied from its traditional location in order to represent the original divine promise which may be overshadowed by its current structures.

9.2.2 Confirming a new doctrine: The shift to infant baptism

While the relativising and corrective effect that Sacred Scriptures exert on ritual could be seen in the first case study, the rite of baptism may serve to elucidate a further insight, namely into the mutually confirming effect between a religious practice and a theological theory. In Volume I, baptism is identified as a rite in which a status changes (*Statuspassage*) and an "identity renewed *ab ovo*" is the result. It is "linked to the act of forgiveness and the promise of eternal life".[674] Its individualising character is emphasised: "The personal decision for baptism and the relevance of the theme of resurrection further amplify (*verstärkt*) the tendency inherent in monotheism of an individualisation of faith".[675]

Yet equally with baptism, there are competing motifs that require integration under a guiding conception in the interest of a coherent understanding of the Christian faith. At its origin with John the Baptist, in view of the Torah regula-

---

673 Freyne, *Expansion*, 186.
674 Habermas, Vol. I, 518.
675 Habermas, Vol. I, 502.

tions of "an annual rite of repentance for all Israel, Yom Kippur, [...] John's activity must be seen as a protest or at least a dissatisfaction with the Temple and its rituals". His symbolic action recalls the rescuing action of God: John "issues a call for repentance of heart on the part of Israel as a whole, introducing a rite of washing as a public statement of such repentance that has echoes of Israel's 'passage' to the Promised Land".[676] The gratitude for being rescued from slavery and from death in the Red Sea has repentance as a consequence and implies a symbolic renewal of purity. Paul's interpretation of baptism in a quasi-mystical sense, namely as "dying with Christ" takes up some of these resonances. By the time of Augustine, the practice has moved to the baptism of infants, and it is here that the construction of a closed circle can be observed, endorsing the theory of a biologically inherited original sin. The term had resulted from Ambrosiaster's erroneous translation of Paul's reflection of the effects of Adam's sin, replacing the Greek original, "*since* all sinned" with the personalising pronoun, "*in whom* all sinned (*in quo omnes peccaverunt*)" (Rom 5:12).[677] This new concept in which Adam's sin is imputed to each individual human as their own is now bolstered by the new church practice of infant baptism, creating a feedback loop between theory and practice. Due to Augustine's conception of damnation, a vicious circle ensued with the practice of infant baptism confirming his extreme position; doctrine and rite in turn served to justify each other. The meaning of this entry rite, to express faith in God's unconditional acceptance of the individual person, regardless of their age and prior to any action of their own, was turned into a fearful rite of protecting against an eternity in limbo. This new location was conceived as a solution to the unacceptable imagination that referred infants who died unbaptised to hell or to purgatory. The fact that their fate continued to be disputed into the Middle Ages, and the practice of separate burial well into the twentieth century are an indication of how important the discursive exchange of arguments is; all the more so when a rite promotes a view of God that undermines the content of the faith and the credibility of its tradition, contravening its own scriptural basis in the Gospels' accounts of its founder who singled out children as examples of faith, not of sin.

---

676 Freyne, *Expansion*, 136. 138.
677 Cf., for example, Ansorge, *Kleine Geschichte*, 218.

9.2.3 Interpreting the Eucharist

With the celebration of the Eucharist, the understanding of the core of Christianity is at stake. Differences between Christologies, doctrines of God and of the Christian church affect its interpretation. This can be seen in Habermas's summary of the organising centre of Christianity which will be discussed first. Secondly, a contemporary interpretation that replaces the Aristotelian substance ontological terms with modern categories of freedom will be indicated in which the literalism, materialism and extrinsicism of earlier proposals is overcome.

As we have seen, Habermas has taken "atonement" to be the encompassing expression shared by Paul with the early church and remaining valid from his time through the subsequent eras. Yet what can be judged on the basis of conjectures about the oral tradition, from the Gospels and from the Didache is that this cultic term, while true of Paul, is not used by the other sources.[678] A hermeneutical warning regarding the reading of biblical texts was not to restrict oneself to terminological searches since the content is conveyed in symbolic expressions and allusions, fluid resonances, not in precise concepts suitable to establish doctrinal continuity. Habermas is aware of the difference between a poetic and a literal approach when he notes the problem of a "realistic" interpretation of the liturgical species of bread and wine suggested by the context of incarnation:

> By repeating every Sunday the ritually renewed community (*Gemeinschaft*) with the atoning sacrifice of Christ, the congregation (*Gemeinde*) reassures itself of the salvation historical cesura (*Zäsur*) of the forgiveness of their sins (*ihrer Sünden*). Incarnation [...] suggests such a realism. In the physical signs – bread and wine – is "embodied" what is symbolised itself – the body and blood of the Saviour. The *realist* interpretation competed with a metaphysical one.[679]

---

[678] Habermas is aware that it is not an unrivalled term but does not give equal weight to the Gospels' interpretation of the resurrection as a vindication by God: "Paul, unlike Luke, does not apply the interpretive scheme of the unjustly suffering prophet, known from the Bible, to Jesus' execution [...] Paul does not object to (*Anstoß nimmt*) the mythical origin of [...] 'sacrificial death' as little as to the idea of the Trinity (*Dreieinigkeit*)." (Vol. I, 504). However, to interpret Paul's conception of the "Spirit" already in the terms of the doctrine of the Trinity elaborated in the fourth century is premature. At the same time, he correctly identifies Paul's own self-understanding: "Of course he understands himself as a Jew and not as the apostle of a new religious doctrine when he takes the words handed on from Jesus as a radical renewal of Judaism; in the light of this radicalisation he attributes a revolutionary meaning to the death on the cross of the Son of Man, which, however, is in no way to break (*sprengen*) the tradition of the Hebrew Bible" (Vol. I, 504–505).
[679] Habermas, Vol. I, 519.

This danger of misinterpreting what is implied in "transubstantiation" is correctly identified. It is worth analysing the reasons for a lesser-known proposal, "consubstantiation", made by Duns Scotus, Ockham, and Gabriel Biel, as an example for the clarity with which the core of the event was located in the two belongings of Jesus Christ: it relates to the two natures of the Son of God and not to a material change in the signs; the Eucharist is to be defined as "consubstantiation" in order to keep the divinity and humanity of God's Son at an equal level, and to avoid the contradiction of attaching changing elements to the Logos.[680] Yet, the term "transubstantiation" of the Fourth Lateran Council of 1215 carried the day, risking the misplaced concreteness of substances assumed to be changing rather than tying the meaning of the ritual to the memory of the crucified and resurrected Saviour. God remains the absolute freedom with the power to rescue and the person of Jesus remains the one ready to risk and suffer death rather than abandon his proclamation of God.

Habermas, in contrast, combines "incarnation" and "atonement", and comes close to Patripassianism in some of his summaries. It is God who takes on the sacrifice that the human creatures would have needed to offer to attain forgiveness for their sins: "According to the Pauline interpretation, God has taken human form because the continuing failure of those generations who had lived [...] in the knowledge of the Law has unveiled the extent of the deep corruption of the human will, only explaining the gracious, contingent-undeserved act of the prevenient atonement (*zuvorkommenden Entsühnung*) of the human person by Jesus Christ".[681] In the following interpretation, revealing the heritage of Anselm, he equally relates the incarnation directly to the death taken on by Jesus Christ voluntarily, eclipsing its relation to his life and proclamation and fixing its meaning to making up for the sin of Adam:

> Augustine [...] neglects the *soteriological* question how the act of atonement (*Entsühnung*) is to be understood through which God's *self* (*selbst*) – in the shape of the crucified Jesus Christ – takes the sins of humanity upon himself. If it is God's self who intervenes into history with this act of an incarnation that vicariously offers itself up (*Akt einer sich stellvertretend aufopfernden Menschwerdung*) and sets a new beginning, this Jesus Christ cannot be "an other" (*ein anderer*) than God.[682]

---

[680] Cf. Ansorge, *Kleine Geschichte*, 211–212.
[681] Habermas, Vol. I, 565. Even in Paul this is not the interpretation offered. As discussed in Chapter Three, the hymn quoted in Phil 2 about incarnation as the *kenosis* of the one who was "in the form of God" has no connection to the forgiveness of sins.
[682] Habermas, Vol. I, 534. In Vol. I, 512, Jesus' crucifixion is even turned into an "epiphany": "In contrast to the Jews, the Christians do not live in the trust of the divine promise of salvation but in the certitude (*Gewissheit*) of the gracious act of atonement (*Entsühnung*) that has already been

9.2 Rituals as anchor points of religion, or as sites of discursive contestation? — 249

The alternative to the restorative Christology implied in Paul's interpretation is, as stated repeatedly before, to take one's lead from the Gospels and interpret Jesus' resurrection as the "vindication" by God of his claim, backed by his life, to express God's will. This logic is reversed when Jesus' divine status is concluded from his crucifixion. While Habermas has perceptively noted the difference between Paul and Luke, the tradition he regards as decisive for the history of Christianity is the Pauline one. It is complemented with elements from subsequent theological approaches, such as Anselm's and Luther's. What has become a problem for a modern understanding of moral accountability, however, is the idea of vicarious substitution. Since Kant, sin and moral guilt are personal deeds and cannot be taken over vicariously by another agent endowed with free will. This is a watershed moment just like the late Middle Ages for which the earlier categories lost their meaning or transported dubious assumptions that were not in keeping with the freedom without which God's love could not be thought. In order to carry through the intentions of the tradition, to express the salvation of humanity as accomplished in the life, death and resurrection of Jesus Christ, conceptions had to change. A different interpretation of the Eucharist had to follow.

Judging the "doctrine of transubstantiation, marked by Aristotelianism, as the most prominent negative example", since "the connotations of 'substance' can barely be protected against a Eucharistic 'materialism'",[683] Pröpper determines the content of this ritual as follows:

> In the eucharistic supper (*Mahl*), the "reception" (*Empfang*) of the love of God takes place. Ultimately accomplished in the pro-existence of Jesus, it continues and is in that instance actualised in a real-symbolic way. It thus constitutes the foundation of a *communio* with God and of the faithful among each other in a symbolically condensed form by including us into Jesus' relationship as Son to the Father which has been opened up to us humans and is present in the Spirit.[684]

The key point is the relationship to God who is glorified and thanked in a ritual that returns the participants to the "everyday life of faith and practice of bringing God's love to one's fellow humans"[685]. This avoids the extrinsicism of a reconci-

---

accomplished [...] it can already rely on the backing (*Rückhalt*) of the past epiphany of the death on the cross". This is not the view transmitted by the Gospels, not even John's in which Jesus' fidelity to his mission is expressed in having "accomplished" it.
683 Pröpper, "Zur vielfältigen Rede von der Gegenwart Gottes und Jesus Christi. Versuch einer systematischen Erschließung", in *Evangelium und freie Vernunft*: 245–265, 246.
684 Pröpper, *Evangelium und freie Vernunft*, 263.
685 Pröpper, *Evangelium und freie Vernunft*, 262.

liation achieved between two external agents, God and Christ, which is then externally reckoned or applied in favour of the sinners, without any need for their internal participation. It also places ritual into the Sunday service as a whole, complete with readings from Scripture, and the inclusion of the concrete contexts from which the participants come and into which they will return. How this positioning of ritual defies an all-too-neat separation of the "everyday" from the "extraordinary" will be treated in conclusion. Such useful distinctions from cultural anthropology and history of religions benefit from being connected to a philosophical framework that allows to take the perspective of subjective agency seriously.

9.2.4 Ritual as on a par with non-linguistic art, or as part of a discursively accessible practice?

As other human practices, ritual is the subject of research in disciplines that use both explanation and understanding as methods of enquiry.[686] Yet by relating to an intangible realm, the categories used for its analysis need to be scrutinised for the premises contained in them. In this interdisciplinary discourse, the criteria of objectivity or truth and methods differ between empirical cultural studies, history, philosophy and the branches of theology. It is important not to foreclose any of these routes by placing religious ritual into a realm that cannot be accessed by categories of agency. This danger appears, however, when religion is assimilated to the realm of art and its discursive signature exchanged for a less defined similarity to "aesthetic experience". While the interruption of everyday life provided by art is an insightful parallel to explore, other aspects of art do not apply to religion. The comparison turns out to be based on presuppositions that fail to account for crucial elements, as two examples will show: the point where the line between the ordinary and the sacred is drawn, and the alleged non-linguistic status of ritual.

It offers a chance to refine the use of binary classifications to check their heuristic potential against the content professed by a religion. While the distinction between God and the world or humans in their finitude is a binary one, unless a monist position is taken, the belief in God's incarnation results in a more

---

[686] As discussed in Chapter One, the clear-cut division, as proposed by Wilhelm Dilthey, between the Humanities as engaged in "understanding" matters produced by the human spirit and the Natural Sciences as marked by "explanation" of data from the world of objects was challenged by Ricoeur, for example in, "What is a text? Explanation and understanding", in *Hermeneutics and the Human Sciences*, 145–164.

differentiated view of what is celebrated in the ritual: in the Eucharist, for example, Jesus Christ is on both sides, a human person like the believers in the community, but as the Son of God embodying God's love for humanity, raised and present through the Spirit. This religious understanding of God's relationship to creation and to the free creatures who can respond to God's love is different from one in which God is experienced in extraordinary natural events like tempests and earthquakes that underline a divine "otherness".[687] Equally, while it remains true that religions designate sacred times, places, persons and events, the phenomena of transition merit attention, to avoid artificial separations. Especially the weekly practice of congregating on Sunday as the designated holy day, in a church as a space designed to celebrate God's presence is misrepresented as an event defined by its separation from everyday life. With its presentation of the Eucharistic gifts as "fruit of the vine and the work of human hands", the liturgy is tied into the participants' ongoing self-understanding and daily practice by core elements: "the petition for forgiveness, the homily, the prayers of the faithful, the preparation of the gifts as well as the dismissal". Being expressly sent back into ordinary daily life is the act with which the ritual that is a "celebration of the presence of God's grace and the glorification of God"[688] concludes.

In Volume I, the phenomena of dealing with the sacred are inscribed into the anthropological tension between individual and community: "Our hypothesis on the origin of the sacred in the change (*Umstellung*) of cognition and coordination of action to a linguistic stage (*Stufe*) of communication postulates at any rate a connection (*Zusammenhang*) between the complex of the sacred on the one hand and a communicative mode of socialisation (*Vergesellschaftungsmodus*) on the other."[689] At the same time, Habermas refers to the "intransparent speechless (*sprachloser*) core of aesthetic experience which is rooted in a symbolic yet non-linguistic (*nicht-sprachlicher*) communication [...] not yet infected by the spirit of language (*Sprachgeist*) [...] The idiosyncratic sense (*Eigensinn*) of ritual practices remains essentially alien (*wesensfremd*) to the discursive form of critique".[690] While the core of ritual seems to be non-linguistic, religion as a whole is seen in "close connection with music, literature and art", based on the "missing or interrupted reference to innerworldly events which distinguishes (*abhebt*) the sacred no less than the modern work of art from profane utterances".[691] An alternative to what appears to be an objectifying observer's perspec-

---

687 Pröpper, *Evangelium und freie Vernunft*, 262.
688 Cf. Pröpper, *Evangelium und freie Vernunft*, 262.
689 Habermas, Vol. I, 272.
690 Habermas, Vol. I, 223–224.
691 Habermas, Vol. I, 224–225.

tive is to connect also non-verbal practices to the continuity of human communication as itself marked by the production of symbolic relations to the world and to others. A static concept of ritual, however, cannot explain the origins of a change in self-understanding which participation in a linguistically interpreted rite may lead to. The way in which new appreciations of God's intention affect the rituals themselves is not accounted for. As the examples of changing historical interpretations of Temple sacrifice, baptism and Eucharist have shown, how rituals are understood within a religious community is subject to contestation. Ritual therefore does not replace, but is subject to an ongoing hermeneutical enquiry into what remains identical in a particular religion throughout the transformations of thought forms and practices. These external, publicly visible enactments do not cause the assumed effects – of solidarity, of connection with a historical deed of rescue, of rededication to a vision – all by themselves but based on the always contested interpretations of the foundational scriptures, accessed inevitably from their theological and practical histories of reception. Ritual as the core performance of the "sacred complex" thus turns out to be part of what is subjected to the interactive determination of the contemporary self-understanding of a religious tradition. Treating it as a stable and self-explanatory "given" misconstrues it, as also religious practice itself shows when inherited forms of ritual, such as confession, either decline or take new forms.

The expectation that they can be used as a resource of meaning by the translation efforts of postmetaphysical thinking reveals a dialectical approach: its very otherness makes religion – as well as art – a candidate for contents that can be appropriated by the opposite mindset of the "knowledge" pole in a way that cuts its ties to its religious origin. A different approach would be to return to the shared ground which Habermas has followed with such subtlety from Antiquity onwards and re-examine the territory mapped out by Kant in the Modern Age: that of philosophy of religion – understood, however, not as the apologetic exercise of a religious tradition[692] but as a discipline within philosophy that thematises the limits of human knowing and acting in relation to an infinite Other.

---

692 Habermas, *Studienausgabe*, Vol. V, *Kritik der Vernunft*, 31.

9.3 "Faith" and "knowledge" as alternatives, or as distinct pursuits of reason?

Among the reasons for following the intricate paths within the history of European thinking up to its current postmetaphysical stage are the following contemporary concerns:[693] first, the need to counter the effects of objectivising instrumental and scientific uses of reason; secondly, to ascertain in the contributory streams contingent motifs and turning points that have influenced contemporary self-understandings. Thirdly, such factors also need to be reconstructed in the non-Western intellectual traditions which constitute other forms of the variety dating from the Axial Age. The peaceful stabilisation of a multicultural world society requires mutual literacy in the foundations of one another's traditions[694] as well as an attitude of working towards agreements, at a level distinct from international legal frameworks.

One outcome that has been achieved in the encounters and learning processes between the strands of European thinking is the overcoming of substance ontology. With the emphasis moving to practical reason from the late Middle Ages onwards, also the participant's perspective gained priority over the observer's view. If, however, a cultural diagnosis spots traits endemic to the processes of rationalisation which pose problems for the development of reason-led identities, this shift to the subject's perspective is at the same time a source of concern. Habermas correctly insists that democracy has its own autonomous justification as well as its proper resources of meaning – not least the insight into historical achievements of moral and legal inclusion;[695] yet the problem of how mentalities of solidarity can be renewed[696] needs responses from all quarters. It is not surprising, he judges, that a system based "on the free flotation of ideas" is marked by "fragility".[697] The aspects to be raised in conclusion are how the alternative to substance ontology is to be outlined (9.3.1), how the

---

693 They appear in the Preface and the Introduction to Chapter 1, Vol. I, 9–16. 23–39.
694 This has been a demand in David Tracy's conception of public theology with its three venues – the university, culture, and the respective churches – and modes of communication which makes this task crucial for the realm of culture that can draw on the "classics" of religious and literary traditions as part of its background understandings. Cf. David Tracy, "Religion in the Public Realm", in Tracy, *Fragments* (Chicago: University of Chicago Press, 2020): 269–287.
695 Kant speaks of "signs of history (*Geschichtszeichen*)". In the Postscript, Vol. II, 790–795, Habermas names some of the learning processes that have led to new standards.
696 Cf., for example, Habermas, "Prepolitical Foundations of the Constitutional State?", in *Between Naturalism and Religion*, 107.
697 Habermas, Vol. II, 766.

question of motivation is to be addressed (9.3.2), and where the otherness of religion is to be located (9.3.3).

9.3.1 Which categories after substance metaphysics?

Habermas's new work admirably spells out the changes in self-understandings and social institutions that religions have brought about in their processes of cultural interaction through the eras. One key transformation that he attributes to the effects of biblical monotheism, despite the circuitous route it took through the patristic engagement with Greek metaphysics as the then valid configuration of general reason, is the critique of "ontology".

> From the beginning the church has fought against (*sich zur Wehr gesetzt*) a subordination of the Christian message of salvation to an alienating (*verfremdende*) ontological view. By insisting on a conceptual clarification of faith that was not assimilating, theology has at the same time given new impetus (*Anstöße gegeben*) to overcoming a narrowing (*Engführung*) of philosophy to the questions of an ontology that had been identified (*ausgezeichneten*) as the basic science. From this interplay (*Wechselspiel*), postmetaphysical thinking will emerge as a winner.[698]

A path has been cleared for the "performative" element which becomes key in the linguistic constitution of the world and the self through intersubjectivity. Increasingly, Habermas has emphasised that the accumulation of facts about the world must be accompanied by the crucial task to attend to *the meaning of knowledge for us*, which is the brief of philosophy.[699] Following Jaspers, the role of self-reflection is a shared feature practised by both formations of the Axial Age, therefore equally a task for religions.[700] As we have seen, the move to categories of subjectivity was presented as one step on the way to postmetaphysical thinking but as itself in need of being superseded by "third" categories, such as language, intersubjectivity and the lifeworld. The question outlined before, in connection with Kant, Schleiermacher and Humboldt, remains: does this change of paradigm de-differentiate aspects that should be kept distinct? For example, the capability to create and to reconstruct the meaning of a proposition is

---

[698] Habermas, Vol. I, 545.
[699] Cf. Habermas, Vol. I, 12–13.
[700] In *Between Naturalism and Religion*, 143, Habermas states that this task is delivered by theology: "The philosophical recapitulation of the genealogy of reason clearly plays a similar role for a self-reflection of secularism as the reconstructive work of theology plays for the self-reflection of religious faith in the modern world."

not the achievement of language but more precisely that of two subjects: the speaker and the listener. And how far is the practice of self-reflection allowed to go? Are Kant's three questions and their synthesis in the fourth, "What is the human being?", still the extent of what a non-scientific philosophy is able to ask?[701] Or have they already been pacified and considered as answered by categories of communicative action? The way in which substance ontology was overcome at long last – even if Aristotelianism and also Platonism have enjoyed a comeback in social ethics and analytic philosophy as well as in Neo-Thomist theology – began with the patristic authors who made the "inner person" a key theme, enriched with accountability in front of God. In Modernity, Schleiermacher and Kierkegaard discovered in their analyses of self-consciousness the facticity of human existence as the philosophical ground where the question of meaning that is inherent in reason arises. At the level of a transcendental analysis of the conditions of the possibility of human pursuits, they used a platform shared between religion and reason. On this basis, Kierkegaard was able to show that the practical option of faith in a Creator God is a decision, not a given presence immediately ascertainable in self-consciousness, as which Schleiermacher had interpreted the results of the analysis. What are the premises and arguments for Habermas that speak against maintaining reason as the capacity to ask beyond what is given, beyond the type of knowledge that is at one's disposition which is produced by the individual sciences? For Kant, in contrast, reason included what can only be thought and not experienced by the senses, such as the ideas of human freedom and of God.

9.3.2 Principled autonomy and its price: Not a case of justification, but of meaning

One reason for insisting on postmetaphysical thinking as "secular" seems to be the distinction between justification and motivation, a second reason the suspicion of a narrowing of universality either to the individual or to the religious community, and a third one, heteronomy.

The first point, that autonomous morality provides its own justification and is not dependent on religion for respecting the other and oneself as ends-in-

---

701 In Vol. II, 767, the "four Kantian questions for humanity (*Menschheitsfragen*) are affirmed as "not lost out of sight also after the end of the age of worldviews". If the fourth question is seen as a synthesis of the first three, the three dimensions – theoretical knowledge, morality, and "hope" as an answer to the question of meaning – are established as being an exhaustive account of the constitutive dimensions of being human.

themselves, is not a case for disagreement. The moral prohibition to instrumentalise is based on the equally original dignity of each human being. The divergence occurs in the weighting given to the question of meaning, for which "motivation" is used as a shorthand term, denoting the readiness to carry out and renew such a commitment even at a cost to oneself.

For Kant's deontological approach, it is not a problem of "motivation", which is already given in the experience of moral obligation.[702] It is a problem of meaning that arises when a moral person in his good will is met with hostility and his intentions fail. This "antinomy" leads to the postulate of the existence of a God, conceived as the moral author of a universe which cannot be completely closed to human endeavour, thus, which is accommodating to their efforts. Habermas has critiqued Kant's highlighting of the dialectics of practical reason as resulting from a concept of morality that overtaxes human agency and as construing a dilemma that requires a God to solve it. He has stood by this position against the questioning of Kantian philosophers and theologians on many occasions.[703] It is surprising that despite Kant's endorsement of a subjective faith – at the level of meaning, not of justifying morality – Habermas seems to include him under "methodical atheism". He singles out Hegel as "being the only one among the great philosophers since the Enlightenment who *turns away* (*sich abkehrt*) from [...] the presupposition of a methodical atheism which *filters out* (*aussortierenden*) knowledge from faith".[704] Thus, the possibility of justifying the relevance of a moral Creator God in order to sustain concrete, anticipatory human action is rejected. From the stance of postmetaphysical philosophy, God does not seem to be even thinkable and faith in God is no longer a live option for reason. If it exists all the same, it does so on a basis other than reason.

Apart from the theory decision against admitting moral action as being threatened by meaninglessness, to which the postulate of the existence of God would have offered a response that generates hope, another concern appears: Religious faith may prioritise its own tradition and a questionable interest in the believer's own salvation, taking away from universality, and turning it into a private quest:

---

[702] In Vol. II, 348, Habermas notes perceptively that "from a deontological view the question why to be moral at all cannot arise *immanently*".

[703] For example, in his "Reply" in *Glauben und Wissen*, ed. Langthaler and Nagl-Docekal, republished in *Postmetaphysical Thinking II*, 122–160, 127–136. This critique is reaffirmed in Vol. II, 333. 348–354.

[704] Habermas, Vol. II, 480.

All religious ethics are orientated towards a salvation (*Heil*) that in principle is promised to all humans but can only be reached through the ethos and allegiance (*Zugehörigkeit*) to their own respective religious community. Insofar the centred universalism of the world religions that extends from a known central point to an unknown periphery is still a limited conception in comparison with a *decentred universalism* which aims at the complete and reciprocal inclusion of foreigners (*Fremden*).[705]

Earlier, a contrast between religions and philosophy was established in the "difference between the binding force (*Bindungskraft*) of a divine authority which promises personal salvation, and a rational (*vernünftige*) authority that convinces through good reasons."[706] However, for Kant, such "good reasons" include the problem of meaning. The quest for absolute meaning, which the author of the three *Critiques* regards as a universally valid human question, is in danger of being delegitimised. The hope for meaning that supports the agency of every individual appears as a private, self-centred search for their own redemption. While it is true that being morally conscious is not an external expectation but part of the individual's self-experience, this does not make it self-seeking. The problem of meaning is connected to struggles for greater justice but poses questions that cannot be answered at the level of a philosophy of history:

> "The human question of meaning, however, is not already satisfied (*abgegolten*) with the hope for a more just future; for the human individuals, it points beyond this dimension of philosophy of history and the question of the destiny of the human species. This is the point where Kant's philosophy of religion begins. The concept of progress of the philosophy of history thus does not take the place of eschatological questions but leaves room for a perspective of meaning and hope beyond it. In every biography there are experiences of the discrepancy between virtue and happiness as well as of failure in relation to one's own moral standards. For Kant, this unavoidable pain of finitude is the site of religion in life [...] locating religion in the practical experience of self."[707]

These readings show how wide a rift exists between an approach that locates itself predominantly in the Kantian school of practical philosophy and those who defend the question of meaning at the levels of personal morality and civic cooperation as a relevant issue of "public reason". It would be in keeping with Habermas's recognition of "what is missing" to acknowledge such problems as open and unresolved.[708] The question arises if they have been sidelined be-

---

[705] Habermas, Vol. I, 477–478.
[706] Habermas, Vol. I, 370.
[707] Nagl-Docekal and Langthaler, "Vorwort", in *Recht – Geschichte – Religion*, ed. Nagl-Docekal and Langthaler: 7–9, 8.
[708] Habermas, *An Awareness of What is Missing*, 15–23, 19.

cause the framework of intersubjectivity has been reduced to "reciprocity" in which gaps, disappointments and failures do not occur and the good will to "go the extra mile" is not relevant for the theory design. From a deontological standpoint, this level is only one of law, of an assured conflict resolution on the basis of the contract the parties are committed to. Even if Habermas asks for sacrifice and solidarity beyond negative private rights,[709] imperfect obligations and duties without counterpart rights may not be sufficiently accounted for in the ideal of social relations. From the perspective of morality, however, what can appear as egocentric is not the interest in meaning but instead the reduction of intersubjective recognition to a legal framework. Because it is guided by the self-interest in strict reciprocity, for principled autonomy, it falls under "heteronomy".[710] This danger looms not only with an authoritarian conception of God and a restriction of the hope for universal salvation to oneself as one of the few elect. It is also present in three moves in discourse ethics that need to be discussed: one, the risk of reducing morality to law when the starting point is taken in actual conflicts, instead of in the individual capacity for self-legislation;[711] second, the "heteronomy" incurred by the expectation to take over the result of a practical discourse and subordinate one's own moral judgement to a joint decision with one's interlocutors; third, failing to account for duties towards oneself which exist in regard of one's autonomy also when no one else is observing one's conduct.[712] Due to the scope of moral commitment, where much more than mere reciprocity is required, Kant's more ambitious position makes hope an integral component of moral agency. By rejecting his demanding design of obligation, Habermas endorses the Hegelian critique of Kant. From the standard of reciprocity, not only Kant but also the New Testament appears as excessive.[713] Jesus' radicalisation of the commandment to love one's neighbour to that of loving one's enemy is judged to be an even greater overburdening of human capacity. The commandments are interpreted as aggravating the consciousness of sin due to an inevitable failure to realise them: "The excessive (*überschie-*

---

709 See above, Habermas, "Prepolitical Foundations", 107.
710 Cf. Nagl-Docekal, *Innere Freiheit*, 86. 96–97.
711 Cf. Nagl-Docekal, *Innere Freiheit*, 17–50, 41.
712 In *Innere Freiheit*, 87–91, in a section entitled "External and internal freedom", Nagl-Docekal elucidates the distinction between legal compliance and moral self-assessment.
713 Kant's categorical imperative implies the readiness for one-sided advance actions in continuing to recognise the other even if this initiative is rejected. As Nagl-Docekal points out in *Innere Freiheit*, 29, in *Groundwork of the Metaphysics of Morals*, BA 13, Kant makes the connection to the "Christian commandment to love of enemy in the sense of unconditional ought of the categorical imperative", identified "as a consequence of unconditioned moral action" (29, Fn. 62).

9.3 "Faith" and "knowledge" as alternatives, or as distinct pursuits of reason? — 259

ßende) claim of Jesus' ethics of love contributes to the human addiction to sin (*Sündenverfallenheit*). With the commandment to love one's enemies it increases normative claims up to a *systematic* overtaxing (*Überforderung*) of human nature", leading to the "consciousness of the sinner to be *unconditionally (unbedingt*) dependent on God's grace."[714] Yet the examples of those whose fortunes will be turned by God's support in the Beatitudes of the Sermon on the Mount – those hungry for justice, the peacemakers, those who mourn – would have allowed a different interpretation to one that replaces human agency with divine grace: assuring them of God's loyalty and vindication of those who go beyond the limits of ethical convention and engage in anticipatory action despite the uncertain success and the risk to themselves.

9.3.3 Finding the "otherness" of religion in history as the location of God's agency

At the same time, religion is acknowledged as a "contemporary form of the objective spirit"[715]. Is this recognition based on its sheer longevity and indestructibility, or on reasons of content? Regarding Christianity, the pillars on which the arcs of salvation history rest are identified with Paul as Adam's Fall, Jesus' crucifixion, and the eschatological vision of the Last Judgement.[716] In contrast to Paul, his resurrection is not mentioned as part of the central pillar, his violent death, and, unlike the Gospels, neither is his life.

From an interest in ethical motivation for which religions are deemed capable of providing resources, the accounts of Jesus' praxis and proclamation would have offered crucial opportunities: ordinary men and women are addressed as able to grasp the meaning of parables; they are capable of action, self-reflection and self-critique, of conversion and healing, and are trusted in their own power of judgement. They can take the point that love of enemy is not passive but an active refusal to react to coercion and violence in kind, opting instead for a way that appeals to the aggressor's own sense of dignity.[717] In contrast, the content that seems to be significant for postmetaphysical thought is identified in the "awkward" truths of sin, grace to compensate for an anthropological pessimism,

---

[714] Habermas, Vol. I, 565.
[715] For example, in Habermas, Vol. I, 75–109.
[716] Habermas, Vol. I, 513.
[717] For the historical and Jewish religious contexts of "turning the other cheek", "going the extra mile" and "giving also one's garment", see Walter Wink, *Jesus and Non-Violence*, referred to above in 2.1.3.4.

atonement, and "dark" motifs like the threat of damnation which make Christianity "other" and explain its difference from reason.

This qualification, here specified in relation to Christian monotheism, appears paradoxical: If religion is "other", how can it still be translatable?[718] With this key demand that treats the historical religions as yet unspent resources of meaning, the question becomes unavoidable: on what shared basis does it become possible for religious and secular citizens to speak to each other, or for an intuition to be recognised as productive even by atheists? As we have seen, in her discussion of Rawls, Herta Nagl-Docekal has identified the "need of reason (*Bedürfnis der Vernunft*)" as the shared basis, expounded by philosophy of religion as the mediating level.[719] It offers categories that historical religions need in order to clarify their understandings, such as the concept of "God" as distinct from the world and from humans in their finitude, and to analyse what makes them receptive to the self-communication of an absolute, infinite freedom.

A critique of the type of "otherness" into which religion is cast by being placed in the opposition of "faith" and "knowledge" is spelt out by Ingolf Dalferth. For him, it is a misleading contrast since "knowledge" is always incremental, while "faith" or belief has a direct opposite in "unbelief".[720] Alternatively, when the contrast is expressed as the relationship of "reason" and "revelation", much more fruitful ground is opened up since the dimension of *history* comes into view. It resonates with Kant's readiness to accept history as the locus of new developments and connects to Habermas's highlighting of the role of history against ontology in biblical and patristic thinking. The promising avenue of history as the location of contingent events that could not be anticipated by reason or "knowledge" is proposed by Georg Essen. He begins with the question whether taking up

---

718 In "Nachmetaphysische Religionsphilosophie", in *Moderne Religion? Theologische und religionsphilosophische Reaktionen auf Jürgen Habermas*, ed. Knut Wenzel and Thomas Schmidt (Freiburg: Herder, 2009): 10–32, 25, with reference to Habermas, *Between Naturalism and Religion*, 143, Thomas Schmidt notes the "conceptual tension" between the "call for 'cooperative translation' or 'rescuing appropriation' and the view that the 'opaque core of religious experience [...] remains profoundly alien to discursive thought'." This conception "overemphasises the difference between religious faith and reasonable knowledge and artificially isolates the realm of the religious from the continuous range and the plurality of human ways of experiencing and their conceptual interpretations."
719 Nagl-Docekal, "Moral und Religion aus der Optik der heutigen rechtsphilosophischen Debatte", 854, quoted in 8.4.2.
720 Ingolf U. Dalferth, "Vom Verkümmern der Vernunft in der säkularen Moderne", in *Religionsphilosophie nach Habermas*, ed. Thomas Schmidt and Matthias Lutz-Bachmann (Stuttgart: Verlag Metzler, forthcoming, 2023).

9.3 "Faith" and "knowledge" as alternatives, or as distinct pursuits of reason? — 261

autonomy unavoidably entails the secularisation of the contents and convictions that reason reflects on. Habermas must be asked whether the genealogy only knows a dual access (*Zugriff*) to history: either reasonable (*vernünftige*) reconstruction that operates in the mode of a figure of sublation, or rational deconstruction that takes place in the mode of destruction? Can reason really only be autonomous when it has transformed (*anverwandelt*) the semantics of historically mediated worlds of faith with a secularising intention? Or can the ordering (*Zuordnung*) of reason, revelation and history also be grasped as a relationship of determination and precisely not as one of mere sublation? [...] According to Habermas, autonomous reason is explicitly interested in a genealogical *self*-pursuit (Selbst*vollzug*) in order to be encouraged by historically mediated "potentials of stimulation (*Anregungspotentiale*)" [...] In other words, also autonomous reason is evidently conscious of the *externality* of its ground of meaning (*Sinngrundes*). It could thus be the case that autonomous reason is directed (*verwiesen*) towards the field of history since in it, a content of meaning is transmitted to reason that is true for it only because its truth cannot be separated from the form of its historical givenness.[721]

As long as the concept of God is not ruled out as no longer accessible within the confines of the "contemporary constellation", history is open to include revelation: events of divine self-communication that are symbolic and thus defy a unitary decoding, but that can be interpreted as signs of God's hidden presence accompanying the lives of persons in their singularity and the entire history of humanity.

This move in turn makes it possible to seek what is distinctive about the Christian message of salvation not primarily in the "dark" elements which contradict especially practical reason. Then Blumenberg would be right that Christianity is marked by an "absolutism of sin"[722] that undermines human capabilities. What is "awkward (*sperrig*)"[723] for reason in the sense of "unprecedented" and of constituting a gift is to be located at a different level: It is the risk God took in the free initiative to create free human counterparts, empowering them with reason and the capability for morality. The story set in motion with them is radically open and undetermined. The first bold arc extends from the first pair of humans to the person of Jesus and the second from him to the end of times. Habermas has perceptively defined the task of judgement as "paradoxical" in its crossing of justice and mercy towards each individual. In his summary of John Rawls's undergraduate thesis he identifies the "demands for equal treatment and complete inclusion" that are present in this religious expectation: "A form of egalitarian universalism is implicit in the powerful image of the Last

---

[721] Georg Essen, Rezension, "Jürgen Habermas. Auch eine Geschichte der Philosophie", *Zeitschrift für Neuere Theologiegeschichte* 28 (2021) (forthcoming).
[722] Cf. above, 7.1.5, J. B. Metz on Blumenberg's critique.
[723] Habermas Vol. I, 783.

Judgement, when God will perform the paradoxical task of pronouncing a differentiated, at once just but merciful (and ultimately redemptive) judgement on the actions and omissions of each person in the light of his or her individual life history."[724] While unresolvable by human judgement, damnation will not be assumed to be its outcome, in view of the significance the two volumes have accorded to the understanding of Jesus' death as atonement.

Habermas's monumental work cuts tracks and uncovers connections, corrects influential assumptions, identifies new projects of enquiry and offers a thought-through combination of disciplines and methods unmatched by other reconstructions. It elaborates an approach to philosophy that marks out "learning processes" as a key endowment of humanity. The edifice he has constructed between past and present conversations over three millennia puts in public view the blocks that make up the groundwork, the connecting rooms and storeys, the processes of cutting new openings or radically rebuilding, while salvaging the keystones that bear the weight and balance the tension. Transposed from the architectural to the literary level which keeps unique events of meaning present, the vital task is to unlock their significance for human history in translations that do not flatten but rise to the original.

---

[724] Habermas, "The 'Good Life' – a 'Detestable Phrase'. The Significance of the Young Rawls's Religious Ethics for His Political Theory", in *Postmetaphysical Thinking II*: 175–188, 182. In Vol. II, 197, Habermas sees three questions as linked in the idea of a Last Judgement: it "connects the problem of the freedom of the will and of conscious historical existence with a third theme: the individualising power (*Kraft*) of the all-penetrating divine glance in front of which every person concerned about her salvation must morally account for her deeds and omissions."

Bibliography

Works by Jürgen Habermas

Habermas, Jürgen. *The Structural Transformation of the Public Sphere*, trans. Thomas Burger. Cambridge, MA: MIT Press, 1989.
Habermas, Jürgen. *Knowledge and Human Interests*, trans. J. J. Shapiro. Boston: Beacon Press, 1971.
Habermas, Jürgen. *Theory of Communicative Action*, Vol. I: *Reason and the Rationalization of Society*, trans. Thomas McCarthy. Boston: Beacon Press, 1984.
Habermas, Jürgen. *Theory of Communicative Action*, Vol. II: *Lifeworld and System: A Critique of Functionalist Reason*, trans. Thomas McCarthy. Boston: Beacon Press, 1987.
Habermas, Jürgen. *The Philosophical Discourse of Modernity: Twelve Lectures*, trans. Frederick Lawrence. Cambridge, MA: MIT Press, 1987.
Habermas, Jürgen. "The Hermeneutic Claim to Universality." In *The Hermeneutic Tradition: From Ast to Ricoeur*, edited by Gayle L. Ormiston and Alan D. Schrift, 245–272. Albany, NY: SUNY Press, 1990.
Habermas, Jürgen. *Moralbewusstsein und kommunikatives Handeln*. Frankfurt: Suhrkamp, 1983. ET *Moral Consciousness and Communicative Action*, trans. Christian Lenhardt and Shierry Weber Nicholsen. Cambridge, MA: MIT Press, 1991.
Habermas, Jürgen. *Postmetaphysical Thinking. Philosophical Essays*, trans. William M. Hohengarten. Cambridge, MA: MIT Press, 1992.
Habermas, Jürgen. *The Liberating Power of Symbols: Philosophical Essays*, trans. Peter Dews. Cambridge: Polity, 2001.
Habermas, Jürgen. *Religion and Rationality: Essays on Reason, God and Modernity*, edited and introduced by Eduardo Mendieta. Cambridge: Polity, 2002.
Habermas, Jürgen. *The Future of Human Nature*, trans. William Rehg, Max Pensky and Hella Beister. Cambridge: Polity Press, 2003.
Habermas, Jürgen. *Between Naturalism and Religion: Philosophical Essays*, trans. Ciaran Cronin. Cambridge: Polity, 2008.
Habermas, Jürgen. *Studienausgabe*, Vol. III, *Diskursethik. Philosophische Texte*. Frankfurt: Suhrkamp, 2009.
Habermas, Jürgen. *Studienausgabe*, Vol. V, *Kritik der Vernunft. Philosophische Texte*. Frankfurt: Suhrkamp, 2009.
Habermas, Jürgen. "Politik und Religion." In *Politik und Religion. Zur Diagnose der Gegenwart*, edited by Friedrich Wilhelm Graf and Heinrich Meier, 287–300. München: C. H. Beck, 2013.
Habermas, Jürgen. *Postmetaphysical Thinking II: Essays and Replies*, trans. Ciaran Cronin. Cambridge: Polity Press, 2017.
Habermas, Jürgen. *Auch eine Geschichte der Philosophie*. Vol. I, *Die okzidentale Konstellation von Glauben und Wissen*. Vol. II, *Vernünftige Freiheit. Spuren des Diskurses über Glauben und Wissen*. Berlin: Suhrkamp, 2019.
Habermas, Jürgen. "Replik." *Deutsche Zeitschrift für Philosophie* 69 (2021): 281–294.

Other works

Adolphi, Rainer. "Das Verschwinden der wissenschaftlichen Erklärung. Über eine Problematik der Theoriebildung in Paul Ricoeurs Hermeneutik des historischen Bewußtseins." In *Erinnerungsarbeit. Zu Paul Ricoeurs Philosophie von Gedächtnis, Geschichte und Vergessen*, edited by Andris Breitling and Stefan Orth, 141–171. Berlin: Berliner Wissenschaftsverlag, 2004.

Ansorge, Dirk. *Gerechtigkeit und Barmherzigkeit Gottes. Die Dramatik von Vergebung und Versöhnung in bibeltheologischer, theologiegeschichtlicher und philosophiegeschichtlicher Perspektive*. Freiburg: Herder, 2009.

Ansorge, Dirk. *Kleine Geschichte der christlichen Theologie. Epochen, Denker, Weichenstellungen*. Regensburg: Pustet, 2017.

Anzenbacher, Arno. *Einführung in die Ethik*. Düsseldorf: Patmos, 1992.

Arens, Edmund. "Rezension: Von der rettenden Gerechtigkeit zur vernünftigen Freiheit: Jürgen Habermas rekonstruiert Konstellationen von Glauben und Wissen." *Ethik und Gesellschaft. Ökumenische Zeitschrift für Sozialethik* 1/2020: Kritik der Identitätspolitik. https://dx.doi.org/10.18156/eug-1-2020-rez-4 (accessed April 14, 2021).

Arndt, Andreas, and Jörg Dierken, eds. *Friedrich Schleiermachers Hermeneutik. Interpretationen und Perspektiven*. Berlin/Boston: Walter De Gruyter, 2016.

Arndt, Andreas. "Hermeneutik und Einbildungskraft." In *Friedrich Schleiermachers Hermeneutik. Interpretationen und Perspektiven*, edited by Andreas Arndt and Jörg Dierken, 119–128. Berlin/Boston: Walter De Gruyter, 2016.

Assmann, Aleida. "Canon and Archive." In *Cultural Memory Studies: An International and Interdisciplinary Handbook*, edited by Astrid Erll and Ansgar Nünning, 97–107. Berlin/New York: Walter De Gruyter, 2008.

Assmann, Jan. "Communicative and Cultural Memory.", In *Cultural Memory Studies: An International and Interdisciplinary Handbook*, edited by Astrid Erll and Ansgar Nünning, 109–118. Berlin/New York: Walter De Gruyter, 2008.

Bannach, Klaus. *Die Lehre von der doppelten Macht Gottes bei Wilhelm von Ockham*. Wiesbaden: F. Steiner, 1975.

Bauckham, Richard. *Jesus and the Eyewitnesses: The Gospels as Eyewitness Testimony*. Grand Rapids, MI: Eerdmans, 2nd edn 2017.

Bauckham, Richard. "Eyewitnesses and Critical History: A Response to Jens Schröter and Craig Evans." *Journal for the Study of the New Testament* 31 (2008): 221–235.

Behrenberg, Peter. *Endliche Unsterblichkeit. Studien zur Theologiekritik Hans Blumenbergs*. Würzburg: Königshausen & Neumann, 1994.

Berner, Christian. "Das Übersetzen verstehen." In *Friedrich Schleiermacher and the Question of Translation*, edited by Larisa Cercel and Adriana Serban, 43–58. Berlin/Boston: Walter De Gruyter, 2015.

Bielefeldt, Heiner. "Verrechtlichung als Reformprozess. Kants Konstruktion der Rechtsentwicklung." In *Recht – Geschichte – Religion. Die Bedeutung Kants für die Gegenwart*, edited by Herta Nagl-Docekal and Rudolf Langthaler, 73–84. Berlin: Akademie Verlag, 2004.

Blumenberg, Hans. *The Legitimacy of the Modern Age*, trans. Robert M. Wallace. Cambridge, MA: MIT Press, 1983.

Blumenberg, Hans. *St Matthew Passion*, trans. Helmut Müller-Sievers and Paul Fleming. Ithaca, NY: Cornell University Press, 2021, German original 1988.

Bongardt, Michael. "Einheit ja – aber welche?" In *Dogma und Denkform. Strittiges in der Grundlegung von Offenbarungsbegriff und Gottesgedanke*, edited by Klaus Müller and Magnus Striet, 85–100. Regensburg: Pustet, 2005.
Breul, Martin. *Diskurstheoretische Glaubensverantwortung. Konturen einer religiösen Epistemologie in Auseinandersetzung mit Jürgen Habermas*. Regensburg: Pustet, 2019.
Breitling, Andris, and Stefan Orth, eds. *Erinnerungsarbeit. Zu Paul Ricoeurs Philosophie von Gedächtnis, Geschichte und Vergessen*. Berlin: Berliner Wissenschaftsverlag, 2004.
Brown, Raymond, and John Meier. *Antioch and Rome: New Testament Cradles of Catholic Christianity*. London: Chapman, 1982.
Brunkhorst, Hauke. "Stand-In and Interpreter." In *The Habermas Handbook*, edited by Hauke Brunkhorst, Cristina Lafont and Regina Kreide, 349–359. New York: Columbia University Press, 2017.
Byrskog, Samuel. "The Transmission of the Jesus Tradition." In *Handbook for the Study of the Historical Jesus*, Vol. 2, edited by T. Holmén and S. E. Porter, 1465–1494. Leiden: Brill, 2011.
Calhoun, Craig, Eduardo Mendieta and Jonathan VanAntwerpen, eds. *Habermas and Religion*. Cambridge: Polity, 2013.
Carroll, Tony. "Review of Jürgen Habermas, *Auch eine Geschichte der Philosophie*, Frankfurt: Suhrkamp: 2019." *The Heythrop Journal* 61 (2020) 882–883.
Casey, Maurice. "Christology and the Legitimating Use of the Old Testament in the New Testament." In *The Old Testament in the New Testament: Essays in Honour of J. L. North*, edited by Steve Moyise, 42–64. Sheffield: Sheffield Academic Press, 2000.
Cercel, Larisa, and Adriana Serban, eds. *Friedrich Schleiermacher and the Question of Translation*. Berlin/Boston: Walter De Gruyter, 2015.
Chadwick, Henry. *Early Christian Thought and the Classical Tradition*. Oxford: Clarendon. 1966.
Chadwick, Henry. *Origen: Contra Celsum*. Cambridge: Cambridge University Press, 1953.
Cross, Richard. *Duns Scotus*. Oxford: Oxford University Press, 1999.
Coppins, Wayne. "Richard Bauckham, Jens Schröter, and Paul Ricoeur on Memory and its Errors." https://germanforneutestamentler.com/tag/schroterposts/ (accessed April 25, 2021).
Crossan, John Dominic. *The Historical Jesus: The Life of a Mediterranean Jewish Peasant*. San Francisco: HarperSanFrancisco, 1991.
Dalferth, Ingolf U. "Vom Verkümmern der Vernunft in der säkularen Moderne." In *Religionsphilosophie nach Habermas*, edited by Thomas Schmidt and Matthias Lutz-Bachmann. Stuttgart: Verlag Metzler, forthcoming, 2023.
Daly-Denton, Margaret. "Singing Hymns to Christ as to a God (Cf. Pliny *Ep*. X, 96)." In *The Jewish Roots of Christological Monotheism: Papers from the St. Andrews Conference on the Historical Origins of the Worship of Jesus*, edited by Carey C. Newman, James R. Davila and Gladys S. Lewis, 277–292. Leiden: Brill, 1999.
Daly-Denton, Margaret. *Psalm-Shaped Prayerfulness: A Guide to the Christian Reception of the Psalms*. Collegeville, MN: Liturgical Press, 2011.
Daly-Denton, Margaret. *John: An Earth Bible Commentary: Supposing Him to Be the Gardener*. London: Bloomsbury, 2017.
Daly-Denton, Margaret. "Instilling the Word." *Worship* 95 (2021): 196–203.

Deidun, Tom. "The Bible and Christian Ethics." In *Christian Ethics: An Introduction*, edited by Bernard Hoose, 3–46. London: Cassell, 1998.
Dunn, James D. G. *The Theology of Paul the Apostle*. Grand Rapids, MI: Eerdmans, 1998.
Dunn, James D. G., ed. *The Cambridge Companion to St Paul*. Cambridge: Cambridge University Press, 2006.
Dunn, James D. G. *Did the First Christians Worship Jesus?* London: SPCK, 2010.
Esler, Philip F., ed. *Modelling Early Christianity: Social Scientific Studies of the New Testament in Context*. London/New York: Routledge, 1995.
Esler, Philip F. *Galatians*. London: Routledge, 1998.
Essen, Georg. *Historische Vernunft und Auferweckung Jesu*. Mainz: Grünewald, 1995.
Essen, Georg. *Die Freiheit Jesu. Der neuchalkedonische Enhypostasiebegriff in neuzeitlicher Subjekt- und Personphilosophie*. ratio fidei 5. Regensburg: Pustet, 2001.
Essen, Georg. "Das Geschichtsdenken der Moderne als Krise und Herausforderung der Christologie. Historische Vergewisserung in systematischer Absicht." In *Der Problemhorizont der Christologie in der Moderne*, edited by Christian Danz and Michael Murrmann-Kahl, 141–155. Tübingen: Mohr Siebeck, 2009.
Essen, Georg. "Autonomer Geltungssinn und religiöser Begründungszusammenhang. Papst Gelasius I. († 496) als Fallstudie zur religionspolitischen Differenzsemantik." *Archiv für Rechts- und Sozialphilosophie* 99 (2013): 1–10.
Essen, Georg, and Magnus Striet, eds. *Kant und die Theologie*. Darmstadt: Wissenschaftliche Buchgesellschaft, 2005.
Essen, Georg, and Christian Danz, eds. *Dogmatische Christologie in der Moderne. Problemkonstellationen gegenwärtiger Forschung*. Regensburg: Pustet, 2019.
Essen, Georg. "Geschichte – Metaphysik – Anthropologie: Diskurskonstellationen der Christologie der Moderne. Eine katholisch-theologische Vergewisserung." In *Dogmatische Christologie in der Moderne. Problemkonstellationen gegenwärtiger Forschung*, edited by Essen and Danz, 9–18. Regensburg: Pustet, 2019.
Essen, Georg. "Rezension Jürgen Habermas, *Auch eine Geschichte der Philosophie, 1–2*. Berlin: Suhrkamp Verlag, 2019." *Zeitschrift für Neuere Theologiegeschichte* 28 (2021) (forthcoming).
Fischer, Johannes. "Über das Verhältnis von Glauben und Wissen. Eine Auseinandersetzung mit Jürgen Habermas' Genealogie des nachmetaphysischen Denkens." *Zeitschrift für Theologie und Kirche* 117 (2020): 316–346.
Flasch, Kurt. *Logik des Schreckens. Augustinus von Hippo: Die Gnadenlehre von 387* (lateinisch/deutsch) (Exzerpta classica 8). Mainz: Dieterich'sche Verlagsbuchhandlung, 2nd edn 1993.
Flasch, Kurt, *Kampfplätze der Philosophie. Große Kontroversen von Augustin bis Voltaire*. Frankfurt: Vittorio Klostermann, 2008.
Frank, Manfred. *Das individuelle Allgemeine*. Frankfurt: Suhrkamp, 1977.
Frank, Manfred, ed. *Schleiermacher: Hermeneutik und Kritik*. Frankfurt: Suhrkamp, 1977.
Frank, Manfred. *Selbstbewusstseinstheorien von Fichte bis Sartre*. Frankfurt: Suhrkamp, 2nd edn 1993.
Fraser, Nancy. "The Theory of the Public Sphere: *The Structural Transformation of the Public Sphere* (1962)." In The *Habermas Handbook*, edited by Hauke Brunkhorst, Regina Kreide and Cristina Lafont, 245–255. New York: Columbia University Press, 2017.

Freyne, Seán. *Galilee, Jesus and the Gospels: Literary Approaches and Historical Investigations*. Philadelphia: Fortress Press, 1988.
Freyne, Seán. "The Early Christians and Jewish Messianic Ideas." In *Messianism Through History*, edited by Wim Beuken, Seán Freyne and Anton Weiler, 30–41. *Concilium* 1993/1. London: SCM Press, 1993.
Freyne, Seán. *Galilee and Gospel*. WUNT 125. Tübingen: Mohr Siebeck, 2000.
Freyne, Seán. "The Jesus-Paul Debate Revisited and Re-imaging Christian Origins." In *Christian Origins: Worship, Belief and Society*, edited by Kieran O'Mahoney, 143–162. Sheffield: Sheffield Academic Press, 2003.
Freyne, Seán. *Jesus, a Jewish Galilean: A New Reading of the Jesus Story*. Edinburgh: T & T Clark, 2004.
Freyne, Seán. "The Galilean Jesus and a Contemporary Christology." *Theological Studies* 70 (2009): 281–297.
Freyne, Seán. "In Search of Identity: Narrativity, Discipleship and Moral Agency." In *Moral Language in the New Testament*, edited by Ruben Zimmermann, J. Van der Watt, in cooperation with Susanne Luther, 67–85. Tübingen: Mohr Siebeck, 2010.
Freyne, Seán. *The Jesus Movement and its Expansion: Meaning and Mission*. Grand Rapids, MI: Eerdmans, 2014.
Freyne, Seán. "How the Early Christians Read the Hebrew Scriptures." In *Reading the Sacred Scriptures: From Oral Tradition to Written Documents and their Reception*, edited by Fiachra Long and Siobhán Dowling Long, 66–78. London: Routledge, 2018.
Gerhard, Volker. "Art. Philosophie." In *Kant-Lexikon. Studienausgabe*, edited by Marcus Willaschek, Jürgen Stolzenberg, Georg Mohr and Stefano Bacin, 433–444. Berlin: Walter De Gruyter, 2017.
Gockel, Matthias. *Barth and Schleiermacher on the Doctrine of Election*. Oxford: Oxford University Press, 2006.
Gordon, Peter E. "Secularization, Genealogy, and the Legitimacy of the Modern Age: Remarks on the Löwith–Blumenberg Debate." *Journal of the History of Ideas* 80 (2019): 147–170.
Gottschalg, Rainer. *"Was nützt die Liebe in Gedanken?" Ekklesiologische Orientierungen zwischen Gnade und Freiheit*. Paderborn: Brill/Schöningh, 2020.
Graf, Friedrich Wilhelm, and Klaus Wiegand, eds. *Die Anfänge des Christentums*. Frankfurt: Fischer, 2009.
Gula, Richard. "Natural Law Today." In *Natural Law and Theology (Readings in Moral Theology No. 7)*, edited by Charles Curran and Richard McCormick, 369–391. Mahwah, NJ: Paulist Press, 1991.
Hadot, Pierre. *Exercices spirituelles et philosophie antique*. Paris: Albin Michel, 2014, 1st edn. 1981.
Häring, Hermann. *Die Macht des Bösen. Das Erbe Augustins*. Zürich/Köln/Gütersloh: Benziger/Gütersloher Verlagshaus, 1979.
Haight, Roger. *Jesus Symbol of God*. Maryknoll, NY: Orbis, 2000.
Hauschild, Wolf-Dieter. "*Kata Eunomiou*." In *Lexikon der theologischen Werke*, edited by Michael Eckert, Eilert Herms, Hans-Jochen Hilberath and Eberhard Jüngel, 425. Stuttgart: Kröner, 2003.
Hengel, Martin. "The Song about Christ in Earliest Worship." In *Studies in Early Christology*, trans. Rollin Kearns, 227–291. Edinburgh: T & T Clark, 1995.

Hengel, Martin, and Anna Maria Schwemer. *Paul between Damascus and Antioch: The Unknown Years*, trans. J. Bowden. London: SCM, 1997.
Henrich, Dieter. *Fluchtlinien. Philosophische Essays*. Frankfurt: Suhrkamp, 1982.
Henrich, Dieter. *Konzepte. Essays zur Philosophie in der Zeit*. Frankfurt: Suhrkamp, 1987.
Henrich, Dieter. "What is Metaphysics – What is Modernity?" In *Habermas: A Critical Reader*, edited and trans. by Peter Dews, 291–319. Oxford: Blackwell, 1999.
Holtman, Sarah. "Öffentlichkeit" in *Kant-Lexikon. Studienausgabe*, edited by Marcus Willaschek, Jürgen Stolzenberg, Georg Mohr and Stefano Bacin, 408–410. Berlin: Walter de Gruyter, 2017.
Honnefelder, Ludger. *Woher kommen wir? Ursprünge der Moderne im Denken des Mittelalters*. Darmstadt: Wissenschaftliche Buchgesellschaft, 2008.
Hooker, Morna D. "Adam Redivivus: Philippians 2 once more." In *The Old Testament in the New Testament: Essays in Honour of J. L. North*, edited by Steve Moyise, 220–234.
Sheffield: Sheffield Academic Press, 2000.
Hübener, Wolfgang. "Die Nominalismus-Legende. Über das Missverhältnis zwischen Dichtung und Wahrheit in der Deutung der Wirkungsgeschichte des Ockhamismus." In *Spiegel und Gleichnis. Festschrift für Jacob Taubes*, edited by Norbert W. Bolz and Wolfgang Hübener, 87–111. Würzburg: Königshausen und Neumann, 1983.
Hübenthal, Christoph. "Autonomie als Prinzip. Zur Neubegründung der Moralität bei Kant". In *Kant und die Theologie*, edited by Georg Essen and Magnus Striet, 95–128. Darmstadt: Wissenschaftliche Buchgesellschaft, 2005.
Hübenthal, Christoph. *Grundlegung der christlichen Sozialethik. Versuch eines freiheitsanalytisch-handlungsreflexiven Ansatzes*. Münster: Aschendorff, 2006.
Hübenthal, Christoph. "Ethische Begründung aus dem theologischen Grund des Säkularen. Eine katholische Sicht." In *Ökumenische Ethik*, edited by Thomas Weißer, 45–63. Fribourg: Fribourg Academic Press/Würzburg: Echter, 2018.
Hübenthal, Christoph, and Christiane Alpers, eds. *T & T Clark Handbook of Public Theology*. London: T & T Clark, forthcoming.
Humboldt, Wilhelm von. *Werke in fünf Bänden*, edited by Andreas Flitner and Klaus Giel. Darmstadt: Wissenschaftliche Buchgesellschaft, 4th edn 1964.
Hurtado, Larry W. *One God, One Lord: Early Christian Devotion and Ancient Jewish Monotheism*. Edinburgh: T & T Clark, 2nd edn 1998.
Hurtado, Larry W. "The Binitarian Shape of Early Christian Worship." In *The Jewish Roots of Christological Monotheism. Papers from the St. Andrews Conference on the Historical Origins of the Worship of Jesus*, edited by Carey C. Newman, James R. Davila and Gladys S. Lewis, 187–214. Leiden: Brill, 1999.
Hurtado, Larry W. *At the Origins of Christian Worship: The Context and Character of the Earliest Christian Devotion*. Grand Rapids, MI: Eerdmans, 1999.
Hurtado, Larry W. *Lord Jesus Christ: Devotion to Jesus in Earliest Christianity*. Grand Rapids, MI.: Eerdmans, 2003.
Hurtado, Larry W. "The Origin and Development of Christ Devotion: Forces and Factors." In *Christian Origins: Worship, Belief and Society* edited by Kieran O'Mahoney, 52–82. Sheffield: Sheffield Academic Press, 2003.
Hurtado, Larry W. *How on Earth Did Jesus Become a God?* Grand Rapids, MI: Eerdmans, 2005.
Jacobi, Christine. *Jesusüberlieferung bei Paulus? Analogien zwischen den echten Paulusbriefen und den synoptischen Evangelien*. Berlin/Boston: Walter de Gruyter, 2015.

Jacobi, Christine. "II. Auferstehung, Erscheinungen, Weisungen des Auferstandenen." In *Jesus-Handbuch*, edited by Jens Schroeter and Christine Jacobi, with cooperation of Lena Nogossek, 490–504. Tübingen: Mohr Siebeck, 2017.
Joas, Hans. "Faith and Knowledge: Habermas' Alternative History of Philosophy." *Theory, Culture & Society* 37 (2020) 47–52.
Junker-Kenny, Maureen. *Argumentationsethik und christliches Handeln. Eine praktisch-theologische Auseinandersetzung mit Jürgen Habermas*. Stuttgart: Kohlhammer, 1998.
Junker-Kenny, Maureen. "Poetics of Culture and Christian Memory: The Relevance of Ricoeur's Thinking for Christian Ethics." In *Paul Ricoeur: Poetics and Religion*, edited by Joseph Verheyden, Theo L. Hettema and Pieter Vandecasteele, 37–66. Leuven: Peeters, 2011.
Junker-Kenny, Maureen. *Habermas and Theology*. London/New York: T & T Clark International, 2011.
Junker-Kenny Maureen. "Memory and Forgetting in Paul Ricoeur's Theory of the Capable Self." In *Handbook of Cultural Memory Studies*, edited by Ansgar Nünning and Astrid Erll, 203–211. Berlin/New York: Walter de Gruyter, 2008.
Junker-Kenny, Maureen. "Jürgen Habermas." In *Religion and European Philosophy*, edited by Philip Goodchild and Hollis Phelps, 141–155. London: Routledge, 2017.
Junker-Kenny Maureen. *Religion and Public Reason: A Comparison of the Positions of John Rawls, Jürgen Habermas and Paul Ricoeur*. Berlin/Boston: Walter De Gruyter 2014.
Junker-Kenny, Maureen. "Schleiermacher und Kierkegaard in der Sicht 'nachmetaphysischen' Denkens." In *Habermas und die Religion*, edited by Klaus Viertbauer and Franz Gruber, 59–77. Darmstadt: Wissenschaftliche Buchgesellschaft, 2nd edn 2019.
Junker-Kenny, Maureen. "What Scope for Ethics in the Public Sphere? Principled Autonomy and the Antinomy of Practical Reason." *Theology and Reason in the Public Sphere*, edited by Christoph Hübenthal, Special Issue, *Studies in Christian Ethics* 32 (2019): 485–498.
Junker-Kenny, Maureen. "Guest Editorial". Special Issue, *Habermas on Religion*, edited by Klaus Viertbauer and Maureen Junker-Kenny. *European Journal for Philosophy of Religion* 11/4 (2019) 1–20.
Junker-Kenny, Maureen. *Self, Christ and God in Schleiermacher's Dogmatics: A Theology Reconceived for Modernity*. Berlin/Boston: Walter de Gruyter, 2020.
Junker-Kenny, Maureen. "The Public Sphere", in *T & T Clark Handbook of Public Theology*, edited by Christoph Hübenthal and Christiane Alpers. London: T & T Clark, forthcoming.
Kant, Immanuel. *Critique of Pure Reason*, trans. Norman Kemp Smith. New York: St Martin's Press/Toronto: Macmillan, 1929.
Kant, Immanuel. "An Answer to the Question: 'What is Enlightenment?'" In *Kant's Political Writings*, edited with an Introduction and Notes by Hans Reiss, trans. H.B. Nisbet, 54–60. Cambridge: Cambridge University Press, 1970.
Kant, Immanuel. *Critique of Practical Reason*, trans. Lewis W. Beck. New York: Liberal Arts Press, 1956.
Kant, Immanuel. *Religion Within the Boundaries of Mere Reason And Other Writings*, edited by Allen Wood and George di Giovanni. Introduction by Robert M. Adams. Cambridge: Cambridge University Press, 1998.
Kasper, Walter. *Jesus the Christ*, trans. V. Green. London: Burns & Oates/New York: Paulist Press, 1976.

Kasper, Walter. *The God of Jesus Christ*, trans. Matthew J. O'Connell. New York: Crossroad, 1984.
Kenny, Peter. "Correcting the History: The Significance of Schleiermacher's Early Hermeneutics Manuscripts." In *New Athenaeum/Neues Athenaeum* 3 (1992): 43–66.
Kertelge, Karl. "Einführung." In *Rückfrage nach Jesus*. Quaestiones disputatae 63, edited by Karl Kertelge, 7–10. Freiburg: Herder, 1974.
Kessler, Hans. *Die theologische Bedeutung des Todes Jesu. Eine traditionsgeschichtliche Untersuchung*. Düsseldorf: Patmos, 1970.
Kimmerle, Heinz. "Interpretationen der Hermeneutik Schleiermachers in den 1950er Jahren in Heidelberg." In *Friedrich Schleiermachers Hermeneutik. Interpretationen und Perspektiven*, edited by Andreas Arndt and Jörg Dierken, 183–196. Berlin/Boston: Walter de Gruyter, 2016.
Kirschner, Martin. *Gott – größer als gedacht. Die Transformation der Vernunft aus der Begegnung mit Gott bei Anselm von Canterbury*. Freiburg: Herder, 2013.
Klauck, Hans-Josef. "'Ein Wort, das in der ganzen Welt erschallt': Traditions- und Identitätsbildung durch Evangelien." In *Die Anfänge des Christentums*, edited by Friedrich W. Graf and Klaus Wiegand, 57–89. Frankfurt: Fischer, 2009.
Kobusch, Theo. *Christliche Philosophie. Die Entdeckung der Subjektivität*. Darmstadt: Wissenschaftliche Buchgesellschaft, 2006.
Kobusch, Theo. *Selbstwerdung und Personalität*. Tübingen: Mohr Siebeck, 2018.
Kögler, Hans-Herbert. "A Genealogy of Faith and Freedom." *Theory, Culture and Society* 37 (2020): 37–46.
Kreitzer, Larry. *2 Corinthians*. New Testament Guides. Sheffield: Sheffield Academic Press, 1996.
Langenfeld, Aaron, and Magnus Lerch, *Theologische Anthropologie*. Paderborn: Schöningh, 2018.
Langthaler, Rudolf. *Nachmetaphysisches Denken? Kritische Anfragen an Jürgen Habermas*. Berlin: Duncker & Humblot, 1997.
Langthaler, Rudolf, and Herta Nagl-Docekal, eds. *Recht – Geschichte – Religion. Die Bedeutung Kants für die Gegenwart*. Berlin: Akademie Verlag, 2004.
Laube, Martin. "'Der Kampf muss ausgefochten werden'. Überlegungen zur historischen Jesusfrage mit einem Verweis auf Ernst Troeltsch." In *Dogmatische Christologie in der Moderne. Problemkonstellationen gegenwärtiger Forschung*, edited by Christian Danz and Georg Essen, 133–152. Regensburg: Pustet, 2019.
Lerch, Magnus. *All-Einheit und Freiheit. Subjektphilosophische Klärungsversuche in der Monismus-Debatte zwischen Klaus Müller und Magnus Striet*. Würzburg: Echter, 2009.
Lerch, Magnus. *Selbstmitteilung Gottes. Herausforderungen einer freiheitstheoretischen Offenbarungstheologie*. ratio fidei 56. Regensburg: Pustet, 2015.
Lindbeck, George. *The Nature of Doctrine: Religion and Theology in a Postliberal Age*. Louisville, KY: Westminster John Knox, 1984.
Lütterfelds, Wilhelm. "Der praktische Vernunftglaube und das Paradox der kulturellen Weltbilder." In *Glauben und Wissen. Ein Symposium mit Jürgen Habermas*, 120–155. Wien: Oldenbourg Verlag/Akademie Verlag, 2007.
McGrath, Alister. *The Making of Modern German Christology: From the Enlightenment to Pannenberg*. Oxford: Oxford University Press, 1986.

Mack, Burton. *The Lost Gospel: The Book of Q and Christian Origins.* New York: HarperCollins, 1994.
Markschies, Christoph. *Die Gnosis.* München: C. H. Beck, 4th edn 2018.
Markus, Robert A. *Christianity and the Secular.* South Bend, IN: Notre Dame University Press, 2006.
Marty, François. "Die Analogie zwischen 'ethischem' und 'bürgerlichem' gemeinen Wesen. Ein Beitrag zur Frage der Erreichbarkeit des höchsten politischen Gutes." In *Recht – Geschichte – Religion. Die Bedeutung Kants für die Gegenwart*, edited by Rudolf Langthaler and Herta Nagl-Docekal, 63–70. Berlin: Akademie Verlag, 2004.
Meeks, Wayne A. *The First Urban Christians: The Social World of The Apostle Paul.* New Haven, CT/London: Yale University Press, 1983.
Meeks, Wayne A. *The Moral World of the First Christians.* London: SPCK, 1987.
Meeks, Wayne A. "Judaism, Hellenism and the Birth of Christianity." In *Paul Beyond the Judaism/Hellenism Divide*, edited by Troels Engberg-Pedersen, 17–27. Louisville, KY: Westminster John Knox Press, 2001.
Meier, John P. and Raymond Brown. *Antioch and Rome.* New York: Paulist Press, 1983.
Mendieta, Eduardo. "The Unfinished Project of the Enlightenment: Jürgen Habermas at 90" in *Los Angeles Review of Books*, August 11th, 2019, https://lareviewofbooks.org/feature/unfinished-project-enlightenment-jurgen-habermas-90/ (accessed April 25, 2021)
Mendieta, Eduardo, and Amy Allen, eds. *The Cambridge Habermas Lexicon.* Cambridge: Cambridge University Press, 2019.
Menke, Karl-Heinz. *Jesus ist Gott der Sohn. Denkformen und Brennpunkte der Christologie.* Regensburg: Pustet, 2008.
Merz, Annette. "Der historische Jesus – faszinierend und unverzichtbar." In *Die Anfänge des Christentums*, edited by Friedrich Wilhelm Graf and Klaus Wiegand, 23–56. Frankfurt: Fischer, 2009.
Metz, Johann Baptist. "Plädoyer für mehr Theodizee-Empfindlichkeit in der Theologie."In *Worüber man nicht schweigen kann. Neue Diskussionen zur Theodizeefrage*, edited by Willi Oelmüller, 107–160. München: Wilhelm Fink Verlag, 1992.
Mitchell, Margaret M. "Patristic Counter-Evidence to the Claim that 'The Gospels were Written for all Christians.'" *New Testament Studies* 51 (2005) 36–79.
Mitchell, Margaret M. "1 and 2 Thessalonians." In *The Cambridge Companion to St Paul*, edited by James D. G. Dunn, 51–63. Cambridge: Cambridge University Press, 2006.
Mitchell, Margaret M., and Frances Young, eds. *The Cambridge History of Christianity: Origins to Constantine.* Cambridge: Cambridge University Press, 2006.
Moyise, Steve. "Intertextuality and the Study of the Old Testament in the New Testament." In *The Old Testament in the New Testament. Essays in Honour of J. L. North*, edited by Steve Moyise, 14–41. Sheffield: Sheffield Academic Press, 2000.
Moyise, Steve, ed. *The Old Testament in the New Testament. Essays in Honour of J. L. North.* Sheffield: Sheffield Academic Press, 2000.
Müller, Klaus, and Magnus Striet, eds. *Dogma und Denkform. Strittiges in der Grundlegung von Offenbarungsbegriff und Gottesgedanke.* Regensburg: Pustet, 2005.
Müller, Sigrid. *Theologie und Philosophie im Spätmittelalter. Die Anfänge der* via moderna *und ihre Bedeutung für die Entwicklung der Moraltheologie (1380–1450).* Münster: Aschendorff, 2018.
Murphy-O'Connor, Jerome. *Paul: His Story.* Oxford: Oxford University Press, 2006.

Murphy-O'Connor, Jerome. "The Origins of Paul's Christology: From Thessalonians to Galatians." In *Christian Origins: Worship, Belief and Society*, edited by Kieran O'Mahoney, 113–142. Sheffield: Sheffield Academic Press, 2003.
Nagl-Docekal, Herta. *Feminist Philosophy*, trans. Katharina Vester. Boulder, CO/London: Westview Press, 2004.
Nagl-Docekal, Herta, and Rudolf Langthaler, eds. Recht – Geschichte – Religion. Die Bedeutung Kants für die Gegenwart. Berlin: Akademie Verlag, 2004.
Nagl-Docekal, Herta, and Rudolf Langthaler, eds. "Vorwort." In *Recht – Geschichte – Religion. Die Bedeutung Kants für die Gegenwart*, edited by Herta Nagl-Docekal and Rudolf Langthaler, 7–9. Berlin: Akademie Verlag, 2004.
Nagl-Docekal, Herta. "Eine rettende Übersetzung? Jürgen Habermas interpretiert Kants Religionsphilosophie." In *Glauben und Wissen. Ein Symposium mit Jürgen Habermas*, edited by Rudolf Langthaler and Herta Nagl-Docekal, 93–113. Wien: Oldenbourg Verlag/ Akademie Verlag, 2007.
Nagl-Docekal, Herta. "Moral und Religion aus der Optik der heutigen rechtsphilosophischen Debatte." *Deutsche Zeitschrift für Philosophie* 56 (2008): 843–855.
Nagl-Docekal, Herta. *Innere Freiheit. Grenzen der nachmetaphysischen Moralkonzeptionen*. Berlin/Boston: Walter De Gruyter, 2014.
Nagl-Docekal, Herta. "Why Ethics Needs Politics: A Cosmopolitan Perspective (With a Little Help from Kant." In *Chiasmatic Encounters: Art, Ethics, Politics*, edited by Kuisma Korhonen, Arto Haapala, Sara Heinämaa, Kristian Klockars, and Pajari Räsänen, 151–169. Lanham, MD: Lexington Books, 2018.
Nagl-Docekal, Herta. "Nach einer erneuten Lektüre: Max Horkheimer, *Die Sehnsucht nach dem ganz Anderen*." *Deutsche Zeitschrift für Philosophie* 68 (2020): 659–688.
Nagl-Docekal, Herta. "Immanuel Kant's Concept of Reasonable Hope." In *Hope: Where does our Hope lie? International Congress of the European Society for Catholic Theology (August 2019 – Bratislava, Slovakia)*, edited by Miloš Lichner, 177–192. Wien: LIT Verlag, 2020.
Oelmüller, Willi, ed. *Worüber man nicht schweigen kann. Neue Diskussionen zur Theodizeefrage* (München: Wilhelm Fink Verlag, 1992)
Orth, Stefan. "Kriteriologie des Göttlichen – Hermeneutik der Zeugnisse. Paul Ricoeur, Jean Nabert und die fundamentaltheologische Diskussion." In *Unbedingtes Verstehen? Fundamentaltheologie zwischen Erstphilosophie und Hermeneutik*, edited by Joachim Valentin and Saskia Wendel, 81–91. Regensburg: Pustet, 2001.
Pannenberg, Wolfhart. "Christianity as the Legitimacy of the Modern Age: Thoughts on a Book by Hans Blumenberg (1968)". In *The Idea of God and Human Freedom*, trans. R. A. Wilson, 178–191. Philadelphia: Westminster Press, 1973.
Petersdorff, Friedrich von. "Verstehen und historische Erklärung bei Ricoeur." In *Erinnerungsarbeit. Zu Paul Ricoeurs Philosophie von Gedächtnis, Geschichte und Vergessen*, edited by Andris Breitling and Stefan Orth, 127–140. Berlin: Berliner Wissenschaftsverlag, 2004.
Peukert, Helmut. *Science, Action, and Fundamental Theology: Toward a Theology of Communicative Action*, trans. James Bohman. Cambridge, MA: MIT Press, 1984.
Peukert, Helmut. "Enlightenment and Theology as Unfinished Projects", trans. Eric Crump and Peter Kenny. In *Habermas, Modernity, and Public Theology*, edited by Don Browning and Francis Schüssler Fiorenza, 43–65. New York: Crossroad, 1992.

Peukert, Helmut. "Nachwort zur 3. Auflage 2009." In *Wissenschaftstheorie – Handlungstheorie – Fundamentale Theologie. Analysen zu Ansatz und Status theologischer Theoriebildung*, 357–394. Frankfurt: Suhrkamp, 3rd edn, 2009.
Pottmeyer, Hermann J. "Zeichen und Kriterien der Glaubwürdigkeit des Christentums." In *Handbuch der Fundamentaltheologie,* edited by Walter Kern, Hermann J. Pottmeyer and Max Seckler, Vol. IV, 373–413. Freiburg: Herder, 1988.
Pröpper, Thomas. *Der Jesus der Philosophen und der Jesus des Glaubens. Ein theologisches Gespräch mit Jaspers – Bloch – Kolakowski – Gardavsky – Machovec – Fromm – Ben-Chorin.* Mainz: Grünewald, 1976.
Pröpper, Thomas. *Erlösungsglaube und Freiheitsgeschichte. Eine Skizze zur Soteriologie.* München: Kösel, 3rd edn 1991.
Pröpper, Thomas. *Evangelium und freie Vernunft. Konturen einer theologischen Hermeneutik.* Freiburg: Herder, 2001.
Pröpper, Thomas. *Theologische Anthropologie*, 2 Vols. Freiburg: Herder, 2011.
Rehg, William. "Critique of Knowledge as Social Theory." In *The Habermas Handbook*, edited by Hauke Brunkhorst, Cristina Lafont and Regina Kreide, 271–287. New York: Columbia University Press, 2017.
Rehg, William. "Cognitive Interests." In *The Habermas Handbook*, edited by Hauke Brunkhorst, Cristina Lafont and Regina Kreide, 489–493. New York: Columbia University Press, 2017.
Ricken, Friedo, SJ. "Postmetaphysical Reason and Religion." In *An Awareness of What is Missing: Faith and Reason in a Postsecular Age,* edited by Jürgen Habermas et al., trans. Ciaran Cronin, 50–57. Cambridge: Polity Press, 2010.
Ricoeur, Paul. "Original Sin: A Study in Meaning" (1960), trans. Peter McCormick. In *The Conflict of Interpretations*, edited by Don Ihde, 269–286. Evanston, IL: Northwestern University Press, 1974.
Ricoeur, Paul. "Freedom in the Light of Hope" (1968), trans. Robert Sweeney. In *The Conflict of Interpretations*, edited by Don Ihde, 402–424. Evanston: Northwestern University Press, 1974.
Ricoeur, Paul. "Schleiermacher's Hermeneutics." *The Monist* 60 (1977): 181–197.
Ricoeur, Paul. "Expliquer et comprendre." *Revue philosophique de Louvain* 75 (1977): 126–147.
Ricoeur, Paul. "What is a text? Explanation and understanding." In *Hermeneutics and the Human Sciences*, edited and trans. by John B. Thompson, 145–164. Cambridge: Cambridge University Press, 1981.
Ricoeur, Paul. "The Hermeneutical Function of Distanciation", in *Hermeneutics and the Human Sciences*, edited and trans. by John B. Thompson, 131–144. Cambridge: Cambridge University Press, 1981.
Ricoeur, Paul. "Philosophies critiques de l'histoire. Recherche, explication, écriture." In *Philosophical Problems Today*, Vol. I, edited by Guttorm Fløistad, 139–201. Dordrecht: Kluwer, 1994.
Ricoeur, Paul. *Figuring the Sacred, Religion, Narrative and Imagination*, trans. David Pellauer, edited by Mark Walker. Minneapolis: Augsburg Fortress, 1995.
Ricoeur, Paul. *The Just*, trans. David Pellauer. Chicago: Chicago University Press, 2000.
Ricoeur, Paul. "Paul apôtre. Proclamation et argumentation. Lectures récentes." In *L'événement saint Paul: juif, grec, roman, chrétien. Esprit* no. 292, 71 (2003): 85–112.

Ricoeur, Paul. *Memory, History, Forgetting*, trans. Kathleen Blamey and David Pellauer. Chicago: University of Chicago Press, 2004.
Ricoeur, Paul. *Reflections on the Just*, trans. D. Pellauer. Chicago: University of Chicago Press, 2007.
Rieger, Reinhold. *Interpretation und Wissen. Zur philosophischen Begründung der Hermeneutik bei F. Schleiermacher und ihrem geschichtlichen Hintergrund*. Berlin/New York: Walter de Gruyter, 1988.
Ringleben, Joachim. "Die Sprache bei Schleiermacher und Humboldt. Ein Versuch zum Verhältnis von Sprachdenken und Hermeneutik." In *Schleiermacher und die wissenschaftliche Kultur des Christentums*, edited by Günter Meckenstock, with Joachim Ringleben, 473–492. Theologische Bibliothek Töpelmann 51. Berlin/New York: Walter de Gruyter, 1991, reprint 2019.
Rosner, Brian. "Paul's ethics." In *The Cambridge Companion to St Paul*, edited by James D. G. Dunn, 212–223. Cambridge University Press, 2006.
Rossi Leidi, Thamar. "Einleitung." In Duns Scotus, *Über das Individuationsprinzip*, trans. from Latin and edited by Thamar Rossi Leidi, VII–LXXXVIII. Hamburg: Meiner, 2015.
Sanders, E. P. *Paul, the Law, and the Jewish People* (Philadelphia: Fortress Press, 1983).
Sanders, E. P. *Paul*. Oxford: Oxford University Press, 1991.
Schleiermacher, Friedrich D.E. *Kritische Gesamtausgabe* (= KGA). Berlin/New York:
Walter de Gruyter, 1980–2011; Berlin/Boston: Walter de Gruyter, since 2011.
Schleiermacher, Friedrich D. E. *Akademievorträge*, edited by Martin Rössler, with Lars Emersleben. KGA I/11. Berlin/New York: Walter de Gruyter, 2002.
Schleiermacher, Friedrich D. E. *Brief Outline of Theology as a Field of Study* (1811 and 1830), trans. and introduced by Terrence N. Tice. Lewiston, NY: The Edwin Mellen Press, 1988.
Schleiermacher, Friedrich D. E. *Brouillon zur Ethik* (1805/06), edited by Hans-Joachim Birkner. Hamburg: Meiner, 1981.
Schleiermacher, Friedrich D. E. *Christian Faith. A New Translation and Critical Edition*, 2 vols., trans. Terrence N. Tice, Catherine L. Kelsey and Edwina Lawler; edited by Catherine L. Kelsey and Terrence N. Tice. Louisville, KY: Westminster John Knox Press, 2016.
Schleiermacher, Friedrich D. E. *Der christliche Glaube* 1821/22, 2 vols., Studienausgabe, edited by Hermann Peiter. KGA I/7.1 und 2. Berlin/New York: Walter de Gruyter, 1984.
Schleiermacher, Friedrich D. E. *Hermeneutics: The Handwritten Manuscripts*, trans. by James Duke and Jack Forstman (Missoula: Montana: Scholars Press, 1977),
Schleiermacher, Friedrich D. E. *Hermeneutics and Criticism And Other Writings*, edited by Andrew Bowie. Cambridge: Cambridge University Press, 1998.
Schleiermacher, Friedrich D. E. *Hermeneutik*, edited by Heinz Kimmerle. Heidelberg: Carl Winter Universitätsverlag, 2nd edn 1974.
Schleiermacher, Friedrich D. E. *Hermeneutik und Kritik, mit einem Anhang sprachphilosophischer Texte Schleiermachers*, edited and introduced by Manfred Frank. Frankfurt: Suhrkamp, 1977.
Schleiermacher, Friedrich D. E. *On Religion: Speeches to its Cultured Despisers*, trans. R. Crouter. Cambridge: Cambridge University Press, 1996.
Schleiermacher, Friedrich D. E. *The Christian Faith* (1830/31), edited by H.R. Mackintosh and J.S. Stewart, trans. D. M. Baillie et al. Edinburgh: T & T Clark, 1928; 1986.
Schleiermacher, Friedrich D. E. *Vorlesungen über die Dialektik*, edited by Andreas Arndt, KGA II/10/1–2 (Berlin/New York: Walter de Gruyter, 2002.

Schleiermacher, Friedrich D. E. *Vorlesungen zur Hermeneutik und Kritik*, edited by Wolfgang Virmond, with Hermann Patsch. KGA II/4. Berlin/New York: Walter de Gruyter, 2012.
Schmidt, Axel. "Der Denkansatz des Johannes Duns Scotus." In *Duns-Scotus-Lesebuch*, Vol. 26, edited by Herbert Schneider, Marianne Schlosser and Paul Zahner, 39–81. Mönchengladbach: B. Kühlen Verlag, 2008.
Schmidt, Thomas. "Religiöser Diskurs und diskursive Religion in der postsäkularen Gesellschaft." In *Glauben und Wissen. Ein Symposium mit Jürgen Habermas*, edited by Rudolf Langthaler and Herta Nagl-Docekal, 322–340. Wien: Oldenbourg Verlag/ Akademie Verlag, 2007.
Schmidt, Thomas. "Glauben und Wissen. Religiöse Epistemologie und spekulative Religionsphilosophie." In *Interesse am Anderen. Interdisziplinäre Beiträge zum Verhältnis von Religion und Rationalität. Für Heiko Schulz zum 60. Geburtstag*, edited by Gerhard Schreiber, 383–402. Berlin/Boston: Walter de Gruyter, 2019.
Schmidt, Thomas. "Nachmetaphysische Religionsphilosophie." In *Moderne Religion? Theologische und religionsphilosophische Reaktionen auf Jürgen Habermas*, edited by Knut Wenzel and Thomas Schmidt, 10–32. Freiburg: Herder, 2009.
Schmidt, Sarah. "Die Kunst der Kritik: Schleiermachers Vorlesungen zur Kritik und ihre Einordnung in das philosophische System." In *Friedrich Schleiermachers Hermeneutik. Interpretationen und Perspektiven*, edited by Andreas Arndt and Jörg Dierken, 101–117. Berlin/Boston: Walter de Gruyter, 2016.
Scholtz, Gunter. "Schleiermacher im Kontext der neuzeitlichen Hermeneutikentwicklung." In *Friedrich Schleiermachers Hermeneutik. Interpretationen und Perspektiven*, edited by Andreas Arndt and Jörg Dierken, 1–26. Berlin/Boston: Walter de Gruyter, 2016.
Schröter, Jens. *Erinnerung an Jesu Worte. Studien zur Rezeption der Logienüberlieferung in Markus, Q und Thomas*. Neukirchen-Vluyn: Neukirchener Verlag, 1997.
Schröter, Jens. "The Gospels of Eyewitness Testimony? A Critical Examination of Richard Bauckham's *Jesus and the Eyewitnesses*." *Journal for the Study of the New Testament* 31 (2008): 195–209.
Schröter, Jens. "Memory, Theories of History, and the Reception of Jesus." *Journal for the Study of the Historical Jesus* 16 (2018): 85–107.
Schröter, Jens. "Der 'erinnerte Jesus': Erinnerung als geschichtshermeneutisches Paradigma der Jesusforschung." In *Jesus Handbuch*, edited by Jens Schröter and Christine Jacobi, with cooperation by Lena Nogossek, 112–124. Tübingen: Mohr Siebeck, 2017.
Schürmann, Heinz. *Gottes Reich – Jesu Geschick. Jesu ureigener Tod im Licht seiner Basileia-Verkündigung*. Freiburg: Herder, 1983.
Schüssler Fiorenza, Elisabeth. *In Memory of Her: A Feminist Reconstruction of Christian Origins*. New York, Crossroad, 1983.
Schüssler Fiorenza, Elisabeth. "Re-visioning Christian Origins: *In Memory of Her* Revisited." In *Christian Origins: Worship, Belief and Society*, edited by Kieran O'Mahoney, 225–250. Sheffield: Sheffield Academic Press, 2003.
Selge, Kurt-Viktor, ed. *Internationaler Schleiermacher-Kongress Berlin 1984*, 2 Vols. Berlin/ New York: Walter de Gruyter, 1985.
Stolzenberg, Jürgen. "Kants Weltbegriff der Philosophie." In *Kantovskii Sbornik/Kantian Journal* 36 (April 2017). http://www.kant-online.ru/en/?p=841 (accessed April 7, 2021).
Stolzenberg, Jürgen. "'Was jedermann notwendig interessiert'. Kants Weltbegriff der Philosophie." In *Protestantismus zwischen Aufklärung und Moderne (FS Ulrich Barth)*,

edited by Roderich Barth, Claus-Dieter Osthövener and Arnulf von Scheliha, 83–94. Frankfurt: P. Lang, 2005.
Striet, Magnus. *Offenbares Geheimnis. Zur Kritik der negativen Theologie*. ratio fidei 14. Regensburg: Pustet, 2003.
Striet, Magnus. "*Wissenschaftstheorie – Handlungstheorie – Fundamentale Theologie*", in *Lexikon der theologischen Werke*, edited by Michael Eckert et al., 812–813. Stuttgart: Kröner, 2003.
Striet, Magnus. "Unterscheidung der Geister. Negative Theologie in der Kritik." In *Jenseits der Säkularisierung. Religionsphilosophische Studien*, edited by Herta Nagl-Docekal and Friedrich Wolfram, 95–107. Berlin: Parerga, 2008.
Teichert, Dieter. "Erinnerte Einbildungen und eingebildete Erinnerungen. Erinnerung und Imagination in epistemologischer Perspektive." In *Erinnerungsarbeit. Zu Paul Ricoeur's Philosophie von Gedächtnis, Geschichte und Vergessen*, edited by Andris Breitling and Stefan Orth, 89–100. Berlin: Berliner Wissenschafts-Verlag, 2004.
Theissen, Gerd. *Die Jesusbewegung. Sozialgeschichte einer Revolution der Werte*. Gütersloh: Gütersloher Verlagshaus, 2004.
Theissen, Gerd. "Die Jesusbewegung als charismatische Werterevolution." *New Testament Studies* 35 (1989): 343–360.
Theissen, Gerd. "Die Tempelweissagung Jesu. Prophetie im Spannungsfeld zwischen Tempel und Land." *Theologische Zeitung* 32 (1976): 144–158.
Thouard, Denis. "Passer entre les langues. Réflexions en marge du discours de Schleiermacher sur la traduction." In *Friedrich Schleiermacher and the Question of Translation*, edited by Larisa Cercel and Adriana Serban, 59–73. Berlin/Boston: Walter de Gruyter, 2015.
Tracy, David. "Theology, Critical Social Theory, and the Public Realm." In *Habermas, Modernity, and Public Theology*, edited by Don Browning and Francis Schüssler Fiorenza, 19–42. New York: Crossroad, 1992.
Tracy, David. *Fragments: The Existential Situation of Our Time. Selected Essays, Vol. 1*. Chicago: University of Chicago Press, 2020.
Tuckett, Christopher M. "Atonement in the NT." In *The Anchor Bible Dictionary*, Vol. 1, 518–522. New York: Doubleday, 1992.
Tück, Jan-Heiner. "Jesus Christus – Gottes Heil für uns. Eine dogmatische Skizze." In Gerhard Hotze, Tobias Nicklas, Markus Tomberg, Jan-Heiner Tück, *Jesus begegnen. Zugänge zur Christologie*, 119–176. Freiburg: Herder, 2009.
Valentin, Joachim, and Saskia Wendel, eds. *Unbedingtes Verstehen? Fundamentaltheologie zwischen Erstphilosophie und Hermeneutik*. Regensburg: Pustet, 2001.
Viertbauer, Klaus, and Franz Gruber, eds. *Habermas und die Religion*. Darmstadt: Wissenschaftliche Buchgesellschaft, 2nd edn 2019.
Viertbauer, Klaus, and Maureen Junker-Kenny, eds. *Special Issue, Habermas on Religion. European Journal for Philosophy of Religion* 11/4 (2019) 1–184.
Virmond, Wolfgang. "Neue Textgrundlagen zu Schleiermachers früher Hermeneutik." In *Internationaler Schleiermacher-Kongress Berlin 1984*, edited by Kurt-Viktor Selge, Vol. I, 576–590. Berlin/New York: Walter De Gruyter, 1985.
Wendel, Saskia. *Affektiv und inkarniert. Ansätze Deutscher Mystik als subjekttheoretische Herausforderung*. ratio fidei 15. Regensburg: Pustet, 2002.

Wendel, Saskia. "Die religiöse Selbst- und Weltdeutung des bewussten Daseins und ihre Bedeutung für eine 'moderne Religion'. Was der 'Postmetaphysiker' Habermas über Religion nicht zu denken wagt." In *Moderne Religion? Theologische und religionsphilosophische Reaktionen auf Jürgen Habermas*, edited by Thomas Schmidt and Knut Wenzel, 225–265. Freiburg: Herder, 2009.

Wendel, Saskia, and Martin Breul, *Vernünftig glauben – begründet hoffen. Praktische Metaphysik als Denkform rationaler Theologie*. Freiburg: Herder, 2020.

Wilckens, Ulrich. "Zur Entwicklung des paulinischen Gesetzesverständnisses." *New Testament Studies* 28 (1982): 154–191.

Wink, Walter. *Jesus and Nonviolence: A Third Way*. Minneapolis: Fortress Press, 2003.

Yarbro Collins, Adela. "The Worship of Jesus and the Imperial Cult", in *The Jewish Roots of Christological Monotheism: Papers from the St. Andrews Conference on the Historical Origins of the Worship of Jesus*, edited by Carey C. Newman, James R. Davila and Gladys S. Lewis, 234–257. Leiden: Brill, 1999.

Person Index

Abraham   20, 35, 48, 51f., 95, 171, 236
Adam   25, 46, 51, 72–76, 82, 98, 114, 117–121, 136, 148, 171f., 186, 234, 246, 248
Adolphi, Rainer   18f., 264
Adorno, Theodor W.   182
Alaric   115
Ambrose of Milan   122
Ambrosiaster   119, 246
Amos   65
Anselm of Canterbury   128
Ansorge, Dirk   108, 113, 115, 117, 119, 121–123, 125–127, 129–131, 140, 143–145, 186, 235, 239, 246, 248, 264
Anzenbacher, Arno   138, 264
Aristotle   12, 87, 102, 124, 127, 132, 134, 139f., 153, 157
Arius   106, 108f., 113
Arndt, Andreas   195, 202, 206–208, 264, 270, 274f.
Assmann, Aleida   11f., 264
Assmann, Jan   10–13, 29, 264
Augustine   1–3, 31, 47, 100f., 112, 114–124, 127, 131, 148, 153, 155, 162f., 167–173, 175–180, 185–188, 230, 233–235, 239–242, 246, 248

Bannach, Klaus   150, 264
Bauckham, Richard   17, 85, 264f.
Baumgartner, Hans-Michael   14
Baur, Ferdinand Christian   52
Behrenberg, Peter   164, 167–169, 264
Benjamin, Walter   182
Berner, Christian   196, 201f., 207f., 212, 264
Biel, Gabriel   248
Bielefeldt, Heiner   184, 186f., 264
Blumenberg, Hans   3, 154, 157–170, 172, 233, 261, 264, 267, 272
Bongardt, Michael   222, 265
Bretschneider, Karl Gottlieb   219
Breul, Martin   178, 231, 265, 277

Brown, Raymond   32–34, 49, 80, 237, 265, 271
Brunkhorst, Hauke   6, 181, 265f., 273
Bultmann, Rudolf   16f., 84, 237
Byrskog, Samuel   85f., 265

Calhoun, Craig   227, 265
Calvin, John   230
Capreolus, John   151, 156
Carroll, Tony   265
Casey, Maurice   60, 265
Chadwick, Henry   265
Chladenius, Johann Martin   205
Clement of Alexandria   100
Cross, Richard   143, 265
Crossan, John Dominic   16, 20, 27, 265
Cusanus, Nicholas of Cusa   167

Dalferth, Ingolf U.   260, 265
Daly-Denton, Margaret   32, 46, 54, 56, 65, 67–70, 74, 84, 96, 265
David, King   10, 55, 57, 70, 75, 87, 96, 184, 253
de Falco, Petrus   151
Deidun, Tom   17, 68, 97, 266
Demeter   75
Dilthey, Wilhelm von   13, 208, 250
Droysen, Johann Gustav   13
Dunn, James D. G.   44, 47f., 56f., 62–67, 77–79, 85, 238, 266, 271, 274
Duns Scotus, John   1, 3, 124, 128, 135, 138, 140f., 143–146, 149, 151, 155, 157, 159, 165–170, 172, 176f., 186, 233, 235, 239f., 248
Durkheim, Emile   242

Elijah   57, 75
Enoch   57, 75
Esler, Philip F.   34, 266
Essen, Georg   13f., 16, 23, 38, 86, 92–94, 110, 126f., 131, 143, 189, 223, 231, 244f., 260f., 266, 268, 270
Eunomius   113f.

Eutyches 108
Ezekiel 42, 244

Feuerbach, Ludwig 61, 167, 214
Fichte, Johann Gottlieb 116, 223
Fischer, Johannes 17, 266f., 270f.
Flasch, Kurt 117f., 120, 240, 266
Frank, Manfred 208f., 222f., 266, 274
Fraser, Nancy 181, 266
Freyne, Seán 19–22, 27–29, 32–42, 44f., 50–53, 65, 78, 80–83, 88, 97, 104, 235, 244–246, 267

Gadamer, Hans-Georg 14, 208
Gelasius I., Pope 110
Gerhardt, Volker 136, 267, 275f.
Gockel, Martin 230, 267
Gordon, Peter E. 267
Gottschalg, Rainer 121, 267
Graf, Friedrich Wilhelm 17, 227, 263, 267, 270f.
Gregory of Nyssa 101, 104, 113f., 238
Gregory of Rimini 150
Gula, Richard 137, 267

Hadot, Pierre 102, 267
Haight, Roger 82, 267
Händel, Georg Friedrich 39
Häring, Hermann 117f., 267
Harnack, Adolf von 100, 229
Hauschild, Wolf-Dieter 113, 267
Hegel, Georg Friedrich Wilhelm 18, 23, 52, 72, 157, 183f., 219, 229f., 256
Heidegger, Martin 158
Hengel, Martin 53, 267f.
Henrich, Dieter 7, 195–198, 216, 221f., 268
Henry of Ghent 151
Herder, Johann Gottfried 3, 18, 31, 61, 90, 94, 117, 123, 129, 136, 178, 190–192, 260
Hobbes, Thomas 186
Hölderlin, Friedrich 222
Holtman, Sarah 181, 268
Honnefelder, Ludger 120, 138–141, 146f., 150f., 268
Hooker, Morna D. 72–74, 268

Horkheimer, Max 182, 184
Hübener, Wolfgang 168, 268
Hübenthal, Christoph 144, 188f., 268f.
Humboldt, Wilhelm von 3f., 189–197, 199–202, 204, 212, 221, 233, 254
Hume, David 1, 3, 122, 178f., 228
Hurtado, Larry W. 54–62, 67, 73, 83, 90, 268
Husserl, Edmund 87
Irenaeus of Lyons 100, 104, 105f., 122, 172, 235, 235f., 238
Isaiah 20, 34–37, 39, 42, 50, 63, 67, 95, 112, 236, 244

Jacobi, Christine 78–80, 85–88, 90, 237, 268f., 275
James, brother of Jesus 29, 32–34, 44, 47, 55f., 62, 77, 79, 85, 96, 182, 206, 222, 237f.
Jaspers, Karl 1, 91, 226, 242f., 254
Jeremiah 37–39
Jesus ben Sira 20
Joas, Hans 269
John the Baptist 36, 38f., 243–245
John, evangelist 13, 16, 20, 27, 29, 32f., 36f., 47, 52f., 60, 64f., 67, 78, 80, 82–85, 95, 97, 104, 109, 112, 137, 143, 173, 186, 237, 241f., 246, 249
Josephus, Flavius 19, 64
Julian of Eclanum 121, 164
Junker-Kenny, Maureen 7, 12, 88, 188, 197, 215, 222, 226, 269, 276
Justin Martyr 100, 106, 115

Kant, Immanuel 1, 3–5, 7–9, 18f., 23, 91f., 94, 121, 139, 154, 157, 159, 168–170, 172–194, 198, 207, 211, 217, 223, 225f., 228, 230f., 233–235, 242, 249, 252–258, 260
Kasper, Walter 109, 113f., 269f.
Kenny, Peter 182, 206, 210, 212, 270, 272
Kertelge, Karl 94, 270
Kessler, Hans 130f., 270
Kierkegaard 23, 225f., 230, 255
Kimmerle, Heinz 206, 270, 274
Kirschner, Martin 129–132, 270
Klauck, Hans-Josef 17, 28–30, 32, 270

Person Index

Kobusch, Theo 100, 102–106, 108 f., 114, 116, 122, 153, 176, 270
Kögler, Hans-Herbert 270
Kreitzer, Larry 74, 270
Kristeva, Julia 70

Langthaler, Rudolf 174, 182–184, 189, 193 f., 197, 200, 202, 216, 221, 223, 225, 256 f., 264, 270–272, 275
Laube, Martin 16, 270
Lerch, Magnus 93 f., 118, 142, 151, 153, 156, 223, 270
Lindbeck, George 241, 270
Löwith, Karl 158
Luke 21, 26, 28, 33 f., 36, 38, 40, 44 f., 52 f., 66, 78, 83, 85, 89, 95, 237, 247, 249
Luther, Martin 29, 81, 150, 173, 175–177, 179 f., 188, 233, 235, 249
Lütterfelds, Wilhelm 184, 270

Mack, Burton 21, 271
Malachi 117
Mark 20 f., 29, 31, 37, 78, 80, 82, 85, 96, 104, 117
Markschies, Christoph 103, 105, 271
Markus, Robert A. 87, 115, 136, 186, 271, 275 f.
Marty, François 106, 181 f., 271
Marx, Karl 230
Matthew 21, 38, 50 f., 66, 78–80, 85, 89, 113, 117, 169, 236
Maximus Confessor 124–126, 137, 153, 235
McGrath, Alister 214, 270
Mead, George Herbert 191, 198, 221
Meeks, Wayne A. 51 f., 271
Meier, John P. 32 f., 227, 263, 265, 271
Mendieta, Eduardo 102, 227, 263, 265, 271
Menke, Karl-Heinz 110, 126, 136, 271
Merz, Annette 28 f., 35–42, 83, 237, 271
Metz, Johann Baptist 41, 100 f., 107, 168 f., 261
Metz, Johann Baptist 41, 100 f., 107, 168 f., 261, 271
Mitchell, Margaret M. 31 f., 271
Moses 29, 50–53, 55, 57, 75, 89, 95, 171

Moyise, Steve 60, 70 f., 265, 268, 271
Müller, Klaus 222 f., 265, 270 f.
Müller, Sigrid 148–152, 156, 271
Murphy-O'Connor, Jerome 44, 51, 77, 271 f.

Nagl-Docekal, Herta 6–8, 153, 182–184, 188 f., 231, 256–258, 260, 264, 270–272, 275 f.
Novalis (von Hardenberg, Friedrich) 222

Ockham, William of 1, 124, 127 f., 138, 147–156, 161, 165, 168, 240, 243, 248
Origen of Alexandria 100, 105, 105 f., 122, 122 f., 238, 241
Orth, Stefan 10, 13 f., 264 f., 272, 276

Pannenberg, Wolfhart 16, 94, 127, 142, 159, 162, 164 f., 168, 172, 214, 270, 272
Paul of Tarsus 1–3, 24–35, 41–54, 56–58, 62–68, 71–84, 87, 89–91, 95–100, 104–106, 111 f., 116–119, 123, 128, 135, 166, 170–173, 179, 188, 233–238, 242, 246–249, 259
Pelagius 115, 121, 164
Petersdorff, Friedrich von 13–15, 17, 272
Peukert, Helmut 182, 272 f.
Philo of Alexandria 29
Plato 101, 105, 108, 140, 173, 201, 204, 235
Pliny the Younger 56, 62, 64 f., 70
Plotinus 123
Pottmeyer, Hermann J. 18, 273
Pröpper, Thomas 31, 90 f., 100, 103–105, 117 f., 120 f., 131, 140 f., 143, 147 f., 173, 220, 223 f., 249, 251, 273

Queen of Sheba 236

Ratzinger, Joseph 100 f.
Rawls, John 130, 188, 227, 231, 260–262
Rehg, William 7, 188, 263, 273
Ricken, Friedo, SJ 47, 273
Ricoeur, Paul 7, 10–18, 43, 82, 87–89, 92, 104, 119, 130, 178, 184, 207 f., 250, 263–265, 269, 272–274, 276
Rieger, Reinhold 209, 211 f., 274
Ringleben, Joachim 212, 274

Rosner, Brian   274
Rossi Leidi, Thamar   151, 274
Rousseau, Jean-Jacques   179
Rüsen, Jörn   14

Sanders, E. P.   20, 49, 274
Schelling, Friedrich Wilhelm Joseph   157
Schiller, Friedrich   204
Schlegel, Friedrich   204
Schleiermacher, Friedrich D.E.   3f., 108, 110f., 121, 156, 173, 176, 188, 190–193, 195–213, 215–226, 228–230, 233f., 241f., 254f., 264–267, 269f., 273–276
Schmidt, Axel   166, 275
Schmidt, Sarah   203–205, 207, 275
Schmidt, Thomas   61, 260, 265, 275, 277
Schmitt, Carl   158
Scholtz, Gunter   195f., 200, 204f., 211f., 275
Schröter, Jens   86–88, 265, 275
Schürmann, Heinz   31, 236, 275
Schüssler Fiorenza, Elisabeth   91f., 182, 272, 275f.
Solomon   75
Stephen, Martyr   32, 43, 63
Stolzenberg, Jürgen   9, 92, 180, 267f., 275
Strauss, Leo   158

Striet, Magnus   134, 140f., 143, 146, 150–153, 156, 182, 189, 222f., 265f., 268, 270f., 276

Tacitus, Publius Cornelius   19
Teichert, Dieter   10f., 276
Theissen, Gerd   36, 38, 276
Theophilus of Antioch   100
Thomas Aquinas   1, 124, 132
Thouard, Denis   195f., 201–203, 207, 209, 212–214, 276
Tracy, David   253, 276
Tück, Jan-Heiner   136, 276
Tuckett, Christopher M.   44, 46, 276

Ulysses   75f.

Viertbauer, Klaus   269, 276
Virmond, Wolfgang   197, 205, 275f.

Weber, Max   6f., 111, 230
Wendel, Saskia   14, 61, 69, 178, 223, 272, 276f.
Wilckens, Ulrich   49, 277
Wink, Walter   42, 259, 277

Yarbro Collins, Adela   56f., 61, 68, 72f., 75f., 277

Subject Index

Adam's Fall   98, 101, 117, 123, 127, 234, 239, 241, 259
agency   2, 4, 7, 11, 22f., 25, 29, 39, 41, 45–48, 51, 67, 70, 81f., 84, 92, 119f., 122–124, 127f., 132, 139, 143–145, 152, 158, 163, 172, 178, 181, 186, 188f., 204, 217, 219, 234f., 250, 256–259
analogy   55, 59, 77, 89, 93f., 133–135, 140–142, 145
analysis of consciousness   242
anamnestic   41, 102
anthropological turn   101, 154, 157, 159, 169, 173f., 177, 180, 205, 214, 228, 233
anthropology   47, 51, 61, 100, 103f., 120, 128, 137, 152, 155, 163, 169, 186, 191, 216, 234, 239, 242, 250
antinomy of practical reason   23, 92, 180, 182, 188
Antiquity   1, 32, 62, 101–103, 121, 124, 159, 161, 164, 232, 238, 252
apocalyptic   20, 35, 39f., 48, 52, 238
apokatastasis panton   122, 230, 241
a priori   13, 93f., 174f., 194, 201
atheism   227, 256
atonement   2, 26, 30, 43–46, 65f., 76, 95, 97, 99, 111, 128, 143f., 234–236, 247f., 259, 262
authority   38, 57, 61, 78–81, 84, 93, 119, 121, 136, 143, 237, 244, 257
autonomy, autonomous   110, 132, 157, 168, 177, 179, 188f., 217f., 255, 258, 260
axial age   1, 157, 167, 226, 232, 242, 253f.

baptism   4, 32, 38, 55, 96, 232, 243, 245f., 252
biblical   1, 3, 5, 9, 15–17, 19, 21f., 25, 31, 37, 40–42, 68, 71, 74, 76, 79, 83–85, 88f., 91, 95f., 101–104, 108, 111, 117–120, 125, 131f., 134–136, 140, 142, 150f., 155, 163, 168f., 171, 176, 182f., 235f., 238f., 241, 243f., 247, 254, 260
Biblical Studies   2, 5, 15, 18f., 30, 34
biography   81, 229, 257

capability   10, 12, 82, 104, 112, 127f., 137, 150, 157, 172, 177, 185f., 198, 209, 234, 254, 261
capacity   4, 7, 10, 14, 47f., 114, 122, 125–127, 136f., 146, 149f., 152, 179, 181, 187, 197, 211, 224, 235, 255, 258
categorical imperative   258
causality   140, 220
cause   14, 22, 29, 55, 58f., 61, 67, 117, 121, 133, 149, 158, 164f., 204, 218f., 252
Christ, Jesus   1–3, 15, 22, 24, 27f., 30–32, 34, 43–51, 53–55, 57–60, 62–64, 66–75, 77, 79–83, 98, 100f., 106, 109–114, 117–119, 121, 123–126, 130f., 136, 140, 142–145, 167, 172, 215, 222, 233f., 237f., 241f., 246–251
Christolatry   27, 54, 69
Christology   24, 51, 54, 60, 64, 67, 69, 71, 74, 76, 82, 95–98, 101, 106, 108, 110, 121, 128, 132, 136, 140, 142–145, 167, 214, 235, 237, 242, 249
church   2, 4, 28, 33–35, 43, 48, 52, 58f., 71, 78, 80, 97, 101, 103, 105f., 108, 110, 115, 119, 121, 123f., 140, 162, 165, 176, 178, 185f., 188f., 229, 239f., 246f., 251, 253f.
citizen   7, 23, 91, 124, 187, 231, 260
civic   32, 124, 154, 230, 240, 257
communication   39, 107, 139, 153, 176, 194, 209, 243, 251–253, 260f.
communicative action / reason   111, 174, 192, 199, 232, 242, 255
community   6, 8, 20f., 24, 32f., 42f., 48–51, 53, 56, 58f., 77–79, 83, 96, 181, 185f., 188, 213, 228, 241, 243f., 247, 251f., 255f.
conscience   181
consciousness   6, 15, 18, 58, 68, 76, 88f., 92, 99, 101, 103, 105f., 110f., 114–116, 120, 122, 131, 137, 145, 155, 169f., 174–176, 179f., 190f., 193–195, 199, 202, 204, 213, 216f., 219–226, 230, 233, 238, 258f.

Subject Index — 283

consensus 24, 45, 91, 237
contingency, see also facticity 14, 92 107, 142, 145–149, 151, 154, 224
contract 258
Covenant 32, 34, 46, 48, 51, 101, 147, 156
creation 20, 29, 40, 48, 73, 75, 80, 82, 97, 101, 109, 115, 122, 129, 131–137, 140, 142, 144–147, 150, 154, 156, 161–163, 165 f., 181, 239, 242, 251
Creator 20, 22, 42, 59, 66, 75, 90, 98, 114, 122, 128, 132, 135, 141 f., 152, 154, 161, 166 f., 188, 224, 240, 255 f.
Critical Theory 182
culture 1, 5, 7, 11 f., 19, 42, 48, 70, 84, 91, 101, 114, 119, 185, 187, 192, 199, 225 f., 229, 233, 243, 253
Cynic, Cynicism 19–21, 27, 39, 84

damnation 115, 117 f., 127, 131 f., 166, 172, 239, 246, 259, 262
decree, divine 121, 125, 143, 155, 166, 171 f., 242
defeatism 4, 92, 183, 226
democracy, democratic 253
demythologisation 17
deontological 156, 170, 178, 181, 256
dependence, absolute 198, 218–221, 223, 229
determination, natural 101, 103, 118, 127, 132, 141, 145, 150 f., 155, 166, 176, 179 f., 198, 211, 213, 218, 227, 232, 234 f., 239 f., 252, 261
disciples / discipleship 29, 32 f., 36, 43, 50, 76 f., 82 f., 85 f., 90 f., 99, 104, 108, 129, 171
discourse 2, 8, 10, 88, 102, 104, 140, 155, 174 f., 190, 227, 232 f., 238, 250, 258
discourse ethics 175, 233, 258
dogmatics 3, 31, 173, 213, 215 f., 220, 222, 228, 241
domination 20, 144
duty 183, 188

education 177, 192, 204, 216
election 36, 118, 163, 166, 230, 241
embodiment 42, 102, 112, 137, 190, 192, 198, 206, 247, 251

Enlightenment 2, 9, 100, 157, 180 f., 198, 226 f., 256
epistemology 4 f., 150
eschatology 45, 116 f., 161, 230, 239, 241 f.
eternal 99, 124, 132, 140, 143, 155, 166, 245
ethical commonwealth 178, 185, 187 f., 235
Eucharist 145, 243, 247–249, 251 f.
evil 39, 42, 48, 82, 117, 119 f., 122, 127, 138, 146, 155, 159, 162–165, 170, 172, 179 f., 185 f., 189, 234, 239
exegesis, exegetical 68, 241
exile 32, 34 f., 42, 121, 244
existence 8, 23, 45, 47 f., 73–76, 91 f., 113, 125 f., 133, 135, 137, 141–143, 148, 150, 152, 156, 158, 162, 184, 191, 200, 214 f., 217, 220, 224, 227 f., 230, 249, 255 f., 262
Exodus 69, 95
experience, religious 15, 37, 39, 42–44, 47, 51, 54 f., 58–61, 66, 68 f., 83, 101, 104 f., 111, 116, 131, 136, 169, 172 f., 175 f., 180, 184, 194, 200–202, 213, 215, 218 f., 223, 250 f., 256 f., 260
extrinsicism 106, 247, 249
eyewitness 5, 16–18, 28 f., 85–88

facticity, see also contingency 93, 153, 220, 224, 225, 255
fallibility 6, 24, 46, 93
feeling of absolute dependence 198, 215, 218, 221
fideism 142, 152, 156, 240
finite, finitude 110, 112, 117, 134, 141, 147 f., 153 f., 169, 179, 184, 198, 200, 214, 214 f., 217–220, 239 f., 250, 257, 260
forgiveness 25, 35, 37, 39–41, 48, 64, 67, 90, 98 f.,104, 112, 129, 147, 232, 243–245, 247 f., 251
form criticism 17, 28 f.
Frankfurt School 182
freedom 2, 25, 40, 47 f., 101, 103–106, 108–110, 113 f., 117, 120–124, 126, 128, 130 f., 135, 137, 139 f., 142–153, 155–157, 161–163, 167, 169, 171 f., 176, 178–181, 190 f., 200, 217–220, 222, 224,

226, 231, 234f., 238, 240, 242, 247–249, 255, 258, 260, 262
friendship   29, 79, 82, 145, 235

Geltung (acceptance) vs. *Gültigkeit* (validity)   11
genealogy   47, 158, 171, 254, 260
Genesis   22, 37, 73f., 80, 95, 101f., 113f., 193, 207, 241
good life / flourishing life   41, 181, 188, 262
good will   106, 147, 256f.
Gospel   2, 16f., 19–22, 24, 26–32, 37f., 43–48, 50, 53f., 60, 63, 65, 67f., 75–90, 95–100, 107, 109, 112, 130, 137, 145, 156, 172, 235–238, 242f., 246f., 249, 259
grace   2, 25, 46f., 63, 67, 82, 98f., 104, 112, 116, 118, 120–122, 129, 134, 137, 144, 146–148, 152, 171f., 239, 251, 259
guilt   118f., 168, 249

haecceitas   143
happiness   8, 92, 178, 183, 187f., 192, 257
Hebrew Bible   20, 24, 29, 40, 50f., 54f., 70, 75, 79, 81, 95, 100, 236, 244, 247
Hellenisation   24f., 100, 235–237
Hellenism   24, 52, 54, 95, 236
heteronomy   21, 126, 177, 255, 258
highest good   117, 121, 123, 185
historiography   9, 13, 15, 77, 83, 88, 91
history of effects   5, 9, 12, 14–16, 22, 29f., 72, 95–97, 104, 117, 128, 176, 185, 229, 235, 238
holy   45, 64, 75, 243, 251
hope   4, 12, 22f., 38, 42, 48, 50f., 68, 92, 101, 122, 136f., 178, 180–182, 184, 187–189, 224, 228, 238, 255–258
human dignity   69, 169, 193, 255, 259
humanity, human species   34f., 42, 48f., 51, 80, 90, 95, 98, 103, 108f., 111f., 118–120, 125–127, 131, 140, 142, 144, 171, 241, 248f., 251, 255, 261f.
human rights   6, 11, 183, 187

identity   11, 21, 29, 42, 81–83, 108, 191f., 202, 212, 233, 241, 245

imagination   10, 14, 52, 78, 82, 85, 130, 206–208, 211, 246
imago Dei   234f.
immediate self-consciousness   176, 198, 213f., 216, 220–222, 224
incarnation   2, 25, 31, 98, 101, 104, 111f., 126–128, 130f., 135, 140, 142–145, 155, 161, 164, 166f., 247f., 250
individuality   143, 155f., 190–197, 199, 203f., 207–212
infinity   147, 219
institution   12, 40, 52, 130, 154, 199, 234, 254
instrumental   186, 253, 255
interiority, inwardness   2, 66, 99, 107, 116–118, 121, 173f., 176–179, 206, 229, 234
interpretation   2–5, 9, 12f., 15–19, 23f., 28, 34, 38, 43–46, 48, 52, 58–60, 64–68, 70–73, 76–78, 81, 84–86, 89f., 92, 94, 96f., 99, 101, 108f., 111f., 117, 119f., 123, 131, 137, 139f., 144f., 149, 151, 161f., 166, 176–178, 180, 183, 185f., 193, 195, 198, 205–217, 221–224, 232–234, 237, 239f., 244–249, 252, 259f.
intersubjectivity   4, 121, 177, 191, 193, 195–199, 221, 223f., 254, 257
intertextuality   68–71
Israel   1, 20f., 28, 32, 34–38, 41–43, 49–53, 65, 69, 95, 98, 236, 243–246

Jesus   15–17, 19–22, 24–91, 93–98, 100f., 106–114, 121, 124–131, 136f., 139f., 142–145, 156, 167, 171f., 234–238, 242–245, 247–249, 251, 258f., 261f.
judgement   7, 24, 33, 39–41, 65, 78f., 86, 94–98, 122, 136, 146, 162, 166, 172, 175, 177, 184, 187, 207f., 214, 227, 230, 235, 238, 241, 258f., 261f.
justice   18, 24, 36f., 39, 41, 90, 105, 117f., 120, 122, 129–131, 134, 141, 143, 145, 148, 155, 168, 182f., 187f., 211f., 215, 220, 226, 257, 259, 261

justification   23, 44, 47f., 61, 67, 74, 86, 90, 120, 132, 135, 140f., 148, 170, 178f., 183, 188, 222, 242, 253, 255

kingdom of God, *see also* reign of God   24, 28, 35–37, 42, 46, 48, 83, 97, 101, 112, 129, 185, 189, 229, 237f.

language system   191, 193, 195, 197–199, 201f., 204f., 212, 214
language theory   155, 199f., 202, 213, 220, 229
Last Judgement   3, 40, 98, 105, 117, 123, 161, 171, 241, 259, 261f.
law   1, 10, 25, 32–34, 41, 46, 48–51, 80, 84, 100, 104, 120, 124, 132f., 137–139, 146, 154, 161, 170, 172, 178, 180, 183–189, 191, 234f., 237, 239f., 248, 258
legal   99, 115, 124, 133, 137, 154, 158, 186–188, 240, 253, 258
legitimacy   129, 157, 167, 186, 244
legitimation   38, 186
liberation   9, 48, 163, 179, 238
lifeworld   4f., 7, 72, 105, 169, 192–195, 199, 216, 225, 230, 254
linguistic turn   3, 5, 177, 190f., 193, 195, 204, 210, 220f., 224f., 233, 241
Logos   1, 76, 97, 103, 106f., 109, 113, 124–127, 136, 143, 248
love   17, 34, 41, 47, 78f., 98, 112, 121, 126, 130, 136f., 140–145, 147–149, 153, 155f., 167f., 170, 236f., 249, 251, 258f.

meaning, question of   5, 7, 14, 18f., 22f., 28, 32, 44, 56, 61, 63, 65, 67f., 70f., 75, 77, 90–94, 107, 111f., 119f., 139, 157, 160, 166f., 169f., 177f., 180, 182, 184, 189f., 192, 197, 199f., 204, 206f., 211, 213, 215, 221, 224, 234, 242–244, 246–249, 252–262
memory   5, 9–13, 15f., 22, 29f., 33, 78, 80, 83, 85, 87–89, 91, 248
metaphysics   101, 104, 107f., 146, 151, 185, 192, 194, 197, 214f., 221, 228, 236, 254, 258
Modernity   1–3, 25, 41, 102, 108, 124, 128, 140, 149, 153f., 156–162, 167, 169, 177, 182, 186, 190, 197, 215, 226f., 229f., 233, 241f., 255
Monism / monist   142, 220, 222f, 232, 240, 250
monotheism   1, 20f., 27, 37, 41–43, 55–60, 65, 67f., 72, 76, 101f., 109, 124, 164, 168, 171, 182, 232, 245, 254, 260
morality   3, 6, 23, 92, 105, 178, 180–182, 186f., 189, 214f., 221, 228, 255–258, 261
Motivation   4, 52, 72, 92, 135, 155, 183, 226, 253, 255f., 259
mystical   78, 81, 83, 93, 172, 246
myth, *mythos* /mythical   11, 13, 16, 85, 98

narrative   2, 17, 19, 21, 27f., 30f., 43, 47f., 76, 81–83, 87–89, 101, 110, 130, 142, 168, 172, 234, 236f., 241
natural   1, 5, 9, 39, 41, 104f., 126, 132f., 137–139, 141–144, 146–149, 152, 154f., 170, 177, 192, 200, 235, 239f., 250f.
naturalism, naturalisation   4, 121, 138f., 216, 225–227, 253f., 260
natural law   1, 132f., 137–139, 146, 154, 170, 235
nature   5f., 40, 93, 105, 107–110, 124–128, 134, 136–141, 143–145, 148f., 152, 154, 158, 161–163, 166, 170f., 185–188, 192, 213f., 239, 241, 248, 258
necessity   117, 127, 129–132, 135, 146, 151, 189, 200, 225, 232
Nominalism   1f., 124, 148, 151, 162f., 168, 233, 240

objectivity   2, 5–7, 9, 19, 46, 86, 211, 223, 233, 250
obligation / ought   138, 179, 180–183, 186, 189, 222, 239, 256, 258
omnipotence   142, 145, 148f., 151, 160, 166
ontology   100, 111, 121, 254, 260
opacity, opaque   174, 260
oral tradition   9, 17, 19, 21, 24, 27, 29–32, 45, 50, 65f., 76–78, 80, 85, 88, 237, 247

original sin 2, 4, 25, 31, 116–120, 169, 172, 177, 180, 234, 239, 246

particularity 51, 202
patristic 1f., 25, 31f., 48, 69, 99–105, 108, 110–112, 115f., 119, 123, 145, 153, 159, 163f., 171, 173, 176, 186, 233, 238f., 241, 254f., 260
performative 107, 109, 174–178, 203, 218, 254
piety 213, 216–218
plot 12–20, 29, 75, 85, 88f.
plurality 2, 8, 25, 41, 57, 84, 114, 136, 139, 260
polarity 17, 115, 152, 195, 199f.
polytheism 1, 27
positivism 5, 9
postmetaphysical thinking 24, 100, 102, 108, 158, 170, 190, 192–195, 198, 213, 221, 226–228, 232, 238, 252, 254–256, 262
postulate of God 182
predestination 118, 122, 155, 162f., 166, 171f.
progress 30, 157, 172, 183f., 220, 257
projection 61, 214
promise 20, 35, 37f., 41, 43, 49, 51f., 82, 92, 95, 101, 122, 135, 147, 159, 164, 168, 183, 226, 230, 241, 244f., 248, 257
Psalms, Psalter 54, 56, 62, 67–71, 96
psychological 129, 173, 178, 198, 203, 205, 207f., 211, 215
public 10, 35, 37, 39, 44, 62f., 92, 125, 131, 177f., 180–184, 187f., 197, 216, 225, 231, 244, 246, 253, 257, 262

rationality 6, 102, 131, 150, 171, 191, 239
reason 1–4, 6–9, 16, 21, 23, 25, 29, 41, 47, 61, 65, 78, 80, 84, 86, 92, 94f., 100–102, 104f., 109, 111, 114, 120–122, 127f., 132f., 135, 137–140, 142f., 145–147, 149–152, 154–157, 159–161, 164–166, 169f., 172–174, 176–192, 194, 197–202, 204, 206f., 209, 211f., 217–220, 224–228, 230–235, 238–240, 242, 248, 252–257, 259–261

receptivity 215, 218–220, 240
reciprocity 49, 181, 219, 257f.
reconciliation 3, 34, 46, 78, 122, 164, 229f., 239, 242
redemption 62, 101, 119, 127f., 130, 134, 145, 162, 168, 242, 257
reflexivity 193, 198
Reformation / Protestantism 1, 132, 165, 168, 171, 179, 229
reign / kingdom of God 24, 28, 35f.,42, 46, 48, 67, 83, 97, 101, 112, 129, 185, 189

sacred 50, 63f., 79, 130, 242f., 245, 250–252
sacrifice 2, 20, 35, 37, 44, 46, 62–67, 89f., 98, 232, 244f., 247f., 252, 258
salvation 2, 30f., 36, 41, 43, 48, 51, 54, 82, 95, 97f., 100f., 104, 107, 109, 111, 120, 125, 131, 135f., 160, 162f., 171f., 175f., 179, 188, 229f., 233, 238, 241f., 247–249, 254, 256–258, 261f.
salvation history 3, 98, 120, 259
science 5–10, 13, 15f., 30, 34, 89, 91, 111, 124, 132, 152, 162, 182, 191f., 199, 201, 203, 227, 242, 244, 250, 254f.
– scientism 6, 253f.
Scriptures 27, 38, 45, 50, 52f., 55, 57, 67, 71, 79, 89, 100, 243, 245, 252
Second Adam 98
Second Temple Judaism 2, 24, 37, 43, 56, 59f., 79, 100, 233, 236f.
Secularity, secularisation and secularism 144, 157, 159, 160f., 164, 168, 190, 227, 254, 260
self-communication / self-revelation of God 127, 142, 153, 260f
self-consciousness 118, 173, 212–215, 217–219, 221–225, 229, 233, 255
self-legislation 177, 179, 185f., 189, 235, 258
self-reflection 48, 116, 146, 175, 223–225, 244, 254, 259
self-relation 197f.
self-understanding 1, 3, 7, 20, 24, 26f., 30, 49, 56, 58, 69, 80, 91, 93, 96f.,

101, 128, 158, 160, 169, 227f., 232f., 235, 241, 243, 247, 251–254
sin, sinner   2, 4, 25, 31, 44, 46f., 51, 64, 66, 82, 89f., 95, 98f., 104, 112, 116–120, 126, 128, 136, 143–145, 148, 155, 166, 168f., 172, 177, 179f., 186, 211, 233f., 239, 241, 246–249, 258f., 261
socialisation   192, 199, 251
solidarity   4, 112, 183, 199, 225, 242–245, 252f., 258
soteriology   31, 43, 101, 106, 111, 128, 135f., 143, 236
Spirit, Holy   24, 28, 48, 54, 58f., 63, 75, 93–95, 104, 110, 112–114, 122, 133, 154, 190, 215, 236, 238, 247, 249–251, 259
state   8, 11, 23, 33, 44, 46, 56, 68, 71f., 86, 90, 93, 107, 110, 115, 117, 121f., 125f., 133, 154, 171, 173, 176, 178, 185–188, 200f., 209f., 219, 224, 231, 234, 240, 245, 253f.
subjectivity, theory of   4, 11, 106, 113, 116, 122, 142, 149, 153, 169, 171f., 174f., 178f., 194, 198, 202, 206, 211, 218–221, 223–225, 228, 242, 254
subject, philosophy of the   1–8, 12, 46, 73, 104, 112, 116, 122, 141f., 157, 160, 173–177, 179f., 185, 189–196, 198–202, 204, 207, 209, 211, 214–216, 218–220, 222–225, 229, 250, 252–254
substance ontology   107, 111, 125, 155, 170, 240, 243, 253, 255
suspicion   61, 85, 153, 203, 205, 255
symbol, symbolic   35, 38f., 54, 82, 111, 236, 244f.

teleological   41, 132f., 138, 144, 153, 157, 162, 169, 181
Temple   20, 29, 33, 35, 37–39, 42, 44f., 53f., 56, 63–66, 96, 99, 236f., 243–246, 252
theocentrism   64, 153, 160f.
theodicy   117f., 159, 162–164, 167–169, 234, 239
Torah   1, 32f., 35, 81, 245
tradition   2, 5, 9, 14f., 17, 20–22, 24f., 27, 29f., 33, 35, 38f., 41, 45f., 52f., 60f.,

63–65, 69, 71f., 74f., 77–80, 85–88, 90–92, 94f., 97, 99, 106, 120, 128, 131, 133, 135, 138, 140, 168, 170, 175f., 179, 183, 194, 217, 222, 225f., 230f., 233, 235–237, 241, 243f., 246f., 249, 252f., 256
transcendental, transcendental method   1, 3, 5, 141, 154, 157, 169f., 173f., 176–178, 183, 185, 189, 191, 193–196, 198–200, 211, 213, 215–219, 221–224, 228–230, 233, 235, 242, 255
translation   24, 41, 46f., 70, 102, 119, 132, 173, 179f., 182, 188, 195f., 200f., 208, 215, 218, 226f., 236, 239, 246, 252, 260, 262
Trinity, doctrine of   110, 114f., 125, 145, 247
truth   6f., 12f., 15f., 21, 89, 101f., 105f., 114, 116, 120, 131, 136, 138–142, 145f., 155f., 158, 163, 165, 168, 174, 194, 197, 216, 226–228, 233, 238, 241, 250, 259, 261

unconditional   38, 136, 246, 258
universality, universalisation   7, 34, 51, 95, 124, 132, 182, 192, 203–205, 236, 244, 255f.
universe   23, 100, 104, 188, 214, 256
univocity   140, 147, 151, 156

validity claim   227, 229
Vernunft see rationality and reason
Verstand (understanding)   150, 207, 211, 239
vindication   26, 30, 44, 66, 89f., 98, 247, 249, 259
violence   41f., 92, 121, 169, 187, 196, 200, 259
virtue   14, 137, 181, 188, 241, 257
Voluntarism   2, 124, 149–151, 161, 166–168, 177

will   2, 4f., 8f., 12–15, 17, 20, 22, 24–29, 31, 35f., 39–43, 47f., 53–59, 64, 67, 69, 76–80, 83f., 90, 92f., 95, 97, 99–106, 108, 111f., 115–117, 121f., 124–130, 133–135, 137–139, 142–157, 159, 161–163, 166, 168–174, 176–180,

185–193, 195 f., 198, 201, 204, 209 f., 213 f., 216 f., 220 f., 225–228, 232, 234–236, 239 f., 242 f., 247–250, 254, 259, 261 f.
wisdom   16, 19–22, 35, 39 f., 75 f., 85, 97, 101, 132, 145, 149, 161, 168, 236

world religions   1, 104, 221, 232, 256
worldview   3, 39, 123, 130 f., 158, 226, 232, 255
worship   24, 28, 32, 38 f., 42, 49, 53–57, 60–67, 69, 71–73, 75 f., 79, 91, 96, 112

www.ingramcontent.com/pod-product-compliance
Lightning Source LLC
Chambersburg PA
CBHW020222170426
43201CB00007B/287